Democratic Delusions: The Initiative Process in America

Richard J. Ellis

University Press of Kansas

Published by the University Press of Kansas (Lawrence, Kansas 66049), which was
organized by the Kansas Board of Regents and is operated and funded by Emporia
State University, Fort Hays State University, Kansas State University, Pittsburg State
University, the University of Kansas, and Wichita State University

Library of Congress Cataloging-in-Publication Data

Ellis, Richard (Richard J.)
    Democratic delusions : the initiative process in America / Richard J. Ellis.
        p. cm.—(Studies in government and public policy)
    Includes index.
    ISBN 0-7006-1155-X (alk. paper)—ISBN 0-7006-1156-8 (pbk. : alk. paper)
    1. Referendum—United States. I. Title. II. Series.
    JF494.E45 2002
    328.273—dc21   2001004659

British Library Cataloguing in Publication Data is available.

Printed in the United States of America

10 9 8 7 6 5 4 3 2 1

In Loving Memory of
Howard S. Robertson

Contents

Acknowledgments

When I entered graduate school in 1983, it seemed that few people cared much about the initiative process. As best I can remember, my graduate training in American politics at the University of California at Berkeley did not include a single book, article, or class session relating to the initiative and referendum. At the time, that suited me just fine; state and local politics seemed a great bore, at least compared to the imperial glamor of the American presidency or the pure glitz of cultural theory. In the intervening years, I've read, taught, researched, and written about the American presidency and political culture, but until recently I have paid little more attention to state and local politics than does the average attentive citizen.

This confession of ignorance prefaces an acknowledgment of my reliance on others far more knowledgeable than myself. All scholarship, of course, depends on the work of others, but that dependence deepens considerably when one ventures into strangely unfamiliar terrain. Deserving of special mention is the seminal work of David Magleby, whose book-length analysis of the initiative process in the United States, *Direct Legislation: Voting on Ballot Propositions in the United States,* remains among the most incisive works on voting in initiative elections. Sadly, the book has been out of print for years and is difficult to obtain because it was never released in paperback. Magleby's comprehensive study, which began life as a Berkeley dissertation in the late 1970s and early 1980s, stood almost alone until 1989, when Thomas Cronin published his lucid and widely read synthesis, *Direct Democracy.* Cronin tends to be less critical of the initiative process than I am, but his readable prose is a model for those who desire to reach beyond a small circle of interested political scientists. Since the publication of Cronin's book, political science research on the initiative process has developed impressively. I have learned a great deal from the work of initiative skeptics like Elizabeth Garrett, Ted Lascher, Ken Miller, and Dan

Smith, as well as from the revisionist work of Shaun Bowler, Todd Donovan, Elizabeth Gerber, and Arthur Lupia. Particularly valuable for my purposes has been the encyclopedic sourcebook by Philip DuBois and Floyd Feeney, *Lawmaking by Initiative,* which was published in 1998. Although unlikely to be read by a large audience, it contains virtually everything one could ever want to know about the initiative process in the United States.

To many of these colleagues I owe far more than just thanks for their fine scholarship. A number of them have patiently acquiesced to my constant badgering for information and clarification, statistics and citations. Dan Smith of the University of Denver generously provided me with Colorado data he had painstakingly gathered and, in countless e-mails, helped me understand Colorado's initiative process. Equally heroic and helpful was Todd Donovan of Western Washington University, who gamely responded to a blizzard of quizzing e-mails, largely though by no means entirely about the Washington initiative process. A number of Californians also answered e-mail queries and shared with me hard-earned data, including Ted Lascher of California State University, Sacramento; Ken Miller at the University of California, Berkeley; and Floyd Feeney at the University of California, Davis. All gave generously of their time and knowledge to help a bewildered novice.

Many elections officials also graciously answered my questions and provided me with data. Among the most helpful were: Virginia Breeze, Public Information Officer in the Alaska Division of Elections; Sandy Claiborne, Programs and Projects Specialist in the Arizona Secretary of State's Office; Penny Ysursa, Administrative Secretary in the Idaho Election Division; Peggy Nighswonger, Elections Director in the Wyoming Secretary of State's Office; and Cory G. Fong, Elections Director in the North Dakota Secretary of State's Office. I also am thankful for the assistance and data provided me by Jennifer Hannan of Oregon's Appellate Court Records and Keith Garza, staff attorney for the Oregon Supreme Court. A number of individuals active in the initiative process also took the time to answer my questions, including Lloyd Marbet, Sherry Bockwinkel, Shawn Newman, Jim Schultz, and Helen Hill. Like almost everyone who researches the initiative process, I owe a debt of gratitude to Dane Waters and the Initiative & Referendum Institute. Their web page (*www.iandrinstitute.com*) provides a tremendous public service.

I am also grateful to colleagues who took the time to read the manuscript in whole or in part. Dan Smith and Ted Lascher gave the book a careful reading and caught a number of mistakes. Several of my colleagues at Willamette University also commented usefully on portions of the book; particularly helpful were the readings by Melissa Buis, Hans Linde, and Fred Thompson. Travis Brouwer, a former student, proved a good teacher and offered a constructive critique of each chapter. When I presented an earlier version of chapter 7 at a 1999 conference in Eugene, Oregon, Jerry Calvert of Montana State University provided valuable early encouragement.

My understanding of the initiative process was deepened by the experience of teaching a seminar on the Initiative and Referendum in the spring of 2000. The arguments advanced here are hopefully more durable by virtue of having been tempered in the forge of undergraduate skepticism. Several student research projects were particularly instructive for me. The work of John Bauer helped sharpen my understanding of the ballot-titling process. Dustin Buehler's senior thesis, which set out to explain why the initiative process has not spread to more states, also influenced my thinking. A number of talented student research assistants helped with the book at various stages; among those who deserve my special thanks are John Bauer, Bryn Berglund, Dustin Buehler, Travis Brouwer, Debu Gandhi, Maegan Lindsay, Elizabeth Lott, and Amelia Porterfield. Also deserving of mention is Arlene Weible, who was until recently the Government Documents Librarian at Willamette University. Arlene showed unfailing grace and consummate skill in helping me and my research assistants locate and retrieve relevant documents.

Willamette University has been a wonderful place to work over the past decade. I have been blessed not only with serious students but with splendid colleagues and supportive administrators. The Mark O. Hatfield Chair in Politics, established in 1999 through a gift from the Meyer Memorial Trust, has provided generous support for my research and teaching. My deepest debt of gratitude is to the late Larry Cress, who, as dean of the College of Liberal Arts, was a model of humane integrity as well as an unfailing source of support to me and to others. We miss him terribly.

Prologue

Over a decade ago, while still living in California, I voted for a proposition that promised to roll back my automobile insurance rates by about 20 percent. Proposition 103 seemed like a wonderful idea at the time. The rates I paid in Oakland seemed high, or at least higher than I would have liked. Of one thing I was sure: a hardworking graduate student needed the money more than any behemoth insurance company. When the measure passed, I celebrated my good fortune along with the other 51 percent of Californians who had voted for it. I began devising ways to spend my windfall, counting the days until the check arrived in the mail. But the check never came. The rollback never materialized. The proposition immediately became entangled in the courts; fighting the initiative cost the insurance industry millions upon millions of dollars, but it produced precious little rate relief for the average California automobile driver. It did create a new and more intrusive regulatory apparatus, but neither I nor most of the millions of other Californians who voted for the measure had any idea that this regulatory scheme was contained within the measure's eleven thousand words. In the end, nobody won. Not the insurance companies, who expended nearly a hundred million dollars fighting the proposition; not the average California automobile driver, who never received a rebate or rate rollback; and certainly not the taxpayers, who ultimately spent millions of dollars over the ensuing years fighting the insurance companies in court.

In the summer of 1990, with Proposition 103 still ensnared in the courts, I headed north to a new home in Oregon, land of rain, green, and, happily, lower automobile insurance rates. During the 1970s, Californians journeying north were met at the border by signs bearing an inhospitable message: WELCOME TO OREGON: THANKS FOR VISITING, PLEASE DON'T STAY. The devastating recession of the early 1980s brought down the signs, but ambivalence toward the colossus of the south lingered. Among the first pieces of advice I received from well-meaning

1

Oregonians was to change my license plates so as not to stand out as a Californian. Oregonians, I quickly learned, prided themselves on being different from Californians. (Californians, in contrast, never give any thought to Oregon, much as Americans barely notice Canada, while Canadians obsess over what makes them different from the United States.) In at least one respect, however, Oregon and California are peas of the same political pod: both are heavy users (and abusers) of the initiative process. No other state in the union comes close to rivaling Oregon and California in the use of direct legislation. Oregonians are, if anything, more devoted to the initiative process than Californians. Indeed, many Oregonians think of the initiative system as their own creation—and with good reason. The first initiative elections were held in Oregon, and for much of the first half of the twentieth century the initiative and referendum were widely known in this country as the "Oregon System."

Within months of my arrival in Oregon, I voted in my first election as an Oregonian. The November ballot included eight initiatives, two of which particularly grabbed my attention. The first was a measure requiring all Oregonians to buckle up. If the four automobile insurance initiatives on the California ballot in 1988 showed the initiative process at its most dubious—poorly designed policies, obscene amounts of money, highly technical measures, unanticipated consequences, and confused voters—the seat belt law represented a more appealing side of the initiative process. The bill was simple, people could use their own everyday experiences to make an informed decision, the money expended to qualify and pass the measure was modest, there was no lengthy and costly court challenge, and the policy change did not produce a host of unintended consequences.

But another issue on the 1990 ballot, Measure 5, which dramatically rolled back property taxes, revealed the less savory side of the initiative process. Having witnessed the impact of Proposition 13 and its many progeny on the provision of public services in California, I found it difficult to believe that Oregon—which prides itself on its progressive image, its parks, and its public services—would want to follow California down the same fiscal path. Prior to Proposition 13, California had consistently been among the nation's leaders in per-pupil spending; by 1990, when Measure 5 was put before the Oregon voters, California, despite its immense wealth, had slipped well into the bottom half of the states. Measure 5 attempted to address such concerns by requiring the state to make up the revenue lost to local school districts, but no provision for an alternative source of revenue was provided for in the initiative. Voters were offered property tax relief and a promise of no reduction in money to public schools. No pain, lots of gain. In the real world of politics, though, there are always trade-offs to be made and negotiated. Making up lost revenues would mean either cutting valuable programs or increasing other taxes, neither of which would be popular with voters (or politicians). No matter how the state came up with the money for schools, moreover, the result would be to centralize funding and thus place control of local schools in the hands of the state. The loss of local control, however, was rarely mentioned in the campaign, and few voters were made aware of that unintended consequence. Although the rhetoric was populist, Measure 5's most devastating impact was on the local governmental bodies closest to the people—city councils, county commissioners, school boards—for whom the property tax is their lifeblood.

Admittedly, Oregon's Measure 5 was nowhere near as radical as California's Proposition 13. Measure 5, for instance, did not require a two-thirds vote of the state legislature to raise state taxes, nor did it mandate a two-thirds majority for any "special tax" increase at the local level. But at least Proposition 13 did have the overwhelming backing of California voters. However unwise the policy might have been, it was undertaken with the broad support of Californians (except for renters, blacks, and the young). Oregon, on the other hand, undertook its dramatic policy departure without anything approaching a statewide consensus. In a bitterly contested campaign, only a bare majority (52 percent) approved the sweeping measure; this narrow victory, moreover, came on the heels of four consecutive albeit narrow defeats (in 1980, 1982, 1984, and 1986) for similar property tax limitation initiatives. The legislature can reasonably be upbraided for ignoring a policy that has the support of two-thirds of the electorate, as Proposition 13 did, but a legislature that fails to enact a measure upon which the electorate is almost evenly divided is arguably doing its job. The many hurdles of the legislative process—committees, the two houses of the legislature, executive veto—are designed to weed out divisive policies that lack widespread support, or at least to modify them so that diverse groups and constituencies feel they can live with the policy change. Particularly when a policy has complex and far-reaching consequences for government and society, the initiative process is a particularly poor lawmaking instrument.

Since arriving in Oregon, I have now voted on seventy-four statewide initiatives in six general elections, which is almost exactly the same number of initiatives I would have been faced with had I remained in California. Although the number of initiatives on the ballot has shown no sign of decreasing since my arrival in Oregon, I now find the voting decision a much simpler one than it was in my relative youth. This is not because I acquired a doctorate in political science in 1990, nor is it a result of greater experience voting in initiative elections. Even with an advanced degree in political science and the wisdom that is said to come with age, I do not begin to comprehend all, or even much, of what is contained in most initiatives. Nor is the simplification of my voting calculus a result of the bewildering variety of pro-and-con arguments included in Oregon's hefty voters' pamphlet. Rather, my life as a voter has been simplified by one very basic decision rule: I vote no. No matter what the measure, no matter what the issue, I just say no.

I hasten to add that I use this decision rule only on initiatives, not on popular referenda or legislative referenda. The popular referendum enables citizens— if they can gather the necessary signatures—to force a public vote on legislation recently enacted by the legislature and signed by the governor. Because the popular referendum adds an additional check to the normal legislative process, it raises qualitatively different issues than the initiative process, which circumvents the legislative process entirely by empowering citizens to place their own issues on the ballot. I have no objection to giving voters the power to veto legislation; my qualms are limited to the problems that occur when the legislative process is routinely bypassed altogether.

Although state ballots do not always clearly distinguish between legislative referenda and citizen initiatives—nor, consequently, do most citizens—the political and normative differences between these two processes are immense. Unlike the initiative process, by which citizens place an issue on the ballot through signature petitions, the legislative referral entails the legislature putting a measure to a vote of the people. A legislature's decision to refer a measure to the voters is often not a choice at all: rather, it reflects the dictates of the law. The overwhelming majority of legislative referenda are constitutional amendments, and in every state but Delaware the legislature is required by law to refer a constitutional change to the voters after it has passed both houses of the legislature. Legislative referenda that make constitutional changes are frequently uncontroversial and are approved by voters at a much higher rate than citizen initiatives. Not that legislative referenda are without problems of their own. Since legislative referrals do not require the governor's signature, legislators sometimes use the referral process as a way to perform an end run around the executive, thus subverting an integral part of the checks and balances of the legislative process. Less sinister but hardly more admirable is the legislature's use of referenda to cover its own cowardice. Unwilling to do the right thing, legistators pass the buck to the voters. There is, in short, plenty to criticize about the use and abuse of the legislative referendum, but these problems are sufficiently distinct from those of the initiative process that I have largely ignored them in this book.

My aim is not to persuade Americans to reject all initiatives. "Just say no" is more a pose than a policy. Rather, my hope is to promote greater skepticism of the populist mantle with which the initiative process is invariably cloaked. If I am less critical of the legislative process it is not because I think it without faults but because I see little need to promote greater public skepticism of legislators. The public does not need a political scientist's help for that. The initiative process, on the other hand, is too often viewed uncritically as the pure, direct expression of the popular will. The initiative process, we are told, belongs to the people. Its results reflect the real voice of the people. According to David Schmidt, whose *Citizen Legislators* is something of a bible among initiative activists, the initiative process "is true, honest, simple self-government." When the public votes for a policy directly, no one, he says, can claim it is "against the public interest." Such naive beliefs are widespread and are too often reflexively accepted. I will have succeeded if I can persuade my fellow citizens to be at least as skeptical of the initiative process as they currently are of legislatures.

1

A Tale of Two Initiatives

Helen Hill had never been one for politics, certainly not for mainstream politics. Born and raised in Missouri, she had never even heard of the initiative and referendum until, at the age of twenty-three, she moved to a small town on the Oregon coast. Her early passions were artistic and literary, not political. Neither in high school nor in college, where she majored in classics, did she run for office or involve herself in campus politics. Her family rarely talked politics. As a young adult she was "a hippie kid," jaded by most of what passed for politics in the United States. Her politics, such as they were, were "of the Jesse Jackson, Ralph Nader variety." Although she voted conscientiously in state and national elections and occasionally wrote letters or called members of Congress, Hill was by her own admission poorly informed about the workings of the nation's political system. She would, she says, have been hard-pressed to identify the three branches of government. Not that she was an uninvolved citizen. Far from it. Although she spent long hours as a mother and waitress, she found time in the early 1980s to write for a local, alternative newspaper, including, most memorably, a hard-hitting investigative report on the effect of herbicide sprays on women's menstrual cycles. In the late 1980s and early 1990s she was active in local efforts to fight short-term property rentals, which were driving up local housing prices and property taxes, and driving out some long-term local residents. But most of her time was absorbed with the mundane everyday life of work, family, and friends. After coming into a substantial inheritance from her father in the mid-1980s, she quit her waitressing job and bought a farm, spending the next decade raising kids and turkeys, working the small, organic farm, painting and printmaking, and volunteering as an art teacher in her children's elementary school.¹

As Hill approached her forty-second birthday in 1997, there was little in her past to suggest that this mother of three would shortly become an initiative heroine, a political figure of statewide and even national importance. By her own account, her life up to that point had been pretty confused and even "screwed up." She had been through three marriages and had tried at least as many occupations: waitress, farmer, and now art teacher. There was even a criminal offense in her not-so-recent past: stealing two ponies. (They were being mistreated, Hill explains.) She had never had any political ambitions, nor had she ever been actively involved in a candidate race or a statewide initiative campaign. Despite the episodes of local activism and the record of involvement in her community, she knew little if anything about how to run a political campaign. When, in the summer of 1997, she drove her old pick-up truck to the state capitol in Salem to file her open adoption records initiative, she had, as she later admitted, "no idea what I was doing." Indeed, she had only been inside the state capitol on one other occasion, when, a few years back, she had taken her kids to visit the state house. The secretary of state's office had to walk her through almost every step of the filing process. Yet in filing those papers Hill launched an initiative that would rock the adoption establishment not only in Oregon but across the nation. By the time it was over, Hill would become something of a minicelebrity, appearing on the *Today* Show, *Good Morning America, The NewsHour with Jim Lehrer,* and *Talk of the Nation,* as well as being interviewed and profiled in many national magazines and newspapers, including *Time, Newsweek, Rolling Stone,* the *New York Times,* the *Los Angeles Times,* and the *Boston Globe.*

The story of how a political neophyte like Hill became the chief petitioner for one of the most talked about and successful initiatives of the 1998 election is a modern-day political fairy tale. At age ten, as Hill tells the story, she discovered adoption manuals stashed away in her parents' bedroom; her mother, clearly embarrassed, told the child the truth: she had been adopted. "Now go to bed and never tell anyone." The subject remained off limits for the rest of their lives, a secret they shared but never discussed.[2] It was not the only adoption secret her mother carried with her. In 1985 Hill's sixty-eight-year-old father discovered that he, too, had been adopted. Salvatore Patti was a second-generation Italian— or so he thought. His parents were Italian immigrants who had arrived in the United States speaking no English, and his father had built up a successful construction business in Kansas City, which Salvatore then took over. Being Italian was not just an ethnic heritage in which Hill's father took pride but a profound part of his sense of self. The trouble was he was not Italian at all but Indian, taken from an Oklahoma reservation when he was three. Worse still, his wife had known the truth their entire marriage but had never divulged the carefully concealed secret. Within six months of discovering that he was not who he thought he was, and that his parents and wife had concealed the truth from him, the old man died—of a broken heart, says Hill.

Although it was at least a decade before Hill learned the whole truth about her father's adoption, his death laid the groundwork for her journey into adoption politics. Hill's father left her a substantial inheritance that not only enabled her to quit her job as a waitress but gave her the freedom and financial resources to seek her birth parents. After almost a decade of searching and spending thousands of dollars on a private detective, Hill finally located them. She summoned the courage to call her biological mother, and several months later she flew out to Iowa to meet her. "I was never at peace," Hill recalls, "until I looked into my mother's eyes."[3] In search of support through this emotionally unsettling time, Hill began to attend meetings of the Oregon Adoptive Rights Association, a search and support group for adoptees, but she quickly found that the group's "pass the Kleenex box" approach was not her style. The meetings were not in vain, however, for it was there that she learned of a new, irreverent website called Bastard Nation, a discovery that would help Hill convert her personal disquiet into public action.

The Bastard Nation website was launched early in the summer of 1996. Like Queer Nation, Bastard Nation used its name not just to provoke but to subvert a wider culture of shame. Rather than wallow in self-pity and victimhood, Bastard Nation "reclaimed the badge of bastardy" as a way of asserting that there was "nothing shameful in having been born out of wedlock or in being adopted." But, unlike Queer Nation, which celebrated difference, Bastard Nation offered a militant assertion of equal rights. "It is the right of people everywhere," boomed the group's mission statement, "to have their official original birth records unaltered and free from falsification, and that the adoptive status of any person should not prohibit him or her from choosing to exercise that right."[4] The group's goal was not individual therapy but fundamental political change in adoption laws across the country as well as in the attitudes and beliefs that sustained those laws. Bastard Nation helped give Hill the language to articulate her feelings and explain her actions. Finding one's birth parents was not just a narcissistic journey of self-discovery, nor was it mere idle curiosity; at stake was an entire culture of shame and secrecy that destroyed families and lives. Hill now saw that she was confronting a fundamental violation of civil rights.

Hill found the website's outrageous humor and brash tone a refreshing contrast to the tears and insipid sympathy of the support groups. She started an e-mail correspondence with leaders of the group, and offered to do a workshop on art therapy at a Bastard Nation conference. The workshop, she confesses, was pretty "lame," and she spent much of the conference hiding in her hotel room, not altogether certain about what she had gotten herself into. But she emerged long enough to hear a lecture by Randy Shaw, whose book, *The Activist's Handbook,* is a widely read primer for a host of progressive groups and is the veritable bible of Bastard Nation. During his talk, Shaw recommended the initiative as one strategy that adoption rights activists might pursue. Hill recalls that "a little light bulb went off" inside her head. Could she do an initiative in Oregon? Shaw and others at Bastard Nation encouraged her to pursue it. When she returned home, she discussed the idea with her children and decided, with their approval, to proceed with the initiative. Just a week or two later, she made the two-hour drive to Salem and filed the necessary legal papers.

In Oregon lots of people file initiatives covering all sorts of issues, but few of these proposals actually make it to the ballot. What made Hill's initiative different? How was she able to make her private passion part of the public agenda? Part of the answer lies in her own determination. She is a remarkably strong-willed person who was determined to see her initiative through to the end. But determination alone was not nearly enough. Also critical was the inheritance from her father. Indeed, in the absence of that pot of money it is highly unlikely that she would ever have begun the initiative; certainly she would never have finished it. But there was a third aspect that went beyond Hill or her money: the Internet. Hill was able to make intensive use of the Internet because adoptees were already organized via the web. Recognizing the enormous search potential of the Internet, adoptees as well as birth mothers had gravitated toward the Internet at an early stage. Because adoptees were already wired, Hill did not have to build an organization from the ground up. Instead she could rely on web-based search and support groups and online chat groups to get out the word, to solicit and coordinate volunteers, and to organize the campaign.

Passionately committed volunteers and a high-tech organization carried Hill only so far, however. The initiative had been approved for circulation at the end of September, but by February 1998 it became clear that highly motivated volunteers would not be sufficient to qualify the initiative. Part of the problem, according to Hill, was that for many of the volunteers this was a highly emotional issue still laced with shame, and that in soliciting signatures they were not only advertising their adoptive status to the world but inviting others to talk with them about it. Many weren't emotionally ready for this sort of coming out. Most of the problems Hill's volunteer campaign confronted, however, were little different from those that face any volunteer signature drive, particularly during the dismally wet winter months, namely, the immense difficulty of getting a substantial number of energetic people to spend a huge number of hours standing in a shopping mall, or in front of a supermarket, begging passersby for signatures. About six months into the campaign, Hill discovered what every experienced initiative user already knows: if one wants to get on the ballot, it is usually necessary to pay people to gather signatures and to hire a professional to coordinate the signature-gathering effort.

Dipping into her father's inheritance, Hill hired political consultant Donna Harris to manage a paid signature-gathering campaign. Harris had learned the signature-gathering business while coordinating the Save-the-Salmon initiative in 1992 and subsequently working for Bill Sizemore's Oregon Taxpayers United, a group that specializes in initiative politics. After the 1996 election, Harris left Sizemore's office to start her own company, Creative Campaigns. From the moment Hill opened her purse strings and hired a professional, qualification of her measure was virtually assured. The cost of qualification was held just below a hundred thousand dollars, in large part because the campaign did not need to gather signatures in the last month, when the price of signatures is routinely bid up as a result of competition among initiative petitions. Although Hill most certainly paid for her spot on the ballot, she could legitimately boast of a substantial volunteer component to the campaign. In the end, about 20 percent of the nearly ninety-five thousand signatures gathered were collected by volunteers, a significant achievement in an era when many initiatives that reach the ballot rely on paid signature gatherers for virtually every signature.

Despite the hired help, the telltale signs of amateurism were not difficult to detect. To begin with, the initiative had been written as a statutory change. Most initiative professionals traffic in constitutional initiatives to prevent the legislature from tampering with their handiwork. When asked why she had not crafted the initiative as a constitutional amendment, Hill naively answered that it was a statutory issue, not a constitutional one. When it was pointed out that most other initiative sponsors had no scruples about writing their causes into the constitution, she admitted that she had been a political novice and had not understood that this was the way the game was played. She conceded that had she understood this at the time she filed the initiative, she probably would have filed the measure as a constitutional initiative.

The actual language of the initiative also stamped it as an amateur effort. The initiative lacked the usual legal jargon and was short enough for the average person to read and understand. Consisting of only two sentences and less than seventy-five words in length, it stated:

> Upon receipt of a written application to the state registrar, any adopted person 21 years of age and older born in the state of Oregon shall be issued a certified copy of his/her unaltered, original and unamended certificate of birth in the custody of the state registrar, with procedures, filing fees, and waiting periods identical to those imposed upon non-adopted citizens of the State of Oregon pursuant to ORS 432.120 and 432.146. Contains no exceptions.

In contrast, the political and legal pros who drafted a medical marijuana measure appearing on the same ballot took thirty-five hundred words and nineteen separate sections of impenetrable legal jargon. The average initiative on the 1998 Oregon ballot was over a thousand words. Nor did Hill try to dress up her measure in pretty packaging. Unlike the unions, for instance, who labeled their two initiatives the Defense of Democracy Act and the Open and Fair Elections Act (who could be against such things?), Hill gave her measure no title at all. The other initiative campaigns all adopted wonderfully alluring names for their measure committees. The medical marijuana advocates called themselves "Oregonians for Medical Rights," advocates of mandatory minimum sentences for criminals were called "Justice for All," and the measure committee for Sizemore's effort to curtail union involvement in politics was called "No Taxpayer Money for Politics." Hill's committee was simply titled "Open '98."

Not that Hill was completely naive when it came to politics. She knew enough to keep Bastard Nation at arm's length during the campaign. Although she continued to rely on the group as an important resource, she insisted that Bastard Nation keep quiet during the campaign. After the election, she promised, she would gladly trumpet the group's praises from every platform. Both sides kept to the bargain. During the election, Bastard Nation kept largely out of sight, never entering the public debate about the open records initiative. Hill never mentioned the group, and the newspapers only rarely mentioned it. After the election, Hill was as good as her word, lauding the group at every opportunity, and the group resumed a more visible role in the postelection public debate, particularly during the legal proceedings, where public opinion was no longer a primary concern.

Hill's tactics were shrewd, even Machiavellian, but her initiative came from the heart, from a deep belief that closed records perpetuated feelings of shame and inadequacy that had ruined and disfigured countless lives. There was no polling the ballot title, as the professionals routinely do, to see whether the title and ballot summary assigned by the state would attract a majority of voters. Nor did she file multiple versions of the same initiative in an attempt to get the best possible ballot title from the state. Such a thought never entered her head. Glossy packaging played a very limited role in the success of the initiative, in large part because Hill couldn't afford the price of such packaging. Several people promised to help Hill with fund-raising, but they failed to come through. In the end the campaign raised a little over seventeen thousand dollars, mostly in relatively small contributions, not nearly enough to mount a slick advertising campaign. The campaign had to settle for a full-page ad in the *Oregonian* that cost Hill ten thousand dollars, and a single, grainy television ad, produced on the cheap by Hill and a producer friend, which aired a handful of times on prime-time television but generally played in the early-morning hours on a cable-access channel. Since the campaign lacked the money for a media blitz, proponents of Measure 58 depended on free media, the kindness of strangers (a pollster who was an adoptee did a poll for free for Hill about three weeks before the election), and Hill's boundless energy. In countless interviews with print and broadcast media, Hill worked tirelessly to broadcast her message to the voters of Oregon.

In November over 57 percent of Oregonians voted in favor of Hill's adoption records initiative, a remarkable triumph for a political novice and an underfunded campaign. Many people close to the campaign felt, as Donna Harris did, that Hill's triumph was inspiring proof that one person can make a difference in politics. For Hill the experience affirmed the possibilities of politics, especially the value of the initiative process. She likens the initiative to the Sword in the Stone. Only the pure of heart, those with a just and true cause, can pull the sword from the rock and wield its tremendous power. Imposters and counterfeits may try but they will be unable to budge the weapon. This marvelous metaphor is tempting, but is it any truer than the mythic tale of Camelot? Or is it, like the Arthurian saga, a captivating fantasy?

Even those who find Hill's personal story immensely appealing may find it difficult to accept that the initiative power can only be effectively wielded by those who possess a pure heart and a good cause. Cynics may wonder whether Hill's story isn't more the exception than the rule. Indeed, Hill's fairy-tale ending was helped by some unusual political circumstances, particularly the lack of an organized or well-financed opposition. The amateurism of the Measure 58 campaign was matched only by the amateurism and disorganization of the opponents of the initiative. Only one measure committee, Concerned Adoption Professionals, was formed in opposition to Measure 58, and it spent less than five hundred dollars, all of which was provided by the group's treasurer, Warren Deras. The committee was made up of a handful of social workers, none of whom had substantial experience in politics. All were from the Boys and Girls Aid Society, an organization that had never before taken a position on a political question in its more than one hundred years of existence. The other adoption organizations in the state, including the Coalition of Oregon Adoption Agencies, a potentially potent political force representing thirty-six private adoption agencies, remained on the political sidelines, reluctant to be drawn into a political battle that pitted birth parents against adoptees. The individuals likely to be most adversely impacted by the measure—birth mothers who did not want their past secrets disclosed to their family—could not publicly fight the measure without losing the confidentiality they wished to protect. Even contributing as little as sixty dollars would force a woman to divulge her identity to the public. Unlike adoptees, who were organized through search and support groups, birth mothers who desired anonymity were impossible to contact, let alone organize. Not that the opposition was completely ineffective. A number of social workers spoke out articulately and passionately against Measure 58. A useful information packet sent out by Concerned Adoption Professionals to newspapers across the state was instrumental in persuading a large majority of newspapers, including the state's leading paper, the *Oregonian,* to oppose the measure. But, lacking money, the opposition could not afford a single advertisement, either in the newspapers or on television. Had the opposition raised substantial sums of money for a concerted advertising campaign, it is likely, as Hill admitted in an interview shortly after the election, that they "could have sunk the measure."[5] Absent such spending, opponents were unable to create the doubt or confusion that generally leads voters to reject a measure. Instead, proponents were able to control the framing of the issue as a fundamental civil right: "our birth certificate: our right" was the slogan that stuck.

For Hill this was no mere slogan but the measure's inner truth. The right of every American to an unaltered birth certificate was a fundamental civil right that could not be denied to adults. In Hill's view there were no tough moral dilemmas or trade-offs, and so compromise was out of the question. "You can't talk about compromise and civil rights in the same sentence and be honest at all," she explained. "You can't make one group's rights supersede those of another." To Hill adoption rights was a black-and-white moral issue akin to the heroic civil rights struggles of the 1960s, in which activists spurned compromise and half measures because they demanded full equality.[6] Just as the white man's desire to discriminate must give way to equal rights for all, so the birth mother's desire to remain anonymous must give way to the equal right to know where we come from.

Yet, upon closer examination this simple tale of right and wrong collapses into agonizing moral complexity. It overlooks the harm done to those birth mothers for whom the dreadful prospect of a call from the child they gave up many years ago is, as one birth mother described it, like "a bomb held over your head." Hill found out that she had been a "love child," the product of a fleeting but passionate romance, but others will not be so lucky.[7] They may unearth emotionally traumatic secrets of rape or incest that the victim has worked a lifetime to put behind her. What right does even the most well intentioned seeker have to tear open such a ghastly wound? One adoption attorney has seen the anguish on both sides: the birth mothers "horrified at the thought they might have to face their child decades later to say their lives must remain separate" and the adoptees "in tears about their need to know their origins and inability to get the information they seek." "I can't imagine not being ambivalent," he adds, "if you've truly listened to both sides."[8] Both sides have desires, fears, and interests that warrant protection. The privacy of some clashes with others' desire to know. Although both sides try to dress up their cause in the absolutist language of rights, at stake are not inviolable constitutional rights but competing preferences and needs. With legitimate concerns and interests on both sides, politics ideally works to balance those rival interests and needs rather than have one side trump the other. But balancing rival interests and concerns is not something to which the initiative process is well suited. It is a winner-take-all process that enables advocates to ignore the interests or concerns of opponents. The legislature, in contrast, is designed to compromise competing interests and weigh intensity of preference.

The legislature in Oregon, like legislatures across the country, had in fact been moving, albeit slowly, in the direction of open records. In 1983 the legislature had established a mutual consent volunteer registry system that allowed both birth parents and adoptees to receive identifying information as well as non-identifying information. Whereas Measure 58 privileged and protected only one right—the right of the adoptee to know—the 1983 legislation explicitly recognized and sought to balance at least five separate interests or rights: the "strong desire" on the part of some adoptees to obtain identifying information about their birth parents; the equally strong desire of some birth parents to obtain identifying information about their genetic offspring; and the "the right to privacy and confidentiality" on the part of those adoptees, birth mothers, and adoptive parents who preferred not to divulge their identities. A decade later, in 1993, the legislature went a step further, adding a "search and consent" procedure that allowed adoptees and birth parents to commission (for a fee of four hundred dollars) the state or the agency that did the adoption to search for and ascertain whether the other party was willing to make contact. The Oregon legislature had not, as neighboring Washington had in the early 1990s, guaranteed open records for all future adoptees, but the legislature's inaction was not due to any resistance to such an idea but rather to the absence of any group taking the trouble to advocate it. Open adoptions had become the norm within the adoption profession. Today it is not uncommon for birth parents to receive a scrapbook of photos charting the adoptee's life, while adoptive parents routinely receive exhaustive information about the medical and social history of their adopted child and the child's family. Adoption rights activists had scant incentive to push for legislation that would do little more than codify the status quo, while possibly making it harder to achieve what they really wanted, to open up past adoption records, often their own.

From Hill's perspective, though, "nothing had happened [in the Oregon legislature] for twenty years." She dismissed the 1993 legislation as "horrible" and "pure extortion." Adoptees were made to pay for something that should have been theirs by right. Moreover, the search process lacked any accountability since the adoptee had no way to determine whether the agency had done a competent search, or that the intermediary handled the contact well. Certainly it is true that as a practical matter the legislation has had a negligible impact on reuniting adoptees and their birth parents; the state agency that handles more than 90 percent of the search requests reports that as of April 2000 only 235 searches had been requested, and of these only a little more than one quarter had resulted in reunions. The voluntary registry may have been an advance when it was first introduced, but in Hill's view it had largely proven ineffective since so many people failed to register. The twenty-five hundred names on the registry represented only a fraction of the people eligible to place their names on the registry of identifying information. According to Hill, any attempt to create a tiered system, with different rules for different adoptees (depending on the date of adoption), meant an unfair "patchwork" system that discriminated against some adoptees. To treat adoptees differently based on their date of adoption was as unacceptable as allowing black people born after 1965 to ride at the front of the bus while requiring blacks born before that date to remain at the back of the bus.

Hill's uncharitable judgment of the Oregon legislature and the adoption establishment contained one essential truth: despite all the progress made toward open adoptions since the 1970s, state legislators, judges, and adoption professionals across the nation remained strongly opposed to abrogating unilaterally the understandings of confidentiality and anonymity that enveloped adoptions from earlier decades. A bill similar in spirit to Hill's initiative had been introduced in the Oregon legislature in the 1997 session and never even received a hearing. In neighboring Washington, where Bastard Nation had focused much of its energies, the legislature had continually rebuffed attempts to open past adoption records. If records were to be opened retroactively, it was abundantly apparent by the late 1990s that the change would not come through the normal legislative process or through the courts, which had uniformly rejected claims that adoptees had a constitutional right to sealed adoption records. A direct appeal to the people appeared the only realistic way to break through the entrenched orthodoxy. Whatever the merits of retroactively opening adoption records, this was arguably the sort of battle between outsider and establishment that supporters of the initiative process had in mind when they brought direct legislation to Oregon at the beginning of the twentieth century.

Measure 58 had many of the problems that accompany so many initiatives. There were the doubts that voters understood the current state of the law, particularly the many options already available under current law to adoptees who sought only nonidentifying medical information. The opposition's lack of money made educating the public particularly difficult. Moreover, since people were not given the option of choosing between competing initiatives, we do not know whether they would have preferred a prospective change to a retrospective one. Most troubling of all, this morally charged question was decided by people who would not be affected by the legislation. The initiative was a species of tyranny of the majority, with a large but unaffected public making a decision that adversely affected a tiny minority of birth mothers. Finally, legislative intransigence on this issue was due not to legislative ineptitude, corruption, or powerful, monied special interests but rather to the power of professional expertise cogently expressed, the legislature's desire to protect an intense but politically vulnerable minority, and legislators' principled commitment to compromises that took into account all affected interests.

Yet despite these problems, aspects of Measure 58 highlight the promise of the initiative process. In several ways it is a model citizen initiative. To begin with, Hill's naive but fortuitous choice to write the measure as a statutory rather than a constitutional change allowed the legislature to respond quickly to the concerns of the losers and craft a compromise amendment, resulting in legislation that both Hill and adoption professionals endorsed. The amendment, skillfully brokered by House minority leader Kitty Piercey, allowed birth parents to file a voluntary contact form where they can indicate either that (1) they would like to be contacted, (2) they would prefer to be contacted only through an intermediary, or (3) they do not want to be contacted. If they choose the third option, they must provide to the state updated, nonidentifying medical and genetic information. When the adoptee receives his birth certificate, he or she also receives the voluntary contact form indicating whether one or both of the birth parents desire contact. Early reports indicated that nearly half of the birth parents who filled out the voluntary contact form indicated they did not wish to be contacted by their offspring. Although Measure 58 took into account only the interests of adoptees, the end result was legislation that also enabled birth mothers to express their desires and needs. The initiative thus proved a spur to policy innovation without taking the place of or preempting legislative action.

Like many successful initiatives, Measure 58 went through an extensive, expensive court challenge. Although the nearly one and a half years of legal challenges were a source of tremendous frustration to many supporters of the measure, the court's actions were a model of judicial self-restraint. The legal challenge, brought on behalf of seven birth mothers, maintained that the initiative violated the contracts clause of the state and federal constitutions and violated privacy rights guaranteed under both constitutions. The Oregon Court of Appeals acknowledged that birth mothers may have "a legitimate interest in keeping secret the circumstances of a birth that is followed by an adoption," but legitimate interests, a unanimous court emphasized, "do not necessarily equate with fundamental rights." Just as there is no constitutional right to have a child adopted, there is no fundamental right to have one's identity concealed from a child one has put up for adoption. As for the question of contract, the court could find no evidence in the statutes that the legislature had intended to or had in fact created a legal contract guaranteeing anonymity to birth mothers. Instead, it found "a legislative intent to balance the interests of all concerned parties rather than to place the interests of one party over those of another." The court did not question that plaintiffs had received assurances of confidentiality from staff at hospitals and private adoption agencies, but it found that such promises of absolute confidentiality were never guaranteed by statute. Throughout this period, for instance, a court order could be obtained that would release birth certificates to adoptees without consultation with the birth mother.[9] The court's refusal to invent an unassailable, fundamental right to anonymity, like Hill's original decision to craft the bill as a statute, kept the issue in the political arena, where competing interests and needs could be balanced and hammered out by affected interests and accountable elected officials.

The most impressive aspect of the tale of Measure 58 remains Helen Hill herself. Fired by a cause she believed in passionately, and at great personal cost to herself and her family, she embarked on a political course that seemed to have no prospect for success. Many of those who shared her goals questioned her tactics; the president of the American Adoption Congress, for instance, warned Hill that her initiative would set adoption reform back twenty years if it lost. Against long odds, and with little if any relevant political experience, Hill persevered and eventually triumphed. In an age of political cynicism, in which people are too quick to believe that ordinary people can't make a difference in politics, one cannot but be moved by her story of faith and commitment. What makes Hill's story particularly appealing is that, having sacrificed and won, she embraced a return to the life she had interrupted for the better part of two years. Unlike those perennial initiative activists for whom direct legislation becomes a way of life, a habit-forming hobby, or a well-paying job, Hill has had enough of initiative politics. Measure 58, she vows, is her last initiative. Not that she plans a retreat to a purely private, self-absorbed existence. The initiative has brought her invitations to speak before groups inspired by her activism, and she has recently purchased an old Masonic temple with the aim of converting it into a community center for art and theater to help ameliorate what she sees as the fragmentation of community. Although the initiative has changed her life, making her something of a local public hero in tiny Nehalem Bay and giving her a self-confidence and sense of direction perhaps previously lacking, the future life she charts for herself is reassuringly similar to the one she lived before the initiative: painting and teaching, hiking and community involvement, and, hopefully, getting the organic farm going again.

THE UNHAPPY TALE OF MEASURE 8

If every initiative sponsor resembled Helen Hill, the initiative process, for all its flaws and limitations, would be in good shape, a valuable supplement to the political process. But the Helen Hills of the initiative world are unfortunately all too scarce. A more typical and sobering tale is the saga of Measure 8, a 1994 Oregon initiative that required public employees to pay 6 percent of their salaries toward retirement benefits, thereby effectively cutting the pay of public employees across the state by 6 percent. In contrast to Measure 58, which garnered a decisive popular majority, Measure 8 passed by the slimmest of margins; fewer than one thousand votes in a state of several million people separated the two sides. Whereas Measure 58 originated with an ordinary citizen, Measure 8 was the handiwork of one ambitious politician, a handful of perennial initiative activists, and an extremely rich patron. When Helen Hill was done, she returned to her regular life; when the proponents of Measure 8 were finished, they immediately turned to their next initiative projects.

Measure 8 had its genesis in a network of conservative political activists who had cooperated on initiative and political campaigns dating back to a 1982 property tax limitation initiative, one of a string of four property tax limit initiatives to fail at the ballot box in the 1980s. In 1984 several of the veterans in the property tax battle turned their attention to public employee pensions and crafted an initiative that would have required the pensions of public employees to be no more generous than the average private retirement plan. Among other things, the initiative would have repealed the PERS (Public Employees Retirement System) "pickup" provision by which a cash-strapped legislature in the late 1970s allowed public employers to pick up the 6 percent employee retirement contribution in lieu of a pay increase. Coordinating the signature drive for the Fair Pay campaign was a forty-four-year-old Australian immigrant, Ruth Bendl. Also involved in a limited way in the signature-gathering effort was a young, politically ambitious man by the name of Bill Sizemore. The effort to qualify the measure failed, as did another attempt to qualify a similar initiative (this time with Bendl as the chief petitioner) in the subsequent election cycle. Over the next few years, Bendl remained active as a volunteer in various state and local initiative drives, but by the late 1980s this small, loosely knit cadre of conservative activists had remarkably little to show for their activism. Even attempts to qualify a property tax limitation failed in 1988, making it the first time in a decade that voters were not faced with a statewide initiative that offered to limit or lower property taxes. But in 1990 the perseverance of the initiative activists finally paid off with the passage of Measure 5, a property tax limitation measure that rocked and shocked the political establishment. The triumph gave the ragtag band of true believers a credibility and swagger they had hitherto lacked and helped persuade a few very rich and conservative businessmen that the initiative process was a wonderful way of changing state policy, with a far quicker and more reliable return on their investment than candidate contributions. The potency of big money mixed with populist righteousness was confirmed by a term limits initiative (Measure 3) in 1992, spearheaded by Measure 5 cosponsor Frank Eisenzimmer, which raised almost 90 percent of its money from four individuals.

The smallest of those four contributions was fifteen thousand dollars from Loren Parks, an eccentric recluse who had made millions manufacturing medical and electronic equipment. Parks had never before contributed to an initiative campaign, but having seen the immediate effect his money had on the process, he now wanted to do more, much more. Bendl, meanwhile, stirred by the triumphs of Measures 5 and 3, was looking to revive her earlier attempts to repeal the PERS pickup. In January 1993, just two months after the term limits triumph, Eisenzimmer—who knew that Parks was in the market for new initiatives in which to invest, and that Bendl was in need of a backer for her public employees initiative—invited the two to his house to meet each other. Parks and Bendl hit it off. Parks was enthusiastic about Bendl's idea to repeal the PERS pickup and agreed to fund the "Pick Up" measure committee that Bendl had formed to qualify the ballot measure. Bendl was soon put on Parks' payroll and paid $750 a month for qualifying initiatives and $750 a month for producing (with Parks's video equipment and facilities) a cable access show called "Taxpayers Speak Out." Bendl's job was not only to coordinate the signature-gathering campaign for the public employee measure but also to help qualify the other four measures in which Parks ended up investing: three criminal justice measures that had been drafted by two state legislators and Eisenzimmer's initiative to require a public vote on all tax increases.[10]

With Parks' fortune securely behind her (in the end Parks would spend over $150,000 on the initiative, including $88,000 for an advertising campaign), Bendl and her allies went looking for political supporters. They particularly needed someone who could spearhead a public campaign to sell the measure to voters. They quickly found their man in thirty-eight-year-old Bob Tiernan, a newly elected Republican state legislator who was making waves in the state capitol with his confrontational style and his eagerness to take on the public employees unions. Tiernan was an employment attorney who had taken a course on retirement plans while receiving a master's degree in labor law from Georgetown University, a background that landed him on the House Commerce Committee Subcommittee on Labor, through which flowed all bills relating to the public employee retirement system. Bendl's original idea had simply been to repeal the

6 percent pickup, but Tiernan wanted to do more. In just his first few months in the legislature, Tiernan had discovered a number of other public employee benefits that he believed were abuses that needed to be exposed and ended. Public employees, he found, were guaranteed an 8 percent annual return on their retirement funds; if the fund performed below that level, the state had to step in and make up the difference. In addition, Tiernan had been shocked to discover that public employees could apply half of their unused sick leave toward retirement. A public employee who had two years of sick leave accumulated could thus retire a year early without penalty. Tiernan insisted on adding two sections to the initiative that would eliminate the guaranteed return and the use of sick leave toward retirement. Working with Sizemore, whom Bendl had recruited to be a chief petitioner, Tiernan revised the initiative throughout the spring before the final version of the initiative was filed in May.

Tiernan had never been involved in an initiative campaign before, but he was no Helen Hill. He had always harbored political ambitions. In college, where he majored in political science, he ran for student body president (he lost). Shortly after returning to Oregon from Georgetown, the thirty-year-old Tiernan ran for the state senate against a powerful Democratic incumbent, Joyce Cohen. He lost, but, undeterred, he ran against Cohen again in 1990 in what was at the time the most expensive state senate race in Oregon history. He lost narrowly, but in 1992, at the age of thirty-seven, he finally achieved his ambition, winning a seat in the state House of Representatives. Taking the initiative route appealed to Tiernan, who dripped contempt for most of his legislative colleagues, whom he regarded as spineless and in the pocket of special interests. In fact, Tiernan liked it so much that within six months of filing the PERS initiative, he had linked up with a fellow legislative renegade, Kevin Mannix, to write and file another three initiatives, each of which, buoyed by the financial backing of Parks and the signature-gathering experience of Bendl, qualified for the ballot.

Tiernan's flamboyant and adversarial style was well suited to initiative politics. In the legislature his abrasive, shoot-from-the-hip political style made it difficult for him to earn the respect of legislative colleagues. Even many of those on the same side of the aisle disliked the freshman legislator's often glib and sometimes strident rhetoric. "He doesn't know what the hell he's talking about," grumbled one veteran Republican legislator. Another experienced Republican member, described as "every bit as conservative as Tiernan," conceded that Tiernan made "great sound-bite material" but cautioned that "we owe it to ourselves to be more responsible with the numbers." Tiernan's inflammatory rhetoric and divisive tactics enraged his opponents. "He immediately goes for the throat," complained one union lobbyist. "His reaction is always to attack, attack, attack." To Tiernan the legislature was bought and paid for by the unions; to the unions Tiernan was "an embarrassment," "an inexperienced lawmaker with poorly written bills and a bad attitude."[11]

If many legislators and lobbyists disliked Tiernan's rabble-rousing style,

Bendl, Sizemore, Parks, and other conservative initiative activists loved it. "If we could clone him, we would," quipped Sizemore. With the legislative session over and the PERS initiative now being circulated by Bendl, Tiernan and Sizemore—who, in the summer of 1993 had been selected by Eisenzimmer to head the newly formed Oregon Taxpayers United (OTU)—began a relentless public assault on public employees. "State workers have a very cushy situation," Tiernan opined. "I'd almost call them spoiled children." Public employee benefits were simply "outrageous." "They're cutting such a fat hog," Tiernan told one reporter. "It galls the crap out of me." And it was struggling taxpayers who were being asked to foot the bill for the extravagance of public employees. "Salary and benefit increases for government workers," Sizemore explained after the election, "have come at the expense of private sector workers and retirees, who have been forced into a lower standard of living because of their heavy tax burden. For some, that has meant their kids have not had braces on their teeth or the family has had to keep its older model car. Others have had to turn down the thermostat and eat a lot more spaghetti and a lot less roast beef."[12] Public employees were fat, comfortable, overgrown parasites, feeding off and weakening defenseless taxpayers and retirees.

The public attacks by Sizemore and Tiernan enraged the other side. Union leaders were galled at having the son-in-law of the owner of PayLess Drug Stores, who resided in a house worth half a million dollars in fashionable Lake Oswego, deride public employees as "spoiled children." Tiernan and Sizemore's charge that public employees had "overly generous pay and fringe benefits" infuriated state workers, who had already had their pay frozen for two years, largely because of the 1990 property tax cut initiative, and who were now being faced with a proposed budget that promised a further two-year salary freeze. Most studies showed that although public employees generally had more generous retirement benefits than private sector workers, salaries (not to mention stock options) tended to be better in the private sector, particularly for high-end jobs. Moreover, the notion that public employees' relatively generous public benefits had come at the expense of taxpayers had it almost exactly backward, at least with respect to the PERS pickup. In fact, the arrangement had been made by the state legislature in 1979 as a way of saving the state money. Rather than increase salaries by 6 percent or more to keep up with rampant inflation, the state kept salaries frozen and instead picked up the 6 percent contribution that public employees paid toward their retirement. By enabling employers and employees to avoid paying additional payroll taxes, social security taxes, and workers' compensation costs, the arrangement benefited state government and state employees as well as taxpayers. The win-win situation pioneered by the state led virtually every one of the state's nine hundred public employers—from cities and counties to school and fire districts—to follow the state's lead.[13] Moreover, the sick leave arrangement that Tiernan had targeted had come at the request of employers, who found that employees nearing retirement were using sick leave to take huge chunks of time off. The arrangement by which employees could use half of unused sick leave toward retirement was a compromise designed to minimize disruptions and save money while at the same time giving employees some compensation for unused sick time.

Government officials and union leaders tried to explain these facts to voters, but they also lashed out at Sizemore and especially Tiernan, whom they vilified as evil personified. As one legislator put it, he became "the Darth Vader for the union movement." Tiernan was accused of "trying to make public employees the Jews and niggers of the 1990s," and both Sizemore and Tiernan received death threats from angry public employees. Following Measure 8's victory, Tiernan announced that for his own and his family's safety, he was "pulling the kids out of school and getting out of here." When state workers went on strike the following spring to protest Measure 8, Tiernan appeared at a press conference in the state capitol with a bulletproof vest and the protection of a plainclothes policeman. The unions also circulated a "rogues' gallery" of contributors to the political action committees supporting Measure 8 (many of whom, it turned out, had given money to OTU to support an unrelated tax measure sponsored by the group and had no idea OTU was also involved with Measure 8), with the implicit and often explicit threat of a boycott, if not harrassment.[14]

The opposition responded with far more than just angry rhetoric and menacing threats. Even before the election took place, public employers and employees began searching for loopholes in the measure—and they were not hard to find. The measure's prohibition against offsetting raises did not take effect until January 1, so governmental employers were free to offer 6 percent raises prior to the new year. Many school and fire districts, as well as cities and county governments, negotiated deals for 6 percent pay increases that were contingent on the measure passing. Moreover, since the measure did not abrogate existing contracts, governmental employers could also renegotiate contracts so as to provide for continued employer coverage of the 6 percent payment to PERS. The Eugene school district agreed to an unprecedented ten-year contract (the norm is two- or three-year contracts) and Columbia County to a twenty-year contract, thereby insulating themselves from the measure for the foreseeable future.[15] By January 1, 1995, the vast majority of the close to nine hundred public employers—including cities, school districts, and counties (though not the state and its many agencies)—had negotiated deals that insulated their employees from the effects of Measure 8.

These efforts to subvert Measure 8 outraged the backers of the initiative and led to a further escalation in the war of words. Sizemore and Tiernan threatened to mount recall efforts against county commissioners who voted for offsetting raises or devised other ways to subvert the will of the people.[16] Drawing on the resources of his campaign committee and the largesse of Loren Parks, Tiernan spent thousands of dollars on ads warning Oregonians that "Local Government Officials Are Selling You Out!" Sizemore, too, ran ads accusing school district officials of sneaky and dishonest behavior.[17] Sizemore was appalled that government officials would place themselves above the law. "The voters have spoken, and they don't care," he charged. Tiernan, too, was outraged at officials' "brazen . . . disregard of the voters." Their actions were "an affront to our democratic system" and would only serve to worsen the relationship between government and the people. Sizemore agreed that such actions would "feed the people's already growing distrust of goverment."[18]

The concern that Sizemore and Tiernan showed for trust in government was not misplaced. State leaders, even those most sympathetic to the plight of public employees, resisted following the lead of local governments and school districts precisely because they feared that it would fuel the fires of discontent. But the most serious damage to voter confidence in government was done by Tiernan and Sizemore, most obviously by their explicit message that government was full of arrogant sneaks who paid no heed to the people, but more profoundly by their slash-and-burn, winner-take-all brand of politics. The loopholes that the unions and public employers exploited were in part due to drafting failures, but the far more important cause of the problem was not technical but political. Having made no effort to incorporate the concerns and interests of public employees in the measure, public employees felt the resulting legislation lacked democratic legitimacy. To them it had been imposed from above by sheer force of numbers. Without an effort to forge a consensus or at least compromise, public employees and local governments could be expected to utilize all legal means to circumvent the bill.

It is because initiatives are rarely crafted to include conflicting interests that so much of initiative politics occurs after the election. Measure 8, like Measure 58, attracted more publicity and media coverage after the campaign than during it. Also like Measure 58, Measure 8 was immediately challenged in court by those who had been defeated in the election. Those legal challenges were triggered in part by ambiguities in the bill. For instance, although Sizemore vehemently insisted there was "nothing retroactive about the initiative," an attorney general's opinion issued after the election determined that the prohibition against applying unused sick leave to retirement applied to all unused sick leave for any worker retiring after January 1. Months before the election, an expert in public-sector labor law had pronounced the initiative "a mess" and predicted that "unquestionably, there will be tons of litigation."[19] His prediction proved correct, but the legal challenges, like the frenetic search for loopholes, owed less to technical deficiencies in the language of the initiative than they did to the political shortcomings of the initiative.

At least half a dozen separate legal challenges were brought against Measure 8 in several different circuit courts. One was filed by the Oregon Education Association; another by the state's police force, prison workers, and parole officers; and a third by a diverse group that included the city of Eugene, the statewide association of cities, the Oregon School Employees Association, a local firefighters union, the mayors of Portland and Salem, and two former governors.

These groups came to court with political grievances dressed up in constitutional garb, and the judges were generally only too willing to provide redress. According to one circuit court judge, Measure 8 was unconstitutional because it was a constitutional revision rather than a single constitutional amendment. Even if the measure had been a single amendment, the judge claimed, it would still be invalid since the subject matter of the measure was not appropriate for a constitutional amendment. In another case the circuit judge held that Measure 8 violated the Contracts Clause of the U.S. Constitution. When these cases arrived at the Oregon Supreme Court, a narrow four-to-three majority agreed with the lower court that requiring employees to contribute 6 percent of their salaries to their retirement unconstitutionally abrogated a contract.

The ruling brought a blistering dissent from Justice Michael Gillette, a well-respected judge with no sympathy for the political aims of Tiernan or Sizemore. "If we were charged in this case with writing on a clean slate," Gillette allowed that he "might well set policy in line with that which results from the lead opinion. But the policy choice in this area is entrusted to another branch of government—the people, exercising their legislative power under Article IV, section 1, of the Oregon Constitution." According to the majority, "The most basic purposes of the Contracts Clause, as well as the notions of fundamental fairness that transcend the clause itself, point to these simple principles: the state must keep its promises, and it may depart therefrom only for a significant and legitimate public purpose." But, as Gillette pointed out, the state never promised to pay the entire PERS contribution in perpetuity, nor did the measure break existing contracts. As for "fundamental fairness," that is a political argument, not a constitutional one. As it happens, fairness was the chief argument of Measure 8 proponents, who complained that the imbalance between the benefit packages of private and public sector workers was unfair. If "fundamental fairness" counts as a transcendent value for the Supreme Court, it is not clear why the initiative proponent's interest in fairness should not count as a significant and legitimate public purpose. The real problem with the provision that workers pay 6 percent of their salaries was not that it violated the Constitution but that it was imposed by the state without entering into negotiations with its workforce. When the old contract expires, nothing in the Constitution stops the state, counties, or cities from offering a new contract with less (or more) favorable terms, but no sensible employer would wish to impose a contract to which employees were violently opposed. Worker morale and loyalty are far too valuable for an employer to squander them through an authoritarian solution, even one clothed in populist dress. But these, as Justice Gillette said, are reasons of politics and policy, not of constitutional law.[20]

Tiernan and Sizemore were understandably outraged by the Supreme Court's decision. They assailed what they viewed as a liberal, activist court, accusing the justices of serving their own self-interest since they were themselves beneficiaries of PERS. Sizemore complained that the Supreme Court's decision meant that "any Legislature or any governor can give away the farm, and there is no relief for the taxpayers. . . . How can we let such an absurdity stand?" Tiernan was so upset by the decision that he decided to run for the Supreme Court. Sizemore and Tiernan were right that the decision was largely politics in constitutional disguise, but the blame for the politicization of the judiciary lies at least as much with initiative sponsors as it does with the judges. Lacking the give-and-take of the legislative process, initiatives too often leave only the judiciary standing between a popular impulse and a grave injustice. Measure 8 was a political not a constitutional injustice, the very sort of injustice that the legislative system is designed to weed out (and in fact did weed out). In the absence of legislative checks, it is hardly surprising that judges often feel it necessary to step in to fill the vacuum created by direct democracy.[21]

The problem with relying on the judicial system to clean up after us is twofold. First, and most obvious, is the threat to the judiciary's legitimacy. By entering ever deeper into the political thicket, the judiciary becomes more vulnerable to the sort of partisan and ideological attacks that occurred after the Supreme Court's ruling on Measure 8. More troubling is that reliance on the judiciary as a remedy often perpetuates the zero-sum, winner-take-all politics of the initiative process. With Measure 8, the courts reversed the roles of winner and loser, but there were still clear-cut winners and losers. Prior to the Supreme Court's ruling, the winners were Tiernan and Sizemore and the losers public employees; after the decision it was the public employees' turn to exult in victory and Tiernan and Sizemore's to bemoan their loss. Winning and losing is, of course, an inevitable part of politics, but one of the distinctive virtues of the legislature is that it tries to craft compromises and build consensus so that it is sometimes hard to tell the winners from the losers. Compromise is what makes the legislative process messy and tortuously slow, but it is also the glue that helps hold together a democratic society containing vastly diverse interests and ideologies.

Neither Measure 8 nor Measure 58 fare well when measured against a benchmark of democratic consensus. Both were divisive and produced clear and unambiguous winners and losers. Both were sponsored by people who had difficulty recognizing the valid concerns and arguments of the other side. Sponsors of both measures raised important and legitimate questions about the status quo, but both offered absolutist solutions that insisted on immediate and sweeping change. No efforts were made to phase in the changes gradually or to make exceptions or allowances for people who might be particularly hard hit. Competing arguments and interests were brushed aside or ignored. Backers of both initiatives converted complex policy issues into simple moral matters of right and wrong.

Yet if both Measures 8 and 58 expose the blunt edges of the initiative process as a policy-making instrument, there remain profound differences between the two campaigns, differences that transcend the wisdom of the particular policies pursued. To begin with, Measure 8 was cynically crafted as a constitutional amendment, even though public employees' retirement benefits are self-evidently a statutory rather than a constitutional matter. There was no reason for Measure 8 to be placed in the state constitution other than the proponents' desire to make sure their handiwork could not be altered by the people's elected representatives. Nor was this an isolated piece of cynicism: virtually every initiative that Sizemore, Tiernan, Bendl, and Parks have been involved with has been crafted as a constitutional initiative. The differences between Measures 8 and 58 are even more clearly illustrated by the contrast between the proponents of the two initiatives. Hill became politicized by her passion for a single issue, pursued that passion with a single-minded commitment for two years, and then returned to her normal life after she had accomplished her goal. In contrast, for the principal players in Measure 8 initiative politics was their life and sometimes their livelihood. When the Measure 8 campaign was over, they immediately sought out new initiatives. In 1996 Parks and Bendl set up a signature-gathering firm, Canvasser Services, which qualified six conservative initiatives—including three written by Parks' employees and associates—and was instrumental in qualifying two others as well as a popular referendum. Even after a falling out between Bendl and Parks following the 1996 election, both continued to be active in initiative campaigns. In 2000, for example, Bendl helped coordinate signature gathering for a spending cap initiative that was spearheaded by Don McIntyre, coauthor of Measure 5 in 1990 and an old friend of Bendl's from the initiative drives of the early 1980s. Parks, meanwhile, continued to be the financial archangel for many conservative initiatives, particularly those sponsored by Sizemore, who has become the eight-hundred-pound gorilla of Oregon politics. In 1996 Sizemore qualified and narrowly passed another property tax limit measure; the following election he ran unsuccessfully for governor and narrowly failed to pass an initiative designed to cripple the political power of unions. Undeterred by either setback, Sizemore returned with a vengeance in 2000, qualifying a record six initiatives.

Tiernan, too, remained active in initiative politics, though not on a Sizemorian scale. After seeing all four of his initiatives triumph at the ballot box in 1994, Tiernan was returned to the legislature for a second term in 1995. In 1996 he spearheaded Measure 32, a popular referendum to repeal a legislatively approved expansion of light rail in the Portland area, and also campaigned actively in favor of Sizemore's property tax cut initiative and a victims' rights initiative sponsored by Representative Kevin Mannix, his collaborator on the criminal law measures from the 1994 election. All three initiatives passed, but the voters in Tiernan's predominantly Republican district had tired of his confrontational act and handed him a stunning setback, throwing him out of office in favor of a Democratic challenger who preached moderation and conciliation. The day after his defeat, though, Tiernan remained upbeat, stating, "It's a great day. . . . Those three measures will do more than the entire Legislature to change the way we do business in this state."[22]

The setback that really rankled Tiernan was the Oregon Supreme Court's decision to strike down Measure 8. Within a month of being turned out of office, he filed an initiative that would overturn regulations restricting judges from raising money directly and from discussing decisions during campaigns. (At about the same time he also filed an initiative that would shift lottery funds from public education and economic development into college tuition—a subject much on his mind at a time when his three children were between the ages of ten and sixteen.) The aim of the judicial initiative was to lift the profile of judicial races, making them more competitive and more politicized, and thereby making it easier for challengers to unseat incumbents. When an opening on the Supreme Court suddenly opened up in the spring of 1998, Tiernan abandoned the initiative in favor of running for the Supreme Court. Funded largely by Parks and two other prominent conservatives, Tiernan smashed the previous records, spending an unprecedented two hundred thousand dollars on the campaign and landing in a run-off election. In a final twist, just two months before the general election Tiernan mysteriously withdrew from the race, citing personal and professional reasons. Although Tiernan is currently involved full time in his law practice (he was a chief petitioner for a "safe neighborhoods" initiative in 2000 but never seriously pursued it), he has no intention of leaving the political limelight. As soon as he is through paying for his kids' college (unfortunately for Tiernan his college tuition initiative never got off the ground), he plans to reenter politics, probably to run for the same state senate seat he failed to win in 1986 and 1990.

When the initiative process first fired the minds of men, it is a safe bet that those men did not have in mind a professional lawyer-politician such as Tiernan, the well-oiled initiative machine of Sizemore, a veteran signature gatherer like Bendl, and certainly not the deep pockets of a Parks. Yet the initiative process today, particularly in states that make heavy use of direct legislation, is dominated by the Tiernans and the Sizemores, the Parks and the Bendls. The Helen Hills who can pry the sword from the stone are few and far between. Where did things go wrong? How did we get to this point, one that seems so distant from the idealism and involvement of ordinary citizens that we still associate or want to associate with direct democracy? Is there anything we can do to rediscover and reclaim the idealism of the initiative process? These are the questions that animate this book.

2
The Initiative Revolution

In the beginning the initiative was widely seen as the province of political cranks and irresponsible radicals. Early proponents of the initiative were almost invariably on the far left of the American political spectrum, beyond where either major political party dared or even desired to tread. The first political party to endorse the initiative and referendum was the Socialist Labor party; next came the insurgent People's (a.k.a. Populist) party. A list of direct legislation supporters in the early and mid-1890s reads like a who's who of late-nineteenth-century American radicalism: Terence Powderly, head of the Knights of Labor for a decade and a half; the socialist labor leader Eugene Debs; the utopian novelist Edward Bellamy; Ignatius Donnelly, the great Populist orator and author of the stirring preamble to the Populists' 1892 platform; James B. Weaver, the presidential candidate of the Greenback party in 1880 and the Populist party in 1892; J. A. Wayland, editor of two of the nation's most important radical newspapers, the *Coming Nation* and the *Appeal to Reason;* the Christian Socialist Benjamin O. Flower, who used his reform journal, *The Arena,* to spread the direct democracy gospel; and Jacob Coxey, who famously led a disgruntled army of unemployed workers in a protest march on Washington. Direct legislation began as the handmaiden of economic radicalism.[1]

THE INITIATIVE'S RADICAL PAST

In South Dakota, the first state to adopt the initiative and referendum, the idea of having citizens legislate directly was pioneered in the mid-1880s by a radical priest and union activist, Robert W. Haire. A member of the Knights of Labor, Haire used the organization and publications of the Knights' local chapter to agitate on behalf of direct democracy. The iconoclastic Haire, who would subsequently enlist in the Populist party and then the Socialist party, was soon joined in the crusade for direct democracy by Henry Loucks, the influential president of the South Dakota Farmers' Alliance (and future president of the national Farmers' Alliance). In addition to running the Farmers' Alliance, Loucks also edited the state's most influential agrarian reform paper, the *Ruralist,* the front-page motto of which was "Socialism in Our Time." Beginning in 1891, Loucks used the *Ruralist* to promote the initiative and referendum as not only "the latest and fullest development of popular government" but as an essential means to achieve the economic reforms necessary to tame economic power and obtain social justice. In 1892 the South Dakota Independent party (which had been formed in 1890 by representatives of the Farmers' Alliance and the Knights of Labor) made the initiative and referendum a central plank of its platform, while a local assembly of the Knights of Labor organized a statewide Initiative and Referendum League, which quickly attracted a wide range of reformers. As the economy skidded into depression in 1893, Loucks' *Ruralist* attributed the farmer's economic woes to the absence of direct legislation: "We are paying $5 more than we ought for each ton of hard coal, 7 cents more than we ought for each gallon of kerosene or gasoline, 25 to 90 cents more than we ought for each telegram, three times as much as we ought for express and easily double a reasonable charge for freight. Why? Simply because we do not have direct legislation by the initiative and referendum in state and nation." Growing popular demands for the initiative and referendum were met with studied indifference from the state's political leaders, particularly from the Republicans, who dominated South Dakota politics. Only after the 1896 election, when the Populists (known as "Fusionists" because the party now included dissident "Silver Republicans" as well as Democrats) secured a majority in the state legislature, were proponents of the initiative and referendum able to muster the votes necessary to refer the matter to a vote of the people. Every Populist/Fusionist legislator voted in favor of the constitutional amendment; only Republicans voted against it.[2]

The radical pedigree of the initiative and referendum was also displayed in New Jersey, a state that can lay claim to being the birthplace of the national initiative and referendum movement in America, even though direct legislation was never enacted there. The initiative and referendum was promoted in the early 1880s by the maverick Benjamin Urner, who had run unsuccessfully as a candidate for the antimonopoly Greenback party in 1882, but it was the formation of the labor-led People's Power League in Newark that gave organized direction to the movement for direct democracy in New Jersey. The People's Power League elected delegates to attend the 1892 Populist national convention to press direct legislation on the fledgling party. The delegation's leader was labor journalist Joseph R. Buchanan, who only a few years earlier had been a leader of the extreme left wing in the Knights of Labor, a prominent figure within the Marxist International Workingmen's Association, and a professed anarchist and revolutionary. Buchanan was named to the platform committee at the Populist convention and—at least so the story goes—refused to yield the floor until the committee included some mention of direct legislation. The Populists agreed to add a supplementary resolution commending the initiative and referendum "to the favorable consideration of the people." However, the People's Power League (soon to be renamed the Direct Legislation League of New Jersey) failed to persuade the New Jersey state legislature to endorse direct legislation. In 1895, when the Republican-dominated state legislature refused even to bring the proposed initiative and referendum amendment to the floor for a vote, and with the state's leading newspapers ignoring or ridiculing the idea, New Jersey's advocates of direct legislation again turned their eyes toward the national stage. Under the leadership and guidance of the socialist Eltweed Pomeroy, secretary of New Jersey's Direct Legislation League, the New Jersey activists spearheaded the creation of the first national organization dedicated to the spread of the initiative and referendum, the National Direct Legislation League. Pomeroy, whose columns on direct legislation appeared regularly in a variety of radical and socialist journals, was promptly elected the league's first president, and the Newark-based *Direct Legislation Record,* which Pomeroy edited, was made the league's official organ.[3]

Arguably the single most important event in the birth of the initiative and referendum in America was the publication, early in 1892, of a small book with the awkward title *Direct Legislation by the Citizenship through the Initiative and Referendum.* So electric was its impact that the title page of the 1893 edition boasted that it was "the book that started the Referendum Movement." Its author, James W. Sullivan, a member of the New York Typographers' Union, explicitly addressed the volume to the "radical world." In the mid-1880s Sullivan, who at the time was a devotee of Henry George and the single tax, had become interested in the Swiss model of direct legislation, and in 1888 he took a leave of absence from his job as editor of a reform weekly to visit Switzerland and investigate the impact direct legislation had had on the nation's economics and politics. Sullivan was not the first to describe the Swiss experience, but he was the first to make the Swiss model seem relevant to the United States. Sullivan's message to American workers was simple and appealing: by empowering the wage-working majority, direct legislation would destroy "the American plutocracy." Under the current system, employees were forced to resort to strikes to improve their wages and working conditions. But the deck was stacked against the striking worker. Arrayed against him "are a ring of employers, a ring of officials enforcing class law made by compliant representatives at the bidding of shrewd employers, and a ring of public sentiment makers—largely professional men whose hope lies with wealthy patrons. Behind these outer barriers, and seldom affected by even widespread strikes, lies the citadel in which dwell the monopolists." Introduce the initiative and the referendum, Sullivan preached, and the walls of the citadel would come crumbling down. The "straightforward politics of direct legislation" had peacefully and simply transformed Switzerland, and there was no reason it could not usher in a similarly bloodless social revolution in the United States.[4]

Among the many American radicals to be captivated by Sullivan's message, none was more important than the founding father of Oregon's initiative and referendum, the blacksmith-turned-lawyer William Simon U'Ren. U'Ren acquired the skills of the blacksmithing trade and a zeal for economic radicalism and political reform from his father, a devoted socialist all of his long life. After reading Henry George's *Progress and Poverty* (1879) in his early twenties, U'Ren became an enthusiastic convert to the single tax on land, the aim of which was to redistribute wealth from idle, parasitic landholders to the common people, who mixed their labor with the land. Upon moving to Portland, Oregon, in 1889, U'Ren soon gravitated toward the nearby Milwaukie farmhouse of Seth and Sophronia Lewelling, which was a magnet for the area's "advanced thinkers." The Lewellings hosted regular séances, Sunday afternoon "salons" that attracted radicals and reformers from across the state, and weekly meetings of the newly formed Milwaukie branch of the Farmers' Alliance. It was at one of these weekly meetings in the late autumn of 1892 that U'Ren encountered Sullivan's recently published book. Although U'Ren had come across the idea of the initiative and referendum a year or two earlier, Sullivan's study fired his imagination. U'Ren felt the veil lift from his eyes. "I forgot, for the time, all about Henry George and the single tax. All these I now saw to be details. The one important thing was to restore the law-making power where it belonged—into the hands of the people. Once give us that, we could get anything we wanted—single tax, anything."[5]

After reading Sullivan's book, U'Ren introduced a resolution at the Milwaukie Alliance's next meeting that called for the establishment of a committee to "agitate and work for the adoption of the initiative and referendum." The idea was to set up a small joint committee that would include one representative from each of five organizations: the Oregon Farmers' Alliance, the State Grange, the Portland Federated Trades, the Oregon Knights of Labor, and the Portland Chamber of Commerce. The latter declined the offer, refusing to become involved with "any (expletived) Populist phantasm," but each of the farm and labor organizations accepted (including the Portland Central Labor Council, which had subsequently been invited), forming the Joint Committee on Direct Legislation, with U'Ren, the Farmers' Alliance representative, as secretary. The committee spearheaded a massive propaganda campaign designed to mobilize popular support for direct democracy. Its rhetoric was unabashedly radical and populist: the legislature was a bastion of "the monied and monopolistic classes," and only direct legislation would "make it impossible for corporations and boodlers to obtain unjust measures by which to profit at the expense of the people." More than just the rhetoric was radical, for the organization also demanded a mandatory referendum that would require all legislation passed at the state, county, or municipal level be approved by voters before becoming law. U'Ren also pressed the direct democracy agenda from within the Populist party. After joining the party in 1893, he was soon selected secretary of the Populist state committee and then

chair of the 1894 Populist state convention. In 1896 he carried the battle directly
to the Oregon state legislature as a Populist state legislator.[6]

FROM THE MARGINS TO THE MAINSTREAM

How did a set of reforms steeped in labor radicalism and agrarian protest movements survive and indeed flourish after the movements that had given birth to
those reforms had begun to decline? South Dakota was the exception; there the
1896 election had brought the Populists into power, albeit briefly. Nationally,
though, the trend was the reverse: toward Populist decline and Republican hege-
mony. Oregon was more typical; after the 1896 election the Republicans still
commanded over two thirds of the legislative seats, whereas the Populists com-
prised only about one sixth of the legislature. By the next election the Populist
party had vanished almost without trace, U'Ren had been defeated in his run for
the Senate, and the state legislature remained firmly in the hands of the Republican party. And yet a funny thing happened in the 1899 session: the legislature
voted in favor of the initiative and referendum by an overwhelming and nonpartisan majority. In 1895 the conservative Republican editor of the *Oregonian,* Harvey Scott, had helped defeat the initiative and referendum by relentlessly
attacking it as "one of the craziest of all the crazy fads of Populism," yet by 1899
Scott, along with a host of other influential figures in the state, had endorsed the
reforms. In less than a decade a dangerous "Pop fad" had become safe, conventional, and consensual.

Since the mid-1880s radicals in the labor movement and agrarian protest
movements had been attracted to direct legislation for its transformative promise.
It would enable farmers and workers to turn the tables on corporate power and
economic privilege, using numbers to defeat money. But so long as the vision
was revolutionary or tied to a specific policy agenda—such as progressive taxation on land, income, and inheritances, or higher wages and shorter working
days—it was difficult if not impossible to gain the support of the establishment:
publishers and editors, bankers, lawyers, professionals, the comfortable middle
class, and party politicians. The widespread economic distress and discontent of
the early 1890s had created a window of opportunity for economic radicalism,
but by 1896 the window was fast closing. If direct legislation were to be established across the country, it would need to appeal to more than just disaffected
laborers and intellectuals; it would have to dance not just with those who brought
it but with those who had initially spurned and spat upon it. After 1896 the initiative and referendum movement increasingly became a political movement
divorced from any particular economic vision.[7]

In Oregon the shift from margins to mainstream was symbolized by the
establishment, in the fall of 1897, of the Non-Partisan Direct Legislation League,
which replaced the faltering Joint Committee. U'Ren, who was by now a nation-

ally known figure in the movement, retained his position as secretary, but the makeup and tactics of the two organizations were radically different. Whereas the Joint Committee had been made up of representatives from labor and farm groups (several of which—specifically the Knights of Labor and Farmers' Alliance—were now insignificant if not extinct), the new league was governed by an executive committee made up of a number of the state's most prominent citizens, including the *Oregonian*'s Harvey Scott, the president of the State Bar Association, and a number of the state's leading bankers and businessmen. The old Joint Committee had unashamedly aligned itself with the Populist party and its agenda, whereas the Non-Partisan League, as its title clearly signaled, carefully adhered to a rigorously nonpartisan policy. Not only did the makeup and tactics of the two groups differ, but so did the groups' propaganda. Whereas the Joint Committee excoriated political representatives as the handmaidens of economic privilege and emphasized the new policies that could be enacted by initiative, the Non-Partisan League tended to justify direct legislation as a safeguard of last resort, remedying the abuses and corrupt excesses that prevented the legislature from operating optimally.[8]

U'Ren's rhetoric and position also shifted during this period. Through 1895 he had vigorously advocated a mandatory referendum on all or nearly all laws. During the 1895 legislative session he was confident that the people "will demand the right to propose and vote direct on *all* remedial legislation." Even after the mandatory referendum was narrowly defeated in the state legislature, U'Ren continued to argue that "no state law save those which the constitution provides to be for maintenance of officers, the penitentiary and asylums, and these on the most economical grounds, should become law until referred to and adopted by the people." In 1896, however, U'Ren suddenly abandoned the mandatory referendum in favor of an optional referendum. Moreover, he began to downplay direct legislation's transformative powers. By the end of 1897, after the state legislature had again failed to act on the initiative and referendum, U'Ren stressed that direct legislation would be used infrequently. Far from citizens becoming political animals, the initiative would allow Oregonians to "give our time to our business and only touch politics occasionally as an incidental duty—and yet do vastly more effective work than was ever done by any amount of labor under the present system." The threat of the initiative and referendum would be sufficient to force the politicians to clean up their act and prevent them from passing wasteful, pernicious, or unjust laws. Direct legislation would be the "gun behind the door."[9]

The shift from margin to mainstream in Oregon was mirrored in developments across the nation. In 1901 George Shibley, founder of the Non-Partisan Federation for Securing Majority Rule, replaced Pomeroy as the leading national figure in the direct legislation movement. Shibley was a tireless advocate for the initiative and referendum, but his rhetoric differed sharply from that used by the leaders of the direct legislation a decade earlier. In Shibley's view, the initiative and referendum should be applied "only to those subjects where the existing state laws are so bad that practically everyone favors a change." On the overwhelming majority of issues the voters should and would stay out of the legislature's way. "It is the representatives," he explained, "who know of the evils in the bills, and it is not the voters in general who know about it." Echoing U'Ren, Shibley predicted that as corruption was eradicated from the representative system, resort to direct legislation would become increasingly rare. In the not-so-distant future "the people in general will pay no more attention to the details of legislation than they now pay to details of medicine or of architecture. Specialists will be employed in both fields. It will be only the broad questions of public policy and the details of installing a new policy that will command the attention of voters."[10]

Shibley's prediction was offered in 1902, several months after Oregon voters had overwhelmingly approved the constitutional amendment establishing the initiative and referendum, making Oregon the third state to adopt direct legislation. (South Dakota was the first, and in Utah, the second, the initiative and referendum did not take effect until decades later because the legislature refused to pass enabling legislation.) In 1904 two initiatives qualified for the Oregon ballot, making it the first state to try out the new tools of direct democracy. Immediately thereafter the floodgates opened: over the next decade Oregonians voted on over one hundred statewide initiatives and popular referenda. Many longstanding friends of the initiative now worried that direct legislation was being abused. Even before the flood had begun, in January 1906, the *Oregon Journal* reminded Oregonians that "the real friends of the initiative law will be slow to invoke its aid, and when they do it will be to remedy a manifest evil that it is ordinarily difficult if not impossible to reach." The *Oregon Journal*'s editor, C. S. Jackson, a Democrat in the Jacksonian mold and an enthusiastic, longtime advocate of direct legislation, repeated the admonition in 1910: "The way to make direct legislation enduring," he cautioned, "is to employ it with discretion." As president of the Taxpayers' League of Portland, Joseph Neal had initially backed the initiative and referendum because it would "prevent extravagance, encourage good government, [and] above all . . . bring to the people a sense of personal responsibility." By 1909, however, he emphasized that "when originally adopted it was generally thought that only measures of great importance and of limited number would be submitted under the initiative." Neal continued to defend direct legislation but hoped "its benefits will . . . be not in its use, but rather in its potentiality." The same message was transmitted by Harvey Scott's *Oregonian,* which admonished the citizenry to remember that the initiative was to be "the medicine of the constitution, cautiously administered when occasion might require; not its daily bread."[11]

This safer, minimalist conception of direct legislation had helped to broaden direct legislation's appeal beyond radical enclaves and protest politics. But there were still many who continued to be attracted by the initiative and referendum's potential for radical transformation. For them Oregon's example was a beacon of hope in a land of concentrated wealth and centralized power. The imagery of a 1908 *Cincinnati Post* editorial was unashamedly biblical: "Behold the people that walked in darkness have seen a great light. Out of Oregon came a sign. A mighty hope has been born. A new and magic watchword has been sounded. 'Back to the people'—that is the blazing banner round which garners today a victorious host." In a similar vein, the editor of *Hampton's Magazine* exulted that "Oregon has shown the way by which the people may deliver themselves from the control of Big Business." Writing in 1911, an admiring C. Frederick Howe overflowed with enthusiasm for Oregon as "the most complete democracy in the world." The outdated machinery of representative government was "so complicated that the people could not make it reflect their will." Checks and balances and the division of powers served only to "baffle and confuse the people" and to prevent them from expressing their will while offering "slight obstacle to Privilege." Oregon had ushered in a wholly new political era by making "every voter a Moses." Now "if you want anything in Oregon you have to 'see all the people.' Neither the boss, the party, nor all the members of the legislature can deliver the goods." A few went even further, imagining the initiative and referendum would lead to the virtual abolition of the legislature.[12]

As states debated whether to adopt the initiative and referendum in the opening decades of the twentieth century, proponents continued to rely upon both millennial and minimalist justifications. The minimalist rationale appealed to those who feared that direct legislation made utopian demands upon the citizenry and subverted representative democracy, or who worried that the initiative process would be used to launch a class war against the rich and well-to-do or to wage a moral crusade against unpopular minorities. Direct legislation, Woodrow Wilson reassured the doubters, was not "a substitute for representative institutions, but only . . . a means of stimulation and control . . . a sobering means of obtaining genuine representative action on the part of legislative bodies." In this minimalist conception, which typically privileged the referendum over the initiative, direct legislation was just another "safeguard of politics," one which citizens would only need to deploy infrequently to keep politicians in check. The minimalist rationale effectively assuaged fears, but the millennial rationale spoke more directly to people's hopes and dreams. Although the Populist party had long since faded away, the Populist vision—which imagined that the initiative and referendum could usher in a radically transformed world "in which equal rights to all shall live on forever, and special privileges shall be known no more"—was still very much alive in the Progressive era. Direct legislation, in this view, would do more than just add another check on the behavior of legislators; it would, in the words of the *Boston Common,* transform politics by enabling "the rising tide of sentiment for social justice" to sweep away "the special interests which now play for delay." In particular, the initiative would be the means by which the people would ensure that government served "the mass of the people" rather than "the greed of corporate wealth."[13]

A mixture of minimalist and millennial arguments helped to enact the initiative and referendum in nineteen states in the two decades between 1898 and 1918, but neither set of expectations proved a reliable guide to the subsequent history of the initiative. Certainly the initiative and referendum, despite notable and undeniable accomplishments, did little to justify the utopian, emancipatory hopes of radical transformation with which so many early advocates began. True, in some states Populist-backed governmental reforms, from direct election of senators to woman suffrage, were achieved through the initiative, but for the most part these reforms came about the old-fashioned way: through the legislative process. Useful reforms in working conditions (especially shorter hours) were sometimes enacted by initiative, but the more sweeping radical panaceas like the single tax were consistently defeated by voters. Moreover, far from disappearing, money, lobbyists, and powerful special interests continued to play a leading role in every state in the nation, whether the state possessed direct legislation or not. Indeed money and special interests usually played at least as prominent a part in initiative campaigns as they did in candidate campaigns.

The early years of direct legislation did little to vindicate the minimalists either. In Oregon in 1912 there were twenty-eight statewide initiatives on the November ballot, a national record that still stands to this day. The flood of initiatives in Oregon (including seventy-two in the three general elections held between 1910 and 1914) led Harvey Scott, among others, to change his mind again and revert to his earlier opposition to direct legislation. Activists in other states rushed to follow Oregon's lead. Coloradans voted on twenty initiatives in 1912, while in 1914 California's electorate faced seventeen initiatives and Arizona's fifteen. In 1920–21 North Dakota, which enacted the initiative in 1914, voted on sixteen initiatives, a record that the state eclipsed a decade later when citizens were asked to vote on eighteen in 1932. Outside of these hotbeds of initiative activity, the minimalist argument often fared much better. In states like Arkansas, Maine, Massachusetts, Michigan, Nebraska, and Nevada, for instance, the initiative was used sparingly in the first few decades of its existence. (See the appendix, which details initiative use by state and decade.)

The minimalist prediction was particularly relevant in the 1950s and 1960s, as Figure 2.1 attests. Had Harvey Scott been resurrected in 1969, he might well have been tempted to switch his position on the initiative once again. Even in Scott's own Oregon, the state that had used the initiative more often than any other, citizens finally appeared to have learned to use direct democracy with discretion. Between 1956 and 1969 Oregonians voted on only nine initiatives and never faced more than two initiatives on the same ballot. Meanwhile, Oregonians took great pride in their government, turned out to vote in large numbers, and had high levels of trust in their public officials. Elsewhere in the nation the story was much the same. In the thirty years between 1942 and 1971, nearly 350 statewide initiatives made it to the ballot, an average of about one initiative every two years for each of the initiative states.[14] During these three decades, direct

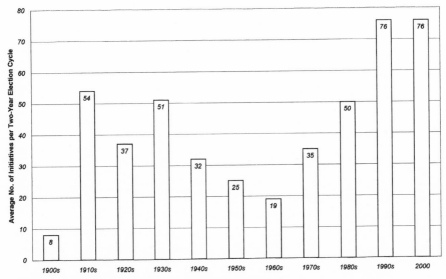

Figure 2.1   Initiative Use in the United States by Decade

legislation did indeed seem to be the gun behind the door that the minimalists had promised, something more valuable for its potential than for its use.

THE SILENT REVOLUTION

Between 1990 and 2000 there were 458 initiatives nationwide. That is over three times the rate at which initiatives appeared on the ballot in the 1940s, 1950s, and 1960s. Today the initiative can no longer be plausibly portrayed as a gun behind the door, at least not in the states that have come to rely most heavily on the initiative process, particularly Oregon, California, Colorado, Washington, and Arizona. In these five states the gun is now madly brandished about and fired in almost every conceivable direction. Politicians scatter, running for cover, desperately trying to keep their heads down. Citizens appear bewildered, unsure what to think. The gunmen cry "power to the people," but few of the people seem to feel more empowered by the blaze of gunfire. To be sure, citizens take a certain delight at the occasional shot lodged in the politicians' posterior, but the gunslingers are not content to threaten only the political class. Vulnerable minorities are at least as likely to be the targets of the shootings as are the rich and powerful. To some it appears that beneath their populist masks, the gunslingers are the very same special interest groups and politicians from which the gun behind the door had promised to protect us.

Table 2.1   Number of Initiatives per Two-year
Election Cycle, 1952–2001

	Mean	High	Low
1952–1971	20	31	10
1972–1975	32	39	25
1976–1987	48	58	42
1988–2001	75	103	61

When was the initiative transformed from a gun behind the door to a weapon of choice for interest groups and politicians? Many observers credit (or blame) California's Proposition 13, the 1978 property tax–cutting initiative that was spearheaded by Howard ("I'm mad as hell") Jarvis. Proposition 13, which passed by an overwhelming majority despite the opposition of virtually every major politician and newspaper in the state, dramatically illustrated direct legislation's enormous power to make public policy as well as to transform the political agenda. And yet Proposition 13 was as much symptom as it was cause. Increased reliance on the initiative, both in California and the nation, was already discernible even before Proposition 13 appeared on the June 1978 ballot. In 1976–77 there were fifty-two initiatives across the nation, the highest number since the 1938–39 election cycle. Californians themselves had voted on ten initiatives in 1972–73; one has to go back a half century to 1922–23 to find more statewide initiatives on the California ballot. Even more telling evidence against the Proposition 13 explanation is that it was not until 1988 that initiative use shifted up into a higher gear nationwide (see Table 2.1). For almost a decade after Proposition 13, the average number of initiatives on the ballot nationally was actually less than the number of initiatives in the two-year election cycle immediately preceding Proposition 13.

Although no single event or year can be unambiguously identified as beginning the modern initiative revolution, there is little doubt about the magnitude of the change. In Oregon, for instance, there were fifty-six statewide initiatives in the five general elections held in the 1990s, an average of over ten per election. That is not far off double the thirty-two initiatives Oregon voters were asked to consider in the 1980s, which in turn was roughly twice the seventeen initiatives on the ballot the preceding decade. In the 1960s Oregonians saw fewer than half that number of initiatives, and none of those were approved. More initiatives passed in the 1980s and 1990s than passed in the previous six decades combined. In 2000 alone Oregonians voted on more initiatives than they did in the twenty-year period between 1956 and 1975. Similarly, in California there were more initiatives on the ballot in the 1980s and 1990s than there were in the previous half century. In fact, more initiatives were approved by California voters in the last two decades of the twentieth century than were passed in the preceding sixty-eight years dating back to the initiative's adoption in 1912. Initiative-made law, once a minor feature of the California political landscape, has become its dominant and defining feature.

Table 2.2   Ranking of the Top Ten Election Cycles in
Initiative Use, 1904–2001

Rank	Election Cycle	No. of Initiatives
1	1996–1997	103
2	1914–1915	92
3	2000–2001	79
4	1932–1933	76
5	1994–1995	75
6	1990–1991	70
7	1992–1993	68
8	1912–1913	67
9	1998–1999	66
10	1988–1989	61

California and Oregon have been the clear leaders in initiative use, but there have been plenty of followers in the past two decades. Even states without a strong tradition of initiative use have increasingly gotten into the act. Idaho, Maine, Nevada, South Dakota, and Utah had more initiatives on the ballot in the 1980s and 1990s than in the previous eight decades of the century combined. Citizens in Maine, for instance, voted on twenty-six initiatives between 1980 and 2000, which is over double the number they had cast judgment on in the previous seventy years. Eight of the nineteen states that have had the initiative power since the early twentieth century experienced as many or more initiatives in the 1990s than in any other decade, and for another four states the 1980s were the peak decade. Across the nation, 35 percent of the approximately two thousand initiatives that have reached the ballot since 1904 qualified in the past two decades. More dramatically still, each of the past seven election cycles rank among the top ten election cycles in initiative use (see Table 2.2). The most recent election cycle (2000–2001) witnessed the third highest number of initiatives in the nation's history.

To be sure, the heavy initiative use of the last two decades is not entirely without precedent. In 1912 and 1914, at the height of the Progressive era, the initiative was heavily used, particularly in the western states of Oregon, Colorado, California, and Arizona. The discontent of the Great Depression triggered widespread use of the initiative in 1932, especially in North Dakota, where there were eighteen initiatives on the ballot. But a focus on these peak years misses the defining difference between initiative use today and initiative use in the early decades of the twentieth century. The ninety-two initiatives in 1914–15 were followed in the next election cycle by less than half that many in 1916–17, tapering off to a mere thirty-three initiatives in the subsequent election cycle of 1918–19. Similarly, the peak years of 1932–33, in which seventy-six initiatives made the ballot, were followed by less than half that number the following two election cycles. Initiative peaks were followed by valleys, and both seemed to bear some rough relationship to the pulse of popular sentiment. In the last decade, however, initiative use has fluctuated relatively little. What states used to see only in occasional bursts of reform enthusiasm or popular discontent, they now experience as a routine part of the policy-making process.

Initiative use indisputably became more widespread in the 1980s and 1990s than it had been in previous decades, but this national pattern is not reproduced in every state. In fact, Arkansas, North Dakota, and Oklahoma used the initiative less often in the 1980s and 1990s than they had in the preceding half century. For a few states it is the 1950s and 1960s that are exceptional, with the 1980s and 1990s representing something of a return to normalcy. In Missouri, for instance, there was only one initiative on the ballot in the 1950s and 1960s, but throughout the rest of the century, including the 1980s and 1990s, the state has consistently averaged about nine initiatives per decade. In other states the absolute number of initiatives remains small despite the increase in initiative use in recent decades. In Utah, for example, almost two-thirds of the state's initiatives appeared on the ballot between 1980 and 2000, but the total number of initiatives in those two decades was only eleven. And just twice during these last two decades has there been more than one initiative on a Utah state ballot. In fact, in 1998–99, eleven of the twenty-four initiative states placed one or fewer initiatives on the state ballot; even in the record-breaking 1996–97 election cycle, in which just over a hundred initiatives qualified for the ballot, there were eight initiative states with one or fewer initiatives. In 2000 seven initiative states had no initiatives at all on the ballot. These statistics help to remind us that when we talk about an initiative revolution we are talking about a phenomenon that has transformed some states while leaving others relatively untouched.

Heavy initiative use remains concentrated in a relatively few states. Between 1980 and 2000 three states (California, Oregon, and Colorado) accounted for 40 percent of the total number of statewide initiatives in the nation. Indeed, Oregon and California alone accounted for 30 percent of statewide initiatives in the 1980s and 1990s and about the same percentage during the rest of the twentieth century. In 2000 these two pace-setting states accounted for close to 40 percent of the nation's initiatives. Six in ten initiatives between 1990 and 2000 came from six states (Arizona, California, Colorado, North Dakota, Oregon, and Washington), and those same six states account for better than 60 percent of the initiatives in the twentieth century. In short, although initiatives are more numerous today than ever before, a handful of high-use states continue to experience the effects of direct legislation in a way that is qualitatively different from other initiative states.

A POPULIST PARADOX

Among the most striking features of the contemporary period is that increased reliance on the initiative has not been accompanied by a rush to adopt direct legislation in other states. This stands in marked contrast to the first two decades of the twentieth century, when high rates of initiative use were accompanied by a rush of states enacting the initiative. In the sixteen years between 1902 and 1918, over two-fifths of the states then in the union adopted the initiative. Only five states have adopted the initiative since then, and four of those (Alaska [1959], Wyoming [1968], Florida [1968], and Illinois [1970]) adopted the initiative between 1959 and 1970, a period in which the initiative was little used across the country. Ironically, only one state has adopted the initiative during the decades of the initiative's greatest popularity. That state is Mississippi, which enacted the initiative in 1992.

More paradoxical still is the antipopulist constraints Misisissippi placed upon the initiative power. The brand of direct democracy enacted in Mississippi bears little resemblance to the populist instrument used in California or in Oregon. To begin with, Mississippi established that no more than five initiatives could appear on any one ballot. The state also refused to permit statutory initiatives or popular referenda. Although voters can change the state constitution by means of an initiative petition, they cannot make laws through the initiative process, nor can they directly negate laws passed by the state legislature. Further constraining voters' ability to utilize the initiative process is a requirement that one-fifth of the petition signatures must come from each of the five congressional districts. The Mississippi initiative process also permits the legislature to place an alternative measure on the same ballot, thereby giving the voters a choice between two bills. To make things even more difficult, the legislature required that the majority in favor of an initiative must comprise at least 40 percent of the number of all voters who cast ballots in that election. Moreover, every initiative that has revenue implications must identify the amount and source of revenue required to implement it; if the initiative reduces revenues or reallocates funding it must specify which programs will be affected. Finally, Mississippi prohibits initiatives that would change the initiative process or alter either the state's bill of rights or its constitutional right-to-work guarantee.[15]

Mississippi's emasculated initiative power resulted from intense opposition by an unlikely legislative alliance of rural conservatives and African-American liberals. Both saw themselves as minority groups who could be harmed by a purely majoritarian system. Blacks feared that whites would use the initiative power to discriminate against them, and legislators from rural districts feared that densely populated urban areas would be advantaged by the initiative. This coalition succeeded in defeating the initiative proposal no fewer that three times in the lower house, and with each defeat the proponents watered down the original proposal still further.

Not surprisingly, persuading legislatures to adopt the initiative process has proved a hard sell, but it is not only legislators who are responsible for the glacial pace of change. Legislators have been able to halt adoption of the initiative precisely because, unlike at the outset of the twentieth century, there has not been a deafening popular outcry in favor of adopting direct legislation. The state that came closest to adopting the initiative in recent decades was Minnesota, a famously progressive state. In 1980, 53 percent of Minnesota voters agreed to adopt the initiative, but the plan failed because a constitutional amendment in Minnesota must be passed by a majority of those who *vote* in the election. Those who showed up to vote but did not vote on that specific measure were effectively counted as "no" votes, and the measure failed. The closely divided Minnesota vote contrasts sharply with the often overwhelming votes in favor of the initiative and referendum at the beginning of the century. In 1902, for instance, Oregonians voted by an eleven-to-one ratio to adopt the initiative and referendum. In Colorado in 1910, over three-quarters of the people voted in the affirmative. The next year, in California direct legislation was also carried by a better than three-to-one vote. Such overwhelming votes in favor of the initiative and referendum were common in the early twentieth century but are nearly unimaginable today.[16]

The increased use of the initiative in the 1980s and 1990s is thus only half the story. If we are to understand the late-twentieth-century initiative process, we must also understand the dog that didn't bark. In the last two decades of the twentieth century, bills to enact the initiative and referendum have been introduced in virtually every state in the nation, but with the exception of Mississippi no state has added the initiative to its democratic arsenal. The initiative's failure to spread to other states has come as a surprise to many political analysts. Interviewed in 1986, three leading experts on the initiative process (including David Magleby, an initiative skeptic, and David Schmidt, an initiative enthusiast) agreed that it was likely that a substantial number of states would adopt the initiative and referendum before the end of the century.[17] Why have such predictions failed to come to pass even while direct legislation is used with increasing frequency in those states that possess the power?

Some initiative proponents might not see this development as paradoxical. In both cases the cause is the same: professional legislators looking out for their own interests or doing the bidding of powerful special interests. In states with the initiative power, this argument goes, the increase in initiative use is attributable to the legislature consistently ignoring popular demands and preferences. And in states without the initiative power, the failure to adopt direct legislation is also a result of the legislature ignoring the popular will. But there is an alternative explanation, namely that the explosion in initiative use in states like California has scared off many who were originally sympathetic to the idea. Certainly that is how many legislators explain their opposition to direct legislation. In Texas, for instance, a Republican state senator from Dallas attributed his change of heart to the effects that initiatives have had in other states. Watching direct legislation in other states convinced him that the initiative and referendum is "not in the best interests of our democratic form of government." On the other side of the aisle, a Democratic state senator from Houston opposed direct legislation because she "did not want Texas to be like California, where propositions have had a negative effect on property taxes, schools, health facilities and other services." The senator also pointed to the huge amount of money spent by business and special interest groups on initiatives across the country. Fears of "Californication," in the phrase of one Minnesota state legislator, have dimmed the ardor for direct democracy.[18]

In the late 1970s and early 1980s virtually every state that lacked the initiative power was giving serious thought to adopting it. In 1977 the United States Senate held hearings on the possibility of adopting the initiative at the national level, which helped put the idea of a nationwide initiative and referendum on the national agenda for the next decade. But at the beginning of the twenty-first century, the idea of a national initiative has dropped almost completely off the national radar. States that seemed on the verge of adopting the initiative in the early and mid-1980s—like New Jersey, Hawaii, and Rhode Island—no longer seem particularly interested. In the 1980s there seemed a strong chance that Texas, the nation's second largest state, would adopt direct legislation, but by 1996 it was being labeled an "impossible dream." The Texas Republican party, which had supported bringing direct legislation to the Lone Star State in the 1980s and early 1990s, reversed itself. The 1996 party platform declared, "We oppose any attempt to introduce direct democracy (I&R) into our state constitution thereby bypassing the legislative process and the checks and balances between the executive, legislative and judicial branches of government."[19]

This is not to say that the initiative and referendum will not spread to other states in the coming years. Throughout the nation, particularly in the South, there are groups and politicians lobbying for the initiative and referendum. Republican governors in Louisiana and New York have come out in support of the initiative. And some antigovernment and antitax groups continue to push the initiative because they believe it is "a great tool for putting handcuffs on the government."[20] But both the left and the right, Democrats and Republicans, are deeply divided over the desirability of the initiative. For every conservative who salivates at the thought of using direct legislation to cut taxes or end affirmative action, there are others who fear it may be used to further the liberal agenda. In Louisiana, for instance, business interests strongly opposed the Republican governor's direct legislation proposal, fearing it would be used to increase the minimum wage or enact environmental regulations that would increase the cost of doing business.[21] And in Texas the Christian Coalition resisted the initiative and referendum because they feared it would be used to legalize gambling. Among liberals, too, fears outnumber hopes. Apart from environmentalists, who have had some notable successes in initiative campaigns—particularly in the 1970s and 1980s (their record in recent years, however, has been decidedly poor)—much of the rest of the left fears that direct legislation will be used to cripple the government's capacity to provide much-needed social services. These kinds of fears were not absent in the early twentieth century, but for the most part they were limited to business groups. As a result, the early-twentieth-century movement to pass direct legislation could plausibly be dramatized as a conflict between powerful special interests and the people. At the beginning of a new century, with groups from all sides of the political spectrum fearful of the initiative's enormous power to make sudden and drastic changes, that populist morality play no longer works as well.

If this analysis is correct, the initiative and referendum will at best be slow to spread across the country, particularly so long as high-use initiative states continue to dramatize the winner-take-all character of direct legislation politics. For most groups, so long as they have a reasonable chance of being heard in the legislature, the thought of what they might lose from direct legislation seems to far outweigh dreams of the world they might gain. The Mississippi experience, moreover, suggests that if another state does adopt the initiative process, intense pressure from interest groups will dilute and restrict the process in ways that make it unlikely that the state would have a large number of initiatives. In short, for the foreseeable future it is unlikely that direct legislation will become an important, let alone dominant, force in the political life of those twenty-six states that do not currently have the initiative. Those critics who fear that direct legislation will spread across the country like a cancer are probably as misguided as the enthusiasts who anticipate national redemption through direct legislation's glorious march from sea to shining sea.

SUPPLY-SIDE POLITICS

If it is possible to speak about the future spread of direct legislation to non-initiative states with a modicum of certainty, it is more difficult to predict the future course of the initiative and referendum within those states that already possess the power. Is the current popularity of direct legislation just a fad or phase the nation is passing through, or is it here to stay as a permanent feature of a transformed political landscape? Will the intensive use of the initiative in the late twentieth century be followed by a period of relatively light reliance on direct legislation, just as the heavy use of the initiative between the 1910s and 1930s was followed by several decades in which the initiative was resorted to infrequently? Or should we expect initiative use in the first decades of the twenty-first century to closely resemble patterns of initiative use in the last decades of the twentieth century? Or perhaps initiatives will become even more common, making the initiative use of the 1980s and 1990s pale in comparison. Will initiative use continue to be concentrated in a handful of states, or will states that have hitherto tended to use direct legislation sporadically now become heavy users?

Our predictions of the future can only be as a good as our explanations of the past. To forecast what will happen in the coming decades, we need to understand what has been driving initiative use over the past several decades. Probably the most common explanation of initiative use focuses on the mood of the voters. When the voters are angry and discontented, the number of initiatives increases. Speaking in 1994, Oregon initiative activist Bill Sizemore explained, "The initiative process heats up when people lose confidence in their elected officials. The present flurry of activity is a tell-tale sign that we don't have that confidence." When the City Club of Portland undertook a study of Oregon's initiative process in 1994, it interviewed over thirty initiative experts and activists. "Witness after witness," it reported, "referred to the current distrust of government as a factor now driving increased use of the initiative."[22] Certainly trust in government has declined at roughly the same time that initiative use has increased. But although trust in government has an intuitive appeal as an explanation, the trust theory loses some of its luster when it is inspected more closely. Trust in government after all has fluctuated substantially over the past several decades, but initiative use has remained relatively immune to those fluctuations. When trust has rebounded, as it did in the mid-1980s and again in the mid-1990s, initiative use has not declined. Nor has anyone provided any evidence that trust in government is lower in states that use the initiative more often. Although popular anger and distrust may have played an important role in triggering the renaissance of the initiative, it is much less clear that continued reliance on the initiative is closely related to levels of popular trust or discontent.

If initiative use seems to remain relatively constant in the face of wide swings in popular mood, we may be better off looking not at the demand side of the equation but rather at the supply side. A supply-side model of initiative use turns our attention away from the mood of the voters and toward those who produce the initiatives. According to this theory, the number of initiatives on the ballot is determined not by the demands of the people but by the suppliers of initiatives: the initiative activists and professionals who place initiatives on the ballot. The professionalization of signature gathering is particularly important in insulating initiative use from popular mood. If anyone with enough money can qualify an initiative for the ballot, then initiative use will vary independently of public demand. If we wish to predict the future of the initiative process in the United States, we must start by understanding the business of signature gathering.

3
The Business of Signatures

Among the most romantic features of the initiative process is the gathering of signatures. One imagines a dedicated band of public-spirited volunteers, committed to their cause, braving rain, sleet, and cold in order to obtain the signatures needed for their petition. What could be more civic-spirited than giving up one's leisure time to stand outside a supermarket or inside a shopping mall, asking fellow citizens to take a moment out of their busy day to consider a pressing public issue? In a world filled with professional politicians, high-paid lobbyists, selfish interest groups, and privatized citizens, the simple act of one citizen beseeching another for a signature seems almost ennobling, purifying our cynical souls. It is grassroots democracy in action.

But the romance and the reality are increasingly at odds with each other. Gathering signatures has become a business, and like any other business it is run for profit. The great majority of those people behind petition tables are not idealistic volunteers but interested mercenaries and bounty hunters who are paid by the signature and remain largely indifferent to the substance of the petition. Many would be as gratified to have you sign a petition that called for an increase in taxes as they would to get your signature on a petition seeking a tax reduction. And they would be happier still if you signed both petitions—and perhaps another two or three while you are at it. The price of your signature will vary, depending on the outcome of the bidding and bargaining between initiative sponsors, signature companies, independent contractors, and signature solicitors. It may be worth as little as seventy-five cents, but if the initiative sponsor is desperate or wealthy enough its value may climb to many times that amount.

So what? We all know that politics is saturated with money. Candidates spend hundreds of thousands or even millions of dollars to run for office. Corporations and labor unions spend cartfulls of cash lobbying the legislature. Why should we grow faint of heart when money is spent in the service of initiatives? "All of politics is run by money," observes Bill Sizemore. "To say it should be different for the people is hypocritical." Lloyd Marbet, a left-wing initiative proponent, agrees with the right-wing Sizemore: "Paying people to petition is no different in my mind than giving money to people to get them elected."[1] These initiative defenders raise an important challenge to those who would criticize the initiative process. Why should we be more wary about the role of money in the initiative process than in candidate elections? Are those who lambast "the initiative industry complex" simply being hypocritical?

The hypocrisy charge misses the mark, for under current campaign finance laws individuals are often sharply limited in what they can give to a candidate, whereas there are no limits on what individuals can contribute to an initiative, either in the signature-gathering phase or in the electoral campaign. If paying people to petition is, as Marbet says, no different from giving money to candidates, then that is an argument for restricting the amount people can contribute to an initiative campaign (or for abolishing laws limiting contributions to candidate campaigns). Only by explaining the difference between paying people to petition and contributing to candidates can we justify the status quo, which leaves money virtually unregulated in initiative campaigns, while subjecting money contributed to candidate campaigns to a dizzying array of restrictions. In thinking about the hypocrisy charge, it must also be remembered that a candidate from a major party appears on the ballot in the general election only after winning a primary election decided by voters from that candidate's party. In contrast, initiatives can appear on the ballot without any show of public support apart from the signatures gathered. If signatures gathered are not an indicator of public sentiment but merely a function of money, then critics are right to single out the role of money in the initiative process. If, as Philip Dubois and Floyd Feeney maintain, "political interests with sufficient funding and professional assistance can qualify nearly anything they want for the ballot," then that raises serious questions about the initiative's role as an instrument of popular democracy.[2]

THE PURPOSE AND VARIETY OF SIGNATURE REQUIREMENTS

All states require initiative petitioners to obtain a certain number of signatures before they can place a measure on the ballot. The primary purpose of signature requirements is to ensure that initiatives that reach the ballot meet a minimum threshold of public support. States vary considerably as to where they set the threshold, but no state has ever dispensed with the threshold. Without a signature requirement, voters would almost certainly be inundated with a flood of frivolous or idiosyncratic measures. Every irate citizen with a pet peeve and a little energy could force his or her obsession upon the voters. Set the signature hurdle too high, however, and committed citizens with genuine, widely shared grievances will be prevented from bringing their issue directly before the people.

The highest signature threshold for a statutory initiative exists in Wyoming, which requires the number of valid signatures to be at least 15 percent of the total number of votes cast in the preceding general election. Much more lenient is North Dakota, where petitioners only need to gather the signatures of 2 percent of the resident population (calculated on the basis of the last federal census) to place a statutory initiative on the ballot.[3] In the vast majority of states, the signature requirement for statutory initiatives ranges between 5 and 10 percent, usually calculated as a percentage of the number of votes cast in the last gubernatorial election.[4] Typically the number of signatures required to get a constitutional amendment on the ballot is greater, though how much greater varies by state. States also differ in the length of time they allow petitioners to gather signatures for initiative petitions. In Oklahoma they have only 90 days and in California 150 days, while in Oregon petitioners have two years and in Florida four years. Three-quarters of the states give petitioners at least a year to gather signatures for an initiative.[5] Half of the initiative states also require that signatures must meet some kind of geographical distribution requirement, the aim of which is to prevent petitioners from obtaining all their signatures in a few heavily populated urban areas. In Nevada, for instance, not only must a proposed initiative receive signatures equal to 10 percent of the number who voted in the preceding general election but it must also achieve that 10 percent threshold in three-fourths of the state's seventeen counties.[6]

Adding to the variation in the signature-gathering experience are the tremendous differences in state size. In California, for instance, the 5 percent signature threshold for a statutory initiative meant that initiative petitioners had to obtain 420,000 signatures to place an issue on the ballot in 2000. The same 5 percent requirement in South Dakota required petitioners to gather only 13,000 signatures. Thus, even though both California and South Dakota have adopted an identical 5 percent signature threshold calculated on the basis of votes cast in the last gubernatorial election, size alone makes the signature gatherers' task in the two states different in kind. Because of its size, petitioners in California have long been heavily reliant on professional signature gatherers, whereas in states like South Dakota and North Dakota petitioners generally have not needed to pay signature gatherers to qualify a measure. A study done by David Schmidt in 1984 found that in California and Ohio—the two most populous initiative states during this period[7]—only 15 percent of the initiatives that appeared on the ballot between 1980 and 1984 had been placed there by signature drives that had used volunteers to gather at least 90 percent of the requisite signatures. In contrast, in the other initiative states more than 80 percent of the initiatives that reached the ballot had relied on volunteers to gather at least 90 percent of the signatures. And of the ten initiative states with populations under two million, more than 85 percent of initiative campaigns during this period relied on volunteers to gather at least 90 percent of the signatures.[8]

THE HISTORY OF SIGNATURE REQUIREMENTS

Schmidt's study seemed to vindicate the grassroots character of most initiative campaigns. According to Schmidt, only about one-quarter of all statewide initiatives between 1980 and 1984 relied on professional circulators to garner more than one-third of the required signatures; and about two-thirds used volunteers to amass more than 90 percent of the signatures.[9] In the early 1980s, then, most initiative campaigns apparently still relied on a large number of dedicated volunteers, people who were working to get the measure on the ballot because they believed in the issue and not because they were being paid. Plenty of initiatives relied heavily, and even exclusively, on paid petitioners, but outside of the most populous states like California, Ohio, and Michigan, these remained a distinct minority.

In a few states the reliance on volunteers during the early 1980s was a product not of choice but of law. Oregon had outlawed paid petitioners in 1935, and it was not until 1982 that a district court decision invalidated the state's ban.[10] Colorado's ban on paid petitioners, enacted in 1941, remained in place until the U.S. Supreme Court ruled in 1988 that the ban was unconstitutional because it restricted free speech.[11] The Supreme Court's decision also effectively nullified Washington's long-standing ban on paid signature gatherers.[12] In 1993 the Washington state legislature responded by modifying its ban to prohibit only the method of paying per signature, leaving initiative campaigns free to pay by the hour. But even this more limited ban on paid signature gatherers was struck down in federal court on free speech grounds.[13] The courts had turned the law on its head. Prior to the 1980s, no federal or state court in the United States had found a ban on paid petitioners to be unconstitutional. In 1973, for instance, both the Washington Supreme Court and the Oregon Supreme Court emphatically rejected the view that a ban on paid petitioners unconstitutionally abridged freedom of speech.[14] Up until the 1980s, banning paid petitioners, like myriad other state regulations of the initiative process, was widely seen as something best left to the legislature and to the people of a particular state.

That a number of states long ago took the trouble to ban paid petitioners tips us off to a simple yet often overlooked fact, namely, that paid petitioners are as old as the initiative process itself. In Oregon, for instance, paid petitioners were used to qualify all of the state's famous good government measures, including the direct primary law of 1904, the Corrupt Practices Act of 1908, and the presidential primary bill of 1912. As the Supreme Court of Oregon observed in 1912, "it is difficult to find citizens who are so devoted to their principles as to be willing to circulate such petitions without compensation." A study of the Oregon initiative process published in 1915 concluded that while "petitions for some measures have been circulated wholly by volunteers . . . such cases have been comparatively few." Even in the initiative's infancy there were already frequent and disparaging references to the "industry" of "petition peddling." The business could be a lucrative one for those gathering signatures. Signature gatherers in 1910 could expect about five cents a signature (equivalent to roughly eighty cents in 2000 dollars). If, as often happened, they carried multiple measures at the same time, their rate might be dropped to closer to three or three-and-a-half cents a signature. As the deadline for submitting the signatures neared, however, the price per signature could climb as high as ten cents or more.[15]

The concerns and anxieties expressed about paid petitioners in the early twentieth century are similar to the ones we often hear today. "Any person with sufficient money," worried the Eugene *Register* in 1913, "knows that he can get any kind of legislation on the ballot." In 1908 the *Oregonian* had lodged the same objection: "The man or group of men who have money to spend, and who are willing to spend it, can secure submission of any measure to a vote of the people." Enlisting "the voluntary service of people in circulating petitions," the *Oregonian* reasoned, was the only reliable way of determining whether "a measure is . . . of sufficient importance and public interest" that it should be brought before the people. Paying signature gatherers effectively gutted the purpose of requiring signatures in the first place. To Republican Senator Jonathan Bourne, a primary problem with paid petitioners was that they choked out the grass roots: "While paid circulation of petitions is the universal custom, there will be few volunteers, for most people will either decline to work without pay while others are paid, or will hesitate to put themselves in the class of paid workers."[16] Paying petitioners degraded the signature gatherer because it came to be seen as a sales job rather than as the precious province of the public-spirited citizen. Knowing they can pay their way onto the ballot, groups do not even attempt the hard political work of mobilizing a dedicated band of citizens. Payment for signatures simplifies the job of the initiative's sponsors—but only at the price of attenuating civic involvement in the political process.

Sentiments such as these, together with concerns about outright fraud and corruption in the signature-gathering process, led to a number of early attempts to ban paid petitioners, some of which were successful. A bill to ban paid petitioners was introduced in Oregon as early as 1909. Similar laws were introduced in legislatures across the nation, including Washington, South Dakota, and Ohio, where such bans were enacted into law between 1913 and 1914. Most states, though, declined to ban paid petitioners, although spectacular cases of fraud or concerns about the control of special interests sporadically forced the issue onto the legislative agenda. In California, for instance, bills to ban paid petitioners were introduced and defeated in 1915, 1917, 1937, 1939, 1953, 1959, 1963, 1965, 1969, 1973, and again in 1987. Banning paid petitioners, opponents warned, would advantage firms that employed large numbers of people and would make it impossible for all but the most popular causes to exercise the right of direct democracy. "Most of these proposals," political scientists V. O. Key and Winston Crouch wryly observed in 1939, "come from that idyllic school of political thought which holds that the political wheels should go round, like the perpetual machine, without money."[17]

Fears that a ban on paid petitioners would cripple the initiative process were particularly acute in a state the size of California. In 1912, the first year in which the tools of direct legislation were made available to Californians, the State Federation of Labor reported that obtaining the required number of signatures had "proved no easy undertaking." "Depending upon volunteer work alone," the federation found, "has proven to be very unsatisfactory."[18] Each of the successful initiatives in California's first initiative election relied heavily on paid signature gatherers. Over the next six decades, just one initiative qualified for the ballot in California using only volunteers, a 1938 measure that promised voters a number of benefits, including improved pensions. California's decision in 1966 to reduce the percentage of required signatures for a statutory initiative from 8 to 5 percent increased the importance of volunteer efforts in California's initiative process,[19] but the effect was short-lived. Volunteer signature campaigns played a prominent—even predominant—role in a substantial number of high-profile initiatives during the 1970s, including the landmark Proposition 13 in 1978, but since 1982 few California initiatives have relied on volunteers for the bulk of the signatures, and it has been the very rare exception that has not used paid signature gatherers. The last volunteer-only initiative in California was a 1990 measure that outlawed the hunting of mountain lions.[20]

DECLINE OF THE VOLUNTEER AND RISE OF THE PROFESSIONAL

California's reliance on paid petitioners today is hardly surprising given the state's size and the relatively short period in which circulators are permitted to gather signatures. It is by far the most populous state, and its 150-day window for circulating direct initiative petitions is the second most restrictive in the nation. The more dramatic story of the past two decades is the change that has occurred in the medium-sized and small initiative states. In Idaho, for instance, which up until 1998 allowed petitioners two years to circulate a petition, paid petitioners were virtually unknown in the postwar era. In the half century prior to 1994, none of the twelve initiatives that made it to the ballot used paid petitioners. In 1994, however, both initiatives that appeared on the ballot—the first establishing term limits for elected officials, and the second establishing state policies regarding homosexuality—used paid petitioners. In 1996 and 1998 five more initiatives appeared on the ballot, each relying on paid signature gatherers to a greater or lesser degree. Virtually overnight the practice of signature gathering in Idaho had been transformed from almost exclusive reliance on volunteers to a heavy reliance on paid signature gatherers.[21]

States generally do a poor job tracking whether or not initiatives rely on paid signature gatherers. Only a handful of states require petitioners to indicate whether they plan to use paid petitioners, and these requirements have generally been enacted so recently that useful data is not yet available. A pioneering exception is the state of Oregon, which for over a decade has mandated chief petitioners to indicate whether they will use paid petitioners in the signature-gathering process. Thus, in Oregon it is possible to document precisely the growth in the number of paid petitioners over the last decade. Moreover, since Oregon requires this information to be submitted before signature gathering has begun, one is also able to examine the reliance on paid signature gatherers among the initiative campaigns that failed to gather the requisite number of signatures.

The number of initiatives in Oregon that rely entirely on volunteers to gather signatures has not changed appreciably since 1988, while the number of initiatives relying on paid petitioners has increased dramatically (see Table 3.1). In 1988 a majority of the initiatives circulating were volunteer-only, whereas between 1994 and 1998 there were twice as many initiatives using paid petitioners as there were using only volunteers. In 2000 there were four times as many initiatives using paid signature gatherers. The big difference, however, between volunteer-only petitions and paid petitioners shows up in their success rate in qualifying for the ballot. Between 1988 and 2000 about one in eight volunteer-only efforts made it to the ballot. Since 1996 only three volunteer-only initiatives have qualified for the ballot, and one of these, a vote-by-mail initiative, was spearheaded by Secretary of State Phil Keisling and other government officials. In contrast, almost half of the initiatives that relied at least partly on paid petitioners have made it to the ballot since 1996. Over the last three elections, 93 percent of the initiatives on the Oregon ballot have used paid petitioners.

The impact of paid petitioners on the success of a qualification campaign is understated by these numbers, dramatic as they are. Petitioners who indicated an intention to pay for signatures but failed to make it to the ballot were generally unable to raise the money to make it possible for them to pay signature gatherers. Among the groups for whom money presented no obstacle, the success rate in qualifying for the ballot approached 100 percent. Overwhelmingly, groups in Oregon that had the money to pay petitioners gained access to the ballot, while groups that did not have the money to pay petitioners found gaining access to the ballot extraordinarily burdensome.

In the neighboring state of Washington, the story is similar. The only initiative to appear on the ballot in 1994—a measure allowing denture makers to sell directly to the public rather than to dentists—spent roughly three times as much as any other initiative campaign. It was also the only initiative campaign willing to violate the 1993 state law prohibiting payment per signature. The other nine active signature-gathering campaigns—which included measures relating to gay rights, abortion, welfare reform, criminal punishment, and legislative ethics—relied entirely on volunteers, and each failed to gather the necessary signatures.

Table 3.1   The Relative Success of Paid Signature Gatherers in Oregon, 1988–2000

Signature Gatherers	Number of Initiatives Circulated	Number of Initiatives Qualified	Percentage of Circulated Initiatives that Qualified
Paid			
2000	40	16	40
1998	20	9	45
1996	28	16	57
1994	31	13	42
1992	18	6	33
1990	15	7	47
1988	13	2	15
Total	165	69	42
Unpaid			
2000	9	2	22
1998	14	1	7
1996	14	0	0
1994	13	3	23
1992	12	1	8
1990	12	1	8
1988	16	3	19
Total	90	11	12

Sherry Bockwinkel, whose signature-gathering firm, Washington Initiatives Now (WIN), collected most of the signatures for the denturists, admitted that "there isn't a chance in the world a volunteer effort is going to make it."[22] The following year Bockwinkel's firm was hired to qualify two initiative campaigns, one relating to commercial fishing regulations and the other to casino gambling on Indian reservations. Bockwinkel publicly boasted, "I can guarantee we'll be on the ballot. . . . I've got the key to the ballot." And Bockwinkel was as good as her word: both measures qualified; indeed, they were the only direct initiatives among the seventeen filed that qualified for the ballot that year. Not coincidentally, they were also the only two to use paid signature gatherers. "You have to pay to play" is Bockwinkel's catchy slogan.[23]

Bockwinkel's boast and bravado notwithstanding, volunteer-only efforts are still possible when an issue captures the imagination of citizens and activists, as the 1998 and 1999 Washington elections showed in spectacular fashion. In 1998 two of the four ballot measures qualified without the use of paid signatures. The first, a ban on partial-birth abortions, gathered the needed signatures in only six weeks and benefited from one of the highest validation rates in state history: a remarkable 90 percent of its signatures were deemed valid. The second, involving a hike in the minimum wage, exceeded the 180,000-signature target by better than 50,000.[24] An even more spectacular refutation of Bockwinkel's slogan came in 1999 when I-695, which proposed to roll back Washington's motor vehicle tax and require voter approval for any tax or fee increase by state or local government, qualified without the use of paid signature gatherers. In fact, the initiative gathered close to 400,000 valid signatures, more than double the number of signatures required and the second highest total in Washington history.[25] A number of other volunteer-only drives succeeded in the 1990s, including a 1996 measure orchestrated by the Humane Society that banned bear and cougar hunting using dogs or bait, a measure similar to ones the Humane Society had qualified using volunteers in Oregon in 1994 and California in 1990. Also noteworthy were the 230,000 signatures gathered by volunteers for a popular referendum on a controversial property rights law enacted by the state legislature in 1995. That number, well over twice the 90,834 signatures the petitioners needed, was gathered within the ninety days allowed for a referendum petition.[26] Not all issues, then, have to pay to play.

Still, of the thirty initiatives that reached the ballot in Washington between 1992 and 2000, only six secured their spot without paid signature gatherers: a 1993 antitax measure, the 1996 hunting ban, the 1998 partial-birth ban and minimum wage increase, the 1999 repeal of the motor vehicle tax, and, in 2000, another Humane Society measure banning certain animal traps and poisons. Considering that prior to 1991 no initiative campaign in Washington had used paid signature gatherers, the practice having been outlawed in the early twentieth century, the transformation is remarkable. Ironically, the first Washington initiative campaign to employ professional signature gatherers after the long-standing ban had been invalidated was a 1991 term limits measure, the aim of which was to throw professional politicians out of the legislature and to give amateurs and ordinary citizens a chance to volunteer for public service. In fact, every term limits measure that has qualified for the ballot in the United States has done so primarily, and often exclusively, by utilizing professional signature gatherers.

The rapid transformation in Washington from volunteer to professional signature gatherers has been replicated with similar speed in Colorado, a state with at least a million fewer people and a substantially lower signature threshold. In 1998 initiative sponsors in Washington needed to gather just under 180,000 signatures, while initiative proponents in Colorado needed less than one third that many. Yet despite the relatively low number of signatures required in Colorado (during the 1990s, initiative petitions needed around 50,000 in a state of well over 3 million people), the lack of any geographical distribution requirement, and the absence of a tradition of paying for signatures (prior to 1988, the practice had been illegal for almost half a century), the Colorado ballot in the 1990s has been monopolized with measures using paid signature gatherers. Between 1990 and 1996 only one of the thirty-one measures (a bear-trapping measure) reached the ballot without paying for signatures, though several (like a 1996 campaign finance reform measure) used volunteers extensively. Initiative activists were quick to proclaim that paid signature gatherers were the only way to reach the ballot. Jim Klodinski, an organizer of a 1994 gambling initiative, justified his measure's reliance on paid signature gatherers by insisting, "If you think you're going to get something on the ballot without paid professionals, you're crazy." Similarly sweeping was another initiative activist's assurance that "it is impossible in Colorado to qualify a petition without using paid circulators."[27]

The activists' exaggerated claims are belied, however, by the success of the Colorado Pro-Life Alliance in using only volunteers to qualify not one but two initiatives for the 1998 ballot, the first requiring parental notification before a minor can obtain an abortion, and the second banning late-term abortions. Calling on "God's people to take a stand for God's righteousness and against abortion," a dedicated cadre of roughly two hundred volunteers collected signatures outside churches, at Christian concerts, and in other venues where God's people were likely to congregate.[28] Moreover, Colorado, like Washington, has had a history of some spectacular volunteer signature drives. In 1982, for instance, an initiative allowing Coloradans to purchase wine at the grocery store gathered over twice the required number of signatures, with most of those coming in two days.[29] Also conveniently obscured by the activists' rhetoric is that in the four elections held between 1982 and 1988, twenty-four initiatives qualified for the ballot in Colorado, and all of them relied exclusively on volunteers.[30] In states like Colorado, where the signature requirements are not onerous, paid signature gatherers are clearly not indispensable to ballot access, at least not for those groups with a sizable and committed band of activists or for those issues that capture the popular imagination.

For many groups and issues, though, paid signature gatherers undoubtedly are essential to reaching the ballot. The main hurdle that most initiative proponents face is finding enough people willing and able to dedicate a large number of hours to gathering signatures. To collect seventy-five thousand signatures (which could safely be assumed to yield fifty thousand valid signatures), one expert has estimated that a volunteer drive would need roughly sixty-six three-hour volunteer shifts (two people) per week, every week, for five months.[31] People might be happy to let denturists sell their wares directly to the public, but few if any citizens would be willing to give up even an hour of their time to circulate petitions on behalf of such a cause. Denturists, who have a sizable economic stake in the outcome, are unlikely to have sufficient leisure time to gather the requisite signatures; moreover, even if all the denture makers in the state or region dropped their tools for six months and devoted themselves full time to signature gathering, their numbers would likely be too few to qualify the measure. Gambling generally arouses more excitement and enthusiasm than dentures, but gaming initiatives also have a difficult time attracting volunteers. Many people like to gamble, but it is apparently not a habit they feel so strongly about that they are willing to devote long, arduous hours to gathering signatures (though an antigambling measure might be more likely to mobilize a cadre of volunteers devoted to eradicating vice); and while gambling interests may have pots of money, they have a comparative dearth of time and numbers.

In opening up the initiative process to issues and interests that could not otherwise play, such as denturists and gambling proprietors, paid petitioners arguably democratize the initiative process, making it more inclusive. Banning paid signature gatherers penalizes those individuals or groups who possess money but lack spare time, while advantaging those short on money but long on time. But why should individuals with lots of spare time be privileged over people with lots of money? Are those groups who have difficulty raising money but no trouble harnessing a cadre of fanatics any more deserving of a place on the ballot than those who have an abundance of cash but lack fervent enthusiasm? Are a small group of denture makers less virtuous than a large band of religious zealots? From this vantage point, the rise of paid petitioners and professional signature-gathering firms promotes democracy by increasing the involvement of a wider diversity of groups.

Yet the complaint persists that permitting paid petitioners means that "anybody can buy their way on the ballot."[32] Allowing rich individuals or well-financed special interests to qualify measures for the ballot regardless of either the depth or intensity of popular support seems to violate the original vision of direct democracy. Grassroots democracy degenerates into "greenbacks democracy"; a system designed to save us from the special interests is captured by those very same interests.[33] The initiative and referendum were not created to promote the sale of dentures and the spread of gambling but rather to make sure legislatures did not ignore widespread popular sentiments for change and reform, and to prevent self-aggrandizement or corruption on the part of politicians and powerful interests. Initiatives such as the ones in Washington aimed at repealing unpopular taxes, saving wild animals, or keeping politicians honest all tap into strong popular feelings, and the signature-gathering requirement allows proponents to demonstrate the depth of public feeling in support of an initiative. Relying entirely on volunteers is no guarantee that a measure has broad support in the population—after all, many volunteer-only initiatives, like the Colorado ban on late-term abortions, are defeated at the polls—but a successful volunteer effort is a virtual guarantee that a significant segment of the population feels passionately about the issue, so passionately that they are willing to relinquish their valuable time to beseech fellow citizens for signatures. Having mobilized their convictions and passions, having risked rejection and courted confrontation, these advocates have earned the right to place their issue before the voters. Those who merely purchase their spot on the ballot have not earned that same moral right, or so the argument goes.

THE COST OF BALLOT ACCESS

Has the initiative process in fact been transformed from a grassroots to a greenbacks democracy? The answer to this question is more complex than the activists on either side are willing to acknowledge. Those who bemoan the capture of the initiative process by monied special interests ignore the reality that organized and well-financed special interests have long been central players in the initiative process, particularly in those states that have made frequent use of direct democracy. Writing in the late 1930s, political scientists V. O. Key and Winston Crouch discovered that the battle over initiatives closely resembled the battle over legislation: both arenas were dominated by organized pressure groups. Proponents of the initiative and referendum, Key and Crouch noted, "thought that 'The People' would circulate petitions and put measures on the ballot for the promotion of the welfare of the average man. The fight would then be over since all measures . . . fell into two well-defined categories, namely, those in the public interest and those for the benefit of some special interests." But initiative measures in California did not originate with "The People." Instead, "initiated measures, like legislative bills, originate with some interest group which has found the existing law unsatisfactory and seeks to secure more favorable legal rules." Groups using the initiative, Key and Crouch reiterated, "have not differed from the organizations lobbying before the legislature."[34]

Moreover, volunteer signature gatherers might be nobler and more altruistic than paid mercenaries, but they are far from free; more precisely, while the volunteers are free, the costs of recruiting, training, and coordinating those volunteers can be substantial. A 1998 "Initiative Cookbook," written to dispense advice to Californians who want to "use the initiative process to advance issues of social and economic justice," recommended that a signature-gathering drive with a large volunteer component would need between $500,000 and $750,000 to qualify an initiative. In 1990 none of the eighteen California initiatives that reached the ballot, including the few that relied heavily on volunteers, spent less than $500,000 in the qualification phase; a gill net measure, for instance, which spent only $21,000 on paid circulators, still spent $620,000 in qualification; and a pesticide measure, which spent less than $200,000 on paid circulators and direct mail efforts, spent an additional 1 million dollars to qualify the measure. Even grassroots democracy, it turns out, needs to be a rich green, at least in California.[35]

Still, volunteer campaigns are generally less expensive than campaigns that pay for signatures—sometimes far less expensive. In Washington in 1999, for instance, the volunteer-only drive that qualified the rollback of motor vehicle taxes (I-695) spent only $78,000 in the qualification stage; its 400,000 valid signatures came at an average price of about twenty cents per signature. In contrast, the previous year a medical marijuana measure in Washington (I-685) paid for all of its signatures and needed over $400,000 to qualify the measure, most of which went to a signature-gathering firm called Progressive Campaigns. The cost per valid signature for I-685 was roughly $2 a signature, ten times as high as the cost of qualifying I-695. If I-685 exemplified greenbacks democracy—the $400,000 came entirely from three out-of-state millionaires, including George Soros, one of the richest men in the world—I-695 was a paradigmatic grassroots campaign. Nobody gave more than $10,000 and half of the campaign's money came from individuals who contributed less than $100.[36]

The success of I-695 shows that the grass roots are not dead. But even among initiatives that rely exclusively or heavily on volunteers, I-695 is the exception. More typical of successful volunteer efforts are the two initiatives that qualified in Washington in 1998: the ban on partial-birth abortions and the minimum wage increase. Unlike Proposition I-695, which was fueled by a combustible mix of populist rage and the entrepreneurial skill and energy of Tim Eyman, the 1998 measures relied heavily on existing organizations. The minimum wage increase was drafted and sponsored by union leaders, and the recruiting and organizing of volunteers was done using the staff and offices of the Washington State Labor Council, estimated by the council to be worth $57,401. Similarly, the antiabortionists relied heavily on a dense organizational network of over two thousand churches to recruit and train volunteers and to reach potential signatories.[37] Neither the Christian conservatives nor the labor unions lacked for clout in the halls of the state legislatures. That volunteer drives are often orchestrated by organized interest groups should not be surprising; it is, after all, special interest groups, not individual citizens, who are in the best position to meet the tremendous organizational demands of a volunteer drive. Ironically, individuals who lack access to the organizational resources of established interest groups are likely to be the ones who are most reliant on greenbacks democracy.

Volunteer signature drives continue to survive for reasons both principled and practical. By helping to reduce the cost of the qualification phase, volunteers can help strapped initiative campaigns save their limited resources for the electoral contest.[38] Volunteer signature drives also often benefit from higher validity rates than paid signature campaigns, thus effectively reducing the number of total signatures needed.[39] More important, involving volunteers in the signature-gathering process can politicize citizens and mobilize groups, making it easier to call upon their assistance later in the process or even in subsequent initiative campaigns. Relying exclusively or heavily on volunteers can also be a public relations coup, a signal to relevant audiences (media, potential contributors, voters) that the measure is a populist, grassroots movement. For some who rely on volunteers, such as the Oregon Citizens Alliance's Lon Mabon (who used volunteers to qualify initiatives in four successive elections between 1988 and 1994 and again in 2000), it's also a matter of principle. "I'm a purist," Mabon concedes. Purity has its costs, though. The OCA's attempt to qualify antigay and abortion measures failed in 1996 and again, narrowly, in 1998.[40]

For every volunteer success story there are scores of failures. The initiative seas are strewn with the hulls of wrecked volunteer drives. Volunteers are notoriously unpredictable, and qualification often hangs in the balance until the closing weeks or even days. Even Washington's I-695 campaign, which ended up submitting over 500,000 signatures, only had 180,000 with less than two weeks remaining. Ten days prior to the July 2 deadline, Eyman was reported as saying that he hoped to raise another 40,000 signatures so as "to provide a cushion"; had he done so, I-695 would likely have failed since an invalidity rate of 20 percent (the actual invalidity rate ended up at 23 percent) would have been enough to drop the initiative below the required 179,248 valid signatures. Fortunately for I-695, Eyman's prediction was off by more than 270,000 signatures. Volunteers and amateurs commonly waste time reinventing the wheel or, worse, make grievous mistakes. In Colorado, for instance, an antiabortion initiative campaign used volunteers to gather 57,000 valid signatures, more than enough to make the ballot, but the measure was disqualified because circulators had mistakenly used outdated forms.[41]

The great advantage in hiring a professional signature-gathering firm is that professionals, by definition, know what they're doing. They can tell the initiative sponsors how long it will take to gather the required number of signatures and what it will cost per signature. An initiative campaign that contracts with a firm like California's Kimball Petition Management is buying the services of a firm that has been in the business of signature gathering for over two decades and has a remarkably successful track record. Professional signature firms drain the mystery and uncertainty from the process. If the initiative proponents have the money, professional signature companies can virtually guarantee almost any measure a place on the ballot, thereby allowing initiative backers to concentrate their energies and attention on other stages of the process. "We handle everything," boasts Dan Kennedy, president of a Colorado signature-gathering firm. "You just give me the petitions and we'll get them back to you, filled out. We've got it down to a science."[42]

No political process, of course, is without uncertainty, and even professionals can miscalculate or encounter unexpected problems. The signature market can be volatile, particularly toward the close of an initiative campaign. Circulators typically carry multiple initiatives and will make the highest-paying initiative petitions their priority. When Philip Morris pays two dollars per signature, as they did in California in 1994 to qualify a smoking initiative, those who are circulating that petition will make sure that it is the one people are asked to sign first. Getting bumped to the rear of the initiative cue can cause an otherwise well run signature drive to stall; many people will sign one, two, or even three petitions but will balk at the fourth, fifth, or sixth.[43] Short on signatures and time, an initiative campaign will be forced (if it can afford it) to hike its per-signature price. Savvy circulators, knowing that the cost of a signature often climbs in the closing weeks of a campaign, have been known to withhold signatures until the qualification deadline nears in hopes of fetching a better price for their wares.

Courts, too, can inject uncertainty into the signature-gathering process. In 1988, for instance, the California Supreme Court struck down a no-fault insurance initiative that had already paid for hundreds of thousands of signatures. The insurance companies were forced to redraft the measure and begin gathering signatures all over again. For most organizations this eleventh-hour judicial setback would have been fatal, but deep pockets enabled the insurance companies to hire a direct mail firm, which gathered more than the required four hundred thousand signatures in just forty-eight days. To achieve this feat cost the insurance industry $2.3 million, a mere drop in the bucket compared to the $14.5 million that the industry reportedly spent on behalf of the no-fault measure in the qualification phase.[44] The ballot titling process can also disrupt well-laid plans. If opponents challenge a ballot title, as often happens with controversial measures, the title is appealed to the courts. The appeal process can be time-consuming, and since signature gathering generally cannot commence until a ballot title has been fixed, initiative campaigns are sometimes left with considerably less time to gather signatures than state law permits.

Despite these uncertainties, however, professional signature-gathering firms rarely fail to reach their signature targets. On those infrequent occasions when they fail to qualify a measure, it is usually because the percentage of invalid signatures is unusually high, the sponsors' money unexpectedly dries up, or the professional firm has been hired too late in the signature-gathering season to rescue a faltering volunteer campaign.[45] One study reported that of the fifty-three initiative campaigns that had retained the services of Kimball Petition Management through 1988, all but one reached the ballot. In that one case the firm met the signature target it had set but had an unusually high percentage of signatures that were declared invalid.[46] A few direct mail firms are so confident of their ability to qualify any measure that they offer a money-back guarantee.[47] The impressive success rates of paid-signature firms make the job security of congressional incumbents seem downright hazardous by comparison.

Not that all initiatives are equally easy to qualify. Individuals do not generally scrutinize the petition they sign—indeed, many do not bother to read it at all—but a popular ballot measure is still easier to qualify than an unpopular or confusing one. A less popular measure may require the signature-gathering firm to charge a higher per-signature price. But if popular appeal affects the cost of the initiative, it generally has little impact on whether an initiative qualifies, assuming the backers have the requisite money. The key variable is not the attitude of those who sign the petition. People sign for lots of reasons that have nothing to do with the substance of the petition. Instead, the most important factor is the number of people who can be solicited. Initiatives proponents who possess the resources to approach enough people can qualify any or almost any measure. The emergence of professional signature gatherers has not made huge sums of money a *necessary* condition of ballot access for all groups or issues, but it has meant money is now a *sufficient* condition of ballot access.[48]

Those who mourn the passing of the grassroots initiative may justly be accused of romanticizing the initiative's past, but stalwart defenders of the initiative as the authentic voice of the people are guilty of whitewashing its present. In California in 1976, the median expenditure during the qualification phase was only $44,861 and the mean was $69,398. In 1978, the backers of Proposition 13 spent even less than that yet still managed to gather a million and a quarter signatures, which remains a record for any initiative campaign. During the 1980s, the median qualification expenditure in California exceeded $700,000, and by 1990 both the median and mean surpassed one million dollars. Throughout the 1990s qualification expenses in California have routinely ranged between one and two million dollars. Unlike in the 1970s, when the bulk of the money spent by an initiative campaign to qualify a measure generally went to support a staff and organization as well as printing and distributing literature, in the last two decades of the twentieth century the cash flowed almost entirely to professional campaign consultants, pollsters, lawyers, and, most especially, professional signature-gathering firms.[49]

Outside of California, of course, the amount of money required to qualify an initiative is usually dramatically less. Expert witnesses testifying before a committee of the Portland City Club in 1996 reported that $100,000 to $150,000 was sufficient to get a measure on the ballot in Oregon. Interviewed in 1999, Rick Arnold, who runs National Voter Outreach, a Nevada-based signature-gathering firm that has been in operation since 1979, estimated that $80,000 to $100,000 was enough to be assured of the necessary signatures in Colorado. In Idaho $60,000 to $70,000 is generally sufficient to secure a spot on the ballot. These are not trivial amounts of money, particularly if one were required to raise the money in relatively small contributions, as federal and many state laws require candidates to do.[50] But since there are no limits on what an individual or group can contribute to an initiative campaign, these amounts are not difficult to reach even for a single (wealthy) individual. In Oregon in 1996, for instance, three initiatives were qualified by a wealthy eye doctor who wrote and bankrolled each of the measures himself. To qualify all three initiatives, none of which received more than 35 percent of the vote, the doctor spent under $200,000.[51] Ironically, the mammoth sums of money required in California may increase the chances that qualification of a measure reflects broader public or group support.

Mountains of cash are not necessarily evidence of a withering of the grass roots. If many, many people are contributing money to an initiative campaign, then money can be one measure (albeit a highly imperfect one) of breadth of support and intensity of preference. Although grassroots purists might prefer to see different, "higher" forms of involvement, like attending meetings or gathering signatures, giving money to political campaigns is one important form of political involvement in our society. The trouble is that by prohibiting any limits on what individuals or groups can contribute to initiative campaigns, the U.S. Supreme Court has created an environment in which initiative campaigns have little or no incentive to seek out smaller contributions. Instead, the legal regime established by the Court encourages initiative campaigns to seek out a few fat cats and sugar daddies who will bankroll the effort and save initiative sponsors the more time-consuming effort of raising money from the little guy (and gal). In California in 1990, for instance, contributions of under $1,000 made up only

6 percent of the total contributions in support of or in opposition to initiative campaigns. Thirty-seven percent (roughly $40 million) of the total initiative dollars came from 19 donors, and 67 percent ($74 million) came from 141 individuals and organizations, each of which gave at least $100,000. Almost as much money came from Anheuser Busch ($8.3 million in opposition to a proposed liquor tax) as was given by the 18,000 contributors who gave less than $1,000. A glance at the 1998 general election in California shows that little has changed. More than half of the almost $10 million raised to support a tobacco tax came from four individuals, two of whom were married to each other. Five of the seven initiatives received an average of 3 or 4 percent of their contributions from donors giving under $10,000; the only two measures to receive a respectable percentage of their support in smaller amounts were a measure forbidding the slaughter of horses for horsemeat (23 percent of its contributions came from people who gave under $10,000) and another banning the use of some kinds of animal traps and poisons (39 percent came from contributions of less than $10,000). Not coincidentally, both of these measures were passed overwhelmingly by the voters: the average support was 58 percent, whereas the mean support for the other five measures was only 44 percent.[52]

Since these statistics refer to overall spending and not just the costs of qualification, they tend to *overestimate* the popular basis of financial support at the qualification phase. For instance, in 1990 Harold Arbit, a wealthy investor, contributed five million dollars in support of "Forests Forever" (Proposition 130), which equaled roughly two-thirds of the total contributions to the initiative campaign. But he bankrolled essentially the entire million dollars it took to qualify the initiative.[53] Arbit's largesse is unusual—his five-million-dollar contribution was at the time a record for an individual contribution to an initiative and was itself a major issue in the campaign—but the pattern of initiative contributions being more concentrated among fewer people in the qualification stage than the postqualification phase is commonplace. Media attention in California and elsewhere tends to focus on the huge sums of money raised and spent in the postqualification stage, particularly as television ads begin to flood the airwaves, but it is the contributions at the qualification phase that should concern us most.

To begin with, money can essentially guarantee a spot on the ballot, whereas no amount of money can guarantee an electoral victory. Huge amounts of money have been spent on spectacular defeats, and vast sums have been spent opposing successful efforts. In Florida in 1994, for instance, over sixteen million dollars was spent to promote a casino initiative that failed miserably, receiving less than 40 percent of the vote. The thirty-five million dollars spent by the insurance industry in 1988 in California on behalf of no-fault auto insurance also went for naught, even failing to prevent passage of a rival auto insurance measure that the insurance companies had hoped to defeat. Tobacco companies have frequently spent mammoth amounts of money in efforts to defeat tobacco tax initiatives, usually without success. In Oregon in 1996, for instance, the tobacco industry outspent the proponents of a cigarette tax increase by almost ten to one, yet the industry lost by a sizable margin. In 2000 thirty-one million dollars (about three-quarters of which came from Tim Draper, a Silicon Valley entrepreneur) was spent in support of a school voucher initiative in California that failed to get above 30 percent of the vote. The same fate befell a voucher initiative in Michigan despite a pro-voucher campaign that spent about thirteen million dollars, well over twice what the opposition spent. Of course, having money is better than not having money, and the evidence shows that heavy and lopsided spending *against* a measure is frequently effective in defeating the measure. But in electoral contests, unlike in qualification campaigns, money is not a sufficient condition for success.[54]

Moreover, although the large sums spent on thirty-second television ads in the closing months and weeks of an electoral campaign may not be pretty, they are essential if voters are to have any chance of arriving at an informed opinion about an initiative. In candidate races many voters can rely on party as a cue to make reasonably informed decisions even with relatively little information. Partisan cues (in the form of endorsements) are available in many initiative campaigns, but they do not come conveniently stamped on the ballot and take more work on the voter's part to ferret out.[55] Television ads, though often obnoxious to the more educated voter, can be essential in giving the less well informed voter a rudimentary understanding of a measure's meaning as well as a rough sense of who is for and against it. Those most concerned about the potential dangers of lawmaking by initiative should be most vigilant not to restrict the flow of money to initiative campaigns, for it is only through spending large sums of money that opponents of a measure can educate voters about the unintended consequences and pitfalls of a bill.

But concentrated spending by one or a few individuals at the qualification stage is conceptually quite another matter. For here money sabotages the purpose of a signature requirement, which is to demonstrate intensity and breadth of popular support. If paid circulators are used to gather virtually all of the signatures, then a campaign's capacity to gather those signatures is no longer a reliable indicator of public interest. Only the task of raising money is left as a meaningful way in which initiative sponsors can demonstrate the existence of public interest in their measure. But if a single individual or a small handful can finance the qualification of an initiative, then this hurdle is also knocked over and rendered useless. If, on the other hand, individuals were limited to contributing no more than one hundred or even one thousand dollars (or perhaps more in a state the size of California) to the qualification of an initiative, then the qualification of a ballot measure—even with paid signature gatherers—could again serve as a useful test of popular interest or support. Unfortunately, states wanting to make qualification a meaningful hurdle have been prevented from doing so by the courts.

THE JUDICIAL PREEMPTION OF POLITICS

The first barriers to a state's ability to make qualification a meaningfully democratic exercise were erected by the U.S. Supreme Court in the landmark 1976 case *Buckley v. Valeo,* in which the Court considered the constitutionality of a host of limitations on campaign finance practices that had been passed by Congress in 1974. In its ruling the Court distinguished between contributions and expenditures, arguing that limitations on expenditures (what a candidate can spend) impermissibly reduce "the quantity of expression by reducing the number of issues discussed, the depth of their exploration, and the size of the audience reached," while contribution limits entail "only a marginal restriction upon the contributor's ability to engage in free communication." A contributor who would like to give five thousand dollars but is limited by law to one thousand dollars has still been able clearly to communicate his message of support for a candidate; in contrast, restricting a candidate's spending to one hundred thousand dollars when he or she could have spent five hundred thousand dollars would drastically limit that candidate's ability to communicate a message to potential voters. Given the more indirect impact on freedom of expression imposed by contribution limits, the Court accepted that the limits were justified by the government's "weighty interest" in preventing "corruption and the appearance of corruption spawned by the real or imagined coercive influence of large financial contributions on candidates' positions and on their actions if elected to office." No such compelling interest exists in the case of expenditure limits, the Court ruled. Neither the government's interest in controlling campaign costs nor in equalizing spending between campaigns could justify the substantial restraints on "the quantity and diversity of political speech" that expenditure ceilings would entail.[56]

Buckley v. Valeo had nothing specifically to say about the initiative and referendum; its subject was candidate elections. The uncertainty as to where *Buckley* left direct democracy was quickly answered, however, by the Court's decision in *National Bank of Boston v. Bellotti* (1978). Under challenge in the case was a Massachusetts law that forbid business corporations from contributing or spending any money "for the purpose of . . . influencing or affecting the vote on any question submitted to the voters, other than one materially affecting any of the property, business or assets of the corporation." The statute explicitly excluded corporations from financial involvement with any measure "concerning the taxation of the income, property or transactions of individuals." Such a statute, a bare majority of the Court held, was impermissible because "the risk of corruption perceived in cases involving candidate elections simply is not present in a popular vote on a public issue." Such sweeping language suggested that even less draconian regulations would have a hard time passing constitutional muster, a suspicion confirmed a few years later in *Citizens Against Rent Control v. City of Berkeley* (1981), in which the Court struck down a city ordinance that limited contributions to ballot measure committees to $250 on the grounds that the threat of corruption was absent in ballot elections. In the Court's view, public disclosure of contributions was sufficient to safeguard the integrity of the political system.[57]

The U.S. Supreme Court's pronouncements in *Bellotti* and *Berkeley* meant that once a measure qualified for the ballot, the states could do virtually nothing to restrict the flow of money to initiative campaigns. So long as states were free to ban paid petitioners, however, they still had the power to restrict the influence of money at the qualification stage. Wealthy individuals could not be prevented from supporting their favorite causes, but by banning paid petitioners a state could stop a wealthy individual from simply buying a place on the ballot. That option was unceremoniously closed by the Supreme Court in *Meyer v. Grant* (1988), which declared that circulating an initiative petition was " 'core political speech,' for which First Amendment protection is at its zenith." Prohibiting paid signature gatherers restricts speech in two ways. First, it directly restricts the amount of speech that occurs during the petition circulation phase; second, it indirectly burdens speech by making it less likely that an initiative will qualify for the ballot, thus reducing the proponents' chances of making their issue "the focus of statewide discussion." In the Court's view, the state of Colorado failed to offer a justification that was sufficiently compelling to warrant the burden on political expression that the ban imposed.[58]

Writing for a unanimous Court, Justice John Paul Stevens cavalierly dismissed Colorado's claim that the prohibition was justified by the state's "interest in assuring that an initiative has sufficient grassroots support to be placed on the ballot." According to Stevens, that interest was "adequately protected by the requirement that the specified number of signatures be obtained." This sweeping judicial pronouncement comes without a scrap of supporting evidence. But if, as we have seen, a single individual can pay a professional signature-gathering firm to qualify virtually any issue, then Stevens is clearly wrong. When there are no restrictions on what an individual can contribute to an initiative campaign, and when paid signature gatherers are permitted, then a signature requirement is no guarantee that an initiative has grassroots support. One could perhaps have sympathized with the Court had it said that the First Amendment right of free expression outweighs the state's interest in ensuring grassroots involvement, but instead it only betrayed its ignorance of the initiative process.[59]

When the U.S. District Court upheld the Colorado ban in 1984, it had emphasized that Colorado ranked fourth in the number of initiatives placed on the ballot, ahead of at least twenty states that permitted paid petitioners. The court might also have pointed out that paid petitioners were banned in two other states in the top six, Washington (number 6) and Oregon (number 1). This evidence suggested to the court that "the prohibition against payment of circulators is in reality no inhibition." The Supreme Court quite rightly countered that these numbers did not preclude the possibility that even more petitions would have made it to the ballot had Colorado not banned paid petitioners. Had the Court known more about the history of the initiative in Colorado, it might also have pointed out that Colorado did not enact its ban until 1941 and that Colorado had as many initiatives on the ballot in its first thirty years with paid petitioners as it had in the next fifty without paid petitioners. Had the Court really wanted to impress, it might also have noted that in Oregon initiatives appeared on the ballot three times as often in the decades before paid petitioners were banned.

Though the Supreme Court was right to reject the district court's empirical argument, Stevens and company then stumbled into a far more egregious error by assuming that if banning paid petitioners makes ballot access more difficult, as it undoubtedly does, then to restrict paid petitioners is to suppress political speech. But as Daniel Lowenstein and his colleagues have pointed out, Stevens' argument "can hardly be taken seriously. The First Amendment prevents suppression of speech but does not require states to place measures on the ballot in order to encourage speech." If Stevens' logic were to be followed, then all effective restrictions on ballot access—including geographical distribution requirements, short circulation windows, or high signature requirements—would be unconstitutional. A state that imposes a 15 percent signature requirement, for instance, does at least as much or more to restrict ballot access than a state that bans paid signature gatherers. Stevens cannot seriously believe that states are under a constitutional obligation to maximize the number of initiatives on a ballot, but unless he is willing to accept this position his argument collapses. The number of initiatives on the ballot is irrelevant to the First Amendment.[60]

The Court's naivete about the initiative process was also evident in its idealized discussion of petition circulation. According to Stevens, a petition circulator will "at least have to persuade [the potential signer] that the matter is one deserving of the public scrutiny and debate that would attend its consideration. This will in almost every case involve an explanation of the nature of the proposal and why its advocates support it." Thus, the activity of signature solicitation is clearly "core political speech." The only evidence the Court provided as to what occurs "in almost every case," however, was the testimony of Paul Grant, an appellee in the case, who claimed,

> You tell the person your purpose, that you are circulating a petition to qualify the issue on the ballot in November, and tell them what about, and they say, "Please let me know a little bit more." Typically, that takes maybe a minute or two, the process of explaining to the persons that you are trying to put the initiative on the ballot to exempt Colorado transportation from [State Public Utilities Commission] regulations. Then you ask the person if they will sign your petition. If they hesitate, you try to come up with additional arguments to get them to sign. [We try] to explain . . . not just deregulation in this industry, that it would free up . . . industry from being cartelized, allowing freedom from moral choices, price competition for the first time, lowering price costs, which we estimate prices in Colorado to be $150 million a year in monopoly benefits. We have tried to convey the unfairness and injustice of

the existing system, where some businesses are denied to go into business simply to protect the profits of existing companies.[61]

The Court uncritically accepted Grant's account while ignoring a vast body of evidence suggesting that most encounters bear little resemblance to the one described by Grant, particularly when (as is usually true with paid signature gatherers) the circulator is pushing multiple, unrelated petitions at once. One initiative "campaign manual" explicitly instructs signature gatherers not to "converse at length with signers or attempt to answer lengthy questions. While such conversation is in progress, a hundred people may walk by unsolicited. The goal of the table operation is to get petition signatures, not educate voters." Ed Koupal, one of the most successful signature gatherers in California in the 1970s, adhered to the maxim that "a signature table is not a library." In an interview published in 1975, he described "the hoopla process" that his signature gatherers use:

> While one person sits at the table, the other walks up to people and asks two questions. (We operate on the old selling maxim that two yesses make a sale.) First, we ask if they are a registered voter. If they say yes, we ask them if they are registered in that county. If they say yes to that, we immediately push them up to the table where the person sitting points to a petition and says, "Sign this." By this time the person feels, "Oh, goodie, I get to play," and signs it.

Similar is the description that Kelly Kimball offers of the training Kimball Petition Management gives its circulators.

> Our training is, the first thing you do is ask [potential signers] which county are you registered to vote in. [Then we ask] will you sign a petition for a California state lottery. For the most part that's all you have to say. If they want more information, you have a second line. California lottery is good for schools. Well, they want more information. At that point you hand them a petition and text sheet. You say come back to me if you want to sign it. After two or three lines it doesn't become cost effective to argue with a person.

People sign, Kimball explains, "because you ask them to sign." Even Paul Grant himself admitted that people were more likely to sign when he told them it was his birthday, a fact that Justice Stevens conveniently left out.[62]

Stevens' rose-colored portrait of signature gathering is offered to bolster his argument that "core political speech" is implicated, but in fact the characterization is largely irrelevant. Even if signature gathering is typically closer to the description offered by Koupal and Kimball than the one pedaled by Grant, the act of gathering signatures in public places would still be a constitutionally protected activity. But Colorado did not restrict a person's right to engage in signature gathering; rather, the state said only that one could not be paid for doing so. The Court's fallback position, relying on *Buckley v. Valeo,* is that paying people to circulate initiative petitions is itself a form of speech and thus warrants heightened First Amendment protection, which creates a burden on the state that is "well-nigh insurmountable." Such is the shadow that *Buckley* casts that the district court judge who upheld the ban also tried to invoke *Buckley* to argue that paying a signature gatherer was more like a contribution than a campaign expenditure and thus did not warrant the same level of constitutional scrutiny.[63] There is little to choose between these two metaphysical positions. Both judicial pronouncements divert us from the important empirical and normative questions, questions that courts are ill-equipped to handle: Does a ban on paid signature gatherers promote grassroots democracy and civic involvement? Does it help ensure that measures reaching the ballot have a sufficiently broad base of support to warrant public consideration? Does it help to promote public trust in the initiative process? Does it help to keep the number of measures on the ballot to a manageable level, or does it mean that the hurdles to ballot qualification are impossibly high? Answers to these questions will surely vary by state; what works in South Dakota will not necessarily be effective or desirable in California. One-size-fits-all court edicts preempt a healthy political debate about the appropriate role of the initiative process in a democracy. By closing down the states as "laboratories of reform," in the famous phrase of Louis Brandeis, the courts limit our ability to discover the relative merits of different ways of regulating the initiative process.

The U.S. Supreme Court, however, shows little sign of extricating itself from the political thicket it has entered. Indeed, judging by its 1999 ruling in *Victoria Buckley v. American Constitutional Law Foundation,* a majority seems intent on plunging ever deeper into the judicial jungle. In *Victoria Buckley* the Court considered the constitutionality of a number of regulations that Colorado had placed on signature gatherers in the aftermath of *Meyer.* Forced by the Court in 1988 to allow paid signature gatherers, Colorado took steps to regulate them, focusing in particular on making it possible for the public to ascertain which initiatives were using paid signature gatherers. If the state couldn't stop them from circulating petitions, at least it could make citizens aware of their presence. To this end, Colorado enacted a requirement that petition circulators must wear an identification badge indicating whether they are being paid for their services and by whom, as well as a requirement that initiative sponsors file monthly and final reports specifying the name, address, and compensation of each paid circulator and the amount of money paid per signature. The Court struck down the identification badge and disclosure requirement as unconstitutional infringements on political expression. In addition, the Court invalidated Colorado's requirement that petition circulators be registered voters, a regulation that is commonplace in initiative states and exists in many states for candidate petitions as well. Colorado's law, which applies to candidate petitions no less than initiative petitions, had been on the books since 1980, when it was approved by the voters in a legislative referendum.[64]

Although the opinion has been hailed by initiative enthusiasts and bewailed by initiative skeptics, the decision was in some ways more limited in scope than was generally recognized in press accounts. In particular, the Court explicitly refused to judge the constitutionality of the requirement that the badge disclose whether the circulator is paid and by whom. Following the court of appeals, the Supreme Court limited its opinion to the requirement that the badge identify the name of the circulator. All nine justices agreed that requiring an individual to wear an identity badge was unacceptable. Indeed, it is hard to see any strong state interest in compelling circulators to display their names on a badge. The purpose of the badge should not be to reveal the personal identity of the circulator but to inform the signer whether the circulator is being paid and by whom. For now at least, Colorado and other states are still free to require circulators to wear badges that indicate whether they are paid and by whom, so long as that badge does not also include the individual's name.[65]

Although the Court agreed that forcing the circulator to divulge his identity at the point of solicitation was unconstitutional, it was sharply divided as to whether the state could compel the circulator to relinquish his or her anonymity in monthly or final reports. In the majority's view, the substantial state interest in maintaining the integrity of the initiative process was served by requiring a measure's proponents to divulge their names and the total amount they spent to collect signatures. The added value of revealing the names of the paid circulators and the amounts paid to each of them "is hardly apparent, and has not been demonstrated." The Court concluded that "what is of interest is the payor, not the payees." Three justices (Sandra Day O'Connor, Stephen Breyer, and William Rehnquist) disagreed. "As a regulation of the electoral process with an indirect and insignificant effect on speech," O'Connor argued, "the disclosure provision should be upheld so long as it advances a legitimate government interest." For O'Connor it was self-evidently obvious that Colorado's "stated interests in combating fraud and providing the public with information about petition circulation" were sufficient to meet this level of review. Indeed, so substantial were these interests that O'Connor affirmed that she would have upheld the regulations even had she believed more exacting scrutiny was required. In the view of the three dissenting justices, whether voters should be interested in the payee as well as the payor was a judgment properly left to the states.[66]

Perhaps the most important and disturbing aspect of the Court's ruling was its decision to invalidate the state's requirement that circulators must be registered voters. It is this aspect of the decision that most clearly reveals the poverty of the reasoning in *Meyer*. For the majority it was "beyond question" that "Colorado's registration requirement drastically reduces the number of persons, both volunteer and paid, available to circulate petitions. That requirement produces a speech diminution of the very kind produced by the ban on paid circulators at issue in *Meyer*." Banning paid circulators, like restricting circulators to registered voters, " 'limit[s] the number of voices who will convey [the initiative proponents'] message' and, consequently, cut[s] down 'the size of the audience [pro-ponents] can reach.' " At a stroke the Court abolished a regulation that had existed for years in all but a handful of initiative states, including every state that used the initiative with great frequency. The Court's decision also would appear to call into question a whole host of state laws that use registration as a means of regulating the political process. Most directly, the decision threatens the requirement that *candidate* petition circulators be registered voters, a require-ment that exists in many states, including a large number that do not possess the initiative process.[67] Also in jeopardy are laws like the one in Oregon which man-dates that only registered voters may file a petition with the Oregon Supreme Court challenging a ballot title.

Given the ubiquity of state regulations that limit political activities (includ-ing voting) to registered voters, it is understandable that the majority's decision provoked something approaching disbelief from the three dissenting justices, each of whom viewed registration requirements as well within the states' power to regulate their own electoral processes. "State ballot initiatives are a matter of state concern," Rehnquist tried to remind the Court, "and a state should be able to limit the ability to circulate initiative petitions to those people who can ulti-mately vote on those initiatives at the polls." What concerned Rehnquist most was the Court's insistence that a state regulation was constitutionally suspect if it either decreased "the pool of potential circulators" or reduced "the chances that a measure would gather signatures sufficient to qualify for the ballot." Under this "highly abstract and mechanical test," Rehnquist pointed out, the validity of almost any regulation of petition circulation is called into question.[68]

The majority tried to blunt Rehnquist's objection by quoting Robert Bork to the effect that "judges and lawyers live on the slippery slope of analogies; they are not supposed to ski to the bottom." The trouble is that the majority opinion leaves state legislatures and lower courts little guidance as to how far down the slope the Court desires to ski. Observers can only wonder why a state can require candidates for office to be registered voters (as the Court has held in a previous case) but cannot require the same of petition circulators. And if states cannot mandate that petition circulators be registered voters, then why can they insist that petition *signers* be registered voters? Would the Court also strike down a residency requirement for circulators? If one rigorously follows the logic of the Court's "abstract and mechanical test," articulated in *Meyer* and repeated in *Vic-toria Buckley,* then residency requirements would seem to be doomed, as would many other initiative regulations. The Court's "sphinx-like silence" on the resi-dency requirement, together with the circumscribed character of its decision regarding the badge and disclosure requirements, suggests that the Court is hes-itant to follow the demanding logic of *Meyer.*[69]

The potential of *Meyer* to transform the entire regulatory environment of the signature-gathering process was immediately grasped by initiative activists. After *Meyer* initiative proponents began to challenge all sorts of initiative regulations,

some of which (like the identification badge and the payee disclosure requirements) were themselves enacted in response to the Court's ban on paid circulators, but others of which has been settled law for decades, sometimes dating back
to the initiative's inception. The *Victoria Buckley* case itself began as a challenge
not only to the three provisions debated by the Court but as a radical assault on
the requirements that the petition circulation period be limited to six months, that
circulators attach to each petition an affidavit containing the circulator's name
and address, and that circulators be at least eighteen years of age. The lower
courts brushed aside each of these challenges, and the Supreme Court refused to
revisit them, even though the length of the circulation period is more important
in determining a measure's chances of qualification than whether circulators are
registered voters. One would be hard pressed to say why a six-month window is
a "sensible" and "reasonable" regulation, as the court of appeals concluded,[70] and
a requirement that circulators be registered voters is unreasonable. Would three
months still be reasonable? What about one month? And even if the circulation
period is not deemed by judges to be "reasonable" or "sensible," if the voters and
elected officials of a particular state decide that they want to organize their initiative process in such a way as to make ballot access extremely difficult, why
should they not be allowed to do so? How reasonable or sensible a particular initiative regulation is depends on a prior political judgment about the desirability
of having a large number of initiatives on the ballot. Courts simply have no business skiing on this particular slope.

WHAT'S LEFT FOR THE STATES?

The U.S. Supreme Court's decisions in the last quarter of the twentieth century,
beginning with *Buckley v. Valeo,* have made it increasingly difficult for states to
craft initiative regulations that stop wealthy individuals from purchasing a place on
the ballot. The most effective way to achieve this goal would be to limit contributions to initiative qualification campaigns in the same way that we do for candidate campaigns, but the Court's decisions in *Bellotti* and *Citizens Against Rent
Control* have ruled out this option. Banning paid signature gatherers was seen by
many states as an alternative way of preventing the rich and powerful from paying
their way onto the ballot, but a decade later this option was also eliminated by the
Court in *Meyer.* The immediate impact of *Victoria Buckley* is less clear. If states
can require circulators to be residents, then the registration requirement may not
be necessary to achieve the goal of preventing out-of-state circulators. And if states
can still require circulators to wear badges that identify them as paid circulators,
then the absence of the individual's name on the badge isn't particularly important. Finally, if states can compel proponents to file monthly and final reports indicating the sources of the money and how much they paid per signature, then the
media and citizens will have the information they need to make informed judg-

ments about the grassroots nature of the initiative campaign. But even if *Victoria Buckley* is given a circumscribed reading, the ruling signals the Court's intention to scrutinize restrictions on the signature-gathering process.

In the immediate aftermath of *Victoria Buckley,* initiative reformers wailed that "the Supreme Court ruling robs states of the ability to fix a defective system,"[71] while initiative activists exulted that states would now have to keep their dirty mitts off signature gatherers. Both reactions are understandable, but if the states' response to *Meyer* is any guide, neither prognosis is entirely accurate. Banning paid signature gatherers severely hampered states' ability to regulate the signature-gathering process, but it also spurred a flurry of efforts to find alternative means to regulate and restrict paid signature gatherers in ways that might pass constitutional muster.

Among the boldest responses to *Meyer* came from several states—Washington and Maine in 1993 and Mississippi in 1996—which prohibited payment per signature but permitted initiative campaigns to pay by the hour or on salary. The courts quickly beat back this subterfuge; the Washington and Mississippi laws lasted barely a year, and the Maine law lasted only five.[72] The same law, however, has so far survived judicial challenge in North Dakota, which enacted its prohibition on per-signature payments in 1987 in reaction to some much-publicized instances of petition fraud associated with a 1986 state lottery initiative, the first North Dakota initiative in many years to rely on paid signature gatherers. The district court judge upheld the pay restriction, reasoning that the state's argument that "a signature-based commission rate of compensation encourages or promotes fraud" has "a common-sense basis," even if the evidence was "primarily anecdotal." The restrictions, he concluded, were not "an impermissible burden" on the free-speech and political advocacy rights of initiative proponents.[73]

The fraud argument worked for North Dakota in district court, but it is a frail reed upon which to rest a challenge to paid signature gatherers, as Maine found out when its prohibition on per-signature payments was struck down in 1999. The Maine law, like the North Dakota law, was challenged in federal court by a coalition of out-of-state groups, including U.S. Term Limits, the Initiative & Referendum Institute, and a California signature-gathering firm. The judge concluded that Maine had "offered no evidence whatsoever that fraud is more pervasive among circulators paid per signature, or even that fraud in general has been a noteworthy problem in the lengthy history of the Maine initiative and referendum process." Similarly, in Washington in 1994 the court emphasized the absence of "actual proof of fraud stemming specifically from the payment per signature method of collection." The Washington judge agreed with the Supreme Court in *Meyer v. Grant* that there was no reason to "assume that a professional circulator—whose qualifications for similar future assignments may well depend on a reputation for competence and integrity—is any more likely to accept false signatures than a volunteer who is motivated entirely by an interest in having the proposition placed on the ballot."[74]

Here the Supreme Court is right. There is no strong a priori reason to believe fraud is more likely among paid signature gatherers than among volunteers. Nor is there any systematic empirical evidence that relying on volunteers reduces signature fraud. Paid signature campaigns often do have lower signature validity rates, but an invalid signature is rarely a result of fraud on the part of the signature gatherer. Moreover, every initiative state already has in place an elaborate system for checking and weeding out invalid signatures, so the presence of invalid signatures poses no great threat to the integrity of the initiative process. Finally, petitioners who knowingly pad a petition with false signatures are liable to criminal prosecution. Far more effective and less restrictive ways to control fraud are available, such as requiring paid signature gatherers to register with the state.

If fraud prevention was the dominant theme inside the courtroom, reactions outside the courtroom showed that for most people these regulations have less to do with preventing fraud than with preserving the integrity of the initiative process by encouraging volunteer efforts and discouraging qualification campaigns that rely only on money. North Dakota's leading newspaper hailed the district court's decision as a victory "for states' rights and common sense." The prohibition against paying circulators by the signature, they explained, was "intended to discourage 'shortcuts,'" and to make it more difficult for people who wanted to buy their way onto the ballot. If North Dakota wanted to promote this end, why shouldn't it be allowed to? "It's nobody's business but North Dakota's." Maine's secretary of state explained his dismay at the Maine court's decision by stressing that "the citizen initiative process is an important part of our democratic process, and it is our responsibility to ensure the integrity of this process for the citizens of Maine. We strive to keep the focus on 'citizens' in the citizen initiative process."[75]

If civic concerns are slighted in the legal arguments, while fraud is invoked, as one lawyer involved in *Victoria Buckley* complained, as "a talismanic incantation,"[76] that is largely the fault of the U.S. Supreme Court, whose decisions have forced states to frame their defense on these shallower grounds. By accepting that a state's interest in assuring an initiative has a broad base of public support is adequately protected by a signature requirement (in *Meyer*), and denying that corruption or the appearance of corruption was relevant to initiative qualification campaigns (in *Bellotti* and *Citizens Against Rent Control*), the Supreme Court effectively ruled out the deepest and most compelling state arguments for restricting or regulating paid signature gatherers. Having reduced democratic concerns about the integrity of the initiative process to little more than the prevention of forgery and bribery, the Supreme Court not only weakens the initiative process but impoverishes political discourse in the United States.

Despite the Supreme Court's rulings, however, the states continue to be laboratories of reform. In Alaska, for instance, where there were five initiatives in 1998 (only the initiative heavyweight states of California, Colorado, and Oregon had more that year), the legislature responded with legislation that restricted anyone from being paid more than one dollar per signature. At the time the bill was enacted in 1998, few if any initiative campaigns in Alaska had paid more than one dollar per signature, but inflation ensures that the limitation, if left alone, will impact qualification drives in the near future. Moreover, since the price of signatures is affected by the number of petitions being circulated, the one dollar limit will be felt most acutely in elections where a large number of initiatives are vying for ballot access; its effect will be relatively slight, however, when the number of initiatives being circulated is small. What impact the law will have on paid signature gatherers and whether it will survive constitutional challenge is still to be determined.

In Oregon paid petition gatherers have recently been redefined as employees rather than as independent contractors, thus making a signature-gathering firm liable for payment of unemployment benefits. This important regulatory change, which increases the cost of gathering signatures, was instituted not by the legislature but by an administrative audit after an individual circulator filed for unemployment compensation and listed a signature-gathering firm as her last employer. The Employment Department's determination that the individual had been an employee of the signature-gathering firm was affirmed by an administrative law judge and then upheld in 1999 by the Oregon Court of Appeals, much to the chagrin of Bill Sizemore, who predicted "it would be a heavy wet blanket on the entire initiative process."[77] The near record number of initiatives on the 2000 Oregon ballot suggests the blanket was nowhere near as suffocating as Sizemore feared.

Even restrictions that *Victoria Buckley* explicitly struck down have not been automatically repealed elsewhere. In April 1999, for instance, a federal judge in Maine upheld that state's power to require that initiative petitioners be registered voters. Unlike in Colorado, where as many as one third of the voting-age population were not registered to vote, in Maine less than 2 percent of the voter-eligible population are not registered. The Maine law was constitutional, the judge reasoned, because unlike the Colorado law it did not significantly shrink the pool of circulators nor make it more difficult to qualify an initiative. Because the burden on initiative sponsors in Maine was at most "slight," a less stringent standard of review was appropriate. It was sufficient that the registration requirement served a "legitimate" state interest in administrative efficiency. The state's residency requirement was more burdensome, but the judge agreed with the state that Maine had a "compelling" interest in "ensuring that Maine is governed by Mainers." Petition circulators, the judge noted, "play a vital role in the process of self-government [and so] the state may reasonably require that such circulators be residents of Maine." A residency requirement also served the state's "important" interest in making it easier for the state to hold "circulators answerable for infractions of its initiative laws."[78]

Despite the Supreme Court's sweeping language in *Meyer*, which seemed to call into question all state restrictions that "make it less likely that appellees will garner the number of signatures necessary to place the matter on the ballot,"[79] courts have shown little appetite for using this test to strike down the most consequential restrictions on circulators, including circulation windows and geographic distribution requirements. Although there have been numerous challenges to such provisions since the *Meyer* decision, courts have consistently upheld geographic requirements and brief circulation periods. Barred by the Supreme Court from directly restricting paid circulators, several states have turned to these other, apparently constitutional, means of making it less likely that initiatives will qualify for the ballot. In 1997 Idaho made life more difficult for circulators by shortening the circulation period to eighteen months and introducing a geographic distribution requirement that mandated the requisite 6 percent of signatures be gathered in half of the state's counties.[80] The following year Maine shortened its circulation window from three years to one, and the Utah legislature stiffened its geographic distribution requirement by increasing to two-thirds (from one-half) the number of counties in which the 10 percent of signatures needed to be gathered. Also in 1998 Wyoming voters approved a legislative referendum that kept the 15 percent signature requirement statewide but added a provision also requiring petitioners to obtain 15 percent in at least two-thirds of the state's counties. Prior to that, Wyoming's geographic distribution requirement had been nominal, as petitioners only needed one signature in two-thirds of the counties.

The irony is that states that are least in need of tighter restrictions seem to be the ones that are most inclined to make qualification even more difficult. Wyoming has the highest signature threshold of any state and has had only seven initiatives on the ballot in three decades. Utah had fewer initiatives on the ballot in the 1990s (three) than any other state except Illinois and Mississippi. A number of high-use states have seriously considered adding geographic distribution requirements or even increasing signature requirements, but the proposals have generally failed. In Oregon, for instance, there were thirty-seven bills relating to the initiative process introduced in the legislature in 1999 and another forty-nine in 1997. The majority of these bills were designed to make it more difficult to get an initiative on the ballot. In 1997 the Oregon legislature succeeded in referring to the voters a proposal that would have followed Mississippi and required one-fifth of all signatures be gathered in each of the state's congressional districts, but the voters resoundingly rejected the idea. In 1999 the only one of the thirty-seven initiative bills to make it out of the legislature was a proposal to increase the number of signatures required for a constitutional amendment from 8 percent to 12, but again the voters repudiated the change.

If courts will allow restrictions that make ballot qualification substantially more difficult—and the evidence suggests they will—that does not answer the harder question of whether such restrictions are good policy. If states make the signature-gathering process more difficult by increasing the number of signatures required or by mandating a geographic distribution requirement, they will advantage those groups with the greatest financial and organizational resources. Signature-gathering firms will be in even greater demand, and ordinary citizens will find it more difficult to place their issues on the ballot. The only way to make signature-gathering firms and money less important in the qualification phase is to relax the signature requirements. But opening the floodgates to more initiatives, particularly in states where the ballot is already crowded with direct legislation, is not an attractive reform option. By forbidding states from limiting contributions to qualification campaigns and then forbidding them from banning paid signature gatherers, the U.S. Supreme Court has created a no-win situation for states wishing to reform the signature-gathering process. Absent a judicial change of heart, what if anything can states do to extricate themselves from the horns of this court-induced dilemma?

WHAT IS TO BE DONE?

"Publicity," Louis Brandeis famously observed, "is justly commended as a remedy for social and industrial diseases. Sunlight is said to be the best of disinfectants; electric light the most efficient policeman."[81] The majority in *Buckley v. Valeo* and the dissent in *Victoria Buckley* both quoted this passage approvingly in their defense of disclosure requirements, and it suggests a place where states could fruitfully concentrate their reform energies without advantaging the rich and powerful. States could enact laws that require petitioners to disclose whether they are using paid petitioners. Oregon enacted such a law in the 1980s, and other states have recently followed suit. Alaska, Missouri, and Utah, for instance, all enacted a similar requirement in 1999. Initiative campaigns could also be compelled to report precisely how much they paid to gather signatures, as well as the number of signatures gathered using paid petitioners and the number of signatures gathered using volunteers. The government, moreover, could be required not just to collect this data but to compile and publish it in a form that is readily accessible and understandable to ordinary citizens. This information could be disclosed to the government immediately after the signatures are submitted, and the government could make the information available to voters at least one month prior to the election. Financial and in-kind contributions to the qualification phase of an initiative campaign could also be made available to the public at the same time. The aim of such laws would not be to prevent fraud but rather to inform voters about how initiatives qualified for the ballot. Under the current legal framework in which one wealthy individual can essentially purchase a place on the ballot, preserving the integrity of the initiative process means that states need to inform voters about whether a ballot measure qualified because a few wealthy individuals paid for signatures or because of the efforts of thousands of volunteers.

Is there anything states can do beyond collecting information and making it more readily available to voters, journalists, and researchers? One radical option, dubbed "the cynic's choice," would be to abandon signature gathering altogether and instead require (or at least allow) petitioners to pay a hefty filing fee. Paid signature-gathering firms would go out of business, states would be saved the considerable expense of verifying signatures, and the amount that would have been spent qualifying the initiative could instead be used by the state for any number of socially useful purposes.[82] The virtue of such a proposal is that it would strip away the populist veneer that masks the financial realities of today's signature-gathering process. Yet the plan obviously does nothing to make the qualification process a more meaningful reflection of citizen interests, nor does it help to make money less important in the process. The proposal does not so much reform the system as admit defeat.

More appealing, perhaps, is a proposal to make signatures gathered by volunteers count for more than signatures gathered by paid petitioners.[83] Allowing for a "volunteer's bonus" would enable states to encourage volunteer involvement in signature gathering without restricting the rights of individuals to hire paid signature gatherers. If done in conjunction with an increase in the number of signatures required, such a two-tiered scheme could simultaneously make qualification more difficult for initiatives relying on paid signature gatherers and easier for initiatives relying largely or entirely on volunteers. Nebraska considered such a two-tiered plan in 1995, but the proposal was eventually defeated amid concerns that the volunteer's bonus might violate equal protection guarantees and that it might prove difficult to administer and enforce. One notable limitation of the proposal is that although it stimulates grassroots involvement and makes it more likely that a qualifying measure has a cadre of devoted partisans who care intensely about the proposal, it does not address the problem that "signatures, whether gathered by volunteers or paid solicitors, are simply not meaningful gauges of public discontent or even interest." What, if anything, can be done to make it more likely that the measures that qualify for the ballot resemble issues that ordinary citizens are most concerned about?[84]

In the initiative's early years, this question frequently prompted the suggestion that petitions be left with county registration officers and signed only in their presence. In part this proposal was intended to reduce fraud, but it was also designed to ensure that an initiative reflected voters' concerns. "Everyone knows," declared the Eugene *Register* in 1913,

> that under the present system petitions do not express real opinion. They are signed for a variety of reasons, among which are desire to be rid of the solicitor or to help him earn a day's wages, and the natural tendency to do that which is requested providing it costs nothing. Petitions signed voluntarily by persons who would take the trouble to go to the registration clerk . . . would be a real call from the people for initiating or referring any measure.[85]

One could make the petitions available at other public locations as well, including public libraries or fire stations. Initiative sponsors could still spend unlimited amounts of money to hire solicitors whose job it would be to explain the measure to interested citizens, distribute relevant literature, and urge citizens to sign. Having learned about the initiative, the individual citizen would then need to make the effort to go to one of the designated public locations and sign the petition. Money would still matter in the qualification phase, but its importance relative to issue appeal (and organization) would be reduced. Of course, without a change in the number of required signatures such a reform would render the initiative virtually unusable. But if this reform was linked to a dramatic reduction in the number of signatures required—as it should be—qualifying a measure could become much easier for initiative sponsors who tap into genuine citizen grievances or concerns. Whereas proponents of popular or controversial issues would find qualification substantially easier, those pushing issues about which people cared little would find the process much more onerous. But if the purpose of gathering signatures is to demonstrate breadth and depth of public support, that is exactly the way the process should work.[86]

In the absence of bold legislative action, the solution rests in the hands of individual citizens, who could refuse to sign an initiative petition until they have read the proposed bill carefully and thought about it for a long while. People should not sign just to be nice or accommodating, or because they feel sorry for the poor man or want him out of their face so they can get on with shopping. Most of all, citizens should not give in to the canard that they should sign so that the people can decide. A signature on a petition is not designed to be a measure of faith in "the people" but rather of support for a particular policy. If citizens sign petitions without scrutinizing the merits of what is proposed, then a ballot packed with initiatives is not a sign of democratic vitality but rather an abrogation of civic responsibility.

4
In the Name of the People

Let us agree that ballot access may be bought. Does that really matter? Ultimately isn't it the people who decide the fate of an initiative? Aren't the resources and the motives of an initiative's backers unimportant in the end? For what matters is not so much how a measure came to be on the ballot but whether voters approve it or not. No matter how an initiative qualifies, if it passes it has demonstrated that it represents the will of the people. Voters always have the final say—or so, at least, the initiative's defenders tell us.[1]

The trouble with this account is that it ignores the power bestowed upon the individuals and organizations who frame the issue. As anyone familiar with polling knows, public opinion on many issues is extraordinarily sensitive to how questions are worded. Ask people whether they support spending for the "poor" and their responses are far more favorable than if they are asked about spending on "welfare." Similarly, people have a much more negative reaction to the term "preferential treatment" than they do to "affirmative action." Most people agree that a terminally ill person should be helped by a physician to "die with dignity," but far fewer support "physician-assisted suicide." The answer a pollster gets depends in large part on the way the question is posed.[2]

Question wording was central to the battle over Proposition 209, a 1996 initiative that banned state affirmative action programs in California. The sponsors were careful not to mention affirmative action; instead, the initiative prohibited the state from "discriminating against, or granting preferential treatment to, any individual or group" on the basis of race or gender. Polls showed that overwhelming majorities supported this language, but support plummeted when respondents were asked about outlawing state affirmative action programs for women and minorities. Conscious of the vital difference that wording makes, Republican attorney general Dan Lungren, a strong critic of affirmative action programs, avoided any mention of affirmative action in the one-hundred-word title and summary of the initiative that appeared on the ballot. Opponents of Proposition 209 took the attorney general to court, and a superior court judge directed Lungren to rewrite the summary because omitting affirmative action misled voters about "the main purpose and the chief point of the initiative." Upon appeal, a district court rejected the lower court's judgment. The title and summary, the court concluded, conveyed to the public "the general purpose" of the proposition. "We cannot fault the Attorney General," the court concluded, "for refraining from the use of such an amorphous, value-laden term" as affirmative action. The decision not to include the words "affirmative action" was among the most critical ingredients in the success of Proposition 209.[3]

The importance of question wording was underlined the following year when a proposition to "end the use of affirmative action for women and minorities" was defeated by voters in Houston. The original language of the Houston initiative had been virtually identical to Proposition 209, and preelection polling showed strong support for the measure. However, Houston's mayor, a supporter of affirmative action, persuaded the city council to amend the proposition so that instead of calling for an end to "discrimination and preferential treatment" in public employment and contracting, the measure called for an end to affirmative action in public employment and contracting. After the measure was defeated, the initiative's sponsor, Edward Blum, complained that the city's rewording had "sabotaged" the initiative, and he took the city to court. As in California, the courts were divided. In 1998 a district court judge nullified the election result on the grounds that the revised wording did not fairly convey the original wording of the initiative petition. The judge required the city to hold a second election but stopped short of telling the city what language to use. The following year the court of appeals overruled the judge, arguing that the new language was not misleading because "by definition, the term 'affirmative action' encompasses minority- or gender-based 'quotas' and preferences." The one thing neither side disputed was that the wording had been a decisive factor in the electoral outcome.[4]

The impact of framing, moreover, is not limited to the phenomenon of question wording effects. Those who write initiatives control the political menu and thereby shape voter choice. Although voters may prefer a particular initiative to the status quo, given a wider range of options they may rank that initiative near the bottom. Given a choice between approving or rejecting Measure A, voters may prefer Measure A, but given a choice between Measures A and B, they may opt for Measure B and reject Measure A. Take term limits. During the 1990s voters in many states approved strict term limit laws that included lifetime bans. Faced with a choice between no term limits and highly restrictive term limits, voters generally favored restrictive term limits. But voters might not have made the same decision if they had been offered a choice between a term limits measure with a lifetime ban and a term limits measure that allowed legislators to return to office after a specified number of years. The power to determine the choices on the ballot carries with it the power to mold the outcome.

Tax-cutting initiatives provide another telling illustration of this same phenomenon. In 1996 Oregon voters were offered Measure 47, which dramatically rolled back property taxes. One critic complained that the measure was like "killing an ant with a bazooka." The problem, as the reporter pointed out, is that for taxpayers "a bazooka is the only weapon at their disposal at the moment." Voters were offered the choice between a large rollback in taxes or no change in their taxes. They were not allowed to choose between a large and a more moderate rollback, or between the proposed measure and a system of rebates for low-income or fixed-income property owners. Nor was the alternative of differential tax rates for business and homeowners put to the voters. So while the vote on Measure 47 reflected the majority's preference for lower property taxes (52 percent supported the measure), the precise policies that were enacted (the extent of the reduction and the restrictions on future increases, the limits on new bonds and replacement fees, and the requirement that property tax levies achieve a 50 percent turnout rate) did not reflect the will of the voters so much as the will of the measure's author, Bill Sizemore.[5]

There is a further reason that popular ratification of a measure cannot erase concerns about the sponsors of initiatives. Passage of a measure reveals nothing about an issue's salience to voters. In 1996, for instance, affirmative action ranked near the bottom of the list of issues that most concerned Californians. Citizens expressed far greater concern about jobs, education, the environment, and taxes.[6] Candidates running for office tend to be far more responsive to the issues that matter most to voters than do initiative advocates. Unlike initiative activists, for whom there is little or no incentive to select issues that are salient to voters, candidates must seek out issues that are not only popular but matter to ordinary voters.

When initiative activists proclaim that "the initiative process belongs to the people,"[7] they obscure political reality behind a fog of populist platitudes. Such claims ignore that what people say may often have more to do with the wording of the question than with their own preferences. What the electorate says is shaped, and sometimes even determined, by the choices that activists frame for voters. The initiative process enables people to express opinions on things that matter to initiative activists but it does not necessarily empower people to express themselves on the issues that they care most deeply about. The initiative literally belongs to the few who write the measures, not to the many who vote.

BROUGHT TO YOU BY A POLITICIAN NEAR YOU

Who brings initiatives to the people? The storybook version is that ordinary citizens, frustrated with legislative inaction, take matters into their own hands and write their own laws. The storybook ending is that, having won at the ballot box, these hardworking citizens return to their regular job and lives. How well does the real world of the initiative process live up to the idealized fairy-tale version?

Occasionally it does. And these stories, as we saw with Helen Hill and Measure 58, can be genuinely inspiring. But more commonly the tale of an initiative's origins bears little or no relationship to this mythical narrative.

Perhaps the most startling divergence from the idealized story of the initiative is the increasingly prominent role played by state officeholders in authoring initiatives. In California in the 1970s and 1980s, for instance, more than one-third of initiatives were initiated by elected officials or candidates for elected office. In 1988 and 1990 over half of the thirty-five initiatives on the California ballot were sponsored by holders or seekers of public office. Before 1970, attests Kelly Kimball, head of California's largest signature-gathering firm, "most California legislators . . . rarely thought about [the initiative process] as a potential option for them to use in pursuing their legislative objectives." Indeed, as Charles Price points out, most legislators "would have viewed initiative authoring by members as a breech [*sic*] of legislative protocol." No longer. Elected officials now routinely reach for the initiative. It can be the weapon of choice for governors who find their bills stalled in the legislature or for legislators who find themselves in the minority. The initiative is particularly attractive to candidates running for office who hope that a popular initiative may increase their visibility, help them raise money, and even increase turnout among critical constituencies.[8]

The most prominent politician to use the initiative process in the 1990s was California governor Pete Wilson, who authored or adopted as his own at least seven high-profile statewide initiatives. To assist his run for governor in 1990, Wilson, then a U.S. senator, became the spokesman for a measure designed to speed up the criminal justice system and reduce the rights of criminal defendants. The Crime Victims' Justice Reform Act (Proposition 115) had its origins in a coalition of crime victims and prosecutors who had come together in 1986 to unseat Chief Justice Rose Bird and two other liberals on the California Supreme Court. Having removed Bird and her colleagues, the group turned to the initiative process as a way of overturning a number of procedural rulings by the Bird court that the group believed had made the criminal justice system too solicitous of defendants' rights and not attentive enough to the victims of crime. The group twice tried to qualify its measure for the ballot but failed both times for lack of money. Enter candidate Pete Wilson, who saw the struggling initiative as an eye-catching vehicle that could be used to frame the upcoming gubernatorial election around the issue of crime, where his strategists believed a Democratic opponent would be vulnerable. A recently enacted initiative (Proposition 73, which was struck down by a federal district court in the closing weeks of the campaign) had placed restrictions on campaign contributions to candidates, but there were no limits on the amount of money that Wilson and his political allies could raise and spend on the initiative. With Wilson's political backing and fund-raising prowess, the initiative became the second fastest initiative to qualify for the ballot in the state's history. In November both Wilson and the initiative emerged triumphant.[9]

In the early spring of 1993, Governor Wilson found himself presiding over a limping economy and trailing his likely Democratic rival, Kathleen Brown, by as much as twenty percentage points in public opinion polls. Focus groups carried out by the governor's campaign showed that two issues, crime and immigration, could help resuscitate his candidacy. Wilson cemented his tough-on-crime profile by signing into law a "Three Strikes and You're Out" measure and by endorsing a Three Strikes initiative (Proposition 184) identical to the bill he had already signed. Wilson's efforts to keep voters' attention focused on the problems of illegal immigration were buoyed by Proposition 187, an initiative that promised to withhold all state services, including public education, from illegal immigrants. Wilson played no public role in helping Proposition 187 qualify for the ballot, but after he officially endorsed the measure in mid-September he became its chief spokesman. As one reporter commented, "It became almost hard to distinguish the YES on 187 campaign from the Pete Wilson campaign." In the closing months of the campaign Wilson spent two million dollars on television ads for Proposition 187. The proposition didn't need Wilson's money to win: polls in September and October showed it ahead by close to a two-to-one margin. Rather, the money was spent to serve Pete Wilson's electoral ambitions by increasing the salience of illegal immigration in the public's mind, thereby making people more likely to vote for Wilson than they would if they were instead thinking about the environment, unemployment, or education. And it worked. Wilson, who had been in a statistical dead heat with Brown in September, ended up winning by a comfortable fourteen percentage point margin, not far off the eighteen percentage point victory for Proposition 187.[10]

After his convincing comeback in 1994, Wilson was immediately touted as a possible Republican presidential nominee in 1996. With visions of the White House dancing in his head, Wilson seized the reins of the anti–affirmative action drive. The newly elected governor engineered the abolition of affirmative action in the University of California system and promised to "do a fundraising package" to help qualify the California Civil Rights Initiative (CCRI) for the primary ballot. The brainchild of two politically inexperienced academics, CCRI required an end to all race and gender preferences in state employment, contracting, and education. The anti–affirmative action measure had languished in relative obscurity for several years until the triumph of Proposition 187 riveted not only the state's but the nation's attention on the apparently potent political power of white male backlash. Republican politicians and operatives across the country eyed CCRI as a possible "wedge issue" that could do for Republican candidates in 1996 what Proposition 187 had done for Wilson in 1994. Unlike Proposition 187, which had relied heavily on volunteers drawn from organizations active in the battle to stem immigration, CCRI had virtually no organizational base and so was almost exclusively dependent on money raised through the Republican party. Over the summer of 1995 the Republican National Committee had begun to lean on some of the party's heavyweight donors, and the money was starting to flow into the qualification campaign, including a fifty-thousand-dollar check that enabled the initiative campaign to place a down payment on the services of an established signature-gathering firm, American Petition Consultants. But just as quickly as the political stars had begun to align for CCRI they threatened to break apart. Unable to generate sufficient national excitement, Wilson pulled out of the presidential campaign and the money flowing into the initiative campaign slowed to a trickle. The CCRI campaign announced it was broke, and American Petition Consultants immediately pulled the petition from circulation. Without money, the lifeblood of its qualification campaign, CCRI faced the grim prospect of dying on the streets a second time. But Governor Wilson had staked too much on the issue to let it die, and he promptly came to the measure's rescue. The governor "offered his mailing list of small donors, asked state legislators to have their staffs collect signatures, and even called on donors himself." One of the leaders in the CCRI campaign observed, "I'll give [Wilson] things I had been trying to do forever, and they're done in a day." Wilson neither initiated nor wrote the measure, but its presence on the ballot was due directly to him and to the Republican party.[11]

Wilson played a similar role with the "Paycheck Protection Act" that qualified for the May 1998 ballot. The measure was drafted by three Orange County conservatives who had been active in efforts to enact school vouchers and take the curriculum "back to the basics," as well as to elect sympathetic school board members. Stymied in the legislature by the clout of the California Teachers Association, the three men drew up an initiative that would require unions to get permission every year from each member before using a member's dues for political purposes. Like Proposition 209, the initiative began as an amateur citizen effort without anything approaching the financial or organizational resources to qualify for the ballot, and like Proposition 209 the initiative was saved by Republican heavyweights who saw the issue's potential to weaken the Democratic opposition. Wilson quickly became the chairman of the qualification drive, hired the same signature-gathering firm that he had contracted in 1996 to qualify Proposition 209, and put his signature to a direct mailing (paid for by Grover Norquist's Americans for Tax Reform, an organization that receives huge sums of money from the Republican National Committee) that solicited petition signatures from over one million California Republicans. Once the measure had qualified as Proposition 226, Wilson became "the poster child of Yes on 226." Wilson personally rewrote the language for the voters' guide and several weeks before the election moved $1.25 million from his personal PAC to the Californians for Paycheck Protection Committee, which he also directed. By the end of the campaign, a Democratic consultant observed, Wilson "was the single source of a lot of the conversation about the issue, even calling reporters and screaming about our ads." Wilson even called voters; the weekend before the election, with support for the once popular initiative slipping away, the governor sent a recorded telephone appeal to a million California homes.[12]

Governor Wilson did more than just adopt stray initiatives, however. If there wasn't an initiative circulating that he could use to serve his political and policy objectives, he wrote his own. After becoming governor in 1990, Wilson repeatedly found himself stymied and stalemated by the Democratic-controlled legislature. Budget agreements were hard to come by, and his budget-cutting proposals were generally rejected. The governor was particularly upset by the legislature's unwillingness to approve his welfare reform plan, which included substantial cuts in welfare benefits. Wilson's response was to draft a proposition (the Taxpayer Protection Act) that substantially reduced welfare benefits and increased the governor's powers in the budgetary process by giving him broad discretion to make spending cuts in case of budgetary shortfalls or stalemate. Wilson poured around two million dollars into the campaign, while the opposition campaign, financed in large part by the Democratic party, launched an expensive advertising campaign that focused on "King Pete." The entire Proposition 165 campaign, as one consultant observed, "absolutely orbits around Governor Wilson." The voters soundly rejected Wilson's "power grab," but only two months later Wilson was threatening the legislature with a new welfare initiative if it failed to accept the welfare reductions he had proposed in his new budget.[13]

During his second term Wilson had greater success with the legislature, and his seventh year (1997) was perhaps his most productive, particularly in the area of welfare reform and education, where he pushed through tougher education standards and reduced class size. But these legislative successes did not dim Wilson's ardor for the initiative process. In October 1997 he announced to the Republican state convention that he would spearhead the drive to qualify the Paycheck Protection Act, and two months later he unveiled two more initiatives: the Permanent Class Size Reduction and Education Opportunities Act and the Gang Violence and Juvenile Crime Prevention Act, both of which he authored. The juvenile crime initiative was mostly a compilation of bills the legislature had previously defeated, including an expansion of prosecutorial discretion to try juveniles as adults, harsher punishment for gang-related crimes, authorization of wiretaps for gang activities, establishment of a registration system for gang members comparable to that used for sex offenders, and a scaling back of the confidentiality of juvenile court records. The governor's education initiative, which included key elements the legislature had never seen before, called for shifting decisions about curriculum and finance from elected school boards to school site councils controlled by parents, creating a statewide Chief Inspector of Public Schools who would be appointed by the governor to a ten-year term, changing how teachers would get credentialed, requiring teachers to submit lesson plans for approval by administrators, and mandating school boards to expel any student caught with drugs (except for first-time offenders in possession of small amounts of marijuana). In addition, Wilson added a provision to ensure that future legislatures could not undo the cap on class size that he had earlier navigated through the legislature. Both of these proposed initiatives were the sort of sweeping overhauls that rarely make it through a legislative process that is designed to favor incremental change and political compromise. Political wish lists are the starting points of the legislative process, never the end point.

In his announcement of the education and juvenile justice initiatives, Wilson promised to submit the proposals to the legislature first, but he made it clear that he would brook no compromise on either measure. The legislature could either enact Wilson's proposal in its entirety or the voters would decide in the fall. The governor undoubtedly hoped that the threat of an initiative would compensate for the handicap of being a lame duck in his last year in office, but the initiatives were also intended to help position himself for another run for the presidency. Wilson designed the measures to keep himself in the public spotlight and to activate the immense political and fund-raising apparatus necessary to run for the presidency. Among the heavy hitters Wilson persuaded to contribute to his juvenile crime initiative, for instance, were corporations with no direct stake in the issue, including Pacific Gas & Electric and Unocal (fifty thousand dollars each) and Transamerica and Chevron (twenty-five thousand dollars each). Although ostensibly contributions to an initiative campaign, they were in fact thinly disguised contributions to Wilson's abortive presidential campaign.[14]

Wilson may have been the most visible politician to use the initiative process for his political advantage during the 1990s but he was far from the only one. Indeed, virtually all gubernatorial candidates in California in the 1990s tried to hitch their campaigns to an initiative. In 1990 Democratic attorney general John Van de Kamp organized his unsuccessful run for the governorship around no fewer than three initiatives. The first of these, the Comprehensive Crime Reduction and Drug Control Act, which allocated billions of dollars for drug enforcement and treatment and prison construction, was created to blunt Republican charges that he was soft on crime. The second, the Clean Government initiative, a highly complex campaign reform measure, was written "to reshape his image as a crusading political outsider rather than status quo insider." The third, dubbed "Big Green" (the initiative's official title was the Environmental Protection Act of 1990), was designed to be so sweeping that Wilson, the likely Republican nominee, would have to oppose it, leaving Van de Kamp with the environmentalist mantle. Like Proposition 187 in 1994 and Proposition 209 in 1996, Big Green was created as a partisan wedge issue that would divide the Republicans while uniting the Democratic base. In the end, Van de Kamp failed to make it out of the Democratic primary, and his orphaned initiatives all went down to massive defeats in the general election.[15]

Dianne Feinstein, Van de Kamp's victorious opponent in the 1990 primary, eschewed her rival's initiative strategy. As she contemplated a second run for the governorship in 1997 (she was now Senator Feinstein, having won the Senate seat that Wilson vacated after he won the 1990 governor's race), she ripped a page out of Wilson's book and unveiled her own sweeping education initiative. Announced in December 1997, just two weeks after Wilson had heralded his own education initiative, Feinstein's initiative made Wilson's ambitious plan look almost timid. The initiative, which she claimed to have been working on for over a year, called for a dollar-a-pack cigarette tax increase to finance improvements in education, including: extending Wilson's class-size reduction program to the fourth-grade; lengthening the school year; ending "social promotion," whereby students are advanced to the next grade even if they are not doing passing work; instituting mandatory summer school for children who are failing; dramatically reducing school size; introducing scholarships aimed at attracting new teachers; and, last but not least, changing the state constitution so as to reduce the required majority on school bond measures from two-thirds to a simple majority. A month later Feinstein announced that she would not run for governor, and shortly thereafter the initiative vanished almost without trace.[16]

Senator Feinstein's Republican opponent in 1994, one-term congressman Michael Huffington, used the Three Strikes initiative to launch and propel his Senate candidacy. A millionaire many times over, the relatively unknown Huffington contributed $350,000 to the qualification of the proposition, which earned him a spot as co-chair of the initiative. The California Three Strikes measure is conventionally told as a tale of an aggrieved father, Mike Reynolds, who lost his daughter to a senseless shooting and embarked on a heroic crusade to put dangerous felons behind bars. Reynolds' commitment and zeal are undeniably a major part of the story of the Three Strikes initiative, but this appealing narrative ignores the dominant role played by the ambition of politicians in writing and qualifying the initiative for the ballot. Of the million dollars raised by the measure, one-third came from Huffington and another large chunk came from Governor Wilson and the Republican party. Moreover, the initiative's primary author, Bill Jones, was a Republican state legislator who also happened to be running for secretary of state. In other words, three of the four individuals most responsible for placing the Three Strikes initiative on the ballot were Republican candidates for three of the highest elected offices in California: U.S. senator, governor, and secretary of state.[17]

Six years later, when Feinstein ran for reelection to the Senate, both of her two leading Republican challengers, wealthy Silicon Valley entrepreneur Ron Unz and U.S. Representative Tom Campbell, used the initiative process to aid their run for office. Unz's involvement with statewide politics began in 1994 with an effort to unseat Wilson as governor. Unz followed his surprisingly strong showing against Wilson in the Republican primary by coauthoring and financing a controversial measure to abolish bilingual education. After Proposition 227 passed resoundingly in 1998, Unz looked for another popular initiative to which he could hitch his ambition for political office. Together with Tony Miller, a former acting secretary of state, Unz wrote and financed Proposition 25, which, among other things, would have restricted contributions to candidate campaigns, banned fund-raising in nonelection years, established a system of voluntary spending limits in candidate campaigns, and allowed for the use of taxpayer money to partially fund initiative campaigns. The effect of the measure would have been to make it easier for wealthy individuals like Unz ("megalomaniacs with megabucks," in the words of Garry South, Governor Gray Davis' chief political adviser) to qualify initiatives and to run for office against well-financed incumbents (like Feinstein and Davis). One month after submitting the signatures for the initiative, Unz formally announced his candidacy for the U.S. Senate. The campaign plan envisioned an "easy primary" during which he would focus on passing Proposition 25, then ride to victory in November on the measure's popularity (and its severe campaign finance restrictions).[18]

But Unz's fond hope for an easy primary was shattered by Campbell's decision to throw his hat into the Republican ring. Support for Unz among Republican leaders evaporated, and within eight weeks Unz had pulled out of the race to focus on his initiative. Campbell didn't have an initiative on the ballot in 2000, but his ability to win the Republican nomination was directly attributable to an open primary initiative he had spearheaded in 1996. A prominent Republican moderate, Campbell had narrowly lost a Senate GOP primary battle in 1992 to the ultraconservative TV commentator Bruce Herschensohn, who in turn had lost the general election to Barbara Boxer, a liberal Democrat. The problem, as Campbell and other moderate Republicans perceived it, was that Republican primary voters were consistently nominating candidates too far to the right to win in the general election. Moderates like Campbell, who might be more competitive in the general election, couldn't get through the conservative activists who dominated the primary. To counteract the power of conservative Republican activists, Campbell sponsored a "blanket primary" initiative that allowed primary voters to select a candidate from any party. Not only could Independents and Democrats help select the Republican nominee, they could choose a Republican senator, a Democratic governor, and a Green secretary of state. Campbell persuaded David Packard and William Hewlett of Hewlett-Packard to put up more than four hundred thousand dollars toward qualifying the measure, the purpose of which, as one political consultant acidly observed, was essentially "to promote the candidacy of . . . Tom Campbell." Campbell's own political action committee kicked in another one hundred thousand dollars. With the new rules in place, Campbell cruised through the Republican party primary, garnering more than twice as many votes as his nearest competitor. Far from being an instrument of the people against the politicians, this initiative was a tool used by some ambitious politicians to defeat other ambitious politicians.[19]

The phenomenon of politicians writing and sponsoring initiatives is probably more widespread in California than in other states, but it is far from uncommon in other initiative states. One of the most accomplished users of the initiative process during the 1990s was legislator Kevin Mannix, who served in the Oregon House of Representatives through most of the decade, first as a Democrat and later as a Republican. He has twice run for attorney general, vying unsuccessfully for the Democratic nomination in 1996 and easily securing the Republican nomination in 2000, only to lose in the general election. The ambitious

Mannix sometimes filed more than one hundred bills in a six-month legislative session, but his greatest impact on Oregon public policy as well as his statewide visibility have come from sponsoring initiatives. In 1994 Mannix was a chief petitioner for four of the sixteen initiatives on the ballot: a measure to establish mandatory minimum sentences for violent crimes; a prison work program that required all able-bodied inmates to work forty hours a week; a measure preventing the legislature from reducing voter-approved sentences without a two-thirds vote; and a proposal to limit free speech protection for obscenity and child pornography. Only the last failed to pass. In 1996 Mannix qualified and passed a victims' rights measure, and in 1998 Mannix qualified an initiative that increased sentences for property based crimes, though it was struck from the ballot at the last minute after courts ruled that the signatures gathered were insufficient.[20]

The beauty of the initiative process, Mannix explained in 1995, was that it "enables you to get through the crap of the legislative system." Mannix may have been thinking specifically of the roadblocks legislators had placed in the way of his prison work program when he introduced it as a bill in the 1993 legislative session. Legislators were wary of the costs of supervising prison inmates and worried that putting prisoners to work might result in job losses for law-abiding citizens. Labor unions were particularly vocal in their opposition, but many small businesses also felt threatened by the competition of prison labor. Legislators were also scared off by the plan's inflexibility. Many other states as well as the federal government had adopted prison work programs since the 1970s, but Mannix's plan went much further in mandating forty-hour work weeks for all inmates who were not mentally ill, physically disabled, or high security risks. In contrast to other federal and state laws, which gave prison authorities the discretion not to employ prison workers in for-profit enterprises if it would displace workers outside prison, Mannix's plan allowed no room for such discretion. Prison administrators were commanded by the law to focus on maximizing employment without regard to cost or consequence. Rather than make the sorts of compromises that legislatures elsewhere in the nation had made to accommodate the concerns of labor and small business, Mannix took his case directly to the people, where he could play all or nothing.[21]

In taking the initiative route, Mannix not only aimed to sidestep the legislative process of compromise and adjustment (the "crap") but also to endow the program with an untouchable status. Once passed by a vote of the people, prison work would be seen less as a policy experiment than an austere and holy commandment. Administrators and legislators who wanted to adjust the program in light of hard-earned experience would be accused of arrogantly thwarting the popular will. The obstacles to experiential learning were made higher still by Mannix's calculated decision to craft the initiative as an amendment to the constitution rather than as a statutory change, thereby making it necessary for the legislature to refer any change in the program to the voters. When the governor or other politicians proposed to alter the program, Mannix immediately brandished the populist sword of righteous indignation, pronouncing himself "ready . . . to do battle to defend the citizens' *demand* that inmates get to work."[22] Yet it was not the citizenry but Mannix the politician who demanded that the measure be placed in the constitution; voters would have been at least as happy to vote for a statutory initiative. And although voters certainly approved of the concept of putting prisoners to work, there is no evidence they preferred Mannix's more ambitious and inflexible plan to other work programs that would give prison officials greater discretion over prison work. In fact, voters overwhelmingly approved a legislative referral in 1999 that amended the prison work program by giving the director of corrections broad powers to curtail for-profit prison work programs that might adversely impact businesses in the private sector or compete with government or nonprofit programs employing persons with disabilities. The same referral also modified Mannix's original measure by allowing nonprofit community work to qualify as prison work. Two years earlier, the legislature had received the voters' blessing for an amendment to the program that prevented inmates from suing the prisons if prison authorities could not find them a job and another that brought the state into compliance with federal law regarding interstate shipment of prison-made products. In the end, then, the legislature produced a prisoner work program that was not only more workable but closer to most voters' preferences.

The poorly written, one-sided initiatives drafted by politicians like Mannix and Wilson should be enough to dispel the myth that the essential difference between the initiative and legislative processes lies in the greater experience and expertise of lawmakers. Although politicians undoubtedly often do have greater experience in drafting laws, the decisive difference lies less in the knowledge of the individual drafter than in the collective capacities of the legislative process. If politicians write good bills, it is not because they are peculiarly virtuous or wise but because they are subject to the rigorous discipline of the legislative process. The long, drawn-out process by which a bill becomes a law—committee hearings, testimony from affected agencies and interests, markup sessions, floor debates, amendments, conference committees to reconcile versions passed by the two chambers, executive veto—is designed to discover and correct mistakes, both political and technical. No individual, no matter how politically savvy or technically brilliant, can anticipate the many objections, some misguided but many valid, that the legislative process will typically bring to light. Politicians are fundamentally like the rest of us: they'd rather have their way and they think their way is the right way. Freed from the sobering discipline of the legislative process, politicians are just as likely as the rest of us to try to enact their own preferences into law.

The opportunity to write laws without the seemingly endless haggling over words and clauses, amendments and riders, is not the only seductive aspect of the initiative process. For some politicians, particularly those with ambitions for higher office, public image and visibility are at least as important as the policy objectives. As Sue Thomas has pointed out, "Win or lose, the initiative can give the sponsoring lawmaker 'Lone Ranger' status as a daring maverick standing up to a self-serving legislature, and affords access to a great deal of free media coverage."[23] Mannix, like Wilson, used the initiative process not only to make public policy in his image but to create a public image that could advance his political ambitions. Prior to sponsoring four initiatives in 1994, the three-term legislator was little known outside his Salem district and the legislative rotunda. His name rarely appeared in newspapers. The crime initiatives gave Mannix the statewide name recognition he had hitherto lacked and made possible his subsequent bids for higher office.

Given the obvious attractions of using the initiative process, it is perhaps surprising that more politicians do not use it. Possibly the self-restraint is due to a feeling, among legislators at least, that using the initiative process is "dirty pool." One veteran California legislator had only scorn for legislators who take to the initiative: "I view it as a form of blackmail—pass my bill or I'll take it to [the] initiative."[24] However, term-limited legislators (virtually every initiative state now has term limits) may feel less institutional loyalty to the legislature; if so, term limits may help to erode the informal norms that have restrained legislators from using the initiative. Moreover, since term-limited legislators can no longer count on building a career within the legislature, for which they need only to be known and respected by their constituents and peers, the ambitious among them are in greater need than ever of the wider name recognition that controversial initiatives can offer. It would certainly be ironic if term limits, enacted in virtually all cases by initiative, encouraged greater use of the initiative process by career politicians.

Although politicians have much to gain from authoring and sponsoring initiatives, the process has its political pitfalls. One danger is that an initiative may more effectively mobilize the opposition than supporters. A gun control initiative in California in 1982, for instance, was widely thought to have boosted turnout in rural counties and thereby helped defeat Democrat Tom Bradley in a close gubernatorial contest against Republican George Deukmejian. A 1997 gun control initiative in Washington apparently had a similar boomerang effect. Propositions 187 and 209 in California, both of which were seized on by Wilson and other Republicans as wedge issues, have had the unintended, longer-term effect of increasing Latino registration and turnout, which has hurt Republican candidates in California. The initiative is a potent weapon in skilled political hands, but the fallout from it is often difficult to predict or control. It is not a process for the risk averse.

Politicians, moreover, have to make choices. A governor who leads an initiative campaign may have less time for other political activities, including campaigning against initiatives that could cripple the state's finances. In 1992, for instance, Colorado's citizens approved Amendment 1, an initiative that severely curtailed the spending and taxing powers of state and local governments. A similar measure had been defeated in the previous two elections, with the opposition in both cases spearheaded by Democratic Governor Roy Romer, who, according to one estimate, gave up to "nine speeches a day" against what he tagged a "terrorist amendment." In 1992, however, Romer was unable to focus his attention and energies on defeating the antitax measure, in large part because he had decided to push his own initiative to help public schools by increasing the sales tax.[25] The initiative, in sum, though often useful to politicians, is anything but a magic bullet. Like any other political process, it has a full range of hazards and rewards, costs and benefits. It is politics, plain and simple, no purer or less political than the maneuvering and scheming that typically occurs in the halls of the state capitol.

THE INITIATIVE ACTIVISTS

That politicians have become accomplished users of the initiative process is hardly surprising. What it takes for an individual to get elected is not radically dissimilar from what it takes to pass an initiative: both require a knowledge of the specialized political underworld of campaign consultants and polling experts, fund-raising, and political advertising. The political skills and organizational connections possessed by experienced politicians are readily transferable to the realm of the initiative. Surveying California initiatives in the 1970s and 1980s, political scientists Charles Bell and Charles Price found that initiatives authored by elected officials were twice as likely to qualify for the ballot as were initiatives submitted by non-officeholders. Part of the reason for this difference, explains Mike Arno of American Petition Consultants, is that "officeholders are more realistic about the difficulties of qualifying initiatives. They understand the need to raise money, and they know how to raise it. Also they don't wait too late before planning their signature drive."[26] Yet for all the advantages elected officials possess, even the most experienced and savvy politician often cannot compete with the resources and specialized knowledge of those initiative activists who have made direct democracy their vocation.

Perhaps the most practiced initiative user in the nation is Oregon's Bill Sizemore. Since becoming head of Oregon Taxpayers United (OTU) in 1993, Sizemore has been responsible for over a dozen measures on the Oregon ballot, including a popular referendum that blocked the expansion of Portland's commuter railway and another that repealed a gas tax hike, as well as a host of initiatives that proposed to cut property and income taxes, reduce public employees' pensions, curtail the power of labor unions to collect money from members, require voter approval of all tax and fee increases, abolish a regional government, and link teacher pay to performance rather than seniority. In 2000 six of the eighteen initiatives on the Oregon ballot were sponsored by Sizemore.[27] Since 1997, when Sizemore established his own signature-gathering business, I&R Petition

Services, Sizemore has made it his business not only to introduce initiatives but also to qualify them—his own as well as other people's. Initiatives have not only become Sizemore's life but his livelihood.

Sizemore's extensive experience with initiative campaigns gives him a tremendous advantage over not just ordinary citizens but seasoned politicians as well. Political experience certainly helps elected officials navigate through the shoals of the initiative process, but there are many legal regulations and technical requirements that are specific to initiatives, and in the face of these even the most experienced politician is prone to make a beginner's mistakes. In Oregon, for instance, state legislator Ginny Burdick's effort to qualify a gun control initiative for the 2000 ballot was initially handicapped by an elementary error: mailing out petition sheets that were not printed on the approved paper stock (white or pastel and at least twenty-pound number one bond). The mailing, which went to seventy thousand households and cost thirty-five thousand dollars, was expected to yield five thousand to ten thousand signatures but only left the initiative's sponsors with red faces.[28] Oregon citizens who wish to use the initiative process for the first time have to pick their way through a daunting thicket of instructions, guidelines, and statutes relating not only to the petition's paper color and weight but also type size, the number of signatures allowed per page, and what material must be printed on the reverse side of the signature page. In the face of these sorts of detailed legal requirements, there is no substitute for the expertise and hard-earned experience possessed by initiative activists like Sizemore.

Experience has also taught Sizemore the importance of starting initiative campaigns early in order to avoid the bidding wars that predictably drive up the price of signatures in the closing months of the initiative season. Those who get into the clubhouse early can qualify initiatives for a fraction of the price that the late starter will likely have to pay. In May 1998, for instance, Sizemore filed five initiatives that he planned to qualify for the November 2000 ballot. He hoped to begin to gather signatures immediately after the July 2 deadline for submitting signatures had passed. "Rather than see that network of petitioners dissipate," Sizemore explained, "we'll just go ahead and take advantage of their presence and just kind of keep the ball rolling."[29] All five of these measures qualified. In fact, six of the first eight initiatives to qualify for the 2000 ballot were Sizemore's. It is the initiative novice who is most likely to have to pay the highest price for securing a place on the ballot.

Sizemore's early start in the initiative season is motivated by more than just economics and efficiencies. It is also spurred by an awareness that "the most important question in a ballot initiative campaign is the wording of the ballot title,"[30] and that it is therefore prudent to "shop" for ballot titles. Sizemore typically files multiple versions of the same measure, each one slightly different, in hopes of securing the most advantageous ballot title. Between September 1996 and April 1997, for instance, Sizemore submitted six slightly different versions of a 1998 initiative that proposed to outlaw public employees unions from using automatic payroll deductions to collect money for political activities. The attorney general drafted a different ballot title for each, giving Sizemore the choice of six certified ballot titles. Sizemore then took the best of the six and appealed that title to the Oregon Supreme Court so that he might be able to obtain a still better ballot title. Such supreme court appeals are a routine part of the way Sizemore plays the initiative game. First-time or infrequent users of the initiative process generally lack the knowledge, resources, and time to manipulate the system in this way. Almost invariably they submit a single initiative, accept the attorney general's title, and get on with the gathering of signatures.

An experienced and well-financed initiative activist like Sizemore has another advantage over the ordinary citizen who decides to launch an initiative: Sizemore knows that there is no reason not to write an initiative as a constitutional amendment rather than a statutory change. Passing an initiative as a constitutional amendment costs a little more than a statutory change (in Oregon signatures for a constitutional initiative must equal 8 percent of the previous gubernatorial vote, whereas 6 percent are required for a statutory initiative), but it has the advantage to the petitioner of making the measure "legislature-proof." Every initiative that Sizemore has written has been crafted as a constitutional amendment. The ordinary citizen, by contrast, is likely to be constrained by an old-fashioned notion that there is or should be a difference between statutes and the constitution.[31]

Sizemore's initiative experience has not always, or even mostly, translated into victory on election day. In 2000, in fact, voters defeated all six of Sizemore's initiatives. But to focus on Sizemore's losses at the ballot box is to ignore the effect that even his failed initiatives have had on the state's political agenda. Although no Sizemore initiative has ever received more than 52 percent of the vote, his measures have often forced politicians and groups, particularly teachers unions and public employees unions, to raise and spend millions of dollars just to ward off disaster. In 2000 unions spent nearly five million dollars to defeat two Sizemore measures that would have made it more difficult for unions to raise money for political campaigns. With union resources overwhelmingly targeted at Sizemore's initiatives, the gap between labor and business spending on candidate races grew from less than two to one in 1998 to nearly three to one in 2000. Moreover, the need to defeat Sizemore influenced the unions' decision not to proceed with a number of initiative petitions of their own. Among the petitions that they submitted to the secretary of state but chose not to pursue were: the Minimum Wage Protection Act of 2000, which would have required, among other things, that the state's minimum wage automatically be adjusted for inflation; the Workplace Safety and Workers' Compensation Fairness Act, which would have made it easier for workers to receive compensation benefits; a State Purchases of Products Made with Child Labor Act, prohibiting the state from buying from vendors who employ children under age fourteen; and a Patients' Bill of Rights. Diverting unions' attention from their own agenda was arguably the primary objective of Sizemore's antiunion initiatives. As one Sizemore assistant exulted after the election, "Imagine the mischief [the unions] could have done in Oregon if they had had that money to spend on something else. . . . They were completely tied up trying to play defense and were not able to play offense."[32]

Even the state's popular governor, John Kitzhaber, who trounced candidate Sizemore in the 1998 gubernatorial election, found himself compelled to react to Sizemore's antitax agenda rather than pursue his own. A year after whipping Sizemore by a better than two-to-one margin, the governor felt it necessary to challenge his defeated opponent to a series of debates focused on Sizemore's bumper crop of initiatives, particularly a proposal to make federal income taxes fully deductible on state tax returns, a change that would have cost the state nearly one billion dollars a year in lost revenues. The need to concentrate his campaigning and fund-raising efforts on defeating Sizemore's antitax initiatives also led the governor to scale back his own ambitious initiative plans, which had focused on ensuring adequate funding for public schools. The costs to the state of enacting a reckless tax cut, Kitzhaber and his allies calculated, outweighed the potential benefits that might be gained by passing his own set of education initiatives. As a frustrated Kitzhaber lamented, "Sometimes I think that my destiny in my eight years as governor is to keep my finger in the dike."[33]

Sizemore's power may be difficult to quantify, but his visibility is more reliably measured. Between 1996 and 2000, only three Oregon politicians received more statewide media coverage than Sizemore: the governor and the state's two U.S. senators. In 2000, only the governor outstripped Sizemore in media attention. Even in 1996, long before he became a gubernatorial candidate, he received more coverage in the state's leading newspaper than Oregon's House members, the secretary of state, and every member of the state legislature. An April 1997 poll found that almost 60 percent of Oregonians could identify Sizemore.[34] Yet for all Sizemore's visibility and influence, voters knew remarkably little about the man behind the many initiatives until he made his ill-advised bid for governor. So long as Sizemore was merely an initiative activist the media never scrutinized his background or character, focusing their attention on his initiatives. Only when Sizemore declared his candidacy for governor did the press subject him to the same level of scrutiny routinely given to serious candidates for high office.[35]

Once reporters began to look closely at Sizemore's record, they quickly found a startling record of business failure, massive debts, poor judgment, and deception. Bankruptcy proceedings relieved him of over $350,000 of debt he had incurred in a failed carpet business in the early 1980s. Unfazed, he immediately started up a risky business in illuminated toys, which did even less well, ultimately racking up almost $800,000 in unpaid bills and outstanding loans. According to several of the individuals who lent Sizemore money for his toy venture, he never disclosed to them that he was in U.S. Bankruptcy Court at the time he was asking for loans to start up his new business. The image of Sizemore that emerged from journalistic sleuthing was that of a smooth talker, at times care-less with the truth, only sporadically attentive to details, and possessed of enor-mous powers of self-deception. When confronted with these facts from his previous life as a businessman, candidate Sizemore tried to spin them positively: "Out of the number of businesses I have tried in my life," he told reporters, "once I didn't succeed. I learned a valuable lesson there. You don't spend money you do not have." When further reporting uncovered the second business failure and the continuing pattern of poor judgment, self-delusion, and half-truths, Sizemore reacted by striking out at the media, blaming his political enemies, and trying to change the subject. When none of these seemed to work, he even began to lash out a bit at the uninformed voter. "The average voter," he explained to a reporter, "doesn't read the Voters' Pamphlet. They don't keep up on election issues. They just go out and vote. I don't think it's any secret there's a large mass of people out there who are uninformed on the issues." Voters, according to Sizemore, were being taken in by Kitzhaber's folksy image and cowboy boots. "Voters agree with me over John Kitzhaber about 2-to-1. They just don't know it."[36]

Sizemore's low estimation of the voters' capabilities was reciprocated by the electorate, which in 1998 handed the Republican nominee the worst defeat by a major party gubernatorial candidate in modern Oregon history. Sizemore received only 30 percent of the vote, losing every county but one. Yet the voters' stunning rejection of Sizemore did not affect his power to place initiatives on the ballot or to shape the state's agenda. His initiative business was largely impervious to the power of the people he so often praised. Sizemore's initiative machine con-tinued to spew out initiatives at an even higher rate than before the 1998 elec-tion. Insofar as Sizemore continued to shape the state's political agenda even after suffering a massive electoral rebuke, he undermined the people's capacity to use democratic elections to set the direction of public policy. Far from being trou-bled by this lack of democratic accountability, Sizemore seemed to glory in his ability to hold onto power despite his electoral defeat: "I know we're holding the cards," he told reporters as legislators deliberated over the state budget under the threat of a new tax-cutting initiative. "The governor," Sizemore gloated, "is kind of a sideline player in this game."[37]

How democratic is a system in which defeated candidates push elected offi-cials onto the sidelines? By what right does an unelected activist and repudiated candidate take a position in the center of the playing field? Faced with such ques-tions about the legitimacy of his power, Sizemore hastily retreats behind a pro-tective cover of populist rhetoric. "I do not pass laws," he points out. "All I do is put questions on the ballot for voters to decide for themselves what kind of Ore-gon they want. Bill Sizemore's plans for this state," he adds, "are no more rele-vant than those of anyone else. . . . Those editors and politicians who are saying that Bill Sizemore has become too powerful are blowing smoke. What they really mean is that the people of Oregon are having too much say in public policy, and they don't like it."[38]

Whether or not Sizemore had become too powerful, there is no question that he had finally found himself a profitable business enterprise. When he was hired as the director of OTU in 1993, he owed tens of thousands of dollars in back taxes and unpaid bills and had just had his car repossessed. By 1998 he sat atop a lucrative initiative business that paid him to write laws, and the more laws he wrote the more money his company could make. To qualify his antiunion measure in 1998, for instance, Sizemore, as head of OTU, paid I&R Petition Services $154,675, two-thirds of which went to a subcontractor who coordinated the actual signature gathering and one-third of which was retained by Sizemore for "overhead." Vertical integration of the initiative business created obvious efficiencies that capitalized on Sizemore's initiative expertise, but at the same time it also created a financial incentive to write and qualify initiatives.[39]

Sizemore's ability to make a living off of the initiative process is admittedly unusual among initiative activists, most of whom, in any event, don't need the income. Far less unusual is the way in which Sizemore has used initiative activism to catapult himself to statewide prominence and influence. In Colorado, for instance, Douglas Bruce, a wealthy landlord and real estate investor, has used the initiative process in much the same way as Sizemore to force his way onto the center of Colorado's political stage, where he has remained for over a decade. In all but one general election between 1988 and 2000, Coloradans have had the opportunity to vote on a Douglas Bruce initiative. At first Bruce's efforts were relatively amateurish. He had difficulty raising money for his initial 1988 tax limitation measure, and in the closing weeks of the campaign he had to dip into his own deep pockets for fifty thousand dollars. The measure was buried in a blizzard of bad publicity, garnering only 38 percent of the vote. But Bruce had the time and the inclination to learn how the game was played. In 1990 he used mailing lists purchased from the Colorado Republican party, which enabled him to raise five times the amount of money he raised from contributors in the previous election; Bruce himself only needed to pitch in fifteen thousand dollars of his own money this time round. The 1990 measure suffered a narrow defeat, but the margin was small enough and the consequences of the draconian initiative severe enough that even in defeat Bruce had become a force to be reckoned with in Colorado politics.[40]

When the legislature convened in 1991, the leadership promptly placed the topic of tax limitation at the top of the legislative agenda. As the legislature deliberated over taxes, Bruce publicly flexed his newfound political muscle by qualifying and passing two tax limitation measures in his hometown of Colorado Springs. He bluntly reminded the state legislators that "the clock is ticking" and threatened another initiative if they did not enact a bill to his liking. When the legislature failed to garner the necessary two-thirds majority required to refer a tax limitation measure to the voters, Bruce was ready with the money and paid signature gatherers (in 1988 and 1990 he had not paid by the signature) to qualify a new version of his Taxpayer's Bill of Rights (TABOR). This time the sweeping and highly complex measure—which required voter approval for most state and local government tax increases and set strict limits on the rate of increase in state and local government spending and taxing—passed with about 54 percent of the vote. Having at last achieved his objective, Bruce might have been expected to ride off into the sunset, content in the knowledge that he had enacted "the nation's most restrictive tax and spending measure."[41] However, he was far too fond of the attention to simply fade away. Instead, he was back in 1994 with another controversial initiative that limited pay increases and government pension plans for elected officials, capped campaign contributions from business and political action committees to fifty dollars, allowed for the recall of judges, and made it easier to qualify initiatives. Bruce's smorgasbord measure was soundly defeated by a three-to-one margin, but that didn't stop him coming back again in 1996 with still another measure, which would have extended the initiative and referendum to school districts, counties, and special districts, and reduced the number of signatures required to force a referendum or initiative election in local government. That, too, was soundly defeated, and in 1997 he even lost big in conservative Colorado Springs when voters there decisively rejected his initiative requiring the city to sell off certain assets.

During this time, polls consistently showed that most Coloradans had little respect for Bruce. A 1995 poll, for instance, showed that although seventy percent of Coloradans were familiar with Bruce, three times as many viewed him unfavorably as viewed him favorably. In 1993 Bruce was convicted of owning a run-down and unsafe building, which brought him a 28-day suspended sentence, 150 hours of community service, six months of probation, and a $2,400 fine; in 1995 the landlord was again convicted of violating Denver's building code, fined $500, and handed a 30-day suspended sentence. This time Bruce was actually jailed for 15 days for contempt of court because he continually violated the judge's instructions about what he could say to the jury. When he ran for office in 1996, challenging Ray Powers, a veteran Republican state senator from Colorado Springs, Bruce was soundly beaten.[42] When the term-limited Powers stepped down in 2000, Bruce again ran for the Colorado Springs seat, losing in the primary to another seasoned legislator. Despite these public defeats and setbacks, Bruce's tenacity, free time, money, and, most of all, initiative experience enabled him to remain a serious if widely reviled player in Colorado politics throughout the 1990s. During this period no state politician in Colorado save Governor Roy Romer received more media coverage than Bruce, who was perpetually appearing before the legislature and threatening lawsuits or initiatives if the legislators altered or circumvented TABOR, or if they proposed to restrict the initiative and referendum process in any way. Bruce stood with the people against the politicians. Despite the people's lack of enthusiasm for Bruce, his rhetoric remained aggressively populist: "It is a question of who should decide how much government we can afford, we the people who earn the money, or the politicians who want to spend it? . . . . The simple rule is that everything the politicians say is a lie."[43]

Were it not for a 1994 legislative referendum, which established a single-subject rule for initiatives, Bruce's impact on state policy and politics could have been greater still.[44] Thirteen initiatives he wrote for the 1998 ballot (actually thirteen slightly different versions of the same initiative) were thrown out by the Colorado Supreme Court for violating the newly enacted single subject rule. In the end, after submitting 165 variations of the same tax-cutting initiative, each of which was rejected by the supreme court or the Ballot Title Setting Board, Bruce's perseverance finally wore down the opposition. Version 166, although much like the previous 165, went forward without a legal challenge,[45] allowing Bruce to begin the process of signature gathering for the mother of all tax cut initiatives for the 2000 ballot. Crafted as an amendment to TABOR, the initiative proposed to cut a wide range of taxes, including taxes on cars, telephone service, heating, electricity, television, real estate, and income. Each tax would be reduced twenty-five dollars the first year and an additional twenty-five dollars each year thereafter, until at some point the taxes would presumably disappear altogether. Experts estimated that the measure, if passed, would reduce state revenue by one billion dollars in the first thirty months and billions more thereafter.

In the end, after nearly two million dollars in opposition spending and a barrage of criticism from a wide range of political and civic leaders, Bruce's measure was soundly defeated, despite beginning the summer with as much as two-to-one support in some polls. But even in defeat Bruce's actions are troubling. Forget the roughly one hundred thousand dollars in taxpayer money that was expended in staff time, publication costs, and legal notices to handle Bruce's 166 versions of his tax-cutting measure. That may be excused as the price of freedom. The more disturbing question is: How many ordinary citizens, with regular jobs, could afford the time that Bruce, a millionaire who lives off of his real estate investments, devotes to this process of perpetual submission? For activists like Bruce and Sizemore, the endless maneuvering of multiple submissions is just part of the way the initiative game is played, but for most ordinary people this legal underworld is as inaccessible as it is incomprehensible.

The populist rhetoric of the initiative activist obscures the tremendous distance that separates the world of the initiative activist from that of the general public. Initiative activists are political elites who possess skills, resources, experience, and influence that citizens typically lack. Of course, the same is true for politicians, but there is a crucial difference. When voters no longer like what a politician is doing, they can vote them out of office. Elections hold politicians accountable for their words and deeds. Citizens have no such control over initiative activists. Sizemore, whose livelihood depends on his initiative activism, is loosely constrained by the marketplace of ideas to seek out plausible initiatives that will appeal to a substantial number of citizens. But for someone like

Bruce, for whom initiative activism is akin to an expensive personal hobby, there is no accountability mechanism. He can stay in the initiative game for as long as he wishes, no matter how embarrassing his actions, outrageous his accusations, or unwanted his proposals. The lack of accountability may explain why, after exploding onto the political scene with a spectacular success, so many initiative activists subsequently offer a string of initiatives for which the voters show little or no demand.

Among the most spectacular recent debuts by an initiative activist was that of Washington's Tim Eyman, who in 1999 brought the state's political establishment to its knees with the passage of I-695, a measure that required a public vote on all increases in state and local taxes and fees and slashed motor vehicle taxes, leaving the state and local governments scrambling to make up six hundred million dollars in annual revenue. In many ways I-695 was a textbook citizens' measure. The signatures were raised entirely using volunteers, the campaign was run on a shoestring budget, and contributions came overwhelmingly from small contributors upset by high motor vehicle taxes. Eyman, only thirty-three at the time I-695 passed, was a relative political novice who had never even voted until 1992, when he cast his first presidential vote for Ross Perot. Unlike Bruce, Eyman did not jump-start or keep his initiative campaign afloat by lending large amounts of his own money to the campaign; and, unlike Sizemore, Eyman was not paid for his initiative activism. Yet upon closer inspection Eyman resembles an aspiring Sizemore or Bruce more than he does the idealized vision of the citizen initiative.

Eyman's first taste of initiative politics came in 1995 while collecting signatures for a petition to force a vote on a proposed new stadium for Seattle's baseball team. In 1996 he watched Pete Wilson and Ward Connerly use the initiative process to dismantle affirmative action in California and decided to try a similar initiative in Washington. Together with Scott Smith, a young and politically inexperienced Republican legislator who had introduced a bill modeled on the California initiative during his first term, Eyman filed his (and Smith's) first initiative. Their inexperience and amateurism showed; although Eyman and Smith devoted themselves virtually full time to qualifying and promoting an initiative that close to 70 percent of Washingtonians said they supported, the campaign raised little money and collected only a handful of the 180,000 signatures needed to qualify the measure. Realizing he was in over his head, Eyman handed control of the initiative over to John Carlson, a prominent conservative talk show host. In the remaining three months Carlson, a veteran of many high-profile initiative campaigns, gathered the necessary signatures and guided the initiative to victory. Meanwhile Eyman, who was now hooked on the initiative process, promptly went in search of another popular cause he could call his own. He found that cause in Washington's motor vehicle excise tax (MVET).[46]

Although Washington's overall tax burden was not particularly high,[47] the state had among the steepest motor vehicle taxes in the nation. The tax dated to the 1930s, but Washington had become increasingly reliant on it in recent decades (in part because the state has no income tax), so that by the 1990s around 2 percent of all state revenue came from the motor vehicle tax. The tax an individual paid depended on the value of the vehicle. If, like Eyman's wife, you owned a brand new Saab, you could pay close to $1,000 a year; if, on the other hand, you owned a ten-year-old Nissan hatchback, as Eyman did, you paid a little under $150. And if you drove a beat-up clunker, you probably would not pay more than $30. Defenders promoted the tax's progressivity: the rich guy driving a $40,000 Mercedes paid a lot and the poor fellow with the broken-down Chevy paid almost nothing. But critics countered that the tax was unfair because the burden fell heavily on some groups (the retired couple with the mammoth motor home might pay $4,000) while leaving others (the young Seattle stockbroker who, because of public transit, can choose not to own a car) untouched. Eyman's simple solution was to repeal MVET.

Despite the unpopularity of the tax, Eyman struggled to attract money and attention. Most of the little money he collected came from auto dealers, but even the state's Auto Dealers Association, nervous about the drastic consequences for the state budget, decided not to endorse the measure.[48] Eyman not only failed to qualify the measure but ended up losing seven thousand dollars as well. The following year he was back, though, with a revised petition (I-695) that replaced MVET with a flat thirty-dollar fee, and added a requirement that voters must approve every tax or fee increase. This time he filed at the earliest possible date, giving himself the full six months to gather signatures rather than the four he had in 1998. He also now had a database of volunteers that he could mobilize. He had begun to learn about signature gathering, raising money, and getting the media's attention. "Reporters don't write nothing down," he explained, "unless it's somewhat provocative." Once the measure had qualified, the fast-talking Eyman became a media fixture, constantly calling reporters and providing them with colorful quotations. "I pump it up as much as I can," Eyman confessed. "I talk about 'ransoming' and use words like 'hostage.' I know reporters don't write down boring quotes. You have to overdramatize and flail your arms to break through the fog."[49]

Even as Eyman was fast becoming a savvy initiative activist, he played up his image as an ordinary citizen outraged by a single injustice. He often told reporters—including on the eve of the election—that after I-695 he would retire from initiative politics and return to his mail order watch business.[50] Whether or not this was ever his true intent, within a month of the election he announced the formation of a political action committee, "Permanent Offense," whose objective was to defend I-695 in court and to push two new Eyman initiatives. The first of these, I-722, dubbed "Son of 695" by Eyman, required the repeal of all tax and fee increases enacted after the date on which I-695 qualified for the ballot; it also strictly limited property tax increases. As an initiative novice in 1997, he had scoffed at pouring money "down a rat hole" to a professional signature-gathering firm, preferring instead his own "revolutionary" method of offering $3,000 to handpicked grassroots organizations that were to gather ten thousand signatures each;[51] now, in 2000, he hired the premier initiative consultant in the state, Sherry Bockwinkel, to run a paid signature campaign to qualify I-722. Hiring Bockwinkel was possible because in just four months Eyman had raised $320,000,[52] more than he had raised in the entire I-695 campaign. At the equivalent point in his first try at the gas tax repeal in 1998, Eyman had only raised $15,000.[53] With I-722, which passed in 2000 by a comfortable majority,[54] Eyman was no longer just another citizen; he had entered the elite ranks of dedicated initiative activists.

Eyman's second initiative in 2000, which mandated that the state spend 90 percent of transportation funds on roads and eliminate all car-pool lanes, ran into immediate trouble. It turned out that many Washingtonians were attached to car-pool lanes as a way to get to work or to a baseball game, so Eyman removed the car-pool provision, which he now dismissed as a distraction to the main point, and promptly refiled the petition.[55] "The thing about initiatives," Eyman explained, "is, you put them out there and see if [they] will play." For Eyman initiatives are "like an IPO," an initial public offering of a stock. "You offer a stock to find out whether there's a demand for it or not. . . . People can tell us what they're worth." Unlike Bruce, who believes feverishly in the antitax cause, Eyman seems more attracted to the initiative process itself than to any particular cause. By his own admission, he had "never given much thought to race or affirmative action" until seeing Ward Connerly talk about Proposition 209 in 1996. A reporter who interviewed him two months before the 1999 election found that the normally voluble Eyman struggled most with the question of why he chose to focus on the motor vehicle tax. "Because it's winnable" was his eventual answer. An old college friend speculates that for Eyman "it's a thrill. He really does enjoy it. There may be a motivation to the actual cause, but I think he's more driven by the challenge, making waves." Eyman does not disagree with this characterization. "You can't do anything well unless you love it. And I mean I love—absolutely love—this initiative [I-695] and the initiative process." His enthusiasm for the initiative seems to be unbounded. "It's fun," he says. "The whole thing is fun. The whole idea is fun."[56]

The depth of Eyman's love of initiative politics is matched only by his contempt for politicians. For Eyman, problems are self-evident and the solutions are obvious: "I just look at a lot of these problems, just like any other citizen does, and say, 'My God, the answer is just as plain as the nose on your face, and you guys aren't fixing the problem.' " Only ineptitude, bad faith, or ulterior motives could explain a failure to "fix" these problems. "The fact is, politicians could solve our traffic problem now, but they choose not to so that we become so angry and frustrated by the traffic mess, they'll force us out of our vehicles and position us for a gas-tax increase." Eyman's vision of politics has no place for legitimate differences in values, beliefs, and interests; instead, it pits a unified and sensible people against an arrogant and indifferent political class. The legislature fails to address problems because "they're a monopoly. [T]here is no competition." As a result, "they'll fix problems when they feel like it." Like most initiative activists, Eyman has no patience with the politician's task of balancing rival goods and interests, including the public services we want and the taxes we must pay. Eyman's world is one in which there are almost no trade-offs, where we can have more of everything: more roads and fewer taxes, more cars and shorter commute times, more freedom and better services. Where the answers seem so simple, the cautiousness of politicians seems pointless. They "just nibble around the edges of change," he complains. But Eyman rejects not only caution but compromise. For him the beauty of the initiative process is that it produces a clear winner: "Either you're gonna win or you're gonna lose. And that's what I like, the finality of it." But this, of course, is exactly what the founders of this country hoped to avoid in devising their complex scheme of checks and balances. They tried to create a political system in which there would be no clear winners and losers in policy-making. Instead, each side would have to engage in a slow process of give-and-take, persuasion and accommodation, until opposing sides could live with the policy. They understood that politics is not like math, where problems can be solved by neat, final solutions. Rather, politics is a messy process in which people fight not just over solutions but over the nature and scope of the problem. Politics, the founders recognized, is not a matter of peering under the hood and fixing the engine; it involves a never-ending debate about the proper number of cars, the size of the engine, indeed, the value of cars.[57]

Eyman insists he will never run for politics. "Never. It just has absolutely zero appeal," he declares. "You have to distrust an elected official who loves his job." Besides, he adds, "My credibility would be shot. It's absolutely never going to happen." That Sizemore and Bruce made similar guarantees early in their careers as initiative activists may lead one to be skeptical of Eyman's pledge, but whether or not he runs for elected office, he is already making his unelected presence felt in the halls of the legislature. Like Sizemore and Bruce, Eyman relishes the power and visibility the initiative process gives him. "They know we're watching every move they make," Eyman boasted to one reporter. Like Sizemore and Bruce, Eyman elicits lots of grumbling from elected officials, who resent his presence and power. A "self-aggrandizing punk" is how one politician uncharitably described him. Instead of "trying to be a Legislature of One [he] ought to run for the Legislature," grouses one legislator. "As much as he said he isn't a politician, here he is being one." Eyman's ability to shape the agenda of the legislature in the wake of I-695 led one rather hyperbolic reporter to describe Eyman as "the de facto governor of the state."[58]

If Eyman never came close to eclipsing the governor in power or media attention, state legislators *were* overshadowed by Eyman in the wake of I-695. In the six months between the victory of I-695 and the close of the 2000 legislative session at the end of April, Eyman received more media coverage than the chairman of the Senate Ways and Means Committee, the two co-chairs of the House Appropriations Committee, and the two co-chairs of the House Finance Committee *combined;* he also received more than the two co-Speakers of the House of Representatives, the Senate majority leader, and the president pro tem of the Senate combined. The only elected official other than the governor whose coverage came close to rivaling Eyman's was Attorney General Christine Gregoire, and a substantial chunk of that coverage came from her role in defending Eyman's initiative from a court challenge.[59] Little wonder that legislative resentment of Eyman boiled over. Not only were legislators spending the session picking up the pieces from the explosion set by Eyman and his "kamikazes," one that had blown a billion-dollar hole in the state budget, but they also were compelled to watch an unelected activist dominate media coverage and dictate the public agenda.[60]

THE SPECIAL INTEREST GROUPS

Flamboyant initiative activists like Sizemore, Bruce, and Eyman frequently capture the media's attention, but equally important if less visible in generating initiatives are run-of-the-mill interest groups. Those who defend the initiative process often point to the clout that special interests exert in the legislature. Because the legislature "is controlled by special-interest groups and lobbyists, corporations and unions," Sizemore reasons, "the only way to pass laws that represent ordinary people is through the initiative process."[61] There is no question that some interests and issues tend to do better behind the closed doors of a committee meeting than in the bright glare of the initiative process. Legislatures, by design, factor in intensity of preference, whereas in an initiative election all preferences are treated equally. Issues for which support is widespread but shallow and opposition is limited in number but deeply felt will tend to fare better through the initiative process than in the legislature, where there are many veto points at which groups can block policies that adversely affect their interests. Similarly, the initiative process tends to be more favorable for issues in which the gains are widely distributed and the costs are borne by a few. Sizemore is right to highlight potential differences between the legislative and initiative processes, but he is wrong to suggest that organized interest groups are not a major source of initiatives.

Labor unions have figured prominently in a number of recent initiative campaigns. In 1998, for instance, the Washington State Labor Council, which is the state federation of the AFL-CIO and represents approximately four hundred thousand members in six hundred local unions, wrote and qualified an initiative that not only raised the minimum wage from $4.90 to $6.50 but, more radically, indexed the minimum wage to the inflation rate, becoming the first (and so far only) state to try this. Nor was this something new for the State Labor Council, which in 1982 had qualified an initiative that would have established a maximum limit on interest rates for bank cards and retail installment loans. The council had also been a major backer of a 1988 initiative that hiked the minimum wage from $2.30 to $4.25. The measure was introduced by a pair of Democratic legislators on behalf of a coalition of special interest groups that included not only the State Labor Council but also the United Farm Workers of Washington State, the Service Employees International Union, the Hotel and Restaurant Employees Union, as well as the National Organization of Women and the Washington Association of Churches. The results were starkly different in the initiative and legislative processes—in both 1988 and 1998 the minimum wage proposals died in the Senate before being passed by the people—but the same special interest groups were the source of the measures in both processes.

In Oregon in 1998, two of the nine initiatives placed before the voters were put there by organized labor, specifically the state's three largest public employees unions: the Oregon Education Association, the Oregon Public Employees Union, and the American Federation of State, County and Municipal Workers. Confronted with a Sizemore initiative (Measure 59) that would have weakened the unions' political power by undermining their ability to raise money from their members, the unions responded with a measure of their own that would nullify Sizemore's if theirs received more votes. The union's initiative (Measure 62) was packaged as a campaign finance reform issue and included a multitude of provisions: campaigns must disclose contributions of over five hundred dollars within seven days; political advertisements or leaflets must disclose who paid for them; initiative campaigns must disclose monthly expenditures and contributions; signature gatherers must be registered voters; and people may not be paid to sign or not to sign a petition. Many of these regulations were already state law, but the unions' intent in pushing the measure was not to reform campaign finance laws but to preserve their own power. These various provisions were included to sugarcoat and disguise the poison pill buried in the middle of the measure's ten complex sections. In section 5 (titled "Individuals' Right to Participate"), the alert voter would find the real intent of the measure, which was to preserve the unions' power to use dues gathered through payroll deductions for political purposes. But nothing in the ballot title ("Amends Constitutions: Requires Campaign Finance Disclosures; Regulates Signature Gathering; Guarantees Contribution Methods") would have tipped off the voter. The ballot summary was equally unhelpful:

> Amends constitution. Existing statutes require disclosing certain campaign finances. Measure adds constitutional requirements for prompter disclosure of contributions $500 or more; more frequent disclosure of contributions/ expenditures for referendum/initiative petitions. Requires disclosing entity authorizing/paying for political advertising. Legislature may regulate, prohibit paying signature gatherers if it finds practice has caused fraud, other abuses. Guarantees individuals' right to make campaign contributions using

certain methods. Secretary of State must promptly publish finance reports. Prohibits payments for signing/not signing petitions. Specifies penalties. Other provisions.

"Guarantees individuals' right to make campaign contributions using certain methods" was the closest the ordinary voter got to the truth that lurked behind that terse phrase. The measure passed by better than two to one, though the number of voters who knew about the contents of section 5 must have been very small.

The unions' other measure on the 1998 ballot was more straightforward: it amended the state constitution to require that any ballot measure mandating a supermajority must receive the same percentage of votes that it would require of other bills. For instance, an initiative that required a two-thirds majority to increase taxes would itself need to secure a two-thirds majority to go into effect. Although the measure never mentioned taxes, let alone Sizemore, its transparent intent was to launch a preemptive strike against a measure Sizemore planned to qualify for the 2000 ballot that would have required a two-thirds vote to approve tax and fee increases. The unions, which had spent $750,000 to qualify Measures 62 and 63, were careful to wipe their fingerprints from the measure. Union officials chose as chief petitioners two government workers who, while active in the union, held no leadership position and had no role in conceiving the measure. The measure committee the unions formed was given the innocuous title Oregonians for Open and Fair Elections. Even the voters' pamphlet gave few clues to the union origins of the measure. The first five arguments in favor were authored by the secretary of state, the head of Common Cause, a representative of the Oregon State Council of Senior Citizens, a vice-president of the Oregon PTA, and the leader of a group called Oregonians for Tax Fairness. Next came an argument submitted by the two chief petitioners, neither of whom were identified with an organization of any sort, least of all the public employees unions. Measure 63, they argued, would prevent "special interest lobbyists" from subverting "the integrity of our elections." The argument signed by Roger Gray, head of Oregonians for Open and Fair Elections, simply listed twenty-three organizations supporting the Defense of Democracy Act, including Common Cause, the Ecumenical Ministries of Oregon, the Oregon State Grange, the Portland Rainbow Coalition, the Oregon Consumer League, and the Oregon State Public Interest Research Group. The few public employees unions included on the list were made to appear as just one interest among many in support of the measure, obscuring the fact that the unions not only wrote the measure but were its sole source of money as well. Compounding the voters' difficulty in identifying the source of the initiative was that the media almost completely ignored the measure. In the few newspaper articles devoted to Measure 63, Sizemore attempted to draw attention to the unions' role as sponsors of the measure, but what little money he had—as in California, business showed little enthusiasm for inciting class war, and the Oregon Republican party, learning from California's experience in the primary election, were wary of an initiative that seemed sure to mobilize core Democratic constituencies—was primarily aimed at defending his own measure against union attacks and, secondarily, at attacking Measure 62. There was no organized advertising campaign against Measure 63, and it received by far the least amount of coverage of any of the initiatives on the Oregon ballot, which was crowded by hot button issues like medical marijuana, adoption rights, clear-cutting of forests, not to mention the most contested of all, namely Sizemore's own Measure 59.

Most of the $4.5 million spent by Oregonians for Open and Fair Elections was spent attacking Measure 59, and essentially all of it came from labor unions: $1.15 million from the Oregon Education Association, $817,000 from the Oregon Public Employees Union, $700,000 from the AFL-CIO, $600,000 from the National Education Association, and about $500,000 from the American Federation of State, County and Municipal Workers. A grand total of $80 came in contributions of $50 or less. The $4.5 million spent by the unions' measure committee was well over twice what was spent by the eight gubernatorial candidates combined, nearly twice what was spent by 32 state senate candidates, and only a million behind what was spent by 129 state representative candidates. More than a third of the $14 million spent by the fifty-five measure committees came from this one committee.[62] Lobbying the people was certainly more expensive than lobbying the legislature, but the unions' victory on all three measures (defeating Measure 59 and passing Measures 62 and 63) showed that unions were every bit as skilled at influencing the public directly as they were at influencing the legislature.

The unions' direct involvement in initiative politics in Oregon is a classic illustration of pluralist models of the role of interest groups in the political process. Groups mobilize politically, the pluralist theory holds, when their interests are threatened by the mobilization of other groups. The galvanizing force that brought the public employee unions together as part of a concerted organizational effort was 1994's Measure 8, which required public employees to pay 6 percent of their salaries toward their pensions. The unions spent heavily and lost narrowly (although they ultimately won in court), but battling the measure propelled union leaders to mobilize their members through phone banks, flyers, door-to-door canvasing, and speeches to local groups, as well as to forge closer connections among the leadership of the different unions. In 1996 unions relied on an aroused membership and the organizational alliances forged in 1994 to qualify and pass an initiative that boosted the minimum wage from $4.75 to $6.50 an hour. Once unions resolved to use the initiative process to advance and defend their interests, they quickly found that their imposing combination of organization and money were well suited to initiative politics, not just for defeating measures but for qualifying and passing them as well.

In 1998 the unions had only a little over two months to qualify their two ballot measures, largely thanks to Sizemore's legal challenges to the ballot titles, which tied the measures up in court for several months. Few organizations could have qualified two measures in so short a time, but with $750,000 available to qualify the two measures, the unions had little trouble gathering the signatures. "If you don't underestimate what it takes, it's not hard to get on the ballot," explained Tim Nesbitt, who masterminded the 1998 initiative drives for the public employees unions and would be rewarded the following fall by being named president of Oregon AFL-CIO. "Once you do your homework, budgeting, planning," Nesbitt opined, "it's very easy stuff really. It's not rocket science. It's not like winning elections, which is really difficult." Moreover, the unions' signature drive didn't pay by the signature; rather, they ran the signature campaign as they would any other campaign, paying an hourly wage plus benefits. Of course, as Nesbitt readily conceded, it helps to have the organizational infrastructure that the unions have. It is this combination of organization and money that allows unions to compete with full-time initiative activists like Sizemore.[63] Far from offering an escape from interest group politics, the initiative process is another arena in which well-endowed special interest groups can struggle over the distribution of material benefits.

The unions' ability to raise money for initiative campaigns (or for candidate races) is impressive, but it pales when compared to the money that some other interest groups have raised on behalf of initiatives. Among the biggest spenders have been gambling interests. Virtually every initiative state has seen expensive battles over gambling initiatives, but none has approached the staggering sums spent by gambling interests in California in the 1998 contest over Proposition 5, an initiative that proposed to allow Indian tribes to expand gambling in reservation casinos to include slot machines and video poker games. The $1.4 billion Indian gaming industry spent about $67 million on behalf of the measure. The opposition, largely funded by Nevada casinos that feared Californians would no longer travel to Las Vegas if they could gamble without crossing the border, spent almost $30 million in an unsuccessful bid to defeat the measure. The total, nearly $100 million, was almost twice as much as had previously been spent on any other initiative campaign. It was double what had been spent by the Republican and Democratic candidates in a hotly contested race for governor, and it was more than had been spent by all candidates for the California state legislature in 1997–98. Put another way, it was as much as the combined amount that the insurance and finance industry, labor unions, oil and gas interests, utilities, real estate, agriculture, transportation, and restaurants and hotels spent lobbying state government between January 1997 and December 1998.[64]

Of course, money spent by special interest groups, in the initiative process no less than in the legislative process, is no guarantee of victory, as Indian tribes discovered in Washington State. In 1995 three tribes spent nearly a million dollars in an attempt to pass an initiative that would have eliminated the state's regulatory authority over tribal gambling, increased the size and number of casinos, allowed casinos to stay open twenty-four hours a day, and removed all limits on bets. The boldest part of the plan was the tribes' proposal to return 10 percent of their annual profits directly to the people who voted in the most recent general election. In government such a plan would be considered an illegal kickback, but bribing the voters in an initiative is perfectly legal, though rather dim politics. Most sponsors of gambling initiatives have the good sense to take a more indirect route to paying off the people, such as offering to devote a share of the profits to increased spending on education,[65] the environment, or social services, or, as in Maine in 2000, pledging to plow a percentage of the profits into property tax relief. When Indian gaming interests returned the following year with a more limited initiative that would have allowed slot machines and video poker at tribal casinos, they were careful to dedicate 15 percent of the gross profits from the machines to salmon restoration, county government, police, emergency services, and charities (though the fine print also allowed the tribes to withdraw much of the promised money if the legislature legalized slot machines or video poker for non-Indians). Despite outspending their opponents by better than 140 to 1, the tribes' 1996 gaming initiative, like the 1995 measure, still managed to lose badly at the polls.[66]

Indian tribes, of course, are not the only, or even the main, gambling interests to invest heavily in the initiative process. At the same time that California tribes were spending their record-breaking millions, riverboat casino companies were smashing spending records in Missouri to pass an initiative that would allow riverboat gambling on boats that were docked or floating in artificial basins adjacent to the river. The casino industry spent $10 million, or about thirty-three times as much as their opponents could muster. The lion's share of the casino money ($8.4 million) came from just two companies, Harrah's Entertainment and Station Casino. While casino money flowed freely into the initiatives, interest groups were prevented by state law from contributing more than $1,000 to candidates for a statewide office; for lesser offices the limit was $250. Even the two major political parties, which raised record amounts of cash in 1998—individuals and groups can give unlimited amounts of money to the parties—spent less supporting all their parties' candidates than a handful of casinos spent on one initiative.[67]

In Colorado, casinos have not had anything like the success they have achieved in Missouri, but it has not been for want of trying. Between 1990 and 1996 gambling interests placed an initiative on the ballot in every general election, and in 1992 they managed to put four initiatives on one ballot. Nearly one in four statewide Colorado initiatives during this period was a measure to expand gambling. The industry's enthusiasm for the initiative process was sparked by a victory in 1990 in which voters approved an initiative legalizing "limited gaming" in three small cities. Gambling interests outspent opponents by twenty to one and raised more money than was spent on behalf of the other four measures on the ballot combined. The following year, gambling interests spent well over $1 million on a more expansive gambling measure; the amount was not enough to win, but it was at the time the second largest spending total in the history of the Colorado initiative process, exceeded only by a 1980 branch banking bill into which state banks had poured over $1.5 million. Only after six successive defeats did Colorado gambling interests finally lose their enthusiasm for the initiative process.[68]

Initiatives to expand gambling fail far more often than they succeed: outside Colorado, only about one in three gambling initiatives passed during the 1990s.[69] But even at those long odds, gambling interests keep playing because of the potentially huge payoffs, as the passage of Proposal E in Michigan in 1996 demonstrated. The initiative, which brought three large casinos to Detroit, was placed on the ballot by gambling interests after they were stymied in their attempt to persuade the legislature to build casinos in downtown Detroit. Few gave the proposition much chance of passing. After all, its backers—several casino and real estate developers and an Indian tribe that already operated five of the twelve casinos in Michigan—had written the measure in such a way that the state was obligated to favor casino license applications from those who financed the petition drive. But pass it did—thanks to over $6 million, which bought the services of a California ad agency, a host of law firms and public-relations consultants, and a Washington telephone bank, not to mention a professional signature-gathering firm. What little money the opposition raised (about $500,000) came largely from two companies, a horseracing track and a sports and entertainment arena, both of which feared the downtown casinos would siphon off customers. By far the biggest chunk of the money in favor of the initiative came from the Chippewa tribe, which contributed over $4.5 million to the campaign, $3.5 million of which was contributed after the late October reporting deadline had passed. By making this last-minute contribution, the tribe was able to conceal better than three-quarters of its contribution until a month after the election, when the final campaign finance reports were due, while enabling the proponents of the measure to embark on a last-minute saturation advertising blitz as well as pay off the debts the campaign had incurred. For the tribe the initiative was worth every penny. Not only did it get the rights to operate a lucrative casino in downtown Detroit, but by making the state extend casino gambling to non-Indian lands it was no longer required to make payments to the state on its other lucrative Indian casinos. A state legislature engineering such a deal would be justly condemned of rank corruption or gross ineptitude, but who can blame special interests for trying to get as much as they can? The fault lies with a system that allows greedy groups to write their own legislation.[70]

Slipping Trojan horse provisions into initiative legislation is nothing new for savvy special interests. In 1984 Scientific Games, the country's leading manufacturer of lottery tickets, wrote, paid for, and passed an initiative that brought a state lottery to California. The lottery was marketed as a way to help education, which in the wake of Proposition 13 was feeling pinched for funding. The opposition argued that the state should not be in the business of directly promoting gambling no matter how worthy the causes the lottery might support.

Unnoticed in the public debate was a provision tucked away in the fine print, in tortuously technical language, that essentially allowed only Scientific Games to supply the lottery tickets to the state of California. The company's first three contracts with the state netted the company nearly $62 million, a handsome return on the $1.4 million investment the company made in qualifying and passing the initiative.[71]

Examples of special interest groups using and abusing the initiative process could easily be multiplied, but the tales would quickly grow tiresome. The aim in recounting these stories of interest group influence is not to contribute to the historically naive, modern-day jeremiad about the "capture" of the initiative process by special interests. The language of capture suggests that there was once a time when the initiative process was not dominated by special interest groups, but there never was such a golden age, a point I shall return to in chapter 7. The jeremiad also ignores the clear evidence that possessing money is no guarantee of victory at the ballot box, as the failure of many gambling initiatives attests. But if the jeremiad warrants a skeptical reception, so does the specious claim by initiative activists and advocates that the initiative process provides an escape from interest group politics. The initiative process does not offer a respite from interest group politics but rather a new venue in which most of the same old interest groups contest for power. The alternative venue certainly has different dimensions and characteristics, and may sometimes favor different players than those found in the traditional legislative arena, but the power of interest groups is every bit as strong.

Indeed, that may be the strongest argument in favor of the initiative process, once one has discarded the naive, misguided hope of abolishing the power of special interests. It is when powerful special interest groups mobilize against an initiative that voters have the best chance of hearing the opposing arguments and making informed decisions. Draconian term limits and "three strikes" initiatives skated through in the 1990s in large part because of the lack of powerful interest groups on the opposing side that were willing to spend money to educate voters about the unintended consequences of these proposals. If money is often crucial to intelligent, informed voting, then instead of longing for the end of interest group politics Americans should be thankful that the same pluralist logic of mobilization and countermobilization of interests that holds true in the legislative arena generally also prevails in initiative politics. Special interest groups are sometimes all that stands between the people and an initiative process monopolized by full-time initiative activists and wealthy individuals with deep pockets.

YOU CAN'T TAKE IT WITH YOU

Money will always follow politics. Individuals with economic resources will try to convert those resources into political influence and power. In states without the initiative process, this will generally take the form of giving money to individual candidates, political action committees, or political parties, or perhaps hiring a lobbyist. Occasionally wealthy individuals will dip into their personal fortunes to run for office themselves. The phenomenon of the self-financed candidate has become more common in recent years because of the rapidly increasing costs of campaigning and the strict limits on candidate contributions in federal and many state elections. Parties often recruit rich candidates because they know the money will be there for a serious challenge. Some voters seem to prefer self-financed candidates, believing they will not be beholden to special interests. A rich person, in any event, does not need the blessing of either the parties or the people to spend millions to try to get elected. So long as contribution limits remain in place and the U.S. Supreme Court refuses to allow limits on what candidates can spend, wealthy individuals will continue to have an advantage in running for political office.

The problem of individual wealth being parlayed into political power is a major challenge for contemporary American democracy. But the initiative process does nothing to solve this problem; indeed, it only exacerbates it. The rich guy who wants to shape public policy in the legislature must either do it indirectly through campaign contributions or directly by running for public office. If he contributes to a candidate, his voice is likely to be only one among many. If he runs for office, he must win twice—in the primary and in the general election—before he is allowed to lay hands upon legislation. Once in office, he is again one voice among many, his personal wealth rendered insignificant. What matters now will be his competence, his persuasiveness, and the respect of his colleagues in the legislature. More important, his actions are now constrained by his role as an elected representative of the people, accountable to them for his actions. The legislative process, in short, tames individual wealth. The initiative process, in contrast, is an open invitation for wealthy individuals to write their own legislation, unburdened by opposing viewpoints and conflicting interests.

In 1994 Gordon Miller, a wealthy Salem ophthalmologist, decided to do something about what he saw as the degeneration of American democracy. According to Miller, the United States had become a "two-pronged oligarchy" of concentrated wealth and elitist academics. To help remedy the situation, he wrote an initiative that would ban candidates from receiving campaign contributions that came from outside the district or (for statewide officers) the state. He wrote the initiative without the help of others and funded it virtually on his own, spending close to $200,000. At the same time, he launched a campaign for an open state legislative seat, spending about $275,000 of his own money to finance the effort. In both the initiative and candidate campaigns only about 2 or 3 percent of the total contributions came from people other than Miller. In the candidate race Miller far outspent his opponent, who raised money the old-fashioned way—from hundreds of individuals and groups—but Miller lost anyway. In the initiative election, however, there was no organized opposition. The only money spent to oppose Miller's homespun measure was the $500 it cost one citizen to pay for an opposing argument in the voters' pamphlet. With interest groups and voters distracted by fifteen other initiatives on the Oregon ballot, including a number of high-profile measures that soaked up media attention, Miller's initiative quietly slipped through, almost unnoticed, with 53 percent of the vote.[72]

Emboldened by his success, Miller was back in 1996 with three more initiatives, each of which he wrote and financed almost entirely on his own. For two of the initiatives, one relating to public employee benefits and the other to student testing, not a single campaign contribution of any amount was recorded. For his third initiative, which proposed to outlaw a particular method by which insurers paid health care providers, Miller attracted a meager $800 from outside contributors. Unlike his successful 1994 initiative, each of these measures directly threatened powerful organized interest groups—insurance companies, doctors, businesses that didn't want to see a rise in health care costs, teacher and public employee unions—that had little trouble beating back Miller's initiatives, none of which got better than 35 percent of the vote.

The 1996 Oregon ballot, which included Miller's three measures, was also host to three initiatives by multimillionaire Loren Parks. Unlike some rich initiative sponsors who revel in the public attention that comes with initiative politics, Parks shrinks from the public gaze. He refuses all interviews and will not allow his name to appear as a chief petitioner. Parks, who made his millions manufacturing medical equipment, first contributed a sizable chunk of money to an initiative campaign in the 1992 election, giving $15,000 to a term limits measure. In 1994 Parks started a political action committee (Conservative PAC) through which he funneled $700,000 to various conservative causes. Much of that money went to five initiatives: two sponsored by Oregon Taxpayers United and three get-tough-on-crime measures sponsored by Representatives Mannix. Rather than contribute money to the measure committees controlled by the sponsors, Parks preferred to establish his own measure committees (with bombastic titles such as "Either Vote On 'Em or Watch 'Em Go Up" and "Maybe If the Politicians Didn't Give Themselves Pay Raises") where he could control the advertising message. Through these committees Parks spent about $230,000 on advertising in support of the five initiatives, easily outstripping what the sponsors' measure committees spent on advertising. All but one of the five measures passed, and in one case (Measure 8, which passed by fewer than a thousand votes) it is possible that Parks' nearly $90,000 advertising campaign was enough to make the difference.[73]

In 1994 Parks had merely been the contributor. But in 1996 he entered initiative politics in a much more direct way. No longer content merely to finance other people's measures, he decided to produce his own initiatives. Parks established a signature-gathering company, Canvasser Services, and hired Ruth Bendl to manage the company and serve as campaign treasurer for each of the measures. Parks also hired an attorney, Greg Byrne, to draft the measures. Bendl and others would appear as the chief petitioners and serve as public spokesmen, but the initiatives and the money to support them belonged to Parks. The first, Measure 33, prohibited the legislature from altering any initiative passed by the voters for a period of five years; the second, Measure 45, raised the retirement age for public employees and reduced their benefits; and the third, Measure 46, amended the constitution to count nonvoters as "no" votes on measures to increase taxes. Parks was virtually the sole source of funding for each measure. He spent $100,000 on advertising for Measure 33, the only one of his three measures that polls showed had a chance to win. In the end, Measure 33 lost by a razor-thin margin, while his other two initiatives went down to overwhelming defeat. The proposal to count nonvoters as no votes gained only 12 percent of the vote, the worst showing of any initiative in Oregon history. Ironically, the name of the measure committee was the "True Majority." But the election had not been a total loss for Parks. He also used Canvasser Services to qualify a popular referendum (which cost him $83,000) nullifying an expansion of Portland's public transit system, and then provided nearly 80 percent of the money for a $192,000 advertising campaign spent by his "Send Back This Piece of Pork & Make 'Em Do It Right" committee. By a narrow margin (and with assists from Sizemore's OTU and Representative Bob Tiernan) Parks succeeded in undoing the legislature's handiwork. He also set up a committee to support a tough-on-crime measure ("Only the Lawyers and Politicians Will Vote Against This One"), and singlehandedly funded the $200,000 advertising campaign on behalf of the successful measure.[74]

Parks remains a major source of funding for conservative initiative campaigns and other causes, although he retreated from direct involvement in sponsoring and qualifying initiatives after a dispute with Bendl over the handling of his money landed him in court. While Parks was away on a cruise celebrating his seventieth birthday, Bendl decided to spend $140,000 of Parks' money to qualify the three measures written by Gordon Miller. Miller had already contracted with Canvasser Services to qualify his measures, but as the signature deadline neared and the price of signatures climbed, it became clear that it would take more than the $174,000 that Miller had agreed to pay to qualify the measures. When Parks returned to find what Bendl had done, he fired her; she retaliated with a defamation lawsuit and won $135,000 in a jury award.[75] Canvasser Services was disbanded, and since that time Parks has limited his role in initiative and referendum politics to funding campaigns for and against other people's measures, including: $85,000 in 1998 to qualify a Mannix measure; $100,000 in 1999 to defeat a $75 million bond issue to expand light rail in Portland; $150,000 in the 2000 primary election to defeat a legislative referral that would have raised the number of signatures required for constitutional amendments; and $500,000 for ad campaigns in support of two Sizemore measures in November 2000.

Parks' involvement in the 1996 election was extraordinary—his money was used to qualify eight measures on the 1996 ballot—but the influence of Parks' millions pales in comparison to the influence that billionaire George Soros has had on drug-related initiatives across the country. Soros, a legendary currency speculator, is estimated to be worth five billion dollars. In one infamous week he is reported to have made a billion dollars speculating on the British pound, earning him worldwide fame as the Man Who Broke the Bank of England. (Soros says he did "the sterling thing to create a platform" so that policymakers would listen to him.) During the 1980s and early 1990s his philanthropy was focused on Eastern Europe, where he has spent over one billion dollars to promote human rights and open, democratic debate, but in the mid-1990s his philanthropic attention began to turn to his adopted country, the United States, which he believes is plagued by "excessive individualism." Soros has given millions to a number of domestic causes, including helping legal aliens and improving inner-city education, but it is his efforts to reorient drug policy that have attracted the most attention and controversy. The war on drugs, in Soros' view, has been an unmitigated disaster, so he has given upwards of thirty million dollars to promote alternative solutions that rely on decriminalizing drug use and focus on drug treatment instead of punishment.

The initiative process is no stranger to attempts to legalize drugs, particularly marijuana. In Oregon, for instance, at least one initiative relating to liberalizing marijuana laws was filed in every election but one between 1970 and 2000. Only once (in 1986) did one of these initiatives make the ballot, and the poorly financed measure was easily crushed by a three-to-one margin. But Soros, together with two other like-minded billionaires, Peter Lewis and John Sperling, have provided the money and the professionalism that had been sorely lacking in previous efforts to decriminalize marijuana. Soros' long-term objective is to break down the "absolutist" mentality he believes surrounds the drug issue. The first obstacle to achieving that goal was not the government or religious fundamentalists but the amateurish drug legalization campaigns led by pot-smoking ex-hippies. Soros needed to change how Americans thought about drugs and the people who use them. Polls and focus groups showed that voters were much more supportive of drug legalization when it was linked to medical purposes, and thus was born the medical marijuana movement. It began in 1996 in California and Arizona. In California Soros personally outspent the opposition by seventeen to one, and together Soros, Lewis, and Sperling accounted for $1.2 million—almost forty times what was spent by the other side. In Arizona the money game was similarly lopsided, with the trio's money going to a more far-reaching measure, crafted by Sperling, which not only legalized the use of marijuana for medical purposes but also required that first- and second-time offenders convicted of possessing illegal drugs be sentenced to probation and a drug education program rather than being sent to prison. After the election, moreover, it turned out that the medical provision applied to all Schedule I drugs, not just marijuana but also heroin, LSD, and at least a hundred others.[76]

After polling to find out which initiative states were likely to be most supportive of legalizing medical marijuana, the trio, acting through the newly formed Americans for Medical Rights (AMR), expanded their crusade to other parts of the country. Doctors sympathetic to the medical use of marijuana were identified and asked if they would be willing to lead an initiative campaign. The trio guaranteed qualification of the measure and the cash necessary to run a successful campaign. The doctor (Rob Killian in Washington, Rick Bayer in Oregon) and sometimes a medical patient (in Oregon it was a woman suffering from multiple sclerosis) became the local spokespersons for the measure. The chief petitioners and paid consultants customized the measure to fit the local situation, but the basic structure of the measure was set by AMR. Invariably the trio's spending dwarfed that of the opposition. In 1998 in Oregon they outspent their opponents by about fifty to one. In Washington Soros, Sperling, and Lewis accounted for about three quarters of a million dollars, and in Oregon they spent close to a million dollars not only to pass a medical marijuana measure but also to stop a law passed by the legislature that would have permitted thirty-day jail sentences for possession of less than an ounce of marijuana. Contributions by others who favored these policy outcomes in Oregon totaled only sixteen thousand dollars.[77]

Soros, Sperling, and Lewis have had remarkable success in promoting initiatives and repealing legislation. So far they have suffered only two defeats at the ballot box. In 1997 in Washington, despite spending nearly fifteen times more than the opposition, they failed to persuade voters to adopt an Arizona-style measure that would allow doctors to prescribe any Schedule I drug (unlike in Arizona, this information was revealed to voters before the election). And in 2000, Massachusetts voters narrowly rejected a Soros initiative that would have made it more difficult for law enforcement officials to seize the assets of drug dealers; it also would have enabled certain "drug-dependent" individuals to receive treatment instead of jail time as well as avoid criminal conviction if they completed the treatment program. In 1998 and 2000, medical marijuana measures passed in every state in which they were on the ballot: Alaska, Colorado, Nevada, Oregon, Washington, and the District of Columbia. In 2000 Soros and his allies also passed forfeiture initiatives in Utah and Oregon, and in California they passed a drug treatment measure similar to the one that failed in Massachusetts.

Perhaps their greatest triumph, though, came in Sperling's home state of Arizona. After it became clear that the fine print of Arizona's 1996 initiative went considerably further than most people initially realized, the Republican-controlled legislature promptly set about gutting the measure. First the legislature passed a law forbidding doctors from prescribing any Schedule I drug, including marijuana, until the Food and Drug Administration approved it. Then they undid the provision of the 1996 initiative that required the release of all first- and second-time nonviolent drug offenders from prison, instead establishing separate drug courts and giving judges discretion over whether the offenders should serve jail time. For $200,000, Soros, Sperling, and Lewis were able to gather the signatures necessary to force the legislature's action to be put to a public vote. Through "The People Have Spoken" committee, which collected not a penny from any people other than Soros, Sperling, and Lewis, the three billionaires spent another $1.5 million pounding home the populist theme that the politicians had violated the will of the people. Supporters of the legislative revisions vainly tried to frame the public discussion around the wisdom of legalizing LSD and PCP, but with less than one-twentieth of the money available to the other side they had little success.

Sperling was not content just to play defense. To teach the legislature a lesson, the self-made billionaire financed another initiative (the Voter Protection Act) that forbid the legislature from repealing any initiative. The legislature, moreover, would only be allowed to amend an initiative if it "furthers the purpose" of the initiative, and only then by a three-fourths vote of the legislature. A group calling itself the Voters Protection Alliance spearheaded the effort. Its carefully chosen public mask was worn by Grant Woods, a maverick Republican attorney general, and Joe Arpaio, "America's Toughest Sheriff," who was described by one wag as "a man drawn to reporters like a Hereford to a salt lick." But beneath the colorful public mask lurked the real impetus and the money behind this alleged "alliance": John Sperling, who, together with his son, contributed all of the $425,000 that the alliance raised. And that was about $425,000 more than the opposition raised. The result: Sperling's initiative squeaked through with 52 percent of the vote.[78]

Men like Sperling and Soros, Parks and Miller, share a deep ideological commitment to the initiatives they finance. Occasionally, though, wealthy individuals have used the initiative process not to advance an ideological agenda but to further their own personal interests. One recent example is Colorado's Phil Anschutz, who funded a 1998 initiative campaign to regulate hog farms. Why, one might wonder, would Colorado's richest man, owner of several sports teams as well as a telecommunications company worth around seven billion dollars, care about pigs? Stranger still, why would a strong conservative side with liberal environmental groups? The answer, it turns out, is that an immense hog farm moved next door to his sprawling ranch. Anschutz did not like the odor of the hog farm and, unable to get the legislature to act, he decided to seize the initiative. By striking an alliance with local farmers, ranchers, and environmental groups worried about corporate hog farms polluting the groundwater, Anschutz was able to dress his personal problem in the garb of the public interest. The group called itself Protecting Colorado's Water and Economy and its public voice was provided by people like Dave Carter, president of the Rocky Mountain Farmers Union, and the aptly named Carmi McLean, state director of Clean Water

Action, but it was Anschutz who supplied over 95 percent of the $425,000 raised in support of the measure.[79]

It is difficult not to be troubled by Anschutz's success in clamping down on corporate hog farms, even if one has little sympathy for such businesses. After all, had the smelly farm been located next door to an average American citizen, hog farms in Colorado would likely still be doing business as usual. But although Anschutz's influence raises the sort of disturbing questions that necessarily accompany the infusion of large sums of money in politics, his hog farm initiative is arguably less problematic than many ideologically driven initiatives. To begin with, Anschutz took on a powerful interest group that could fend for itself rather than taking aim at defenseless groups with little clout—like prisoners, for example—or at an equally defenseless political process that no group has a vested interest in defending. The hog farmers not only outspent Anschutz by better than two to one (the National Pork Producers Council alone more than matched Anschutz, contributing $440,000), they also offered up their own competing initiative designed to confuse voters and upend the Anschutz measure. Moreover, even though Anschutz put up the vast majority of the money, the crafting of the initiative as well as support for it was the work of a disparate coalition of farmers and environmentalists. The Environmental Defense Fund, the League of Conservation Voters, and a group called the Colorado Environmental Coalition contributed almost $100,000 in in-kind contributions. In addition, Protecting Colorado's Water and Economy received nearly two hundred small contributions from individuals concerned about the threat to land and water posed by vast numbers of swine. In contrast, the hog farmers' money came entirely from one interest group, pig farmers, and most of that from three or four mammoth corporate farms. Neither side in this contest much resembled a grassroots movement, but in spite of Anschutz's deep pockets, the backers of Amendment 14 were closer to the genuine article than the opposition, and certainly closer than the self-financed initiatives of a Parks or a Miller.

WHAT'S LEFT FOR THE ORDINARY CITIZEN?

Once one takes away the initiatives engineered and sponsored by politicians and initiative activists, interest groups and the very rich, what is left for the ordinary citizen? How many initiatives resemble the idealized process whereby a concerned citizen or group of citizens spearhead an initiative in order to remedy a social injustice that has been ignored by an unresponsive political system, and then, having triumphed over the politicians and special interests, return to the ordinary life of a citizen? The story of Helen Hill, described in chapter 1, is a tale that does closely mirror the initiative ideal. She is precisely the sort of average citizen that many of the original architects of the initiative process hoped to empower. But how typical is her story? A quick glance at the other initiatives that appeared alongside Hill's measure on the 1998 Oregon ballot shows how rare are the Helen Hills of the world.

None of the other measures were sponsored by political novices like Hill. Two were authored by government officials: a vote-by-mail measure spearheaded by the secretary of state and a mandatory minimum sentence law authored by a state legislator. One was pushed by Sizemore and another (the medical marijuana measure) was crafted and funded by Soros. Four were written by well-organized interest groups. A proposal to make it easier for groups to force a legislative review of administrative rules was authored by a "wise use" group, Oregonians in Action, which claims about nine thousand members and regularly lobbies the legislature. Indeed, a spokesman for the group estimated that it generally introduces between twenty and thirty bills in a single legislative session. A coalition of conservation groups was responsible for drafting an initiative earmarking a certain percentage of lottery funds for parks and saving the salmon. And two measures were written, qualified, and paid for by labor unions. That leaves only one 1998 initiative, a measure banning clear-cutting on public and private land, that bears even a family resemblance to the Progressive ideal.

The measure's chief architect, Gary Kutcher, is certainly not rich, nor did his initiative rely on wealthy backers. Apart from $17,000 contributed by rock stars Don Henley and Brian Wilson, the largest contribution to the campaign was $1,200. Almost 80 percent of the $122,000 contributed to the campaign came in amounts of $50 or less. Not a penny came from Kutcher himself. He did run for office in 1996 as the Pacific party candidate for the U.S. Senate (he received slightly more than 1 percent of the vote), but he has never held elective office and nobody is likely to mistake this middle-aged hippie for an aspiring politician. A number of environmental groups—including the Sierra Club, the Oregon Natural Resources Council, and the Rainforest Action Network—endorsed the measure, but these groups played no role in drafting or qualifying it and provided no financial or organizational support to the campaign. Press accounts described Kutcher as the director of Oregonians for Labor Intensive Forest Economics (OLIFE), but this was not an organized interest group so much as a political action committee that he was required to set up to support the measure. Kutcher was also no Sizemore; indeed, he did not even hire a signature-gathering firm. Instead OLIFE hired a cadre of young enthusiasts to work full time doing door-to-door canvasing. They collected signatures while at the same time asking for donations to support the measure. The money raised paid the canvassers' salaries, and the little money left over went to support the low-budget campaign. The grassroots campaign was buried at the ballot box under a $3.3 million avalanche largely financed by the timber companies.

Yet despite Kutcher's grassroots credentials, he is more akin to the initiative activist Sizemore than to the apolitical Hill. Unlike Hill, who was activated by a single issue and then returned to her life as an art teacher, Kutcher's vocation, like Sizemore's, is that of the political activist. Ever since he arrived in Oregon in

1979, Kutcher has been active in initiative campaigns. His maiden initiative was a 1980 antinuclear initiative, and throughout the 1980s he continued to work as a full-time organizer and canvasser for antinuclear initiatives (Oregon had six such initiatives on the ballot between 1980 and 1986). In 1986 Kutcher put his organizing skills to work in spearheading a successful local initiative campaign to make the city of Eugene a nuclear-free zone. In the late 1980s Kutcher's activism began to shift from antinuclear to environmental causes, from the threat of nuclear power to the devastation of clear-cut logging. Working for a group called the Forest Conservation Council, Kutcher was involved with the group's efforts in the early 1990s to amend the Forest Practices Act. When three bills to amend the act went nowhere in the 1993 legislative session, Kutcher promptly turned once again to the initiative process. His effort to qualify an initiative in 1994 got held up in court, and the 1996 version garnered about half the required signatures. He finally made it in 1998. Despite getting crushed in the 1998 election, Kutcher was back again with a substantially revised version for the 2000 ballot, though this one, like the 1996 attempt, failed for lack of signatures. Kutcher, in short, is hardly your average citizen. He is a full-time political activist. Like Sizemore, he makes his living from political activism, though unlike Sizemore, the income from this activism barely lifts him above the poverty line. At the time I interviewed him he was being paid ten dollars an hour by the Sustainable Forestry Project (which was OLIFE with a new name) to work half time, but since he works between forty and sixty hours a week on his sustainable forestry initiative, his real salary was below minimum wage. Given the huge amounts of time it takes to conduct an initiative campaign the old-fashioned way, it is hard to imagine anyone but committed activists having the time or energy for the game.[80]

In neighboring Washington State, single-issue political novices have also been a rarity in recent elections. Perhaps the closest fit to the idealized model is Jim and Fawn Spady, a husband-and-wife team who wrote a charter school initiative that appeared on the ballot in 1996. The couple had children in the Seattle public school system and got fed up with what they saw as the mediocrity of the education being offered. First they pulled their kids out of the public schools and then launched their Education Excellence Initiative. Initially they planned a volunteer effort fueled by parental outrage and civic spirit, but when the signature deadline passed, the Spadys had collected only about ten thousand signatures. When they filed again, they decided to use paid signature gatherers. Unlike Kutcher, the Spadys had money: Jim Spady was an attorney and vice president of Dick's Drive-In Restaurants, a Seattle chain owned by his family. But they were not among the superrich, nor were they willing to spend the family fortune. They promised to spend a hundred thousand dollars if they could get contributions to match that gift. "I'm not going to do this unless I know other people are going to stick with us," Jim Spady explained at the time. Unlike the self-made millionaire Ron Taber, who qualified a private school voucher initiative the same year, the Spadys had neither the desire nor the resources to go it alone. Also unlike Taber, who needed the publicity of an initiative campaign to propel his 1996 run for the state superintendent position, the Spadys had no political ambitions; they were solely committed to advancing charter schools and improving public education. They spent long hours in the state house trying hard to persuade legislators to support charter schools. The last thing the couple wanted was an expensive election that would drain their family savings. For them the initiative process truly was a last resort.[81]

Unlike Taber, the Spadys managed to attract significant outside contributions for their measure, but not nearly enough to defend the measure against an onslaught of union spending. Like Taber's measure, the Spadys' initiative was easily routed, losing by thirty percentage points. But the Spadys' dedication to their cause was undiminished, and in 2000 they came back with a more moderate version of the initiative that they hoped would attract financial support from Seattle's high-technology community. With only a few months remaining before the signature deadline, they had raised just sixty thousand dollars and still had to hire paid signature gatherers. But then they caught the big one: Microsoft cofounder Paul Allen, who promised to spend six hundred thousand dollars to get the Spadys' measure on the ballot and pledged more of his millions to pass it. The Spadys were kept on as advisers, but they were no longer involved in the day-to-day operations. It was now the Allen family's initiative; the Allens hired the signature-gathering firm, the political consultants, and the admen, and these hired professionals then orchestrated the show. Ironically, it was only by ceasing to become a classic citizen initiative that charter schools became a viable initiative.[82]

The best place to find genuine amateur citizen initiatives is not on the ballot but in the large number of initiatives that get filed but never make it to the ballot. These are people like Aaron Durland, a twenty-five-year-old college student in Oregon who believed that government had no business telling people to wear seat belts. His personal crusade never made it into any newspaper. He had no money and never raised a penny. The only signatures he collected were the handful he gathered himself. He tried contacting a few groups, including a motorcycle group that was opposed to wearing helmets, but got nowhere and eventually abandoned the idea.[83] Or consider the fifty-four-year-old Milo John Reese, a one-man antiprostitution crusader in Nevada who filed an initiative petition in 2000 to prohibit prostitution, which is legal in twelve of Nevada's seventeen counties. Unlike Durland, Reese did manage to draw media attention to his efforts, primarily by abandoning his car near a Reno brothel, breaking a side window, and leaving bloodstains on the seat. Police spent ten days looking for Reese, only to be told when they found him that he had staged his disappearance "to publicize his claim that prostitutes are leaving their legal brothels in rural counties to work illegally in Las Vegas and Reno." Reese's unfamiliarity with the initiative process was evident early on: when he submitted the requisite papers to the secretary of state's office, he mistakenly indicated that signatures were to be sent to the Coalition for the Protection of Marriage, a group that was circulating an initiative to prohibit same-sex marriages. Evidently he had borrowed one of their signature sheets but neglected to delete the reference to the marriage protection group.[84]

Some citizens aren't content with just one initiative. In 1994 Washington's David Henshaw, a self-described Renaissance man, filed no fewer than eight initiatives on a dazzling array of topics. One initiative would have required state lobbyists to pay a million-dollar license fee and entitled employees to time off to testify before the legislature. Another would have set aside a million dollars in state funds to pay for embryo transfers as an alternative to abortion. A third would have required anybody buying a gun to take a firearm safety course, a fourth would have mandated an increase in the hourly wage for anyone working weekends and nights, and a fifth would have assessed fines based not only on the nature of the offense but on the income of the person convicted. Kurt Weinreich of Olympia, Washington, filed five measures in 2000, one of which would have voided all municipal ordinances and state administrative codes that "applied to flesh and blood people." Another eliminated the requirement that lawyers must pass the state bar examination, and still another required that "all trees growing and producing oxygen on publicly owned lands be forever preserved to supply voters with essential life-sustaining oxygen." The record, however, probably belongs to Patrick O'Shaughnessy of San Francisco, who in one week in 1973 filed twenty different initiatives on a wide variety of subjects. None of these ever came close to qualifying for the ballot.[85]

Some amateurs are quite persistent. In Washington, for instance, Elizabeth Patrick has pedaled a pair of initiatives involving the national security apparatus in every even-year election since 1994. Clarence Keating submitted variations on the same tax initiative every year between 1987 and 1996, totaling nine initiatives in all. Antitax crusader Donald Carter circulated six property tax cut initiatives between 1995 and 2000. When Carter kicked off his 2000 initiative drive on the steps of the state capitol, three people showed up for his "Storm 2000" rally. Winton Cannon has submitted nine tax-related initiatives between 1997 and 2000, including one that resembled the motor vehicle tax initiative with which Eyman hit pay dirt. None of these initiatives have qualified for the ballot. In California Robert Wilson, a cement contractor-turned-studio artist, has submitted close to thirty gambling initiatives over the last thirty-five years in an attempt to replicate his 1964 success, when he managed to qualify a statewide lottery initiative, only to see it fail by a better than two-to-one margin. Wilson freely admits that he has made no effort to qualify many of these thirty initiatives. "I kept reintroducing them," he explains, "because this was my idea—my way of maintaining a kind of patent on the idea."[86]

Most of these citizens have about as much chance of qualifying an initiative as they do of winning the jackpot in the state lottery. Indeed, winning the lottery or coming into a substantial inheritance (as Helen Hill did) may be the only way these individuals will be able to place their pet ideas before the people. The list of initiatives filed is filled with the names of ordinary if sometimes eccentric citizens, people who never get their names in the newspaper or have anybody of political importance pay attention to them. But when it gets to the serious business of qualifying and passing initiatives, initiative politics is no place for amateurs—excepting rich amateurs. In that respect, one might say that it is little different from ordinary, legislative politics. Both are dominated by organized interest groups, political activists, and elected officials. And that, to repeat, is precisely the point. The initiative process is no freer from the struggle between societal and political groups than is the legislative process. Interest groups, money, political activists, and politicians are the lead and supporting actors in both political dramas. The real problem is not that the initiative process has been perverted by interest groups, activists, or even money—none of these can be eliminated in a free and democratic society—but rather that too many Americans are seduced by a populist rhetoric that insulates the initiative process from critical scrutiny. Americans inexplicably check their hardy skepticism about politics at the initiative door.

5
Majority Rules

Majority rule is a bedrock principle of democratic government. From grade school on we are accustomed to a show of hands and then abiding by the majority's decision. As a method of settling disagreements, it certainly beats fisticuffs and bloodshed. Rarely do we have the time or energy to wait for a consensus to emerge; indeed, on many issues no amount of discussion or deliberation can bridge the differences of opinion and belief that divide citizens. The appeal of majority rule, though, goes beyond the negative virtues of avoiding violence or stalemate. For majority rule is also a principle with a strong ethical basis in an egalitarian society. If we are all political equals, then each of our opinions should count equally. Majority rule is thus the political expression of a liberal commitment to treat each individual equitably.

Liberal democracy is inconceivable without majority rule, but it would be a mistake to reduce liberal democracy to majority rule. American government modifies and even abandons the principle of majority rule in countless ways. A strictly majoritarian system would have no need for a bicameral legislature or even legislative committees, let alone the executive veto or judicial review. Supermajorities are sprinkled throughout the Constitution: a two-thirds vote is required for the House or Senate to expel a member; two-thirds of the Senate must vote to convict the president in order to remove him from office; two-thirds of the Senate are also required for the ratification of treaties; and presidential vetoes may be overridden only with a two-thirds vote in both houses of Congress. Even where the Constitution is silent, American political institutions have often adopted supermajority rules to govern their proceedings. Up until 1936, for instance, the Democratic party national convention required presidential and vice-presidential candidates to receive the votes of two-thirds of the convention delegates in order to secure the party's nomination. Three-fifths of the Senate must vote for cloture in order to terminate a filibuster, an institution which in and of itself is a glaring violation of the principle of majority rule.

Each of these departures from majority rule reflects the nation's historical commitment to safeguarding minority rights and interests, as well as promoting democratic deliberation and good public policy. Unchecked majority rule may become majority tyranny, as Madison famously worried in *Federalist 10*. It was never the founders' intention to leave the protection of minority rights entirely or even primarily to the courts; the legislature itself, a bicameral body with different representational bases and terms of elections, was engineered with an eye to preventing tyranny of the majority. Requiring supermajorities (or successive majorities in separate institutions) not only helps to protect a minority from the majority but also encourages the majority to confer and compromise with those who hold different views. By slowing down the legislative process, the aim is not just to protect minorities but to promote the public welfare by transcending narrow partisanship or temporary political advantage.

Requiring supermajorities is particularly common when it comes to making constitutional changes. A two-thirds vote of both houses of Congress as well as ratification by three-fourths of the states is required to amend the U.S. Constitution. States also commonly require supermajorities to amend their constitution. Only ten states allow the legislature to pass a constitutional amendment with a simple majority vote; most require a three-fifths or two-thirds vote, or a majority vote in two successive legislative sessions. Even those states that demand only a majority vote in a single legislative session require the legislature to submit the amendment to a vote of the people. In only one state (Delaware) can the legislature amend the constitution without a popular vote, and in that state a constitutional amendment must be approved by a two-thirds vote in each legislative chamber in two consecutive sessions. These additional hurdles reflect a widespread belief that constitutions, unlike statutes, should not be lightly or hastily amended. We may wish to experiment with our laws, but constitutions should reflect a considered judgment that commands widespread and deep public support.[1]

Is it undemocratic to put obstacles in the way of majorities wishing to change a constitution? Many Progressives at the turn of the century certainly thought so, believing with J. Allen Smith that "every scheme under which the power of the majority is limited means in its practical operation the subordination of the majority to the minority." There is "no middle ground," Smith argued. "We must either recognize the many as supreme, with no checks upon their authority except such as are implied in their own intelligence, sense of justice, and spirit of fair play, or we must accept the view that the ultimate authority is in the hands of the few." Alternatively, one might concede that supermajority requirements are deviations from the democratic norm yet argue that Americans have wisely given up a little democracy in order to secure certain fundamental rights. Liberal constitutionalism, in this view, protects not only the minority from the majority but also saves the majority from itself. But there is a third possible answer, one that challenges head-on the equation of democracy with majority rule. To begin with, as political theorist Stephen Holmes emphasizes, constitutional limitations established by one generation may limit the majority in the next generation and thereby preserve majority rule for subsequent generations. "To safeguard the choices available to distant successors," Holmes explains, "constitution makers restrict the choices available to proximate successors." Moreover, by creating institutional guarantees that opposition voices will not be punished or silenced, constitutions enable the sort of vigorous, searching public debate without which democracy would be a sham as well as short-lived. Certainly few Americans would define as democratic a system in which the majority ruled and outlawed all rival political parties, terrorized dissenting voices, and did away with freedom of the press and freedom of assembly.[2]

Whatever one's definition of democracy, it is clear that supermajority requirements are commonplace in American politics, particularly when it comes to constitutional changes. Yet even though Americans live quite happily with all sorts of deviations and departures from the principle of majority rule, the defense of supermajorities still strikes many as deeply undemocratic and unfair—even un-American. My view is different: far from restricting democracy, supermajorities in initiative elections can promote genuine majority rule.

THE DEMOCRATIC WISH

If one compares the process of amending the constitution through the legislature with amending it by initiative, one difference immediately stands out: no state allows a simple majority in the legislature to amend the constitution, yet almost every state that permits constitutional amendments to be made by initiative allows the constitution to be modified by a single, simple majority vote of the people. The same contrast is evident with statutory changes as well. In all but six states it takes an extraordinary majority of both houses to override a governor's veto, yet relatively few states that allow for statutory changes by initiative require anything more than a simple majority in one election for a measure to become law. Why are supermajorities an integral part of the regular amending and governing process yet rarely employed in the initiative process? Why do Americans apparently believe that supermajorities are necessary to check legislatures but the people acting directly do not need any such check?

The short answer is that Americans don't trust politicians, and never have. Look up "politician" in *The American College Dictionary:* "one who, in seeking or conducting public office, is more concerned to win favor or retain power than to maintain principles." *Merriam-Webster's Collegiate Dictionary* offers an equally unattractive definition: "a person primarily interested in political office from selfish or other narrow usu. short-sighted interests." Among the synonyms listed in *Roget's Thesaurus* are "party hack," "grafter," "spoils-monger," "power broker," "influence peddler," "wheeler-dealer," "finagler," and "wire puller." Distrust of politicians is as old as the republic. In 1791 a Virginia politician by the name of Richard Henry Lee declared that politics was "generally speaking . . . the Science of fraud" and politicians were "the Professors of that Science." Another famous Virginian politico, John Randolph, lamented that "we [politicians] are on the way to becoming the only degraded caste in this society."[3]

Public opinion polls show that such attitudes remain prevalent in the United States. A national survey conducted in 1944 found almost seven in ten agreeing with the statement "I didn't raise my boy to be a politician," while fewer than one in five said they would like to see their son go into politics. Another poll conducted in the same era found 70 percent of parents agreeing that they "would rather see their children sweep streets than enter politics." More recent surveys show more of the same. If anything, attitudes toward politicians have become even more negative in the past several decades. One survey from the 1970s, for example, found that the only groups of people who were thought to have standards of ethics and honesty on a par with public officials were advertisers, car salesmen, and union leaders. In another survey that examined public attitudes toward twenty-six different groups and institutions, politicians placed rock bottom not only in perceived "honesty, dependability, integrity" but also in "ability to get things done." In the minds of most Americans, politicians are not only corrupt but inept.[4]

But Americans' skepticism is selective, not congenital. Their hardened skepticism about politicians and politics often goes hand in hand with a naive innocence about "the people." The same individuals who openly parade their mistrust of politicians will hardly think twice about displaying an unqualified faith in the will of the people. Power to the people promises to bypass politicians and bureaucrats, conflict and coercion. "The people" are imagined as a harmonious and homogenous whole, completely unlike the political arena of government that is disfigured by competing self-interests and group interests, loud squabbling and unseemly fighting. The checks and balances, so necessary to control the avarice and ambition of politicians, are not needed when the will of the people can be directly expressed. And if the people do err on occasion, the courts are there to prevent them from doing away with fundamental rights. The "democratic wish," as James Morone calls it, enables Americans to sublimate their dread of government.[5]

ARE INITIATIVES SPECIAL?

Should laws enacted through the initiative process be treated differently than laws enacted through the legislative process? Are such laws or amendments more legitimate or more deserving of deference by virtue of having been approved by a popular vote? Many people certainly think so. In 1995 Congress held hearings on a Republican-sponsored bill to require that state laws or amendments passed by initiative or referendum, when challenged in federal court, must be heard by a three-judge panel rather than the normal single judge. As the bill's proponents explained, "State laws adopted by referendum or initiative, reflecting the direct will of the electorate of a State on a given issue, should be afforded greater reverence than measures passed generally by representative bodies."[6]

A few states endow laws enacted through the initiative process with a special, almost untouchable, legal status. The most notable example is California, which forbids the legislature from amending or repealing an initiative without submitting the change to another vote of the people. In 1998 Arizona amended its constitution to prohibit legislative repeal and to require a three-fourths vote by the legislature to amend an initiative-made law. Initiative laws are also placed on a legal pedestal in Michigan and Arkansas, both of which require the legislature to marshal a supermajority (a three-fourths vote in the former, a two-thirds vote in the latter) to amend or repeal an initiative. In a few other states the initiative's protected status is time-limited: in North Dakota the requirement of a legislative supermajority lapses after seven years; in Nevada the legislature can't touch an initiative for three years; and in Alaska and Wyoming legislatures are forbidden from repealing an initiative for two years, though they can amend by majority vote at any time. Even in those states where statutory initiatives are granted no special protection (as is true in a majority of the twenty-two states that permit statutory changes by initiative), state legislatures are usually extremely reluctant to tamper with voter-approved laws.[7]

No state court is required to give greater deference to voter-approved laws, though in the early twentieth century the Colorado and Nevada constitutions did attempt to bar judges from invalidating laws or amendments approved by the people. Still, some state courts have occasionally shown a tendency to treat voter-approved initiatives with great deference, particularly in states where judges are not only elected but subject to recall. As one unseated California Supreme Court justice lamented, "It is one thing for a court to tell a legislature that a statute it has adopted is unconstitutional; to tell that to the people of a state who indicated their direct support for the measure through the ballot is another."[8]

Some legal scholars agree that laws enacted through the initiative process should be treated differently than legislatively enacted statutes, but they argue that initiatives deserve *less* and not more deference from the courts. "Because the system of direct democracy lacks many of the checks imposed on raw majoritarianism by the federal constitution," explains law professor Julian Eule, "laws enacted through such a system must be subjected to a more rigorous judicial check." The legislature's judgment is due greater judicial deference because the laws it enacts have survived a rigorous system of checks and balances (especially bicameralism and the executive veto) designed to prevent bare majorities from enacting ill-considered or self-serving plans. Because laws enacted through the initiative process have not had to run the same institutional gauntlet as laws enacted through the legislative process, judges should compensate for the lack of institutional checks by applying a heightened level of scrutiny to initiative-made law.[9]

Eule and other legal scholars who advance this view are right to point to the absence in the initiative process of reliable institutional checks on transient, bare majorities. They are also right that the framers of the Constitution would not have looked favorably on the initiative process for this very reason. Where they err is in assuming that the proper remedy is with the judiciary. Courts have no business adopting a different standard of scrutiny just because a law was passed through the initiative process. How a measure became a law should be immaterial to the determination of whether the law is constitutional or not. The shortcomings of the initiative process should not be remedied by expanding the role of the courts but rather by modifying the process itself so that it contains more of the checks on "raw majoritarianism" that are a standard part of the legislative process. One way of doing this is to require some type of supermajority for an initiative to become law.

THE SUPERMAJORITY SOLUTION

This proposal is not as unprecedented as it may sound. Several states have used or currently use some form of supermajority voting to protect against bare and transient majorities achieving their policy preferences through the initiative process. In Illinois, which only permits the initiative to be used for constitutional changes, an initiative must be approved by either three-fifths of those voting on the measure or a majority of those voting in the election.[10] Up until 1980, the state of Idaho, which only allows the initiative to be employed for statutory changes, required that an initiative must achieve not only a majority of the vote cast on that measure but also a majority of votes cast for governor. Wyoming, which adopted the statutory initiative in 1968, has a similar requirement that the majority in favor of an initiative must also be a majority of the total number of people who turn out to vote in the general election. This means that if 10 percent of the voters in Wyoming do not vote on a given initiative, the supermajority required for that initiative to pass will be about 55 percent. If drop-off climbs to 20 percent, an initiative would require around 60 percent of the vote to pass, whereas if drop-off shrinks to 5 percent the supermajority required would only be about 52 percent.[11]

The first time in Wyoming's brief experience with the initiative that a measure fell afoul of the supermajority requirement was in 1996, when a term limits measure failed despite getting 54 percent of the vote. Drop-off was about 10 percent on the measure. The initiative sponsors immediately challenged the

Wyoming law in federal court on the grounds that it violated equal protection and free speech rights. Since the Wyoming law essentially counts all voters who do not vote on a particular initiative as a "no" vote, the terms limits proponents argued that the law deprived citizens of the right to abstain on an issue. The U.S. Court of Appeals for the Tenth Circuit rejected this argument, instead agreeing with the original trial judge that "Wyoming has a legitimate and reasonable interest in seeing that an initiated measure . . . is not enacted into law unless it is approved by a majority of those voting in the general election in which the initiated measure is being considered. . . . If Wyoming wants to make it 'harder' rather than 'easier' to make laws by the initiated process, such is its prerogative." It was reasonable, the court concluded, for the state of Wyoming to wish to minimize "abuse of the initiated process and make it difficult for a relatively small special-interest group to enact its views into law." The U.S. Supreme Court affirmed the lower court's ruling without comment.[12]

What impact would a law like Wyoming's have if it was adopted by other initiative states? In the early years of the initiative, the requirement that a statutory change receive a majority of votes of those going to the polls would have had a devastating impact on the number of successful initiatives. In Colorado's first initiative election in 1912, drop-off on the twenty statewide initiatives on the ballot averaged an incredible 62 percent. Only a statewide Prohibition initiative had a drop-off rate below 45 percent, and even on this highly charged issue almost three in ten of the people who voted for president did not bother to mark their ballot on this measure. Under a Wyoming-style law, none of the twenty initiatives would have come close to passing, including an initiative limiting women to an eight-hour workday, which received an impressive 77 percent of the vote. Because almost half of those who cast presidential ballots did not bother to vote on the eight-hour workday initiative, only a little over 40 percent of presidential voters registered their approval of the measure. One initiative relating to civil service reform passed despite getting the votes of fewer than 15 percent of those who showed up at the polls.[13]

Drop-off in initiative elections today, however, is much, much smaller than it used to be. In Oregon in the 1990s, for instance, the percentage of voters who showed up at the polls but did not vote on a particular initiative was never above 12 percent and frequently as low as 2 or 3 percent. The mean drop-off was under 5 percent. Between 1990 and 2000 only two out of twenty-seven successful initiatives would have lost if Oregon had in place a law identical to Wyoming's. The first of these was Measure 8, which attempted to scale back pensions for public employees. The 1994 measure, which passed with only 50.04 percent of the vote and was subsequently declared unconstitutional, is a classic illustration of why bare and transient majorities need political and not just judicial checks. Ironically, the other measure that would have failed was a 1998 measure that mandated a supermajority vote for all initiatives that required a supermajority. Although 55 percent approved, drop-off was relatively high (12 percent) on this

Table 5.1   Percentage of Voter-Approved Initiatives That Would Have Survived a Supermajority Requirement, 1980–2000

	Supermajority Requirement		
	55%	3/5	2/3
California (n = 50)	68	40	8
Oregon (n = 41)	71	49	29
Colorado (n = 25)	56	40	20
Washington (n = 22)	77	45	32
Arizona (n = 21)	71	52	19
Average	69	45	20

more technical measure. As long as drop-off rates remain low, there is no reason to expect a Wyoming-style supermajority to have much of a deterrent effect on the number of initiatives on the ballot, but it would serve the valuable purpose of weeding out initiatives that were only supported by narrow majorities, particularly for those issues that the public did not feel strongly about or attracted relatively little media attention and hence had relatively high drop-off rates.

Requiring an initiative to receive a supermajority of three-fifths or two-thirds of those who voted on a measure would produce more dramatic results, as Table 5.1 illustrates. In Oregon, for example, between 1980 and 2000 slightly under half of the 41 successful initiatives would have passed had a three-fifths majority been required for passage; had a two-thirds supermajority been required fewer than three in ten would have become law. Instead of initiatives succeeding nearly four in ten times, as they did in Oregon during this period, a three-fifths supermajority would drop the passage rate for initiatives to less than two in ten; a two-thirds supermajority would result in about one in ten initiatives passing. In California a supermajority requirement would have had an even greater impact. A two-thirds supermajority requirement would have resulted in the defeat of all but four of the fifty initiatives passed in California between 1980 and 2000. A three-fifths supermajority would have been far less Draconian but would still have resulted in the defeat of 60 percent of the voter-approved initiatives in California.

Obviously, then, a supermajority requirement of three-fifths or two-thirds would dramatically alter the role of the initiative in state politics. The higher threshold would likely curtail the number of initiatives placed on the ballot. In states inundated with ballot measures, like Oregon and California, this might be counted as a plus, though in most states the number of initiatives on the ballot at any one time does not tend to be unmanageable. It would also help to ensure that an initiative that became law represented a widely held popular preference that was not being addressed by the legislature. Also, the initiative would retain its agenda-setting power. Even if the measure fell short of the supermajority, an initiative that gained a substantial majority would likely grab the attention of legislators and prod them to take action.

These gains would come at a significant cost, however, since requiring large supermajorities would make it difficult for many groups to use the initiative process successfully. All issues are not created equal, and a supermajority requirement would affect some kinds of initiatives far more than others. Generally the initiatives that tend to win by more than three-fifths or two-thirds are those where there is not an intense, well-organized, and well-financed minority on the other side. In the Oregon *Voters' Pamphlet,* the twelve initiatives between 1992 and 2000 that received at least 60 percent of the vote attracted a total of only 45 arguments in opposition (for three hundred dollars any person or group can have half a page in the voters' pamphlet to present an argument in support or in opposition), whereas the twelve initiatives during that same period that passed with less than three-fifths attracted 158 arguments in opposition. Even more striking, the median number of opposing arguments for an initiative achieving a three-fifths supermajority was one, whereas the median for initiatives that passed with less than three-fifths of the vote was thirteen.

Among the least well organized and least powerful groups in society are those behind bars; not surprisingly, then, six of the twenty Oregon initiatives that passed by greater than a three-fifths vote between 1980 and 2000 involved stiffening criminal punishment. Four of the twelve initiatives that achieved a two-thirds supermajority during this same period involved reforms of the political process—term limits (70 percent), campaign finance reform (72 percent), vote by mail (69 percent), and voter registration (67 percent)—where there was little organized opposition by interest groups. Initiatives that faced well-organized or well-financed opposition rarely succeeded in gaining a three-fifths supermajority. In this category were economic initiatives that limited property taxes (52 percent in both 1992 and 1996) or increased cigarette taxes (56 percent), reduced public employee benefits (50.04 percent) or raised the minimum wage (57 percent). Also prominently represented are contentious moral questions such as the medical use of marijuana (55 percent), physician-assisted suicide (51 percent), the death penalty (56 percent), and homosexual rights in employment (53 percent). The only Oregon initiative during the past decade to achieve a three-fifths supermajority despite strong, well-financed opposition was a 2000 initiative to expand background checks for gun sales.

One could argue that Oregon would be better off without many or all of the laws that failed to achieve a supermajority, particularly those that failed to garner even 55 percent of the vote. On the other hand, in states such as Oregon that do not restrict the legislature from amending or even repealing a statute passed through the initiative process, the rationale for a supermajority seems weak. If the law is bad, then the legislature can fix it.[14] Where the initiative amends the constitution, however, the case for a supermajority becomes much more compelling, for where there is no possibility for the legislature to amend an initiative it becomes important to ensure that the initiative represents a deeply considered and widely held public judgment rather than a fleeting or ill-informed whim of a bare majority. Moreover, to the extent that constitutions are expected to reflect more fundamental and enduring law, a supermajority requirement is a reasonable way to make it more difficult to change a state's foundational document.

The principle that it should be more difficult to amend a constitution than a statute is recognized in every state. No state requires ordinary laws to be submitted to the people, yet every state but one requires constitutional amendments to be approved by the people. A few states even require the vote of the people to be either a majority of those voting at the election (Minnesota and Wyoming) or a two-thirds supermajority (New Hampshire). Only ten states, as noted earlier, permit a bare majority of legislators to refer a constitutional amendment to the people; the rest require either a supermajority vote or mandate that the legislature pass the amendment in two separate sessions. Of the eighteen states that allow citizens to use the initiative process to change the constitution, eleven require the legislature to muster more than a simple majority vote before it can refer a constitutional amendment to the people. With the exception of Colorado, moreover, every state that allows voters to use the direct initiative for both constitutional and statutory changes requires that more signatures be gathered for a constitutional amendment than for a statutory change.

Although the differential in signature requirements expresses the principle that it should be harder to change the constitution than to change a law, the difference between statutory and constitutional signature requirements is rarely large enough to have much impact on the calculations of experienced or well-heeled initiative users. Increasing the signature differential by raising the number of signatures for constitutional amendments would probably have a negligible impact on well-organized and well-financed groups' ability to amend the constitution, while crippling less well-endowed groups. A far more equitable means of protecting the constitution is to require that an amendment receive a supermajority. Indeed, a supermajority could be combined with a reduction in the required number of signatures, thereby lowering barriers to entry into the initiative marketplace. Such a reform would allow states to recognize the difference between constitutional and statutory law without punishing citizen groups that lack deep pockets.[15]

As attractive as such a proposal might appear in theory, it runs into several practical problems. To begin with, a supermajority requirement would make it more difficult to remove the constitutional clutter that currently exists in many state constitutions. If constitutions already contain provisions that belong in statutory law rather than in the basic framework of government, a supermajority requirement would give these provisions enhanced protection. Requiring a supermajority would make it harder for future generations to misuse the constitutional framework, but only at the cost of fortifying the abuses of past generations. The more a state's constitution has been abused in the past, the greater the cost of making it more difficult to amend in the future. Short of a constitutional convention, there is no easy escape from this dilemma.[16]

Another problem with the supermajority idea is that it is doubtful whether it could be enacted, particularly in states where the initiative is an ingrained part of the political culture. No state has yet enacted a supermajority for the approval of initiatives. Wyoming's stealth supermajority comes closest, but it is a less egregious affront to majoritarian sensibilities since, in form at least, it still requires a majority, albeit not a majority of those who vote on the initiative but a majority of those who go to the polls. In 1996 Colorado voters decisively rejected a legislative referendum that would have required a 60 percent popular majority to amend the state's constitution. Other state legislatures have considered similar proposals but have failed to garner sufficient support to refer the measure to the people, in large part because legislators anticipate almost certain defeat and fear being viewed as trying to restrict the people's rights.

The difficulty of establishing a supermajority for initiatives has less to do with a popular aversion to supermajorities than with popular devotion to the initiative process. Supermajorities are a hard sell when they are seen as a restriction on the people's will, but when they are used to restrict less popular targets, like government spending or taxes, opposition to the idea of supermajorities melts away. The use of supermajorities to restrain local spending has a long history in this country. In the latter part of the nineteenth century a number of states responded to the growing problems of municipal indebtedness by requiring supermajorities in bond referendums. Today about twenty states require a supermajority for local bond measures.[17] In recent years supermajorities have become a favorite tool of antitax and antigovernment activists looking to rein in government spending and taxation. The Republicans' 1994 Contract with America included a proposal for a constitutional amendment to require a three-fifths supermajority vote in both the House and Senate to raise taxes. Although Republicans never came close to mustering the supermajority necessary to pass the proposed amendment, the Republican majority in the House opened the 104th Congress by amending the House rules to require a three-fifths supermajority to pass any increase in income tax rates. During the 1990s ten states enacted supermajority requirements to increase taxes, eight requiring legislative supermajorities and two requiring a supermajority in a vote of the people. Colorado requires both a three-fourths legislative supermajority and a majority vote of the people before any tax increase can take effect. Most of these statewide supermajority requirements have been enacted by initiative, and virtually all have happened in states that possess the initiative power.[18]

The trouble with this recent brand of policy-linked supermajority requirements is that they are generally not designed to promote deliberation or to protect minority interests or rights. Rather, they represent a power play by the current majority to alter the playing field so that its policy preferences will prevail even when they become the minority. Using supermajority rules to advantage a partisan political ideology is deeply undemocratic. These supermajority schemes are particularly difficult to defend when the supermajority requirements are passed by small and partisan majorities. In Oregon the supermajority requirement on tax increases was narrowly passed on a largely party line vote by the legislature (16 to 14 in the Senate and 33 to 27 in the House) and then referred to the voters, where it received 54.7 percent of the vote in the May 1996 primary election. Since only 38 percent of registered Oregonians went to the polls, and nearly 9 percent of voters declined to vote on the measure, the total number who voted for the supermajority requirement constituted only 19 percent of registered Oregon voters.

The perceived unfairness of a majority protecting its preferred policies through enactment of a supermajority requirement led to the passage of Oregon's Measure 63 in 1998. As was noted in the previous chapter, the measure required that any proposal establishing a supermajority requirement must pass by the same supermajority that the measure would impose on other measures. Sponsored by public employee unions, the initiative was a preemptive strike aimed at Sizemore, who was in the process of gathering signatures to qualify an initiative for the 2000 ballot requiring that any tax increase be referred to the electorate and approved by two-thirds of the voters. While Measure 63's supermajority requirement was every bit as politically motivated as the Sizemore initiative it hoped to forestall, the union-backed measure had the virtue of being formally neutral as to policy outcomes. The amendment did not advance one partisan political ideology over another. Instead it laid down a neutral rule that supermajority requirements should only be imposed by supermajorities. Adherence to this principle obviously makes it more difficult to enact a supermajority requirement, but it also helps to ensure that adoption of a supermajority requirement reflects a societal consensus rather than a contested partisan ideology.[19]

THE NEVADA MODEL: SUCCESSIVE MAJORITIES

Is there an alternative way of achieving the benefits of a supermajority scheme without its clear costs? One little-noticed state model suggests that it is possible to achieve greater deliberation in the initiative process while still remaining faithful to majority rule and avoiding many of the practical pitfalls that beset the supermajority idea. That underappreciated model can be found in Nevada. Since 1962 Nevada has required that initiatives amending the constitution must receive a majority not just in one but in two successive elections.[20] The idea has a distinguished pedigree in American history. Oregon was one of many states at the turn of the century that required two successive legislatures to pass a constitutional amendment before it could go before the people. In fact, the initiative process itself had to pass through the gauntlet of the double majority before Oregon voters adopted it in 1902. Although Oregon did away with its double majority provision in 1906 (through the initiative), fourteen states still require a constitutional amendment proposed by the legislature to pass in two consecutive sessions.[21]

The logic behind the idea is compelling. First, by requiring two majorities rather than one it recognizes and sustains the difference between statutory and constitutional law. Without violating principles of majority rule, it helps ensure that the majority in favor of a measure is not acting on a passing whim but on a settled and considered opinion. The double majority also prevents a measure from squeaking by without adequate scrutiny, as arguably happened with Measure 8 in Oregon in 1994. Had the issue been presented again to the voters in 1996, the measure would likely have lost and the state would have been saved a protracted and expensive court battle. The hurdle of having to win two elections would also be an incentive for sponsors to craft the initiative as a statutory rather than a constitutional change, thereby furthering the goal of not cluttering the constitution with partisan policy objectives.

That, at least, is the logic. Because Nevada has been a relatively light user of the initiative, our experience with the impact of the double majority provision is limited. The infrequency with which Nevada has used the initiative process to amend the constitution, however, cannot be attributed to the double majority requirement. In the almost half a century that Nevada had the initiative prior to adopting the double majority requirement, there were only three constitutional amendments that made it to the ballot using the initiative. In contrast, since 1962 Nevada has had twelve constitutional amendments qualify for the ballot. Another measure of the infrequency with which Nevadans have historically used the initiative power is that there have been only thirteen statutory initiatives in the state's history, and only three since 1962. There is no evidence, in short, that the double majority requirement has scared off citizens from using the initiative process.

Of the twelve constitutional initiatives that have qualified for the ballot since 1962, one was defeated in the first election, a second was subsequently removed from the ballot due to a U.S. Supreme Court decision, and a third will be voted on in the 2002 election, leaving nine initiatives that have been subject to the double majority requirement. In all but two cases the majority on the second vote was smaller than the majority in the first election, but generally the difference in the vote margin has been small. In 1980 Nevadans overwhelmingly voted to exempt household goods and furniture from taxation; they reached the same decision in 1982 by a virtually identical three-to-one margin. Equally decisive was the voters' rejection of a personal income tax; in 1988 the initiative passed with 82 percent of the vote, and in 1990 it again sailed through with 72 percent approval. In 1994, 77 percent of Nevada voters approved a package of campaign finance reform measures, and in the 1996 election 71 percent still backed the proposal. Another 1994 initiative, which required a two-thirds vote of both houses to increase taxes, passed by overwhelming margins (78 percent in 1994 and 71 percent in 1996) in both elections. In each of these four elections there is little question that the result reflected the will of the people. The second vote was neither necessary nor harmful.

On three occasions, however, the double majority provision had a decisive impact on the result. In 1978 a measure limiting property taxes passed with close to 80 percent of the vote, yet when the voters faced the same question in 1980 the initiative was decisively defeated. The same pattern manifested itself in a 1980 proposal to exempt food from taxation. After overwhelmingly approving the initiative, the voters changed their minds in 1982 and soundly defeated the measure. Finally, in 1994 voters agreed to establish term limits for state and local officers by a better than two-to-one margin. But in 1996, after a judge split the measure into two ballot questions, voters decisively rejected the plan to establish term limits for judges, and only barely passed term limits for executive and legislative officers. What happened to make the voters reconsider? Why, in particular, did the electorate in one of the most tax-averse states in the nation (Nevada has no income tax) do an about-face twice and decide not to cut taxes?

Nevada's Question 6 was closely modeled on California's Proposition 13: it limited property taxes to no more than 1 percent of the property's value; rolled back the assessed value of property to 1975 levels; and limited increases in the assessed value of a property to no more than 2 percent a year unless the property was sold, at which point it could be assessed at the market value. In addition, like Proposition 13, Question 6 stipulated that the legislature could not create or raise taxes without a two-thirds vote of the legislature and forbade local governments from imposing new taxes without a two-thirds vote of the people. That Nevada voters approved the measure in 1978 surprised no one; virtually no major Nevada politicians opposed the measure, and the state's leading newspapers backed it as well. So why did Nevada voters reject the same measure in 1980? Had voters decided that high property taxes really were not so bad after all? Hardly. Rather, the legislature had responded to the voters' message with legislation that achieved much of the property tax relief promised by Question 6 but without its worst excesses and without enshrining tax policy in the state constitution. The double majority mechanism enabled Nevada's voters to vent their outrage at rising property taxes while still benefiting from legislative deliberation, compromise, and expertise in the formulation of public policy.[22]

Citizens in both Nevada and California ended up with real, substantial property tax relief, and both states have had to turn to other taxes and fees to compensate for the lost revenues, but Nevada's law has avoided some of the more perverse inequities and unintended consequences introduced by Proposition 13. For instance, by only allowing property to be reassessed when it changes owners Proposition 13 created huge discrepancies in property tax bills among Californians owning properties of similar or identical value. Proposition 13 forced new residents to subsidize the provision of public services for the entire community. Even more troubling has been Proposition 13's impact on business property. By levying a higher tax on new businesses and privileging established businesses with lower property taxes, Proposition 13 impedes competition. Rather than reward new businesses and encourage new investment, Proposition 13 dampens the entrepreneurial spirit. Intending to protect retirees on fixed incomes, the voters ended up distorting the marketplace in ways no one intended but any reasonably competent legislative analyst could have predicted. Nevada can thank its peculiar system of successive majorities for enabling it to avoid California's fate.[23]

In 1980 media attention in Nevada was strongly focused on Question 6. Even though the legislature had passed a property tax relief bill the previous year, the initiative's sponsor was far from satisfied with half a loaf. As debate raged over Question 6, another tax measure, which exempted food from the state sales tax, slipped by without serious scrutiny. In the two months prior to the election, the state's leading newspaper, the *Reno Evening Gazette,* did not publish a single letter to the editor relating to Question 9 and only ran a couple stories on the issue. In contrast, the newspaper published countless articles and many letters to the editor relating to Question 6. As Question 6 was going down to defeat, Question 9 cruised to victory. Who, after all, could be in favor of taxing food at the grocery store? In fact, in 1979, in the same piece of legislation that reduced property taxes, the legislature had already removed the sales tax on groceries. The trouble was that Question 9 was worded so broadly that it also seemed to apply to restaurant food and possibly liquor, even if that was not the authors' intention. (The proponents insisted they only intended to place the exemption for food in the state constitution where the legislature could not touch it.) Nevada's secretary of state had pointed out this problem in 1980, but media and public attention was fixed on Question 6 and no one seemed to notice. In 1982, with Question 6 no longer on the ballot, citizens began to take a closer look at the measure, and they did not like what they saw. Nevada is heavily reliant on tourists from outside the state, and 80 percent of restaurant food is bought by tourists. The food exemption, if interpreted to include restaurants, would cost the state between seventy-five to eighty million dollars, and the lion's share of the savings would go to people who were not residents of Nevada. The successive majority requirement gave Nevada's voters a chance to focus their attention more closely on the arguments and to reconsider the wisdom of their initial decision. Close to 60 percent of the voters rejected the measure in 1982, twice the number that had opposed it in 1980.[24]

The successive majority scheme works in Nevada, but its utility in states that are heavier users of the initiative process may be more limited. Requiring an initiative to achieve majorities in two successive elections would make a crowded ballot even more crammed. Since the media, political elites, and voters can only give serious scrutiny to a limited number of issues on any ballot, the incentive would be to ignore a measure at its first appearance on the ballot and only begin to organize opposition and focus voter attention the second time around. One way to make a successive majority scheme work without cluttering the ballot would be to allow statewide initiatives to appear on primary ballots, in special elections, or at odd-numbered November elections.[25] An obvious drawback, though, is that turnout is typically much lower in primaries or odd-numbered election years, so that the majority in such an election may represent only a small fraction of the population. Even if heavy-use states like Oregon, California, and Colorado cannot easily import the exact mechanics of Nevada's successive majority scheme, they can still learn from Nevada's experience with tempering ill-considered or transient majority preferences.

THE MASSACHUSETTS MODEL: THE INDIRECT INITIATIVE

Massachusetts provides an alternative model for restraining transient or narrow majorities from using the initiative process to amend the constitution: the indirect initiative. In the Bay State an initiative amendment does not go before the people until it has first been submitted to a joint session of the legislature and approved by a quarter of the legislators in two successive legislative sessions. The first legislature may amend the initiative amendment with a three-fourths vote, but the second legislature cannot modify the amendment in any way. It can, however, offer a substitute measure, which is then paired on the ballot with the original initiative and identified as a legislative alternative. In Massachusetts, then, the legislature is enlisted to provide some of the checks missing in the initiative process.

Garnering a quarter of the votes in the legislature, even in two successive sessions, may not seem like a high hurdle, but it has proved to be a substantial check on initiative amendments. Of the dozen or so constitutional initiatives that have been presented to the Massachusetts legislature with the requisite number of signatures, only three have been approved by the legislature and forwarded to the people. The first of these, approved in 1938, established biennial legislative sessions; the second, enacted in 1974, authorized the use of state highway revenues for mass transit; and the third, which was soundly rejected by voters in 1994, proposed a graduated income tax. These numbers, however, understate the impact of the initiative because a number of constitutional amendments referred to the people by the legislature were triggered by the initiative process. The most notable example was an initiative introduced in the legislature in 1966, which called for a reduction of the membership in the lower house from 240 to 160. Although the proposal narrowly secured the necessary one-fourth vote in 1968, it failed by a single vote in the second session in 1970. However, under considerable public pressure and the threat of a second initiative, the legislature referred its own "House Cut" plan to the electorate in 1974, and it was overwhelmingly approved by close to 80 percent of those who voted on the measure (although a quarter of those who turned out to vote did not care enough about the issue to mark their ballots). The legislative amendment reduced the number of House members by exactly the same amount as was called for in the original initiative, though the measure did not take effect until 1978. Massachusetts' cumbersome amendment process meant its citizens had to wait almost a decade to secure the desired change; on the other hand, the system worked, even with an amendment that directly threatened the livelihood of every state legislator.[26]

The most impressive result of the Massachusetts system has been to encourage citizens to craft their demands in the form of statutory law rather than constitutional amendments. Fifty-eight of the sixty-one initiatives in Massachusetts have been statutory initiatives. None of the other fifteen states that permit both constitutional and statutory changes by initiative has a comparable record. In Oregon and California about 45 percent of initiatives have been constitutional amendments, and in many states the percentage of constitutional initiatives is closer to two-thirds or three-quarters. Even more striking is Massachusetts' record over the last several decades, a period in which many states have seen an increase in the percentage of initiatives that are written as constitutional amendments. Only one of the thirty-two initiatives that qualified for the Massachusetts ballot between 1978 and 2000 has been a constitutional amendment. This stands in stark contrast to Oregon, in which nearly 60 percent of the seventy-four initiatives that made it to the ballot between 1990 and 2000 have been constitutional amendments, or Colorado, in which constitutional initiatives have accounted for 80 percent of the forty-three initiatives that reached the ballot between 1990 and 2000.[27]

The Massachusetts data are particularly noteworthy since the number of signatures required for a constitutional initiative is lower in Massachusetts than in any other state. Massachusetts is also the only state where it takes more signatures to qualify a statute than a constitutional amendment.[28] If one wishes to divert more of the initiative traffic into statutory changes and away from constitutional amendments, manipulating the differential between statutory and constitutional signature requirements will have only a limited impact. Oklahoma, the state with the greatest differential, also has a high percentage of constitutional amendments (roughly three-quarters over the last two decades). There is no statistical correlation between the signature differential and the relative percentage of constitutional amendments. One thing that does matter is whether the state requires an indirect initiative for statutory changes. The three states (Michigan, Nevada, and Ohio) that require indirect initiatives for statutory changes while permitting constitutional amendments by direct initiative have a high percentage of constitutional amendments. Thus, whatever advantages may be gained from the indirect initiative for statutory changes have to be weighed against the cost of creating an incentive for activists to craft initiatives as constitutional amendments that bypass the state legislature.

The Massachusetts model is probably too strong a medicine for most American states. Although nine other states use the indirect initiative,[29] Massachusetts is the only one that gives the legislature the right to prevent an initiative from reaching the ballot. In each of the other states that employ the indirect initiative, the legislature can only stop the initiative from reaching the ballot by adopting it. Generally the legislature also has the option of putting before the voters an alternative plan so the electorate can choose between the initiative and the legislative alternative. Moreover, only Mississippi follows Massachusetts in requiring the indirect initiative for constitutional amendments. In each of the other states the indirect initiatives can only be used to alter statutes. Although it is easy to understand why states might find the Massachusetts model too restrictive, it is harder to comprehend why states have limited their use of the indirect initiative to statutes. The mystery deepens when we find that Switzerland, the cradle of the initiative process, has always used the indirect initiative for constitutional amendments.

THE SWISS MODEL

American proponents of the initiative have long pointed to the Swiss as evidence of the benefits of the initiative process. As we saw in chapter 2, early advocates of direct democracy in the United States were strongly influenced by the Swiss experience with the initiative and referendum. After visiting Switzerland in the late 1880s, the journalist and social reformer James W. Sullivan rhapsodized about the Swiss system. Having abolished "the lawmaking monopoly," the Swiss had "rendered bureaucracy impossible" and driven out "the chief evils of governmental mechanism—class rule, ring rule, extravagance, jobbery, nepotism, the spoils system, every jot of the professional trading politician's influence." The Swiss model once again came to the fore in the 1970s as Americans debated the desirability of a national initiative. Congressman Jack Kemp, one of the leading proponents of a national initiative, lauded Switzerland as the "one country of the world that has more democracy than the United States." In Kemp's view, the existence of a national initiative explained why Switzerland was also the one nation that was "more peaceful and prosperous than the United States."[30]

Yet few of the people who tout the virtues of Swiss democracy seem to have any knowledge of how the Swiss system actually works. Nor do they recognize how radically different it is from the system which exists in the American states. Although Americans pride themselves on their system of checks and balances, the U.S. initiative system is distinguished by its lack of checks on majorities, checks that are commonplace in the Swiss initiative system, particularly at the federal level, where the initiative power is limited to constitutional amendments. Initiatives at both the federal and cantonal level in Switzerland are indirect, that is, they must first be presented to the legislative assembly. Although the federal assembly cannot stop an initiative from reaching the ballot, the legislature is given four years to deliberate upon the measure before sending it to the people. If the federal assembly approves an initiative, it is presented to the voters with the legislature's stamp of approval, but this rarely happens. Between 1891 and

1991 only three of the approximately one hundred initiatives that reached the voters carried the legislature's official blessing; the last initiative to receive the legislature's endorsement was in 1928. The Swiss assembly is not required to take a position on an initiative measure but almost invariably does. There were only two initiatives during this one-hundred-year period on which the assembly failed to take an official position. In contrast, American states with the indirect initiative usually pass the initiative along to the voters without taking a position. When sending an initiative to the voters, the Swiss assembly will typically include an explanation of why it believes the initiative should be rejected. The legislature also has the option of placing its own counterproposal on the ballot along with the citizen initiative (in which case the legislature is allowed five rather than four years to take action). The Swiss assembly has offered the voters a counterproposal about a quarter of the time, and voters have adopted the counterproposal more often than not. In only two cases did voters approve the citizen initiative and reject the legislative counterproposal.[31]

When the Swiss people are offered a legislative counterproposal together with a citizen initiative, they are asked to indicate which they prefer if both measures gain a majority of votes. As a result, a citizen initiative can receive a majority, even a large majority, and still not become law if more citizens indicate a preference for the legislative alternative. A more blatant constraint on majority rule is the Swiss requirement that a federal initiative (or the legislative counterproposal) be approved not only by a majority of those voting but also by a majority of cantons.[32] Since the population of Swiss cantons varies enormously (five of the twenty-six cantons contain well over half of Switzerland's population, and the largest, Zurich, has more than twice as many people as the ten least populous cantons combined), an initiative can readily achieve a majority of the votes and yet fall short of a majority of the cantons. Not surprisingly, the percentage of federal initiatives that are successful is exceedingly small. Of the approximately one hundred citizen initiatives voted on by the Swiss people between 1891 and 1991 only ten were successful.[33]

The success rate is even lower when one considers the large number of initiatives in Switzerland that are submitted to the federal assembly with the required number of signatures but are withdrawn by the sponsors before the legislature submits the initiative to the people. In fact, almost as many qualified initiatives are withdrawn as reach the ballot. Reasons for withdrawing a measure vary, but probably the most common is that the assembly has promised or taken legislative action that satisfies the initiative's sponsors. In many of these instances the objective of the sponsors in presenting the initiative is more to prompt a legislative deal than to take the issue to the voters. The initiative in Switzerland is thus an integral part of the legislative process and is often used as a spur to get a majority in the legislature to heed the concerns of minority groups that have previously been thwarted in the assembly. Unlike in the United States, where the initiative process is a baldly confrontational, zero-sum game, in Switzerland it is often employed to arrive at a consensus by facilitating legislative deliberation and compromise.[34]

Far from being a hothouse of direct democracy, then, the Swiss initiative system, particularly at the federal level, is a model of deliberative democracy and is radically unlike the American initiative system. American defenders of the initiative process are right to point to Switzerland's long and successful experience with direct legislation, but the lessons to be drawn from that experience are very different from the ones drawn by initiative enthusiasts. Far from vindicating the American initiative system, a close look at the Swiss initiative process reveals the limitations of the American-style initiative and perhaps points the way to possible reforms.[35]

INTERPRETING THE SINGLE-SUBJECT RULE

The initiative process is attractive because it allows voters to cobble together issues or policies in ways that make sense to them rather than in ways that make sense to more ideologically consistent party elites. In 1998 in Washington, for example, voters approved an increase in the minimum wage (a liberal issue) at the same time they voted to end racial preferences (a conservative issue). In a candidate election, voters would likely be faced with a choice between a Democrat who favors the minimum wage and affirmative action and a Republican who opposes both the minimum wage and racial preferences. Voters, though, are less likely to have ideologically consistent preferences. For the less ideological voter who approves of one liberal policy and one conservative policy, a candidate election, particularly in a polarized two-party system, will often present an uncomfortable choice. Does the citizen vote for the Republican, in hopes of abolishing affirmative action, or the Democrat, in the hope of achieving a hike in the minimum wage? Thus, in theory at least the initiative process allows the political system to produce policy outcomes that more closely mirror the policy preferences of the public.[36]

But for the majority to express itself clearly, the initiative must contain only one question or issue. If an initiative contains two or more distinct questions, it becomes virtually impossible to determine what the majority meant to say in approving or rejecting an initiative. It is for this reason that most initiative states have a single-subject rule of some sort. The Oregon constitution, for instance, specifies that "a proposed law or amendment to the Constitution shall embrace one subject only and matters properly connected therewith," while California requires that "an initiative embracing more than one subject may not be submitted to the electors or have any effect." Other state constitutions, as in Massachusetts, mandate that the parts of an initiative be "related or . . . mutually dependent." What constitutes a single subject or even "mutually dependent" parts is not obvious, however; only through court rulings have these vague formulations been given concrete meaning.

Most state courts have, at least until recently, approached single-subject provisions with tremendous trepidation. In Washington the state supreme court operated for many years on the assumption that the single-subject rule, which says that "no bill shall embrace more than one subject," did not even apply to initiative measures. Not until 1995 did the Washington Supreme Court rule that the single-subject provision in fact applied to initiatives. In October 2000 Tim Eyman's I-695, which combined a reduction of motor vehicle taxes with a public vote on most tax and fee increases, became the first initiative in Washington State history to fall victim to the single-subject rule. The supreme court swept aside the argument of initiative proponents that the two parts of the measure were rationally related because requiring a public vote on taxes was necessary to prevent the state legislature from simply imposing new taxes or tax increases to replace the lost revenues from the reduction in the motor vehicle taxes. The court was unmoved, countering that the provisions had different purposes and that neither provision was necessary to implement the other. A few months later a superior court judge, relying on the supreme court's newfound weapon, struck down another Eyman initiative that limited property tax growth to 2 percent a year and ordered local governments to refund tax and fee increases imposed in the second half of 1999. To Eyman and the state attorney general, who had to defend the initiative in court, the single subject was limiting taxes, but to the court the two provisions lacked a "rational unity."[37]

A similar transformation in judges' willingness to use the single-subject rule to strike down initiatives may also be occurring in California, where for the first time in history the state supreme court used the single-subject rule to nullify an initiative in December 1999.[38] Unlike in Washington, where single-subject challenges to initiatives have been a rarity, in California the courts have repeatedly been offered opportunities over the last three decades to strike down initiatives on single-subject grounds. And yet until recently they have repeatedly rejected those invitations. Among the California initiatives that survived single-subject challenges was the twenty-thousand-word Political Reform Act of 1974, which contained no fewer than eight separate elements: (1) establishing a Fair Political Practices Commission, (2) mandating disclosure of candidate contributions, (3) limiting candidate spending, (4) regulating lobbyists, (5) enacting conflict-of-interest rules, (6) adopting rules regarding argument summaries in the voters' pamphlet, (7) fixing the ballot position of candidates, and (8) detailing the enforcement provisions and penalties. Each of these separate parts, the California Supreme Court ruled, was "reasonably germane to the subject of political practices" and therefore did not violate the single-subject requirement. A few years later the high court upheld the "Victim's Bill of Rights," passed by initiative in 1982. This bill, according to the court's own summary, contained eleven separate topics, including a constitutional guarantee of safe schools, a right to restitution for crime victims, abolition of the diminished capacity defense, stiffer sentences for habitual criminals, abrogation of most of the state's evidentiary exclusionary rules, limits on plea bargaining, and repeal of provisions regarding "mentally disordered" sex offenders. In 1991 the court upheld an initiative that limited legislative terms, eliminated legislative pensions, and restricted legislative costs. These provisions were deemed reasonably germane since each dealt with the legislature.[39]

The California Supreme Court's liberal interpretation of the single-subject rule was not without its critics. Three of the seven California justices dissented in the 1982 *Brosnahan* ruling on the Victim's Bill of Rights, arguing that the appropriate standard should have been whether the parts were "functionally related" or "interdependent" rather than "reasonably germane." Under this more stringent standard, the dissenting justices would have invalidated the Victim's Bill of Rights, as well as a number of other initiatives that came before the court. According to the dissenting justices, the court had set the hurdle so low that virtually no initiative could fail to clear it. "There is no measure, no matter how heterogenous," objected Justice Stanley Mosk, "that is incapable of bearing some label, so long as that label is defined broadly enough." In the eyes of Mosk and others, the court had rendered the single-subject rule a virtual dead letter.[40]

One can sympathize with the critics' exasperation at a single-subject rule that permits multifaceted initiatives that may thwart majority rule. But as a constitutional matter the court majority was probably right to insist on using the same standard for initiative-made law as for legislative acts. Although the single-subject rule for initiatives was not adopted in California until 1948, a single-subject provision relating to acts of the legislature had been a part of the California constitution since the state's beginnings in 1849. In *Perry v. Jordan* (1949), the California Supreme Court ruled that the same liberal "reasonably germane" standard should apply to initiatives that applied to legislative acts. Nothing in the legislative record suggests that the drafters of the 1948 amendment intended the single-subject provision to be interpreted differently for initiatives than for legislative actions. To adopt the more stringent standard advocated by the dissenting California justices would not only mean overturning decades of settled law but, more important, would put the courts on a collision course with the legislature unless the court could develop a rationale for why the single-subject rule should be interpreted more stringently for initiative-made law than for law made by the legislature.[41]

In Florida the state supreme court has advanced a rationale for a stricter interpretation of the single-subject rule for initiatives that rests, in part, on the difference between the initiative and legislative processes. In *Fine v. Firestone,* a 1984 case invalidating an antitax initiative for violating the single-subject rule, the court reasoned: "We should take a broader view of the legislative provision because any proposed law must proceed through legislative debate and public hearing. Such a process allows change in the content of any law before its adoption. This process is, in itself, a restriction on the drafting of a proposal which is not applicable to the scheme for constitutional revision or amendment by initiative." This may be an accurate appraisal of the differences between the legislative and initiative processes, but it is not the sort of judgment that properly belongs to the courts. It is a political judgment that is best made by legislators and citizens.[42]

There are sound reasons to establish a stricter single-subject rule for initiatives than for legislative acts, but the relative levels of public debate or scrutiny in the two processes is not among these reasons. Legislatures have been known to rush bills through at the end of session with little debate or with only perfunctory hearings. This is particularly true in states like Oregon, where a part-time legislature meets for only six months every two years. Moreover, the public debate surrounding initiatives in the months immediately preceding the election is frequently robust. Even in states that use the initiative process frequently, the number of initiatives pales in comparison to the huge number of bills introduced in the legislature, arguably making it easier to scrutinize initiatives than most legislation. To be sure, the Florida court is correct that legislative debate and hearings will often result in amendments and improvements to the legislation, whereas public debate in the initiative process can only lead to a yes or no vote. This is certainly an advantage of the legislative process, but it is unclear how this advantage warrants the conclusion that a single-subject rule should be construed more stringently for initiatives than for legislative acts. After all, it is amendments or riders to bills made on the floor that may receive the least scrutiny since they receive no committee hearings and may attract no debate. One could argue with as much justice that because the legislative process allows for last-minute amendments, it should be held to a more exacting single-subject standard than the initiative process.[43]

The case for applying the single-subject rule more strictly to initiatives should rest on the different purposes of the initiative and legislative processes. The sole justification for a successful initiative is that a majority of voters approve of the measure. Without a strict single-subject rule, it is generally impossible to know which if any parts of a successful initiative express the majority view. The rationale behind a law produced by the legislature is more complex than simple majority rule. Legislatures are designed to produce compromises among competing interests. The final law may well be nobody's first choice yet be preferable because it represents a consensual second choice with which most everybody can live. Social peace and political harmony may be objectives that are given precedence over majority rule. Or, to assuage the objections of an intense minority, legislation may include concessions that are designed to protect the interests or rights of the minority. Safeguarding minority interests and accommodating intensity of preference may legitimately be pursued by the legislature, even at the expense of strict majority rule. A stringently enforced single-subject rule could thus prevent the legislature from carrying out important parts of its job: creating coalitions out of diverse interests and beliefs, forging law that is widely supported, and safeguarding minority interests. Because the initiative is designed to be a bluntly majoritarian instrument, a strict single-subject rule is essential to the integrity of the initiative process. The legislature, in contrast, is designed not only to advance the interests and views of the majority but also to serve minority interests and protect minority rights, to piece together coalitions, and to factor in intensity of preference. Balancing these multiple objectives requires a loose interpretation of the single-subject rule.

The 1996 election in Nevada provides an instructive example of the problems that can result from an initiative containing more than one question. After the state supreme court separated the term limits question into two questions, the voters responded by approving term limits for legislative and executive officers and rejecting them for judges.[44] Had the court not separated out the two questions, the fate of these two distinct issues would have been tied together. If the amalgamated initiative had passed in 1996 (as it had in 1994), the will of the majority would have been thwarted because judges would have been subject to term limits even though a majority opposed the idea. If the combined initiative had failed, the will of the majority that preferred term limits for legislative and executive officers would have been denied. By insisting on two separate questions, the judges enabled the will of the majority to prevail; had the justices not intervened, the will of the majority would have been thwarted. More pernicious still, the minority would have been dressed in the misleading garb of the majority will.

Oregon provides another, more significant example of a state supreme court decision furthering majority rule. In 1996 59 percent of Oregon voters approved Measure 40, a victims' rights initiative that, among other things, allowed for eleven-to-one jury verdicts in murder trials, prohibited unregistered voters from serving on juries, gave prosecutors the power to demand a jury trial for a criminal defendant, relaxed the immunity law so that more evidence against a defendant would be admissible in court, and restricted a criminal defendant's right to pretrial release. Since all of the provisions of the constitutional amendment dealt with crime victims' rights, the new law seemed relatively safe from a single-subject challenge. But as a constitutional amendment the initiative had an additional hurdle because Oregon law requires that "two or more amendments" must be submitted "separately" to the voters. Just because an amendment satisfies the single-subject rule, the Oregon high court decided, does not mean that it satisfies what it called the "separate-vote" requirement. The latter, in the court's view, was a "narrower restriction than the requirement that a proposed amendment embrace only one subject." Since Measure 40 changed five different sections of the Oregon constitution and implicated a number of distinct constitutional rights, it violated the people's right to vote on different amendments separately.[45]

The decision in *Armatta v. Kitzhaber* was met with a volley of abuse from the initiative's backers as well as from other initiative activists.[46] The court was assailed for foiling the will of the majority, but subsequent events suggest that the court's decision enabled majority rule. After getting over the initial shock and disappointment, the initiative's chief petitioner, state legislator Kevin Mannix, responded by breaking up Measure 40 into seven different amendments, pushing each through the legislature, and referring them to the voters in November 1999. The results of the election are a cautionary tale for those who had blithely assumed that Measure 40 represented the will of the people. Three of the seven measures—the eleven-to-one jury verdict in murder trials, the weakening of immunity law, and the prosecutor's right to insist on a jury trial—were comfortably defeated. In the case of the prosecutor's power to demand a jury trial, close to 60 percent voted in opposition. The remaining four measures passed, in all but one case by roughly the same margin as Measure 40.[47] Far from depriving people of their voice, the high court had enabled people to speak more clearly and to express their preferences more accurately. In *Armatta* the court acted not to protect minority rights but to further majority rule.

The wisdom of the *Armatta* decision is that it does not rest on a judicially imposed distinction between the legislative and initiative processes. Instead, it develops a judicial standard that rests on the important difference between constitutional amendments and statutory changes. Nor is this distinction developed out of whole judicial cloth. Rather, it stems from a concrete constitutional provision specifying that the separate-vote requirement only pertains to constitutional amendments. *Armatta* thus serves not only to preserve and protect majority rule but also creates an incentive for initiative sponsors to craft initiatives as statutory changes, where the hurdle will be a lenient single-subject rule, rather than as constitutional amendments, where they will face a more exacting "separate-vote" requirement.[48]

The *Armatta* decision demonstrates that in states where constitutional provisions permit, the courts can play an important role in protecting majority rule. But we should not ask the courts to do our dirty work for us. Legislatures and citizens should be the ones to determine whether the single-subject rule is to be a more stringent restriction on the initiative process than on the legislative process. Although the Florida high court justified its decision in *Fine v. Firestone* on the grounds that it believed that legislators and citizens intended to set the bar higher for initiatives, the court was forced to squeeze a lot of political meaning from precious little in order to reach this conclusion. The Florida constitution mandates that initiatives "embrace but one subject and matter *directly* connected therewith," while legislative bills must "embrace but one subject and matter *properly* connected therewith." If the legislature, which proposed the amendment, and the people of Florida, who approved the amendment, intended to establish a higher standard for initiatives, they chose an extraordinarily subtle way to articulate the standard. More likely the Florida court invented a standard that was far from the minds of the people or their elected officials.[49]

The Florida Supreme Court's stringent interpretation of the single-subject rule has resulted in the court striking down a substantial number of initiatives, which in turn has brought howls of protest from initiative backers. In other states, such as Arizona, Colorado, and Washington, the single-subject rule has become an increasingly important obstacle to initiative proponents. Courts would seem, at first blush, to be natural enemies of the initiative process. After all, the initiative process is the most direct expression of the people's preferences, whereas the judiciary is the political institution most insulated from those popular preferences. Yet the irony, as we shall see, is that expansion of the initiative process, sometimes labeled as "the fourth branch of government," has made the political system more reliant on the judicial branch.

6
The Initiative Goes to Court

Today we tend to see the courts as the backstop of American politics. If anything gets by the catcher, the courts will protect the bystanders from harm. Ironically, the initiative process, in the name of empowering the people, tends to exacerbate Americans' tendency to rely on the least democratic branch of government to secure their liberties. When confronted with the potential harms that direct democracy may cause to minority rights or interests, defenders of the initiative process instinctively reach for the courts. There is nothing to fear from the initiative, we are assured, because the courts will make sure the people don't take their prejudices out on a hapless minority. Critics of the initiative, meanwhile, look to the courts to place a brake on the runaway initiative train. Having failed at the ballot box, opponents routinely turn to the courts to repair the damage. In fact, since 1960 about half of successful initiatives have been challenged in court. In California the number has been closer to two-thirds.[1]

Better than half the time the challenged initiative is struck down either in whole or in part. To initiative critics this statistic may be reassuring, and it may also provide solace to initiative advocates anxious to allay fears of majority tyranny. But few acts are better calculated to breed popular frustration and anger than that of unelected or even elected judges striking down popularly enacted laws. When initiative advocates meet a setback in the courts, they predictably lambast the judges for judicial arrogance, for legislating from the bench, and for flaunting the public will. Yet in bypassing the legislature, initiatives push judges onto the political front lines, where they are invited to make the sensible political judgments the legislature was denied the chance to make. A politicized judiciary can offer short-term relief for badly written or mean-spirited initiatives, but that relief is often purchased at the expense of judicial legitimacy and integrity.

BEFORE THE BALLOT

Judicial involvement in the initiative process generally only becomes visible to the public after an initiative passes and is then challenged and struck down in court. But the courts' involvement with the initiative process begins much earlier. The extent of that judicial engagement varies considerably from state to state, but in a number of states the courts have become increasingly entangled in the task of writing ballot titles. Nowhere is this development more marked than in Oregon, where one-fifth of the court's opinions between 1998 and 2000 related to initiative ballot titles.

In Oregon the attorney general is required by law to write a ballot title, which includes a 15-word caption, two 25-word statements describing the result of a yes vote and a no vote, and a summary of not more than 125 words. If either a proponent or an opponent of the measure is dissatisfied with the attorney general's ballot title, either can ask the state supreme court to review the ballot title. The court must take the case and conduct the review of the ballot title "expeditiously" so as to "ensure the orderly and timely circulation of the petition." In practice this has meant that the court immediately moves ballot title cases to the top of its docket. The court can either certify the ballot title as written by the attorney general or, if the title fails to "substantially comply" with statutory requirements, it can rewrite the ballot title. Over half of the ballot titles certified by the court in the late 1990s were rewritten by the court.[2]

The justices understandably resent the immense amount of time that is now involved in hearing ballot title cases and rewriting ballot titles. In the 1999–2000 election cycle, of the 146 ballot titles that were certified by the attorney general's office 92 were appealed to the court. In March and April 2000, according to the supreme court's staff attorney, the justices and the staff dedicated virtually all their time to ballot title cases.[3] Crowding the judicial docket with ballot title cases means less time to hear other cases and justice delayed for those cases the court does hear. Those justices who sat on the court in the 1980s and early 1990s can still recall a time when ballot title cases made up only a small fraction of the court's caseload. The mushrooming of the court's ballot title caseload is due only in small part to the increase in the number of measures submitted. Far more important has been the growing professionalization and sophistication of those who use the initiative process. This growing sophistication has given rise to "ballot shopping," whereby initiative advocates submit multiple versions of the same measure to increase their chances of getting a favorable ballot title. Opponents of ballot measures are often equally savvy and cynical, challenging the title so as to delay by two to three months the date on which proponents can begin to gather signatures. Proponents and opponents now recognize the state supreme court as the first (and last) important battlefield in the long, protracted initiative war.

This transformation has not only left the court overloaded but has drawn it into the slippery and unavoidably political terrain of writing ballot titles. The court valiantly strives for impartiality, but there is no unbiased or nonpolitical way to decide between whether, for instance, the term "racial preferences" or "affirmative action" more accurately describes a measure. Within the court deep divisions have emerged over the past decade about the wisdom and constitutionality of having the courts involved in what appears to more closely resemble a legislative rather than a judicial function. Those divisions became public in *Rooney v. Kulongoski,* a 1995 case in which both the chief petitioner, Lon Mabon, and the opposition, the ACLU, challenged the ballot title the attorney general had written for a measure that would have forbid governments from making sexual preference a civil right classification. The attorney general's caption (in 1995 the caption was limited to only ten words) read "Amends Constitution: Homosexuality, Other Sexual Behavior not Civil Rights Basis," whereas Mabon preferred "Amends Constitution: Prohibits Minority Status Based on Sexual Behavior, Desires," and the ACLU wanted "Amends Constitution: Forbids Civil Rights Protection Based on Homosexuality." The court decided that none of these would do and opted instead for "Amends Constitution: Restricts Local, State Government Powers Concerning Homosexuality." The court also rewrote the attorney general's summary in a number of ways. "Government cannot . . . spend public funds in [a] way expressing approval of homosexuality," for instance, was changed to read "Government cannot . . . spend public funds approving homosexuality." Rather than say that "pro-homosexuality books" would be banned from public libraries "unless books met established local community standards," the court preferred to state that such books would be available at public libraries "to minors with parental supervision" so long as they "meet local standards per review process." These and other changes were justified in forty pages of densely argued text.[4]

The majority's opinion brought a biting dissent from Justice Richard Unis. Absent some explicit provision in the state constitution authorizing the court to write ballot titles, Unis wrote, the court's involvement in writing ballot titles violated the principle of separation of powers. The state constitution explicitly provided that "no person charged with official duties under one of these departments [the legislative, executive, and judicial] shall exercise any of the functions of another, except as in this Constitution expressly provided." In writing ballot titles, Unis argued, the court was performing an act that was clearly "legislative in nature." Drafting a ballot title was "akin to the writing of a title for a legislative bill." Moreover, Unis pointed out, it is the ballot title and not the actual text of the measure that appears on the official ballot cast by voters. In addition, the ballot title "becomes part of the legislative history that courts utilize in interpreting measures that are approved by voters." The majority did not dispute Unis' point that writing ballot titles was fundamentally a legislative function, but it found authority for the court's actions in the constitutional provision that "Initiative and referendum measures shall be submitted to the people as provided in this section and *by law not inconsistent therewith.*" The court, said the majority, was responsible for hearing challenges to the government's ballot titles and ensuring that the titles were in "substantial compliance" with the relevant statutory requirements. The majority's pragmatic approach has so far triumphed, but though Justice Unis retired in 1996, his position has gained support on the court in recent years. As of 2000, three of the court's seven justices have indicated that they do not believe the court has the constitutional authority to write the ballot titles that shape the public vote.[5]

Even if the constitutional question can be surmounted, there remains the thorny question of how broadly or narrowly to interpret the stipulation that the ballot title must be in "substantial compliance" with the legal requirement to summarize the ballot measure impartially and concisely. On its face such a standard suggests a less than exacting threshold. One would expect that the highly trained, expert legal staff of the attorney general's office, which has extensive experience drafting ballot titles, would be in substantial compliance with the law a reasonably high percentage of the time. Attorney generals who managed to comply with the law less than half the time would be deemed by most people to be incompetent in most contexts. Nobody on the court really thinks the attorney general's office is incompetent, yet between 1996 and 2000 the justices nonetheless rewrote the attorney general's ballot title in over half the cases they decided. What should be the exception has become the rule. The result, not surprisingly, has been to encourage the advocates and opponents of an initiative to appeal virtually every title to the court in hopes of getting a more advantageous ballot title. The judicial wounds that have resulted from the mushrooming caseload are in important ways self-inflicted.

In rewriting large numbers of ballot titles, the Oregon Supreme Court has not only plunged into a political morass of subjectivity but has spent scarce resources on large numbers of ballot titles that never even made it to the ballot, let alone became law. Fewer than one in five of the ballot titles that are appealed to the court end up appearing on the ballot, and only a minority of these are passed by voters. More troubling than the judicial time expended on measures that never reach the ballot or become law is the impact that the court's involvement in the preelection phase can have on the postelection challenges to a successful initiative. This problem becomes particularly acute when the court not only drafts the ballot title but also writes the five-hundred-word explanatory statement, which is drawn up after the measure qualifies for the ballot. This statement is drafted by a five-member committee made up of proponents and opponents of the measure, but if an interested party does not like the outcome it can appeal directly to the state supreme court, which can rewrite the statement if it deems it unclear, misleading, or insufficient.[6] In such cases the court drafts a key statement that the judiciary will later rely on to interpret the meaning of the statute or amendment should it pass and then be challenged in court. The court, in other words, ends up interpreting its own words.

Oregon's ballot title situation in the late 1990s is admittedly extreme, at times bordering on the dysfunctional. But in other states, too, courts have become increasingly involved in the writing of ballot titles, even in states where there has been little or no tradition of court involvement in the titling process. In Colorado, for instance, prior to 1990 the state supreme court was only infrequently drawn into the politics of ballot titles, and in those few cases where it was asked to decide it almost always affirmed the title set by the Title Board, a three-member committee composed of the secretary of state, the attorney general, and the director of the Office of Legislative Legal Services. Between 1970 and 1989 fourteen initiative ballot titles were appealed to the Colorado Supreme Court, and in all but two of those cases the court affirmed the board's title. The 1990s, though, saw a dramatic change in the court's role. Whereas in the 1980s, ballot title cases made it to the court at a rate of about one a year, by the close of the century the court was deciding an average of ten ballot title cases each year. Initially the increase in the number of initiative challenges did not appear to affect the court's deferential attitude toward the board. In 1992, for instance, the court heard thirteen ballot title cases and affirmed all but one. Between 1993 and 1998, though, about a third of ballot title cases resulted in the court reversing the board. And in 1999 and 2000 over 60 percent of such cases resulted in reversals. A big part of this increase in the reversal rate stems from a 1994 constitutional amendment that applied the single-subject rule to initiatives. Indeed, over three-quarters of the reversals between 1995 and 2000 were due to the state supreme court ruling that the board should not have prepared a title and summary because the measure violated the single-subject rule. But the Colorado high court has also become increasingly vigilant during the last decade about ensuring that the board sets ballot titles that "correctly and fairly express the true intent and meaning" of the initiative, even when there is no single-subject violation. In fact, in most of the cases where the court found a single-subject violation they also found the ballot title to be inadequate.[7]

Prior to the 1990s the court was guided by the principle that "all legitimate presumptions must be indulged in favor of the propriety of the board's action." In practice, this meant that the court routinely affirmed the board's actions even when the titles were perhaps a little dubious. For instance, in 1984 the court affirmed a ballot title for a measure that would have raised the drinking age for fermented malt beverages from eighteen to twenty-one and would have allowed such beverages to be sold until two in the morning rather than until midnight. The title crafted by the board highlighted the increase in drinking age but made no reference to the change in hours during which the beverage could be sold. The court concluded that although the title was "perhaps not [a] model . . . for future draftsmanship, [it was] adequate to meet the statutory requirements of fairness and clear expression of the true meaning and intent of the proposed law." The court's job was not to draft the best possible title but rather to ensure that the board had met its statutory responsibility to provide a fair title.[8]

The Colorado court today continues to reaffirm the principle that "the Board's actions are presumptively valid" and that the court should not be "second-guessing every decision the Board makes in setting titles." But the reality is that the court now regularly second-guesses the board. In one recent case, for example, the court invalidated the ballot title of a controversial measure that would have given Spanish-speaking students a year of intensive English instruction before mainstreaming them into regular classes. The court allowed that the measure did not contain more than one subject, but it insisted that the title and summary were unclear and misleading and contained a "prohibited catch phrase." The court indicted the board both for what it left out and for what it included. By including the measure's exhortation that public schools should teach English "as rapidly and effectively as possible," the board had included an impermissible catchphrase that "works to a proposal's favor without contributing to voter understanding." By excluding the provision that "no school or school district shall be required to offer a bilingual education program," the board failed to alert voters that, as a practical matter, students might not be able to opt out of the English immersion program even though the ballot title (and measure) said they could.[9]

In the case of the English immersion initiative, the court did not attempt to rewrite the initiative, but in most other remanded cases during the 1990s the court dictated to the board the precise language it must use in rewriting the ballot title.[10] Unlike in a 1980 ballot title case, in which the court left it to the board's discretion to use either the court's suggested language or "a statement of similar import," during the 1990s the Colorado court typically left the board with no discretion when it remanded a case. In 1990, for instance, the court faulted the board for not including the proponents' definition of abortion in the ballot title. The court instructed the board to change the ballot title from "An Act Prohibiting a Procured Abortion upon an Unemancipated Minor until at Least 48 Hours after Written Notice to the Parent(s) or Guardian(s) of Such Minor" to "An act (1) prohibiting a procured abortion upon an unemancipated minor until at least 48 hours after her parents or guardians receive written notice of the procedure and (2) defining 'abortion' as the use of any means to terminate the pregnancy with knowledge that the termination will, with reasonable likelihood, cause the death of the minor's unborn offspring at any time after fertilization." To take another example, in 1994 the court heard a challenge to an initiative that would have allowed local governments to exercise tighter control over obscenity. The board had assigned the title "An Amendment to the Colorado Constitution Stating That the State and Any City, Town, City and County, or County May Control the Promotion of Obscenity to the Full Extent Permitted by the First Amendment to the U.S. Constitution," language taken virtually verbatim from the amendment itself. The court ruled that the title did "not contain sufficient information to enable the electorate to 'determine intelligently whether to support or oppose such a proposal,' " and directed the board to add the words "And Thereby Preventing The Colorado Courts from Interpreting the Right of Free Expression More Broadly under The Colorado Constitution than under the First Amendment to the United States Constitution in the Area of Obscenity." The judicial rewriting of the ballot title brought a sharp dissent from two of the justices, who believed that the original ballot title "fairly and accurately" reflected the initiative's purposes, and that the court should thus have affirmed the board's title.[11]

The injection of the single-subject rule into ballot title reviews after 1994 has increased the importance of the Colorado Supreme Court in the ballot titling process, but it has also meant that the court often has less need to rewrite ballot titles. If the court finds that an initiative contains more than one subject, the entire title and summary is struck and the proponents must revise the initiative before asking the board for a new title. In 1993, for instance, perennial initiative activist Douglas Bruce proposed an omnibus initiative that, among other things, would have rolled back compensation for elected officials, provided tax credits for campaign contributions, reduced the size of the state senate, increased the size of the state house of representatives, changed the legislative reapportionment process, and altered a host of laws relating to initiative and recall petitions. The board did its best to set the title for this multifaceted initiative, but the court still felt compelled to rewrite four separate parts of the ballot title and summary. After the single-subject rule had been added to its quiver in 1994, the high court as well as the board could (and did) refuse to title such measures, thereby reducing the judiciary's involvement in the process of rewriting ballot titles and summaries.

Also helping to prevent Colorado's high court from following Oregon down the path of judicial hyperactivity is the requirement that the initial appeal of a ballot title must first be heard by the board. The board is thus given the opportunity to hear objections and to reconsider the title and summary it has drafted in light of those objections. Only after the board has had a chance to remedy possible deficiencies in the title can the case be brought to court.

In some states, like Arizona, no statutory provision at all is made for appeal of a ballot title, although legal suits can still be brought if interested parties feel the drafting body has failed to meet its legal obligation to provide a neutral ballot title. The courts in such states generally adopt a deferential standard of review toward ballot titles and explanatory statements. Typical is a 1998 ruling by the Arizona Supreme Court, which overturned a lower court ruling and sustained the secretary of state's ballot title and the accompanying analysis of the measure written by the Legislative Council. "By their very nature," the court explained,

> most disputes over ballot proposals are contentious. Thus, proponents and opponents are often dissatisfied with the [Legislative] Council's analyses. We cannot settle each of these disputes; our function is only to ensure that a challenged analysis is reasonably impartial and fulfills the statutory requirements. . . . The question is whether reasonable minds could conclude that the Council met the requirements of the law, not whether we believe the judicial system could itself devise a better analysis.

Absent evidence that a ballot summary or analysis is "tinged with partisan coloring" or clearly argues "for one side or the other," the court should defer to the drafting body.[12] Even in those rare cases where the Arizona court has found that the drafting body failed to meet its statutory duty to be evenhanded, the justices have been scrupulously careful not to "draft and order the Council to adopt any particular language," instead contenting themselves with directing the drafting body to reconsider and then to adopt "a truly impartial analysis and description."[13]

But even in Arizona the courts have become more aggressive in recent years. Just two months before the 2000 election, and days after the voters' pamphlet had gone to press, the Arizona high court struck from the ballot Proposition 107, which would have abolished the income tax, required voter approval of any replacement taxes the legislature might pass, and allowed federal candidates to indicate on the ballot their position regarding repeal of federal income taxes. It was the first time in over sixty-five years that the Arizona Supreme Court had used the single-subject rule to keep an initiative off the ballot. Prior to 1994, the Arizona high court had also never second-guessed the Legislative Council's analysis of an initiative and its effects, believing that such descriptions were a legislative task. In 2000, though, the court repudiated parts of the Legislative Council's analysis of three separate initiatives.

In the case of Proposition 202, which required cities and counties to adopt growth management plans, the court rejected the entire first paragraph, which described recent changes made by the legislature in planning and zoning requirements. The court also rejected the fiscal impact statement prepared for Proposition 204, which proposed using tobacco settlement money to finance various health care programs, including a requirement that the state provide health care to anyone making less than the federal poverty level. The Joint Legislative Budget Committee staff, which prepared the fiscal impact statement for the publicity pamphlet, estimated that tobacco settlement funds would be insufficient to meet the anticipated costs beyond 2003, and that other state funds would have to be tapped to make up the difference after that time. The court ruled that the fiscal impact statement, along with the Legislative Council's analysis based upon the estimate, was not impartial and should thus be stricken from the voters' pamphlet. The two-page court order promised that "in due course" (i.e., after the election) the court would issue an opinion explaining its order. The court order refrained from rewriting the analyses or even suggesting wording changes; instead it said only that any replacement wording must avoid "argument or advocacy." Because the court's decision came just weeks before the voters' pamphlet was due to go to the printers, the Legislative Council lacked adequate time to revise its analysis, and so the offending portions of the analysis were simply deleted from the voters' pamphlet. The legislative analysis of Proposition 203, which mandated an end to bilingual education, suffered a similar fate when, one week prior to the printing of the voters' pamphlet, the court ruled that the analysis misstated how many children were currently entitled to bilingual education.

Unable to fix the analysis on such short notice, the State Elections Director was compelled to delete the first paragraph of the analysis.[14]

Even in Utah, where the initiative process is infrequently used, the state supreme court has recently begun to insert itself into the ballot titling business. Prior to the 2000 election, the Utah Supreme Court had never rewritten an initiative ballot title, but in August 2000 the court rewrote the ballot titles of both initiatives that qualified for the ballot. Although "well aware" that it was not its job "to substitute our editorial judgment" for that of the Legislative Office of Research and General Counsel (LRGC), which was charged by statute with writing ballot titles, the court nonetheless proceeded to completely rewrite the one-hundred-word ballot titles for both measures on the grounds that the existing titles were not "a true and impartial statement of the purpose of the measure." So, for instance, the court agreed with the measure's proponents that the LRGC's language stating that Initiative A would "make English the sole language of government and require all official state and local government documents and actions to be in English, with specified exceptions," would mislead voters into thinking the measure was broader than it really was. The court thus substituted its own language, which explained that the measure would "exempt those documents and actions required by the United States and Utah constitutions; federal law and regulations; law enforcement, public safety, and health requirements; public and higher education; certain judicial proceedings; economic development and tourism; and libraries." Although the court's language is certainly more specific than the LRGC's wording, it is hard to see how one is truer or more impartial than the other. The court's willingness to overhaul the entire ballot title drew a short but sharp dissent from the court's chief justice. "Both of the initiatives," the chief justice pointed out, "have a number of purposes. There is no one correct and complete way to express the most important of those purposes." Therefore the court should "grant LRGC some deference as to its judgment on what purposes should be included in the ballot titles. Any corrections or additions we deem necessary should be made from the draft composed by LRGC." Even if the ballot title fell short of the "true and impartial" test, the court should amend the existing title rather than rewrite it entirely.[15] The court's unprecedented intervention in the ballot titling process was predictably rewarded several weeks later with another invitation to intervene. This time initiative proponents complained that the Office of the Legislative Fiscal Analyst's estimate was inflated in such a way as to "seem almost deliberately intended to undermine the voters' fair consideration of the initiative." With over a million voters' pamphlets due to go to the printer, the court denied, without explanation, the proponents' request to enjoin the printing of the voters' pamphlet.[16]

The erosion of judicial deference toward ballot titles is also marked in Washington, where state law requires the attorney general to write a twenty-five-word ballot title and seventy-five-word summary, and allows any dissatisfied person to appeal to the superior court and request that the court amend the title or summary. Prior to the 1990s, no Washington judge had rewritten a ballot title. In 1994, however, a superior court judge rewrote three ballot titles, two relating to restrictions on gay rights and a third concerning a waiting period for abortions. For instance, instead of the attorney general's title—"Shall government be prohibited from protecting homosexuals against discrimination; from awarding homosexuals custody of their own or other children; and from discussing homosexuality as acceptable?"—the judge substituted his own preferred title—"Shall certain rights based on homosexuality; adoption or custody of minors by homosexuals; and government approval of homosexuality be prohibited?" According to a news source at the time, "several officials present at the hearing felt [the judge] may have set a dangerous precedent in writing ballot titles rather than ruling in favor of either the complainant or the attorney general." According to these officials, the decision "would allow any group not satisfied with the attorney general's ballot title to challenge and have it rewritten."[17]

These fears have proved warranted. In 1998 the same judge found himself wrestling with the intractable question of whether the word "abortion" should appear in the ballot title of a measure that would ban partial-birth abortions. The attorney general's title read: "Shall abortion of any fetus located wholly or partly in the birth canal be a felony, except where necessary to prevent the pregnant woman's death?" The initiative's author objected to using the word "abortion" in the ballot title, arguing that "once the fetus leaves the womb, it's no longer abortion, it's infanticide." The proponents instead preferred: "Shall the killing of a child in the process of being born be a felony?" The judge apparently agreed that the term "abortion" might be misleading, and so wrote his own ballot title: "Shall the termination of a fetus life during the process of birth be a felony crime except when necessary to prevent the pregnant woman's death?" Although one might prefer the judge's language to the attorney general's, it is hard to see how the attorney general's language failed to meet the statutory requirement for impartiality. There is, of course, no perfectly neutral way to describe such an emotionally charged issue. The National Abortion and Reproductive Rights Action League (NARAL) objects to the use of the phrase "partial-birth" because its considers it emotionally loaded, while pro-life advocates believe the term "fetus" loads the deck against them. The battle over language is an inherently political battle, and it is not at all clear that it is good for the courts or for society to have the judiciary serve as the arbiter of this political struggle.[18]

THE JUDICIAL VETO IN FLORIDA AND ARKANSAS

The considerable power of the courts to shape ballot titles in states like Oregon, Colorado, and Washington pales, however, in comparison to the preelection veto power that courts have assumed in a few states, most notably Arkansas and Florida. Unlike Oregon and Washington, Florida is a relative newcomer to the initiative process, only having adopted direct democracy in 1968. In the first fifteen years of its existence, the initiative power was infrequently exercised in Florida; through 1987 Florida's citizens had voted on only four statewide initiatives, three of which related to the establishment of casino gambling and a state lottery. Things began to change in the late 1980s when nongaming interests and conservative activists started to make their presence felt in Florida initiative politics. An initiative making English the official language and another placing limits on noneconomic damages went before the voters in 1988. Then, in the early 1990s, interest in the initiative process began to grow in earnest. In 1992 voters passed a term limits initiative and a property tax limit. In 1994 three initiatives reached the ballot, and in 1996 four more made it. The number of petitions circulating increased even more dramatically. To many observers it appeared that Florida might become the next California. Indeed, given that Florida allowed signature gatherers four years to complete their task, in contrast to the mere 150 days allowed in California, it seemed possible that Florida might become an even more attractive haven for initiative activists. Instead, the momentum building in the early and mid-1990s was stopped almost dead in its tracks. No initiatives qualified for the ballot in 1998 and only one in 2000. What happened?

The answer lies not with initiative activists—a record forty-one initiatives were placed in circulation for the 2000 election—nor with a stiffening of signature-gathering requirements—the legislature made no changes in the law—but rather with the seven unelected individuals who make up the Florida Supreme Court. Unlike in Oregon and Washington, where ballot titles are reviewed by the court prior to the gathering of signatures, in Florida initiative proponents must first gather 10 percent of the required signatures before submitting the ballot title for approval. And unlike in most other states, initiative proponents in Florida write their own ballot title, consisting of a fifteen-word caption and a seventy-five-word explanatory statement. The attorney general is required by a 1986 statute to seek an advisory opinion from the court as to whether the initiative complies with the single-subject requirement and the statutory requirement that a ballot summary be written in "clear and unambiguous language." In addition, the caption must express the way in which "the measure is commonly referred to or spoken of."[19] The court cannot rewrite the ballot title, but if it deems the measure fails to meet these legal requirements, the signatures are invalidated and the initiative proponents must start from scratch.

Between the time when the 1986 statute took effect and 1993, the court offered advisory opinions on five initiatives and upheld all five, spurning invitations from opponents and, on at least one occasion, from the attorney general to invalidate the petitions. In the last of these five cases, in which the court upheld an initiative prohibiting the use of gill nets, one of the justices wrote a concurring opinion that revealed the justices' growing unease with the increased use of the initiative process. He agreed that the gill-net measure did not violate the single-subject rule and that the ballot title was legally sufficient, yet he volunteered his opinion that the amendment was "more appropriate for inclusion in Florida's statute books than in the state constitution." (Florida is unusual in that it only allows the initiative to be used for constitutional change.)[20] Gingerly acknowledging "the sovereignty of the people," he nonetheless felt "compelled to express my view that the permanency and supremacy of state constitutional jurisprudence is jeopardized by the recent proliferation of constitutional amendments. [Since] the technical requirements, such as the single-subject rule and the requirements of [a clear ballot title] appear insufficient to prevent abuse of the amendment process," he offered his heartfelt "hope that the next Constitutional Revision Commission might have the opportunity to establish some criteria regarding the subject matter of initiatives that will preserve the constitution as a document of fundamental laws." Three other justices concurred in this strikingly personal opinion.[21]

Since neither the legislature nor the Constitutional Revision Commission came to the constitution's aid, the court took matters into its own hands by interpreting more stringently the "technical requirements" of the single-subject rule and a clear ballot title. After upholding the gill-net initiative, the court was asked to judge the validity of an unprecedented nine measures in the space of a year. Had the court upheld each of these measures, many of which had already gathered the required signatures at the time of the court's review, Florida's voters could have faced as many as ten initiatives in 1994, which would have matched, in a single election, the total number of initiatives in the state's history. The initiatives, moreover, would largely have been the work of conservative activists. Of the nine initiatives the court considered in 1994, six were clearly identified with conservatives: three were attempts to make it more difficult for the government to raise taxes, one was a property rights measure, another called for an end to the early release of criminals, and the sixth attempted to restrict gay rights. The court invalidated all but one of these (a proposal to eliminate the single-subject requirement for taxation measures) and also threw out the lone identifiably liberal measure, an initiative that would have imposed a tax on the sugar industry to pay for cleaning up the Everglades.

Among the measures the court rejected was one that called for voter approval of all new taxes. The measure's caption read: "Voter Approval of New Taxes: Should New Taxes Require Voter Approval in this State?" The sixty-four-word summary stated: "This provision requires voter approval of new taxes enacted in this State. New taxes include initiation of new taxes, increases in tax rates and eliminating exemptions to taxes. It does not limit emergency tax increases, lasting up to 12 months, which are approved by a three-fourths vote of a taxing entity's governing body. The amendment is effective two days after voters approve." Drawing on principles articulated in the 1984 case *Fine v. Firestone*, the majority concluded that the initiative should be struck from the ballot since it did not identify each of the other parts of the constitution that would be affected by the measure. For instance, neither the initiative nor the explanatory statement indicated that it would eliminate the constitutional requirement that certain local taxes beyond a constitutionally specified amount require a public vote. Moreover, the question in the ballot caption was positively misleading since it implied that there currently were no such requirements for voter approval. The court went on to list a string of other constitutional provisions that would be "substantially affected" by the measure, including:

> (1) article VII, section 1(a), which confers upon the legislature, without the requirement of a referendum, the power to impose taxes by general law, e.g., sales taxes, cigarette taxes and liquor taxes; (2) article VII, section 1(b), which confers upon the legislature the authority to impose taxes without a referendum on the operation of motor vehicles, boats, airplanes, trailers, trailer coaches, and mobile homes; (3) article VII, section 2, which provides legislative authority to impose some forms of intangible personal property taxes without a referendum; (4) article VII, section 5, which provides, with restrictions, legislative authority to impose estate and inheritance taxes to the extent that they are credited towards the federal tax, and, in addition, this section provides for a corporate income tax up to 5% and authorizes a rate in excess of 5% if approved by three-fifths vote of both houses of the legislature; and (5) article VII, section 7, which provides legislative authority to impose pari-mutuel taxes.[22]

Since neither the summary nor the measure itself alerted voters to the impact the measure would have on these other constitutional provisions, the court concluded that it was duty bound to remove the initiative from the ballot.

Two justices on the court, however, saw their legal duty differently. Drawing on a 1986 ruling that upheld the ballot wording of an initiative establishing a state lottery, the dissenting justices insisted that "failure to state every specific ramification of a proposed amendment is not fatal where the summary adequately explains the amendment's chief purpose." The justices did not find the ballot summary at all confusing or misleading. To them it clearly apprised voters "of exactly what the amendment purports to do—require a public referendum on all new taxes."[23] Although the dissenting judges lost, their view was far closer to the language of the statute, which required only that the summary be a clear explanatory statement of "the chief purpose of the measure." The word "chief"suggests that there is no expectation that every aspect of the measure must be embodied in the summary. More important, the word "purpose" suggests that it is the aim or intent of the measure that must be captured in the summary, not the myriad effects or unintended consequences. Flushing out the unintended consequences of a measure is the task of those who oppose a measure. If campaigns consistently fail to make these unintended consequences known to voters, that is an indictment of the initiative process and a reason for reforming the process. But that reform should come from the people and their representatives, not judges.

The majority's new standard of review has made it much more difficult to qualify an initiative in Florida. All but one of the twelve measures brought before the court for preelection review between 1997 and 2000 were rejected. Among these were four initiatives that would have barred the use of race and sex as criteria in public education, public employment, and public contracting. Rather than bundle these aims into a single initiative, as had been done successfully in California and Washington, the proponents attempted to get around the Florida court's strict interpretation of the single-subject rule by creating four separate measures: one that barred using race as a criteria in public education, a second in public employment, a third in public contracting, and a fourth that barred both race and sex in all three areas. Voters could then decide the question of race separately from the question of sex and could differentiate between using race as a factor in college admissions and using it in public contracting or public employment. But even this extraordinary effort was swatted down by the high court.

The court held that an initiative that applied only to race in public education still violated the single-subject rule because it affected more than one branch of government (the legislature as well as the judiciary) and multiple levels of government (state universities as well as local school districts). In addition, the measures failed because neither the text of the measure nor the ballot summary identified the other constitutional provisions that would be affected by the initiative. For instance, it failed to alert voters that it would affect Article 1, section 21, which provides that "the courts shall be open to every person for redress of any injury, and justice shall be administered without sale, denial or delay." To appear on the ballot, the measure and summary must tell voters that it would directly impact this constitutional provision by "strip[ping] the judiciary of its powers to provide redress for injuries emanating from discriminatory practices."

The court also found that the ballot captions and summaries were misleading since they implied that "there currently is no . . . constitutional provision barring discrimination based on the enumerated classifications," when in fact Article 1, section 2, of the Florida constitution "prohibits deprivation of rights based on race, religion, national origin, or physical disability." Captioning an initiative as the "Amendment to Bar Government from Treating People Differently Based on Race in Public Education" or the "End Governmental Discrimination and Preferences Amendment" misleads voters into thinking that people currently can discriminate based on race. The problem with the title, the court argued, is not what it says but rather "what it does not say." How the caption was supposed to say these things in fifteen words was not explained by the court. Also not explained was why an initiative should be invalidated for giving "the negative implication that the government is presently practicing discrimination" when this is precisely what the initiative's advocates believe, namely, that affirmative action is government discrimination. To make this the basis for striking an initiative from the ballot is to cloak a fundamentally political judgment in the guise of a narrow technical requirement.

Perhaps sensing the weakness of its position, the court reached for still more reasons why the initiatives should not be allowed on the ballot. The ballot summary of the measure outlawing preferences based on sex as well as race was faulted for failing to define its terms adequately. In particular, the justices objected that the summary's statement that the measure "exempts bona fide qualifications based on sex" was undefined, thus "leaving voters to guess at its meaning." The court conceded that "bona fide qualifications based on sex" was a common legal phrase but noted that since "voters are not informed of its legal significance" they "would undoubtedly rely on their own conceptions of what constitutes a bona fide qualification." The judges were unmoved by the fact that the measure itself clearly indicated what it regarded as a bona fide qualification exception, namely, a "classification that (a) Is based on sex and is necessary for sexual privacy or medical or psychological treatment; or (b) Is necessary for undercover law enforcement or for film, video, audio, or theatrical casting; or (c) Provides for separate athletic teams for each sex." To expect the law itself to provide a definition of the excepted classifications is reasonable; to expect each of the exceptions to be detailed in a seventy-five-word summary as a precondition for appearing on the ballot seems more difficult to defend. The court, though, had little difficulty finding a precedent for its decision. It cited as authority its 1997 decision in which it invalidated (for the second time) a measure requiring voter approval of new taxes on the grounds that the summary's "definition of new tax as 'increases in tax rates' did not distinguish between an increase in the amount of payments on taxable property or an increase in the actual rate at which the property was being taxed." Whether most voters would have found such a distinction helpful in understanding the chief purpose of the amendment is highly debatable.

Even more strained was the court's finding that the ballot title was misleading since the caption and summary spoke of "people," while the text of the measure referred to "persons." As improbable as this seems, the court could again point to a number of cases it had decided in the previous few years in which it had invalidated measures for as little cause. In 1998, for instance, it had struck down a health care initiative because, among other reasons, the ballot title spoke of "citizens" while the text referred to "every natural person," which "leaves voters guessing whether the terms are intended to be synonymous or whether the difference in terms was intentional." In the case of the affirmative action measures, the court was concerned that by using the term "people" in the summary, proponents had failed to give voters notice that corporations might also be prohibited from receiving preferential treatment since they could be construed as "persons" under the law.

Such reasoning evidently struck even some members of the court as rather labored, for although all seven justices concurred in the result, only three concurred with the reasoning articulated in the court's opinion. Three justices agreed with the result but joined no opinion, leaving the measure's proponents in the dark as to why the justices believed the measure should be struck from the ballot, or what they needed to do to bring their measure into compliance with the law. The seventh justice wrote a separate opinion, rejecting the court's reasoning and its reliance on the single-subject rule but expressing, in even more vehement terms, his belief that the ballot title and summary were "fundamentally misleading." In the name of nondiscrimination, the justice complained, the measure actually undermined existing civil rights protections for minorities. The real problem, as one justice put it during oral arguments, was that the measure was "a wolf dressed up in sheep's clothing."[24] But this was not so much a problem with the ballot title and summary as it was an objection to the substance of the initiative itself. For the justices affirmative action or racial preferences were legitimate and valuable ways of redressing past discrimination or promoting diversity, and the initiatives, no matter how they were dressed up, would set back the cause of racial equality. For the measures' proponents, on the other hand, affirmative action was decked out in the misleading garb of civil rights. The initiatives, from this point of view, would help to restore the color-blind vision of the original civil rights movement. This was the thorny and divisive policy question the voters would have been asked to decide had the measures been allowed to remain on the ballot.

The court's decision drew justifiable outrage from the measure's proponents. Ward Connerly, accustomed to the far more accommodating courts of California, vehemently criticized the court's "disgraceful display" of judicial over-reaching: "If ever there were a case of judicial malpractice, this is it. I swear to you, if I were a resident of Florida, I'd start an impeachment process tomorrow. It's such a partisan court, it's unbelievable." But many Floridians were happy not to see Connerly's measure reach the ballot. Liberal Democrats, for obvious reasons, were overjoyed that the court had saved them from the prospect of voters abolishing affirmative action. Many leading Republicans also expressed relief. Republican Governor Jeb Bush, though opposed to racial and gender preferences in contracting, hiring, and university admissions, was thankful that the court had helped the state avoid a battle that would have been "unnecessarily divisive." Bush and other Florida Republicans feared that Connerly's initiatives might— as Proposition 209 had in California—mobilize the minority vote and damage Republican prospects in 2000 and beyond.[25] The court helped Bush rid himself of the meddlesome Connerly, leaving him free to pursue his own, less sweeping One Florida plan, which would end affirmative action programs in hiring and contracting decisions by state agencies and end the use of race as a factor in university admissions. Was Florida better off without Connerly's four sweeping initiatives? Almost certainly. But as the dissenting judge in *Adams v. Gunter* (1970) warned, "As a court, we can't 'play God' for the people and 'wet-nurse' them on the supposition that if we don't they will make egregious errors."[26] Liberals (and conservatives) do not do themselves or the judiciary any favors in looking to the courts to win their political battles for them. And the court takes grave risks with its own legitimacy and the democratic process when it treats the people as defenseless, dumb sheep.

The court has also assumed the mantle of defender of the people in Arkansas, the first and, until Florida gained the initiative, the only southern state to possess the initiative power. In Arkansas, unlike Florida, the state supreme court will not hear a challenge to a ballot title until after all the signatures have been gathered. If the court finds the ballot title deficient, it does not attempt to rewrite it but rather disallows the qualified initiative from appearing on the ballot; the petitioner must begin again, with no guarantee that the next ballot title will fare any better. If the court adopted a deferential standard of review, this process might be workable, but the Arkansas high court has become increasingly stringent in recent years about what constitutes an impartial and fair ballot title. Between 1994 and 2000 the court ruled on the ballot titles of twelve initiatives, rejecting all but three.[27]

The Arkansas Supreme Court, unlike courts in most other states, has a history of judicial activism on ballot titles that stretches back to the early 1930s. In fact, the Arkansas high court had set about emasculating the initiative and referendum immediately after its adoption in 1910. In the first initiative election in 1912, the court voided two of the three statewide initiative amendments that qualified for the ballot. The court's reasoning was that an 1874 provision limiting to three the number of amendments submitted in any one election applied to initiated amendments as well. Since the legislature had already placed two amendments on the 1912 ballot, there was only room for one initiated amendment. In addition, the court voided all the local initiatives that had qualified for the ballot, even though the Arkansas initiative amendment included a clause that explicitly extended the initiative and referendum to local elections. According to the court, "the words 'each municipality' and 'each county' were ineptly thrust into the amendment . . . in a way that they express nothing and mean nothing." In a 1915 case the court also ruled that initiative amendments, like legislative amendments, must receive a majority of the total vote and not just a majority of the votes cast on the particular amendment, this despite the unambiguous wording of the 1910 amendment declaring that "any measure referred to the people shall take effect and become a law when it is approved by a majority of the votes cast thereon." According to the court, "any measure" referred only to statutory measures, not to constitutional amendments. Among the many initiatives to fall short as a result of the court's ruling was a new I&R amendment in 1920 that was designed to fix the court's creative jurisprudence. Although approved by nearly two-thirds of those who voted on the measure, the amendment failed to gain a majority of those who cast ballots in the election. It was not until 1925 that Arkansas' citizens at last obtained the power of direct legislation they thought they had secured in 1910, when a specially selected supreme court (the regular justices had recused themselves because one of the amendments under challenge was a legislative amendment authorizing the legislature to add two judges to the court) overturned the court's 1915 ruling and retroactively validated the 1920 I&R amendment.[28]

Prevented from eviscerating the initiative and referendum, the high court next turned its attention to scrutinizing ballot titles. In 1931 the court voided a popular referendum on the recently adopted Three Months' Divorce Law, a statute that amended existing law by enabling residents of Arkansas to file for divorce after living in the state for three months rather than the full year that the state had previously required. The court ruled that the title of the referendum was misleading because unsuspecting citizens, reading the description of the law as "an act to permit the granting of divorces after a residence in the State for three months," might erroneously believe that the act made residency the only criterion for the granting of a divorce. As the two dissenting judges pointed out, the majority's reasoning only made sense if the court assumed a citizenry of almost subhuman intelligence. The dissenting justices allowed that there could conceivably be "a few voters who would not understand from the ballot title what act they were voting for or against," but that would be true of any measure submitted to the people of an entire state. The court's ruling, the dissenters concluded, threatened the court with relativism—"probably no two persons would prepare the same ballot title for any measure," they pointed out—and would "defeat the very purpose" of the initiative and referendum.[29]

The principle that the majority laid down in the 1931 case—that a ballot title must "convey an intelligible idea of the scope and import of the proposed law, and ought to be free from any misleading tendency, whether of amplification, of omission, or of fallacy, and must contain no partisan coloring"—was generally adhered to in subsequent cases, but the court often showed little sign of agreeing as to what those words meant. In 1934, for instance, the court invalidated another referendum that would have voided a legislative act abolishing "the State Board of Education elected by the people," instead creating "a new State Board of Education appointed by the Governor." According to the majority, the "only purpose" for using the words "elected by the people" was "to lend partisan color to the position assumed by the petitioners." "It was and is wholly immaterial," the court opined, "whether or not the abolished board was elective or appointive." Similarly, the words "appointed by the Governor" were "partisan and colored" since "the undue emphasis placed upon 'appointed by the Governor' does not add to or detract from the merits or demerits of the act." Moreover, the title was misleading since it did not disclose that the appointment was with the advice and consent of the senate. The dissenting judges found this interpretation absurd. After all, the old state board *was* elected by the people and the new state board would be appointed by the governor. Since the ballot title "contained no misstatement of a fact, and there is no omission or amplification or partisan coloring calculated or intended to mislead," the dissenting judges insisted the ballot title should be upheld.[30]

In 1936 the adequacy of a statewide initiative ballot title was challenged in court for the first time. The initiative, which levied a 2 percent sales tax and appropriated a third of the proceeds from horse and dog racing to fund a pension for the aged and blind, was invalidated by the court because the thirty-two-word ballot title failed to reveal how the pensions would be funded. The case for a misleading title was far stronger than in its two earlier referenda rulings, yet even in this case the court remained split on the sufficiency of the title. In subsequent

cases the court evolved a more liberal interpretation of the ballot title requirements than was evident in the 1931 and 1934 referenda cases, though disagree-
ment among the justices remained common and the court still periodically struck
initiatives because of inadequate titles. In 1952, for instance, the court voided a
consumer credit initiative, and in 1958 it struck an unprecedented four initiatives
from the ballot. In the early 1980s the court removed two initiatives, including
an antiabortion measure, from the ballot because of faulty titles. But these occasions of judicial activism were, until recently, episodic. Between 1960 and 1992
the Arkansas Supreme Court heard eleven ballot title cases and voided only three
initiatives because of inadequate ballot titles (one initiative was struck from the
ballot because of signature inadequacies, but the ballot title was upheld). As
notable were the twenty-one initiative ballot titles that went unchallenged in the
courts. All told, then, petitioners gathered sufficient signatures for at least thirty-
one initiatives in the three decades between 1960 and 1992, and the court only
voided about one in ten of those initiatives. In contrast, during the four elections
between 1994 and 2000, only one initiative title went unchallenged and the court
voided over two-thirds of the thirteen petitions that successfully overcame the
signature barrier. The episodic has become routine.

Initiative proponents in Arkansas consequently face an immense judicial
hurdle today, as the proponents of a 2000 initiative to repeal the state sales tax
on used goods and require public votes on future tax increases were the most
recent to discover. Just two weeks before the 2000 election, the state supreme
court struck Amendment 4 from the ballot, ruling that the ballot title failed to
inform voters of "the far-reaching consequences of voting for this measure." In
particular, the court faulted the title for not making it clear to voters that "by
approving this measure, he or she may risk losing valuable government services."
Moreover, the ballot title failed to clearly define what counts as a "tax increase"
and what counts as "a regularly scheduled statewide election"; the voter could
thus not know for certain what acts would trigger the voter approval provision
and when those votes would take place. According to the court, "the ultimate
issue is whether the voter, while inside the voting booth, is able to reach an intelligent and informed decision for or against the proposal and understands the consequences of his or her vote based on the ballot title."[31] One can agree with the
court about the importance of voters making informed decisions; that is the reason we have campaigns. It is less clear, though, that the decision about whether
voters are capable of making informed decisions should be left to judges.

THE DAY AFTER

The judicial role in the preelection process varies greatly from state to state, but
the court's place in the modern postelection process is more consistently consequential. Every state that makes heavy use of the initiative process today expe-

riences frequent court challenges to voter-approved initiatives. In California, where there are law firms that specialize in initiative challenges, about two-thirds of the voter-approved initiatives between 1960 and 2000 have been challenged in court. In other high-use states, such as Oregon, Washington, and Colorado, the percentage of challenged initiatives during this same period has been somewhat lower but still substantial, ranging between 40 and 50 percent.[32]

Postelection legal challenges to initiatives are nothing new. In 1904 temperance advocates in Oregon used the newly created initiative process to enact a local option liquor law that allowed residents of a county or town to initiate a local plebiscite to prohibit the sale of "intoxicating liquors." The constitutionality of the measure was immediately challenged in court by those unhappy with the proliferation of "dry" towns and counties. A suit brought by a licensed liquor dealer argued that the measure violated the constitution because the constitution did not permit state laws to be put into effect upon the vote of a county or subdivision of a county. The plaintiff maintained that the sale of liquor in a locality could only be prohibited by popular vote if it was a vote of all the people of the state. A separate constitutional challenge to the law was brought on the grounds that it granted special privileges or immunities to some state citizens that were denied to others, and that the ballot title did not accurately convey the content of the measure. Each of these challenges was rejected by the state supreme court, which was careful to exercise great self-restraint despite its misgivings. The court agreed that an accurate ballot title was vitally important in the initiative process, concluding:

> The majority of qualified electors are so much interested in managing their own affairs that they have no time carefully to consider measures affecting the general public. . . . We think the assertion may safely be ventured that it is only the few persons who earnestly favor or zealously oppose the passage of a proposed law initiated by petition who have attentively studied its contents and know how it will probably affect their private interests. The greater number of voters do not possess this information and usually derive their knowledge of the contents of a proposed law from an inspection of the title thereof, which is sometimes secured only from the very meager details afforded by a ballot which is examined in an election booth preparatory to exercising the right of suffrage.

Although essentially conceding that many voters may not have understood the implications of the measure—though billed as a local option measure, the initiative allowed a county to shut down the sale of alcohol throughout the county, even in local towns or precincts that had opted not to go dry—the court concluded that the title was a "fair index of the subject-matter of the act." Nor did the court find a constitutional violation in the fact that the measure, in the guise of allowing the people to decide, loaded the deck in favor of prohibition by allowing a local precinct or county subdivision to go dry even if the county as a whole voted to remain "wet." The initiative may not have been good policy, but the justices concluded that "with the wisdom, policy and expediency of the legislation the courts can have nothing to do. That is a matter purely and solely for another department of state—the lawmaking body, the legislative assembly—or, under the initiative and referendum amendment, for the people themselves to determine, and their determination in that regard is final and conclusive, save by an appeal to the same authority or department."[33]

The court's self-restraint was again on display a few years later when it refused to accept the ambitious argument that the initiative process itself violated Article 4, section 4, of the U.S. Constitution, which guaranteed to every state "a Republican Form of Government." The frontal assault on the initiative process emerged from a 1906 initiative that required telephone and telegraph companies to pay an annual 2 percent license fee on gross receipts. The Pacific States Telephone & Telegraph Company refused to pay the tax, and the state took the recalcitrant corporation to court. In defending its actions, the company argued not just that the particular measure was unconstitutional but that the initiative and referendum process itself was "repugnant" to no fewer than ten separate sections of the U.S. Constitution. The court brushed aside such arguments, referring to its own earlier 1903 decision in which it had declared that

> the initiative and referendum amendment does not abolish or destroy the republican form of government, or substitute another in its place. The representative character of the government still remains. The people have simply reserved to themselves a larger share of legislative power, but they have not overthrown the republican form of the government, or substituted another in its place. The government is still divided into the legislative, executive, and judicial departments, the duties of which are discharged by representatives selected by the people.

In these early decisions the Oregon court clearly signaled that it had no interest in entertaining arguments that would allow the courts to eviscerate the newly created initiative process.[34]

Indeed, it would be several decades and over a hundred initiatives later before the courts would strike down the first Oregon initiative. Writing in 1915, the political scientist James Barnett observed that since laws adopted by the people are subject to the same constitutional restrictions as ordinary legislation, "there is a possibility . . . that the courts may find popular legislation to be unconstitutional, although so far, in actual practice, this possibility has scarcely been realized at all." Instead, he noted a tendency on the part of the courts to jealously guard against "any interference with the 'people's laws.' "[35] It was not until the appearance of a 1922 initiative that required all students to attend public schools (a measure clearly targeted at Catholic parochial schools) that the courts intervened, and even then it was the federal courts—and ultimately the U.S. Supreme Court—and not the state courts that invalidated the initiative.[36] Federal and state courts struck down a number of other high-profile initiatives in the first half of the twentieth century, but such involvement pales against the pattern of judicial activity that has emerged in the last third of the twentieth century and has only intensified during the last decade.[37]

California's Proposition 62 provides an instructive example of the litigious nature of contemporary initiative politics. Drafted by Howard Jarvis and passed in 1986, Proposition 62 required public votes on all new local taxes: special taxes required a two-thirds public vote, while general taxes required a majority vote as well as a two-thirds vote of the local governing body. The impetus for the measure was an earlier state supreme court decision that had restricted the scope of Proposition 13, the landmark property tax limitation measure passed in 1978. Among the many ill-defined provisions of Proposition 13 was a requirement that any "special tax" imposed by a local government must be approved by a two-thirds vote of the electorate. Since Proposition 13 did not specify what constituted a special tax, it was left to the courts to interpret the meaning of the term. In a 1982 decision the high court accepted a narrow definition of special taxes that enabled local governments to raise taxes without seeking voter approval. The aim of Proposition 62, Jarvis explained, was to "bring back rights the State Supreme Court took away from us, which we won with Proposition 13." But Proposition 62 started out exactly where Proposition 13 had ended up: mired in the courts. Even before the sample ballots had been printed, Jarvis had filed suit against the legislative analyst's interpretation, which argued that since Proposition 62 was a statutory change and not a constitutional amendment, the measure could not apply to chartered cities, thus freeing the state's biggest cities from its stringent requirements. As soon as the measure passed, it was the opponents' turn to resort to the courts, which promptly invalidated several key provisions. According to one appellate court ruling, "the requirement that local tax measures be submitted to the electorate by either referendum or initiative would be a gross interference with the fiscal responsibility of local governments."

For almost a decade legal challenges to Proposition 62 continued, while the law remained largely moribund. Encouraged by the California Supreme Court's refusal to hear appeals from two appellate court decisions, most local governments continued to operate as if Proposition 62 had never passed. In 1995, however, nearly a decade after passage of the measure, the California Supreme Court finally accepted an appeal and reversed the lower court, finding the measure to be unconstitutional. Not that the justices were of one mind. The conservative chief justice Malcolm Lucas issued a rare and strong dissent, lamenting that the court had "seriously undermined the ability of local government to finance sorely needed projects and improvements through local tax measures." A second dissenting justice opined that the measure was plainly an effort to circumvent the constitutional ban on tax referenda. Even after the high court's final decision, the legal wrangling was not over. Immediately after the court's decision, the Howard Jarvis Taxpayers Association was back in court in an effort to annul local taxes that had been enacted during the previous decade. At the end of the decade, after several conflicting rulings, the court finally decided that the statute of limitations began from the moment the tax was enacted, not from the date of the court's 1995 decision, and so rejected the suit brought by the Jarvis Taxpayers Association.[38] The final chapter on the fifteen-year legal battle over Proposition 62 had at last been written.

Why do so many initiatives get entangled in the courts? Part of the answer lies in the technical deficiencies of many initiatives. Although initiatives are sometimes drafted by coalitions made up of diverse interests, the initiative process in most states lacks the institutional structures of a legislature through which the perspectives of opponents, interested parties, and experts are brought to bear on the drafting of a bill. Staff analysis, committee hearings, and mark-up sessions are designed, in part, to ferret out drafting flaws and uncover unintended consequences. Of course, as initiative proponents are quick to point out, not all legislative bills receive the same high level of scrutiny, particularly those bills that are pushed through in the hectic final days of a legislative session. It is also true that the level of staff expertise available in a legislature varies a great deal; some states, like California, possess highly professionalized staff, whereas other state legislatures possess precious little in the way of professional staff. And in states with term limits (which today is virtually every state with the initiative power), the legislative experience and policy expertise of legislators is often much less than it would have been a decade ago. State legislatures, in short, are imperfect. Yet for all their manifest imperfections, legislatures do generally force ideas through an elaborate institutional winnowing process, which helps to weed out and revise legislation with the sorts of obvious flaws that invite legal challenge.

Had Proposition 62 been taken through the normal legislative process, for instance, staff analysis would have alerted legislators that a constitutional change was necessary to alter the way chartered cities did business. The legal expertise of the legislature would have made the court challenge unnecessary. Another feature of Proposition 62 that invited legal challenge was a provision that retroactively applied the measure's requirement to any taxes enacted after July 31, 1985, fifteen months before the measure was approved by voters. The proponents' aim was to prevent cities from trying to rush through tax increases in anticipation of the measure's passage, but the means selected retroactively criminalized a legal act. The courts predictably struck down Proposition 62's retroactive provision, as other courts in other states have consistently done when faced, as they often have been, with similar retroactive provisions.

At times the legal flaws in initiatives are obvious to virtually all parties, occasionally even to the proponents themselves. In 1998 California's ballot was home to an initiative that instructed elected federal and state legislators to propose and support a specific congressional term limits amendment to the U.S. Constitution. In addition, it required that candidates who failed to pledge support or to vote for the proposed amendment would have the phrase "Disregarded

Voters' Instruction on Term Limits" or "Declined to Pledge to Support Term Limits" placed adjacent to their names on the ballot. Similar provisions had been ruled unconstitutional in a number of other states. After the U.S. Supreme Court refused to review these decisions, the measure's proponents finally accepted the unconstitutionality of what they were doing and used the ballot pamphlet to urge voters to oppose the measure since "passage of this measure will likely result only in needless and costly litigation." The measure passed anyway, a result that may say more about the importance of the ballot pamphlet than all the academic studies combined. Predictably the state supreme court invalidated the measure the following year.[39]

Legal flaws were likewise glaringly obvious in "The Compassionate Use Act," a 1996 California initiative that clearly contravened federal law by legalizing the use of marijuana for medical purposes. Under federal law, cultivation and possession of marijuana are illegal. Marijuana, moreover, is a Schedule I drug, which is defined as a drug for which "there is a high potential for abuse, no currently accepted medical use in treatment in the United States and a lack of accepted safety for use under medical supervision." States do not have the power to approve or distribute drugs that the federal Food and Drug Administration has not approved. As one law professor remarked, "medicinal marijuana would not be legal in California unless we were also to secede from the union. Federal law in this area could not be cancelled by our initiative, however well intentioned."[40]

The conflict between state and federal drug laws created by the passage of Proposition 215 engendered tremendous uncertainty among doctors, patients, and law enforcement officials about what was allowable. Although federal law trumps state law, the federal government's guidelines stipulate that federal law enforcement officers should not get involved in cases involving fewer than five hundred marijuana plants. State and local officials could not enforce the federal law without violating their own state law, not to mention ignoring the will of the voters. In this environment of legal uncertainty, California's Democratic attorney general, the chief law enforcement official of the state, publicly informed San Francisco officials that medicinal marijuana distribution in the city can proceed "if it is done discreetly, so that federal authorities do not feel the need to intervene."[41] The federal drug czar, meanwhile, threatened doctors with the loss of their licenses to prescribe controlled drugs if they prescribed marijuana, leaving them caught between the threat of federal prosecution and the demands of their patients to take advantage of the new law. The calculated legal chaos created by the initiative could, of course, only be settled by the courts.

The ill-defined or ambiguous language of Proposition 215 only exacerbated the many legal uncertainties. In contrast to a bill approved by the legislature in 1995 (and vetoed by the governor) that limited the use of medical marijuana to patients suffering from cancer, AIDS, glaucoma, and multiple sclerosis, Proposition 215, drafted by a longtime advocate of marijuana legalization, permitted marijuana use for "any . . . illness for which marijuana provides relief." What counted as an illness or even relief was not specified. Moreover, whereas the legislature's version granted a medical exemption only to patients who had received written permission from a physician, the initiative required only a written or oral *recommendation* from a physician. Further complicating matters was that the initiative nowhere defined who is to count as a "physician," opening up the possibility that homeopaths or other nonlicensed medical practitioners could make the recommendation. The initiative also permitted cultivation and possession of marijuana by the patient's "primary caregiver," defined as the person whom the patient designates as having "consistently assumed responsibility for the housing, health, or safety" of the patient. According to the measure's chief author, Dennis Peron, his Cannabis Cultivators Club, which in 1997 reportedly distributed marijuana to between five hundred and one thousand patrons a day, was such a "primary caregiver." Since the initiative itself failed to delimit clearly who would qualify for the medical exemption—shortly after the election Peron was quoted as saying that "all marijuana use is medical, except for kids"—the job of determining the meaning and scope of the measure was left to the courts, which, after nearly five years, eventually did sort out the legal mess created by Proposition 215.[42]

The legal and technical deficiencies of initiatives are an important factor in the large number of initiatives that end up in court, but probably more important still are the political deficiencies. Some bills skate through the legislature with virtually no serious opposition, but on contentious issues, the sort that routinely appear on initiative ballots, legislation does not normally get passed without significant concessions to opponents. Amendments are the majority's way of co-opting opposition and building winning coalitions. The opposition, in turn, gets a chance at a bill that it can live with even if not love. By amending or moderating a bill to take into account the political objections of affected interests, the legislative process makes it less likely that these groups will seek to challenge the law in court. The legislative process of compromise and consensus-building thus helps to keep what are fundamentally political disputes from being fought out in the courts. The main reason Proposition 62, for instance, would not have been produced by a legislature and signed by a governor is that it never generated anything approaching political consensus.[43]

The political and technical inadequacies of most initiatives may help to explain why so many of them are challenged in court, but they do not explain why initiatives are more likely to be embroiled in court challenges today than they were at the beginning of the twentieth century. For that piece of the puzzle one needs to examine not the inherent limitations of the initiative process but rather the changing relationship between the judiciary and direct democracy. In the early decades of the century, as has already been noted, courts rarely invalidated initiative legislation. This judicial deference, moreover, probably acted as a deterrent toward those who might have wished to challenge an initiative. Why challenge a measure if you know the cost is high and your chances of success extremely low? Today the costs remain high, but the odds look much better. Litigants know that about 50 percent of the time they will succeed in persuading a judge to invalidate an initiative at least in part, and about 25 percent of the time they will succeed in invalidating the initiative in its entirety. Those are the kind of odds that, together with the rapid increase in the absolute number of initiatives, have encouraged the emergence of what Kenneth Miller has described as an "initiative bar," that is, "lawyers who specialize in legal challenges to initiatives."[44]

In this environment, the election itself becomes almost an interlude between the main legal dramas that occur prior to a measure's qualification and immediately following the election. Voters tune in during September and October so as to be able to make intelligent judgments in November, but the legal maneuvering that began months and often years before voters were paying attention will often continue long after they have tuned out. Although citizens take the popular vote to be the final, determinative decision, legally savvy opponents know that the election is just one of several veto points along an extended political route. In the normal way of things, those veto points are stops along a legislative trail—committees, the house and senate, and the governor's desk—but in the initiative process those legislative veto points are replaced by the multiple levels of appeal within the judicial branch. The trouble occurs when participants—litigants as well as judges—treat the judicial process as a surrogate political process.

A TALE OF JUDICIAL HUBRIS

In 1990 California voters approved an initiative that established strict term limits for state legislators and other statewide offices. State senators as well as the governor were limited to two four-year terms, and members of the assembly could serve no more than three two-year terms. Once public officials reached their term limit, they faced a lifetime ban from that office. The initiative passed by a narrow margin and was immediately challenged in state court. The California Supreme Court upheld the initiative, rejecting only the provision that would have eliminated the legislators' pension system. Not all the justices agreed with the majority, however. Justice Stanley Mosk argued that term limits would "fundamentally alter a fundamental component of the state constitutional system" by putting " 'citizens' . . . in the Legislature in the place of 'politicians.' " This change amounted to a constitutional revision, which was not permitted by means of the initiative process. This implausible interpretation—if it is so fundamental, why is it that neither the California constitution nor any other state constitution prescribes a particular level of political experience for legislators?—dressed up policy questions as constitutional judgments. The judge's insistence that "the wisdom of Proposition 140 is of no consequence to the analysis" rang hollow.[45]

The court's decision was hailed by the measure's backers and their cheers were redoubled when in the following year the U.S. Supreme Court turned down an appeal of the case. But that was only the beginning of the legal saga. In 1995 a Democratic assemblyman, who was prevented by the new term limits law from running for reelection the following year, filed a lawsuit in federal court on the grounds that the law violated his First Amendment rights to run for office. To the surprise of many, Federal District Judge Claudia Wilken agreed that term limits were unconstitutional because they limited voters' fundamental right to elect the candidate of their choice. "Ending legislative careerism," the judge pronounced, "is not a substantial or compelling State interest." Nor, the judge said, did the state have a compelling interest in ending legislative careerism, rotation in office, increasing the number of candidates running for office, or making legislators more ideologically representative of the people. Even where the state had legitimate and compelling state interests in "defining its own political institutions and . . . in reducing the unfair electoral advantages incumbents enjoy," the judge still rejected the lifetime ban because it was not narrowly tailored to these legitimate state interests. Even more clearly than Mosk's dissent, Wilken's opinion cloaked political or policy judgments in constitutional garb.[46]

Wilken's surprising judgment was immediately appealed to the United States Court of Appeals for the Ninth Circuit, where a three-judge panel invalidated the initiative by a two-to-one margin, though for reasons altogether different than those offered by Wilken. Although describing Wilken's decision as "a careful and thoughtfully reasoned opinion," the appeals court panel dodged the question of the constitutionality of lifetime term limits, deciding instead that the more basic problem with the initiative was that voters were not adequately informed that the initiative contained a lifetime ban. Because the measure, if enacted, would "severely limit" fundamental voting rights, the court was compelled, as "a matter of federal constitutional law," to "carefully scrutinize" the measure to make sure "that sufficient notice has been given that fundamental rights will be so burdened." Noting that the phrase "lifetime limits" did not appear in the text of the amendment, the proponents' ballot arguments, or the official statements prepared by the state, the court concluded that it was "likely that the number of voters who were not aware of the initiative's principal effect was sufficiently large that it could have affected the outcome of the election." In a matter as important as the right to vote, "the state simply must tell its citizens what they are voting on." Because the state had failed in this duty, the court explained, it was left with "no choice" but to invalidate the measure.[47]

The court's claim that it had "no choice" but to strike down the measure was transparently specious. Indeed, the opinion rested on the highly dubious proposition that federal judges should decide whether voters of a state understood an initiative. Judges have many virtues, but they possess no special insight into the hearts and minds of voters; if we desire to know what voters think, we should ask pollsters and not judges. If voters fail to understand an initiative, then the remedy lies with the voters, who can either vote against the measure because of its ambiguity or can seek out more information prior to casting their vote. If voters have neglected to inform themselves about the impact of an initiative (or the positions of a candidate), that is a lamentable failing of democracy, not the occasion for a judicial remedy.[48]

In the end, the court system corrected its errors. Concerned about the soundness of the panel's opinion, the justices of the ninth circuit voted for an en banc review, which entails rehearing the case before an eleven-judge panel selected at random from the appellate justices of the circuit. Although the decision was fractured by six separate opinions, the court decisively reversed the decision of the three-judge panel and the district court judge. The court argued that voters were given ample notice as to what they were voting on, and, more important, that lifetime term limits were not a severe limitation on fundamental voting rights that warranted exacting judicial scrutiny. The court agreed with the state of California that term limits were "a neutral candidacy qualification," much like age or residence. The law did not discriminate between voters or office seekers on the basis of race, ethnicity, religion, or gender, nor on the content of their political speech. The court allowed that the political wisdom of California's term limits law was certainly open to question, but the choice between policies was properly left to the people of California and their representatives. Lifetime bans might be bad policy, but a judicial regime of fabricated rights that prevents people from exercising self-governance is far worse.[49]

The reactions of disappointed legislators after the appeals court's decision neatly revealed the fundamental policy dispute that had always lurked just beneath the creative claims of constitutional rights. Tom Bates, who brought the original suit against the term limits law, confessed he was disappointed "because the effect of term limits is to shift power from the legislative branch to the executive branch, bureaucrats and lobbyists." Although Bates offers a compelling reason why voters should oppose term limits, it is no justification for courts to save voters from themselves. Term limits may be, as one Democratic legislator put it, "the dumbest thing that's ever happened," but in a democracy, unfortunately, the people sometimes do dumb things.[50]

A JUDICIAL CATCH-22

The framers of the U.S. political system were well aware that people in a democracy will often act in ways that are, if not dumb, at least unwise. People will sometimes vote for candidates or policies that serve their short-term interests or fleeting passions at the expense of their longer-term needs or more considered reflections. A democratic people may make decisions they later regret either because at the time they lacked vital information, or because they were angry or fearful, or because they allowed hope to get the better of their reason. Those democrats who deny that the people can act unwisely are dangerous demagogues. They blame external forces—intellectuals, government, foreigners, judges, bureaucrats, politicians—anybody but the people. The founding fathers were democrats who understood the danger of demagogues.

Deliberation protects democracy from the demagogue. The political institutions the framers designed were intended to cool inflamed passions and to delay the ill-considered plan. Democratic institutions such as representation, bicameralism, and the executive veto would help to force the decision taken in anger or haste to be justified and reconsidered after the rage had dulled or the enthusiasm subsided. A legislative system in which power was divided between two houses, each with different terms of office and different constituencies, was not only a vehicle for expressing majority preferences but also an instrument for distinguishing transient moods from settled convictions. By promoting deliberation, democratic political institutions could balance majority preferences and minority rights, democratic rule and individual liberties. Courts were an important part of the founding institutional structures designed to check the ill-tempered or myopic majority, but they were only one part among many, and by far the least democratic part at that. Indeed, it was precisely because courts were so blatantly antidemocratic that so many framers were reluctant to rely heavily on the judiciary to safeguard the new democracy.

In bypassing the representative institutions that the framers relied upon to safeguard democracy, direct democracy has ironically contributed to our increasing reliance on the least accountable branch of government. Judges more and more find themselves in the glare of the populist spotlight, asked to serve as the main check against the populist will. A burden that was shared among the branches of government is now handed over largely to judges. Although courts are well equipped to protect constitutional rights, they are not well suited to the more subtle screening and filtering of popular interests and passions that take place in the normal legislative process. Judges are placed in an unenviable position: they can either fill the legislative role that has not been performed, thereby becoming liable to well-earned accusations of judicial activism and overreaching, or they can stick to a more limited, constitutional role and allow poorly written, ill-conceived, misleading initiatives to crowd the ballot, statute books, and state constitutions. For the courts and for our democracy, the predicament is a Catch-22 situation in which nobody wins.

7
The Myth of a Golden Age

Even the most severe critics of the initiative process often look nostalgically back to a golden age of the initiative at the turn of the century, when direct democracy was uncorrupted by special interests, big money, paid signature gatherers, misleading ballot titles, and thirty-second television ads. In the old days, the story goes, legislatures were hopelessly corrupt, dedicated only to the interests of large corporations and the whims of political party bosses. The initiative and referendum were the tools of the people, enabling them to clean out the political stables. Through the initiative the people obtained the right to elect their senators directly and to participate in primary elections, women achieved the right to vote, and corporations were made to serve the people.

Although this mythic narrative is not without some basis in fact, the real history of the initiative process is far more complex and much less romantic. To begin with, this mythic portrayal exaggerates the corruption of state legislatures. If early-twentieth-century legislatures were as nefarious and unresponsive as is sometimes asserted, then how, one wonders, did voters ever obtain the initiative and referendum in the first place? Although a number of states (Arizona, Massachusetts, Michigan, Ohio, and Oklahoma) achieved the initiative and referendum through constitutional convention, the great majority of states obtained direct legislation in the early twentieth century by the legislature referring the matter to a vote of the people. In Oregon two successive legislatures (in 1899 and 1901) approved the initiative and referendum before the measure was enacted into law by a vote of the people in 1902. In many states the percentage of the legislature voting in favor of the initiative was higher than the percentage of the public who approved the measure. In 1901 only one Oregon legislator voted against the initiative and referendum. Similarly, in California in 1911 only one legislator voted to oppose referring the initiative and referendum to the people. Of course, in Oregon and California, as elsewhere, there were many legislators who would have loved to smother the initiative in its infancy, but their unwillingness to act on these impulses is itself evidence that turn-of-the-century legislatures were not impervious to public opinion or popular pressure.

THE INITIATIVE'S FIRST DECADE IN OREGON

The first initiatives in the United States were placed on the ballot in Oregon in 1904. Voters there were asked to decide two initiatives: the first would establish a direct primary and direct election of U.S. senators; the second was a local liquor option law. The direct primary initiative fits the mythic narrative quite closely. During the 1903 session the legislature had bottled up several bills to establish a statewide direct primary, and when voters received the opportunity to vote on the issue, they overwhelmingly approved the ballot measure. Legislative opposition to the direct primary, however, is not evidence of corruption; rather, it reflected a principled and wholly justified fear on the part of legislators that the direct primary would cripple political parties, which legislators believed to be essential to a healthy democracy. On this issue, though, the Oregon legislature was out of step with voters.[1]

The other measure on the ballot, however, reveals a different and often forgotten face of the early initiative process. The Oregon state legislature, buffeted by rival interests and passions, had consistently resisted Prohibition legislation. Antiliquor activists thus turned to the initiative process, cleverly cloaking Prohibition in home rule. Under the initiative, each locality would be free to decide for itself whether to become "dry" or "wet." Although the initiative passed, the narrow margin of victory indicated that the legislature's inaction reflected not perversity but the divided state of public opinion. Of those who showed up at the polls, only 44 percent voted in favor of the initiative, while 40 percent opposed it and 16 percent had no preference. Moreover, many of those who supported the initiative did so in the belief that local option meant that residential neighborhoods would go dry, not that entire counties would, as happened in 1905 when Prohibition carried in six of the twenty-three counties that voted on the subject. The public policy reached by initiative was certainly different from that enacted by the legislative process, but it is difficult to argue either that the legislature was out of step with public opinion or that the policy enacted through the initiative was superior to the legislature's inaction.[2]

Moreover, far from damming the rivers of reform, the Oregon legislature had enacted a series of ameliorative measures during the preceding 1903 legislative session. Over the heated objection of the railroads, for instance, the legislature unanimously enacted a law which established that railroad companies were liable for any worker injuries that might occur through the neglect or malice of a fellow worker. In addition, the legislature acceded to the demands of the State Federation of Labor in passing bills that set up a Bureau of Labor as well as a Commissioner of Labor, limited hours of female laborers to ten working hours a day, and banned employment of children under fourteen. Other legislation passed in the 1903 session protected union employees and prevented employers from blacklisting workers. Most of these pro-labor bills passed by lopsided margins and with little dissent. The legislature also passed an inheritance tax, which only one legislator voted against, and established a state Board of Health. William U'Ren, direct democracy's founding father in Oregon, claimed that the legislature acted on these measures only because of the threat of the initiative; it was the "gun behind the door." Perhaps so, but in the following legislative session the gun must have been firing blanks because the legislature stalled on a range of issues important to reformers.[3]

The Oregon initiative's proudest moment came in 1906, the year in which the golden age thesis is strongest. Of the ten initiatives on the ballot that year, seven passed and none of these received less than 72 percent of the vote. Two initiatives that levied taxes on transportation and communication corporations received over 90 percent of the vote. When the same ideas had been introduced in the 1905 session of the legislature, they had been soundly defeated after a vigorous lobbying effort by the affected corporations. The new system worked well but far from perfectly. The People's Power League was responsible for half of the ten measures. One of them, which prohibited railroads from distributing free railroad passes to elected officials, had been drafted by U'Ren in such haste that he had inadvertently left out an enacting clause. As a result, the measure never took effect.[4] Another trouble sign was that the number of voters who went to the polls but did not vote on a particular initiative ranged from about one in five to almost one in three in the case of a measure extending initiatives to the local level. Expanding the scope of the initiative and referendum excited reformers but evidently did not interest a large chunk of the electorate, particularly less educated and lower-income voters.

The dark side of the initiative is also glimpsed in a measure entitled "A Law to Abolish Tolls on the Mt. Hood and Barlow Road and Providing for Its Ownership by the State," which, unlike the other nine initiatives on the ballot, had never been brought before the legislature. Few toll roads remained in Oregon, and so the initiative perhaps seemed reasonable enough on its face. It turned out, though, that the measure was sponsored by the owners of the road, who, if the measure passed, were to be paid twenty-four thousand dollars to unload the road and its upkeep on the state of Oregon. It was, as one observer noted, "the first trick bill tried on the Oregon electorate"—it would not be the last. Fortunately for the voters, the scam was exposed by the newspapers and the measure went down to defeat.[5]

The initiative may have been (relatively) golden in 1906, but there was no enduring golden age. In 1908 only one of the eleven initiatives matched the lowest winning percentage in 1906, and that was an amendment instructing legislators to vote for the popular choice for U.S. senator; the legislators had done so in 1906, when they selected Republican Jonathan Bourne as senator, but there was understandable concern that the overwhelmingly Republican legislature might be less inclined to follow the popular will if the people's choice turned out to be a Democrat or an Independent. On this issue the initiative was an invaluable tool in helping to ensure that the legislature follow the public's wishes. The public also strongly backed the recall and, to a lesser extent, the Corrupt Practices Act, both of which the legislature had opposed.

Although the initiative process proved important in securing the electorate's ability to control governing institutions—through the direct primary, direct election of senators, the Corrupt Practices Act, and the recall—it played a relatively minor role in securing the Progressive policy agenda. The Oregon legislature continued to resist proposals that were perceived as gutting the power of the political parties (as with the direct primary and direct election of senators) or undermining representative democracy (as in the case of the recall), but the legislature proved reasonably responsive to popular concerns about substantive issues like working conditions and unchecked corporate power. The centerpiece of the 1907 legislative session, for instance, was a proposal to create a statewide railroad commission. Over the heated objections of the railroads and their lobbyists, both the house (unanimously) and the senate (with one dissent) passed the legislation. The legislature also provided for state regulation of banking, enacted a pure food law, limited working hours of state and county employees, further regulated employment of women, regulated work underground, and tightened regulation of insurance companies. Not only in Oregon but in other states as well the representative process was generally effective in securing the right to safe working conditions, reasonable hours, child labor laws, workmen's compensation, and a host of other related Progressive causes.[6]

Where the early initiative was used to achieve substantive policy objectives, the results were often less than edifying. In 1908, for instance, voters were faced with two rival initiatives regulating salmon fishing on the Columbia River. The first, which effectively banned the use of gill nets by downriver fishermen, was placed on the ballot by upriver fishermen who relied on fish wheels for their catch. Not to be outdone, the gill net fishermen responded with an initiative of their own, one which would ban the use of fish wheels on the upper river. The proponents of both initiatives cloaked their motives in the altruistic mantle of protecting the salmon, lamely trying to disguise their true aim, which was to drive their rivals out of business and increase their harvest of fish and thus their profits. The voters ended up passing both measures, thereby bringing salmon fishing on the Columbia to an almost complete halt, which was neither the intention of the initiative sponsors nor, in all likelihood, the desire of a majority of voters. The trouble was not with the voters, who acted reasonably enough, but with the initiatives themselves, which had structured the voters' choices in such a manner that there was no opportunity for intelligent action or sensible compromise.[7]

As early as 1906, even supporters of the initiative in Oregon began to express alarm at the overuse and abuse of the instrument. George H. Williams, former president of the Direct Legislation League, admitted that "the people would suffer no injury if they were to vote down the whole batch of the proposed amendments." Direct legislation, Williams believed, should be resorted to only in rare circumstances when no other alternatives were available. Another former backer of direct legislation, A. L. Mills, who had been president of the Direct Primary Nominations League, also protested that voters were passing too many laws with too little consideration. Other Oregonians complained about U'Ren's leading role. "There is too much of the 'one man initiative,'" the *Oregon Statesman* objected. The 1908 election further fueled the growing resentment against the overuse of the initiative.[8]

Despite these problems and criticisms, initiative supporters who surveyed the first three election cycles could make a reasonable case that even if the initiative had not been a panacea, it had brought to Oregon a number of important governmental reforms that had been resisted by the legislature and were supported by a large majority of the public. Between 1904 and 1908 all but three of the seventeen successful initiatives passed with more than 60 percent of the vote, suggesting that the legislature was ignoring issues with widespread public support. After 1908, however, this case for the initiative collapses. In the next three general elections (1910, 1912, 1914) Oregonians were asked to vote on seventy-two initiatives (and one hundred measures overall, counting legislative referrals and popular referenda). Of these seventy-two initiatives only eighteen passed. Only four garnered better than 60 percent of the votes: two in 1912 relating to the employment of prisoners; one in 1910 permitting counties to vote bonds for permanent road improvement; and the fourth establishing a workmen's compensation bill. Only the last of these measures, which had been killed by business interests in the 1909 session (with an assist from the AFL), fits the mythic picture of the initiative process. But even in this one case it is important to remember how much the legislature had already done to help improve working conditions during the previous few sessions. In addition, the initiative at best meant the bill was enacted a year or two earlier than it otherwise would have been, since in 1911 Progressive forces for the first time captured control of both houses of the legislature. In 1913, in fact, the legislature showed its strong commitment to labor by passing a comprehensive workmen's compensation law and a minimum wage law, and by providing the enabling clause that had been left out of a 1912 initiative, which established an eight-hour workday for public employees. In addition, the legislature passed a sweeping law that limited all employees to a ten-hour workday and sixty-hour work week, allowing overtime only if paid at time and a half.[9]

Had the initiative been functioning as a safety valve for a recalcitrant legislature damming up the popular will, one might have expected a dramatic drop in the use of the initiative immediately after the Progressives gained control of both houses of the legislature in 1911 and then cemented that control in 1913. In fact, initiatives continued to flood the state, with a record twenty-eight in 1912 and another nineteen in 1914. This tidal wave of initiatives inundated voters with many issues that they had not even the remotest interest in deciding. Eight of the initiatives in 1912, for instance, involved readjusting boundary lines between counties, all of which were overwhelmingly rejected by the voters, who were understandably perplexed that they were being asked to adjudicate such matters. In many cases, moreover, voters were being asked to decide issues that they had already rejected in previous elections; by one estimate, as many as a dozen of the measures on the ballot in 1914 had previously been before the voters in one form or another. Frustrated voters found themselves, like the sorcerer's apprentice, awash in initiatives and unable to halt the black magic that kept bringing them more. Only when they discovered the magic word "no" did the threatening floodwaters begin to subside. In 1914 the electorate emphatically said "no" to all but two of the nineteen initiatives on the ballot; the average margin of defeat was more than two to one. It would be more than seventy years before Oregonians would again be faced with more than eight initiatives on a ballot.[10]

Few Oregonians in the early 1910s thought that they lived in a golden age of the initiative. On the contrary, a chorus of criticism rained down on the initiative from all directions during this period, most but not all of it focused on the initiative's overuse. "It is generally admitted," observed the Eugene *Register* in 1912, "that the initiative and referendum are being abused." Even members of U'Ren's People's Power League had become concerned enough that they drafted an initiative in 1910 that included a provision allowing no more than twelve direct legislation measures to appear at any election. The Grange had been among the earliest and most vocal supporters of the campaign to bring the initiative to Oregon, but a spokesman for the organization now reflected that it was "far better that even needed reforms be a little delayed than that many untried and not well understood measures be submitted at any one time under the Initiative."[11]

By 1910 U'Ren's People's Power League had begun to wear out its welcome with the people. Ten of the twenty-three initiatives Oregonians voted on between 1904 and 1908 had been drafted by U'Ren, and not one of these had come close to being defeated by the voters. In 1910, though, voters turned down three of the four measures placed on the ballot by U'Ren, and the one measure that passed, creating a presidential primary, squeaked by with only 51 percent of the vote. Among the defeated U'Ren initiatives was a sweeping measure that, among other things, would have allowed voters to recall the entire legislature, made it much more difficult for the legislature to use an emergency clause to avoid a popular referendum, and established proportional representation as well as annual sessions for the state legislature. Particularly paradoxical, given the league's purported desire to ensure legislative responsiveness to the people, was the plan to increase the term of all legislators to six years. None of these aspects of the plan were as unpopular, though, as the measure's proposal to triple the pay of state legislators.[12]

Defeat did not deter U'Ren from trying again, in 1912, with another measure no less ambitious. Suffering from the same hubris that often afflicts self-anointed spokesmen of the people, U'Ren tried to rewrite the entire Article 4 of the Oregon constitution. He again proposed proportional representation and annual sessions for the state legislature. "The lawgiver," as U'Ren's admirers styled him, also proposed abolishing the state senate and creating a unicameral legislature in which members' terms would be four years, making the governor and defeated gubernatorial candidates ex-officio members of the legislature, and permitting only the governor to introduce appropriation bills, except those the legislature referred to the voters. Just how out of touch U'Ren was with the people he claimed to empower was clear on election day, when the people of Oregon buried the initiative by better than a two-to-one margin. In 1914 the voters rendered an even clearer judgment, handing U'Ren an ignominious fourth-place finish in his run for the governorship. With only 4 percent of the vote, U'Ren fared even worse than the Socialist candidate.[13]

In 1914 U'Ren championed the single tax. He had shelved his passion for the single tax while he worked to bring the initiative to Oregon, but he never forgot his first love. Indeed, for U'Ren the point of having the initiative was, in part, to enact the single tax since legislators, who were in the deep pockets of the propertied elite, would never enact this populist policy. But it turned out that the people themselves were the biggest obstacle to U'Ren's dream of a single tax, for they defeated it in 1908, 1912, 1914, 1916, 1920, and 1922. In none of these elections did the single tax come close to passing. Its best showing was in 1908, when it went down two to one; its worst in 1920, when it lost five to one; and its average defeat was by a margin of four to one.[14] So why did an issue with so little popular appeal keep coming back? Clearly it had nothing to do with the intransigence of legislatures. The most charitable explanation is that the supporters of the single tax were idealistic men who wanted to keep the issue before the people in hopes that they might someday see the light; a more cynical explanation might focus on the egos or self-interest of leaders, who needed the issue far more than the people needed them. Either way, the sorry saga of the single tax is a far cry from the mythic narrative of the initiative's golden age.

Even less uplifting is the story of the one initiative related to the single tax that did pass. Having witnessed the thrashing of even a modified single tax in 1908, in 1910 the Oregon Single Tax League decided to try a little trickery. "No poll or head tax," the initiative began, "shall be levied or collected in Oregon." The actual effect of this provision would be minimal since the dollar poll tax had already been abolished and the three-dollar county road poll tax, while still on the books, was not enforced in much of the state. Still, abolishing any poll taxes that did exist was a good idea and was sure to draw votes to the initiative, as indeed it did. The second clause of the initiative, another provision bound to appeal to voters, asserted that "no bill regulating taxation or exemption throughout the state shall become a law until approved by the people of the state at a regular general election." Only if voters continued to the end of the proposed amendment would they discover the true purpose of the initiative, which was to allow individual counties to adopt a single tax and prevent the state legislature from altering these local decisions. It was essentially "a local option law for single taxers," although nowhere did the initiative mention the single tax. By having the State Federation of Labor file the measure, the Oregon Single Tax League further obscured its role in authoring the measure. Through these Trojan horse tactics the single taxers achieved (with barely 51 percent of the vote) their aim of paving the road to a single tax, even though only a relatively small fraction of Oregonians showed any interest in the destination favored by single taxers.[15]

In the absence of a single-subject rule, a provision that was only added to the Oregon constitution in 1968, there was nothing to stop initiative sponsors from trying to sugarcoat a bitter pill. Defenders of the initiative howled at the evils of legislative logrolling and vote trading but saw nothing wrong with combining completely different subjects in the same initiative. Abolishing poll taxes was unrelated to the cause of the single tax, just as creating proportional representation was an entirely different question from raising legislative salaries. When such radically different subjects showed up in the same measure, there was no way to know what the voters meant to say when they passed (or rejected) an initiative.

The less regulated environment of the early twentieth century often meant that fraud and corruption were widespread, at least in terms of the circulation of petitions. The most infamous case was a popular referendum in 1912 that aimed to nullify an appropriation the legislature had made for the University of Oregon. The circuit court that heard the case concluded that over 60 percent of the thirteen thousand signatures gathered for the referendum were fraudulent. Even the defendants themselves conceded that about 30 percent of the signatures had either been forged or fabricated. It is difficult to determine how typical or pervasive such corruption was because under a 1907 law—which had been passed at the urging of county clerks, who objected to the workload of checking signatures against registration records—petitions were verified by the signed affidavit of the circulators. Whatever signature gatherers were willing to swear, the state, absent a legal challenge, was bound to believe. Ironically, the Corrupt Practices Act, which had been passed by initiative in 1908, applied only to candidates for elective office, thus doing nothing to stem corruption or even the role of money in the initiative and referendum process. The result, worried the Eugene *Register* in 1913, was that "fraud and forgery [are] becoming an annual scandal . . . that threatens to bring popular government into disfavor."[16]

In the initiative's infancy there was no requirement that an initiative campaign reveal to the public how much money it had received and from what sources. Until 1913 the secretary of state was not even required to record who had filed the petition for an initiative. As a result, often nobody knew which interests were sponsoring, let alone bankrolling, an initiative. For instance, a 1915 study of the Oregon initiative and referendum found that the authors of four of the five referenda on the ballot in a special election in 1913 were "generally unknown or uncertain," as were the identities of the authors of the three referenda in 1912. The liquor industry feverishly tried to conceal its sponsorship of a 1908 "open-town" measure that would have modified the 1904 local option law by giving cities exclusive control over the regulation of saloons, pool halls, and theaters. The problem of concealing initiative sponsors was widespread enough to prompt the *Oregonian* to editorialize: "This evil should not be tolerated by the people of this state. The voters have a right to know the persons who are boosting every bill that appears on the ballots. The only reason for concealment makes this public knowledge necessary, for in each case some designing group of persons is trying to hoodwink the public by covering up the real purpose of the measure."[17]

It was a sobering moment when Oregonians realized that the initiative and referendum were being used by many of the same special interests that the process had been designed to thwart. Contrary to the mythic narrative, however, the initiative's loss of innocence occurred not in its later, mature years but in its very infancy. Even in those early years, as the Eugene *Register* noted at the time, the initiative and referendum "gives the interests that can command money a practical monopoly of the business of petition making." Getting an initiative on the ballot had less to do with "the existence of a general demand for the legislation that is contemplated" than it did with whether an individual or interest had "money enough at hand to pay for the circulation of the petitions." And nobody, as the *Oregonian* pointed out, could raise this money more easily than powerful special interests. "The corporation, the 'vested interest' or 'big business,' when it takes a hand in law-making, dips into a well-filled cash box and never misses the money."[18]

Nor was the early initiative process any stranger to the large out-of-state contributions that so many decry today. Far from being a late, oligarchic perversion of an originally uncorrupted, democratic system, the practice of out-of-state individuals and interests bankrolling initiatives was tightly woven into the original fabric of the Oregon initiative process. In 1910 and again in 1912, for instance, the single tax initiatives on the Oregon ballot were financed by Joseph Fels, a multimillionaire Philadelphia soap manufacturer. In 1912 Fels provided a forty-thousand-dollar war chest (today equivalent to about two-thirds of a million dollars) to get the measure on the ballot and publicize it throughout the state. Apart from Fels, the single tax campaign received only seventy-six dollars in contributions. The *Oregonian* felt the problem was serious enough to warrant immediate reform: "There is a need of a law which will prevent foreign organizations and residents of other states from employing attorneys or lawgivers to draft initiative measures, paying the stipends of petition hawkers, hiring press agents, spending vast sums for literature in behalf of their own and against other specific measures." The concern over the role of "foreign" money also manifested itself in the 1913 legislative session, where there was a concerted if failed effort to forbid individuals outside the state from contributing to either side of an initiative campaign.[19]

In at least one important respect the early days of the initiative were closer to a dark age than a golden age. During the past several decades (as noted in chapter 5) voter drop-off in Oregon initiative elections has averaged a mere 5 percent and has never been higher than 12 percent. In the early twentieth century, the number of voters who failed to vote on initiatives was far higher. On the typical initiative, approximately 20 to 25 percent of voters would fail to indicate a preference. In the first three decades of initiative use in Oregon, there were only two occasions—the vote on prohibition in 1914 and the Ku Klux Klan–sponsored compulsory education initiative in 1922—in which drop-off went below one in ten voters. On many occasions drop-off on initiatives reached three in ten, and sometimes it reached four in ten voters. On a few occasions, like the vote to create Hood River county in 1908, the percentage of voters not voting on a measure was higher than either the yes or no vote. The high rate of drop-off, together with the declining margins of initiative victories, meant that between 1916 and 1930 no initiative received a majority of the votes of those who showed up at the polls, even though eleven initiatives passed and became law. These high rates of drop-off, particularly on initiatives that passed by relatively small margins, raise serious questions about how well these initiatives reflected public opinion.

In sum, there was no golden age in Oregon, or if it did exist the moment was fleeting. Within only a few elections the initiative and referendum system was showing most of the same problems that plague the system today. Before the initiative process was a decade old, the most common defense of the initiative seemed to focus less on the positive good it could accomplish than on the damage it had not done. By and large it was true that voters did reasonably well under the onslaught, avoiding most of the traps and land mines laid for them. They did this primarily by quickly developing a healthy skepticism of initiatives and a strong predisposition to vote no. Between 1914 and 1940, Oregon voters approved only 22 percent of the seventy-nine initiatives put before them. If there is anything about this early period that citizens might try to recapture or rekindle, it is, first and foremost, Oregonians' robust skepticism about the initiative process and their plain talk about the limitations of government by initiative.

TAKING THE INITIATIVE IN THE GOLDEN STATE

Oregon's experience with the initiative was highly atypical in one important respect, for the initiative process in Oregon became established as an important statewide political instrument prior to the high tide of Progressivism that swept the nation between about 1910 and 1914. By the end of 1910 Oregonians had already voted on forty-eight statewide initiatives and passed twenty-five. In the rest of the country, in contrast, there had been a total of nine initiatives in three states (six of which were in Oklahoma), and only two of those had been successful. It was not until the elections of 1912 and 1914 that the initiative became an important national phenomenon. California was typical. It adopted the initiative in 1911, becoming the twelfth state in the union to do so. In 1912 California voters faced only three initiatives, but in November 1914 they voted on seventeen, a state record for a single election that still stands today.

Was the initiative in the old days any more golden in the Golden State? There are good reasons one might expect this to be so. After all, the California legislature was famously corrupt, a captive in the iron grip of the monopolistic Southern Pacific Railroad. The company's long tentacles of control were memorialized in Frank Norris' novel *The Octopus* (1901): "They own us . . . they own our homes; they own our legislatures. . . . We are told we can defeat them at the ballot box. They own the ballot box. We are told we must look to the courts for redress; they own our courts."[20] California, then, would seem to be an ideal stage for the mythic tale of the initiative: in one corner immensely powerful special interests and a corrupt, recalcitrant legislature; in the other the People, armed only with righteousness and the initiative. Uplifting the tale might be, but the truth is that the statewide initiative played no role in slaying the monster railroad or in ridding the state of legislative corruption. Instead, the Progressive reformation happened the old-fashioned way: through electing representatives who did the people's bidding.

The transformative event in California politics was the 1910 election, in which Progressives not only won control of both houses of the state legislature but also the governorship. Under the leadership of newly elected governor Hiram Johnson, the California legislature approved in a single session twenty-three constitutional amendments, which, as the state constitution required, were then referred to voters in a special election in 1911. Among the constitutional amendments passed by the legislature were those amendments that established the initiative, referendum, and recall as well as women's suffrage, stiffened regulation of railroads and public utilities, reorganized and strengthened the state railroad commission, strengthened employers' liability law, and mandated government inspection of merchandise and food quality. All but one of the twenty-three legislative referrals were approved by the people, and most by very large popular majorities. Almost at a single stroke the legislature had reshaped the contours of California politics without any assistance from the statewide initiative.[21]

By the time California voters were given the statewide initiative and referendum, most of the hard work of refashioning a more responsive government had already been accomplished. A direct primary bill had been passed by the legislature in 1909, an achievement that had been instrumental in paving the way for the sweeping victory of Progressive candidates in 1910. During the 1911 session, legislators amended the direct primary law to allow voters also to state their preference for U.S. senator. In addition, legislators established a presidential primary election and removed the party designation from the ballot. Parties were further weakened by the legislature's decision in 1911 to make all elections for nonpolitical offices nonpartisan. The legislature went one step further in 1913 by making all county and township elections nonpartisan, thereby leaving only the governor, state legislators, and a handful of state officials to be selected on a partisan basis. That same year the legislature also passed a law permitting cross-filing, which allowed candidates to enter a primary in either or even both political parties. The crippling of party organization that occurred in Oregon by initiative was executed in California through the normal legislative channels.[22]

Nor was California particularly unusual in this respect. Other than Oregon, only four states enacted a direct primary law by means of the initiative: Maine in 1911, Montana and South Dakota in 1912, and Arkansas in 1916. Similarly, the statewide recall, which was enacted in eleven states between 1908 and 1926, arrived by initiative in only two states: Oregon in 1908 and Colorado in 1912. In three cases the recall was actually enacted in states (Wisconsin, Kansas, and Louisiana) that possessed neither the initiative nor referendum, although in Louisiana the recall came courtesy of a constitutional convention rather than the legislature.[23] Oregon's use of the initiative to assert the right of the people to vote for their U.S. senator was emulated only in Montana and Oklahoma, in 1912 in both cases. Montana was also the only state other than Oregon to use the initiative to allow voters to express a preference for their presidential nominee directly. In the other states that enacted these Progressive reforms they largely came, as they did in California, through the legislature.

The 1911 California legislature did not limit itself to reforming the political process. It also reshaped labor law, enacting no fewer than thirty-nine bills that had been backed by labor groups to improve the working conditions of California's labor force. Among these were a workmen's compensation act, an eight-hour law for women, restrictions on child labor, an act requiring employers not to withhold wages for more than fifteen days, and the creation of an Industrial Accident Board. The legislature also beat back an antiunion bill that would have restricted the ability of workers in utilities and other public service corporations to strike.[24] Some labor advocates wanted still more and took their cause to the people through the initiative route, placing a measure on the ballot that would have established an eight-hour day and forty-eight-hour week for all workers and another that called for "one day of rest in seven." Both initiatives were overwhelmingly defeated by the voters, and no other initiatives to improve workers' lives were placed on the ballot during this period. Nor was there any initiative dealing with the Southern Pacific Railroad or any other corporate power. Having granted the railroad commission broad new powers to establish rates and standards of safety, the legislature had evidently done enough to satisfy most citizens.

The statewide initiative, in short, played little role in advancing the Progressive agenda in California. Of the thirty initiatives on the ballot in California between 1912 and 1919, only eight (27 percent) were enacted into law, and three of these—a constitutional amendment abolishing the poll tax, a usury law, and an amendment facilitating the consolidation of city and county government—passed by only the slimmest of margins, suggesting that the legislature's failure to act in these areas did not represent a failure to heed the people's voice. Of the remaining five initiatives, four were relatively inconsequential. One was rendered immediately irrelevant since it only would have taken effect if Prohibition had passed, which it did not; another, which banned boxing matches in California, was repealed by initiative a decade later; a third was a relatively noncontroversial bond issue for the University of California; and the fourth was an ineffectual measure relating to the arcane law of land titles.

Only one of the eight successful initiatives in the 1910s fits comfortably into the mythic narrative of the initiative past, and even here the story has an ironic twist. Passed in 1916, this initiative prohibited any legislator from "holding any office, trust, or employment" from the state while he served in the legislature. Progressives had long been critical of the Southern Pacific Railroad's political machine, specifically its practice of rewarding legislative supporters with state jobs. But now that Progressives controlled the levers of government, their ardor for abolishing lucrative state patronage had diminished. Suddenly it was the turn of the former "ins" to complain about legislative corruption. Ironically, it was the former machine elements who were the primary sponsors and proponents of this "good government" initiative.[25]

If Californians generally did not use the initiative to reform the governmental process, regulate the railroads, or improve working conditions, what *did* they use the initiative for in its early days? The issue that dominated the early statewide initiative process in California was Prohibition. In the three elections between 1914 and 1918, Californians voted seven times on initiatives relating to the consumption and prohibition of alcohol. And in each of these three elections voter interest and turnout was highest on the measures relating to Prohibition. In this respect California was wholly typical. In virtually every state, one of the first issues to be placed on the ballot was Prohibition; in fact, in every state that enacted the initiative between 1904 and 1916 an alcohol-related initiative was on the ballot by the second election. Yet, oddly, Prohibition is usually left out of the mythic narrative of the initiative. This is particularly ironic because Prohibition is in many ways an issue for which the initiative is well suited. The question of Prohibition is not a complex or technical one; it is an issue about which most people have personal experience and even expertise. Voter drop-off on Prohibition initiatives was negligible. In fact, sometimes more people voted on Prohibition than on the gubernatorial contest. Moreover, the initiative process allowed voters to settle an emotionally volatile dispute in a way that an action of a state legislature, no matter what its decision, could not. Those who are interested in looking backward to find the initiative's potential uses would do well to look more closely at Prohibition, even if it means dimming the initiative's heroic luster.

THE CASE OF WOMEN'S SUFFRAGE

One of the most frequently claimed success stories of the early initiative process was woman suffrage. Scholars as well as activists have often uncritically repeated this tale. According to Thomas Cronin, "citizen-initiative politics brought us women's suffrage." John Dinan agrees that "the initiative served . . . as the vehicle for extending the suffrage to women." Woman suffrage, echoes Lynn Baker, was one of a number of "initiative-forced reforms."[26] The truth of the matter, however, is that the initiative was less hospitable to the suffrage movement than were state legislatures. Only two states, Oregon and Arizona, granted women the right to vote using the initiative process. And a closer look reveals that only in Arizona can it be said that the initiative rushed in where the legislature feared to tread.[27]

In Oregon the initiative was as much if not more of a hindrance than a facilitator of woman suffrage. To be sure, Oregon voters narrowly approved an initiative in 1912 granting women the right to vote. But what is less often remembered is that Oregon voters defeated similar initiatives in 1906, 1908, and 1910 by increasingly large margins. A more important omission is that more than a decade earlier the Oregon legislature had twice (in 1895 and 1899) passed a bill calling for a constitutional amendment giving women the right to vote. In the 1899 session only six of the seventy-eight legislative votes were cast against the amendment. So why did Oregonians have to wait until 1912 for women to have the right to vote? The answer is that the Oregon constitution required a constitutional amendment to pass not only in two successive legislative sessions (the 1897 session had failed to organize itself, so the 1895 and 1899 sessions counted as consecutive sessions) but also to be approved by a vote of the people. And when the amendment was referred to the people in 1900, the people voted it down despite the fact that only one newspaper and precious few politicians in the entire state opposed it. By the time Oregonians got around to approving woman suffrage in 1912, its neighbors immediately to the north (Washington in 1910), south (California in 1911), and east (Idaho in 1896 and Wyoming in 1890) had already done the deed through the legislature.[28]

Four other states (Oklahoma in 1910 and Ohio, Missouri, and Nebraska in 1914) tried and failed to achieve woman suffrage by initiative. Ohio is a particularly instructive case. In 1912 a constitutional convention was convened and proposed a woman suffrage amendment, but a decisive majority of 58 percent of voters rejected the amendment. After more than 60 percent of voters rejected a suffrage initiative in 1914, the suffragists turned their attention back to the legislature. In 1917 they managed to secure passage of a bill that gave women the right to vote in presidential elections, and the bill was duly signed by the governor. Opponents of woman suffrage, particularly saloon keepers and bartenders, worried that giving women the right to vote would mean more votes for Prohibition, and immediately set to work gathering signatures to launch a popular referendum that would repeal the act. Despite widespread evidence of signature-gathering fraud, 58 percent of Ohio voters voted to nullify the legislature's handiwork. The new tools of direct democracy were thus used in Ohio to undo women's right to vote after it had already been achieved through the regular legislative process.[29]

Throughout the country, legislators, with their sensitive political antennae attuned to potential new voters, were almost invariably more willing to accede to woman suffrage than was the electorate. In each of the eleven states that enacted full woman suffrage by legislative referral (Colorado in 1893, Idaho in 1896, Washington in 1910, California in 1911, Kansas in 1912, Montana and Nevada in 1914, New York in 1917, and Michigan, Oklahoma, and South Dakota in 1918), the legislative majority was greater than the popular majority. In California, for instance, the woman suffrage amendment, which had been passed by well over 80 percent in both houses of the legislature, barely squeaked by in the 1911 election with less than 51 percent of the vote. The narrow margin of victory is particularly striking since all five political parties that had run candidates in the 1910 elections endorsed the woman suffrage amendment. The 1911 vote made California the sixth state to enact woman suffrage, but had constitutional amendments not required popular approval, woman suffrage would have come to the Golden State a decade and a half earlier. In 1895 the requisite two-thirds of both houses had passed a woman suffrage amendment, only to see it decisively defeated in 1896 when the amendment was referred to the people.[30]

The story was much the same in Washington, which in 1910 had become the fifth state to enact woman suffrage. But for the electorate, however, Washington would have had woman suffrage a decade or two earlier. An 1889 constitutional convention submitted a woman suffrage amendment to the voters, only to have it beaten by a two-to-one margin. In 1897 80 percent of the state house members and two thirds of the senate voted for a woman suffrage amendment. After the governor affixed his signature to the amendment, it was submitted to the voters, who again decisively rejected the act. When Washington voters finally assented to woman suffrage in 1910, the emphatic two-to-one margin in favor of the amendment was far less than the almost four-to-one margin of victory the amendment had received in the state legislature.[31]

Had state constitutions allowed legislatures to amend the constitution without a vote of the people, woman suffrage would have advanced far more rapidly than it did. Between 1870 and 1900 ten suffrage amendments were passed by state legislatures and referred to the voters for approval. In only two cases (Colorado in 1893 and Idaho in 1896) did the voters accept the amendment. By the time the Nineteenth Amendment to the Constitution was enacted in 1920, state legislatures had referred woman suffrage amendments to voters on at least thirty-five occasions, but the voters had given their approval less than a third of the time. Had the people approved all the suffrage amendments referred to them, there would have been thirty-two states with full woman suffrage by 1920 rather than the fifteen states that had granted full woman suffrage at the time the Nineteenth Amendment was ratified.[32]

It might be objected that this calculation is misleading, for by referring a constitutional amendment to voters state legislatures were not necessarily endorsing woman suffrage. They may have been merely ducking the contentious issue and leaving it for the voters to decide. To some extent, this is true, but there is also a lot of evidence to suggest that legislatures were far more progressive on this issue than most voters. In twelve states where full woman suffrage amendments had failed to pass muster with the voters, legislatures and governors took matters into their own hands by passing laws that permitted women to vote in presidential elections, thereby bypassing the voters and enfranchising eight million women. Many legislatures also enacted laws that gave women the right to vote for state officers that the state constitution did not specifically identify as needing to be elected by men, and in a few one-party states, such as Texas and Arkansas, state legislatures gave women the right to vote in primaries. Legislatures were more supportive of woman suffrage than voters not because they were more naturally virtuous or open-minded but because they were doing what a legislature does best: respond to well-organized, intense pressure from mobilized groups.[33]

In sum, state legislatures in the late nineteenth and early twentieth centuries did not hold back a popular tide in favor of woman suffrage. Although state legislatures bottled up, rejected, and sabotaged woman suffrage, aside from Arizona these obstructionist actions appear to have accurately reflected the preferences of a majority of their voting constituents. Moreover, to the extent that legislative and popular preferences diverged, legislatures were generally far more receptive to female suffrage than the people.

HISTORY LESSONS

An accurate understanding of the initiative process today must begin with a realistic appreciation of its history. It may serve particular political agendas to draw an invidious contrast between a mythic golden age and the fallen state of politics today, but such mythmaking only obstructs an honest, searching evaluation of the strengths and weaknesses of the initiative process. Once we strip away the rhetoric, we find that direct legislation at the beginning of the twentieth century suffered from most of the same defects that it does today, including congested ballots and confused voters, deceptive titles and multiple subjects, paid signature gatherers, rich individuals bankrolling pet initiatives, and the pervasive influence of organized special interest groups. With a few exceptions (most notably voter drop-off), the problems that plagued the initiative process at the outset of the twentieth century are still with us at the beginning of the twenty-first century.

Epilogue

Calls for initiative reform are as predictable as the swallows returning to San Juan Capistrano. Crowded ballots, misleading titles, simplistic campaigns, the influence of money, poor public policy, and interminable court battles are a constant spur to the reform-minded. At least three times in the 1990s distinguished commissions studied and recommended reforms of California's initiative process.[1] Each produced a host of intelligent, well-reasoned reform proposals, none of which were adopted. Hope, however, springs eternal among reformers. Just ten days before the November 2000 election, California's speaker of the assembly, Democrat Robert Hertzberg, announced the formation of yet another commission charged with improving the state's initiative process. "Those who gave California's voters this powerful tool for reform," Hertzberg explained, "would have a hard time recognizing the initiative process we know today, where powerful interests clutter the ballot with contradictory proposals incapable of passing constitutional muster." The panel's task was "to find ways to restore public confidence in the [initiative] process."[2]

Only a few days before Hertzberg's press release, two Republican state representatives in Colorado unveiled Respect Our Constitution, an organization whose mission was to educate the state's citizenry about the uses and abuses of the initiative process. Their message, like Hertzberg's, was that a system originally designed to battle powerful interests ("timber and railroad barons" in particular) had been hijacked by well-heeled special interest groups. "Our organization," one of the representatives explained, "is going to work hard to make sure our voters understand the process and aren't going to be easily swayed by glitzy ad campaigns." To educate the voters, the group planned a series of town meetings and advertising campaigns, including one ad campaign featuring "Olivia the Ostrich" proclaiming that trying to decipher all the ballot initiatives is "for the birds." Their aim, one of the group's founders said, is not to make it more difficult to place initiatives on the ballot but rather to make citizens more cautious about signing petitions that propose changes to the Colorado constitution.[3]

In Arizona, too, talk of initiative reform was in the air, particularly after Republican governor Jane Hull suggested, in an August 2000 press conference, that "it's time we go back and look . . . at how easy it is to run initiatives. . . . We need to rethink this whole process to keep the initiative process alive and well in Arizona." Too many ballot measures confused rather than empowered voters. Hull estimated the voters' pamphlet would be the size of a phone book to accommodate the pro-and-con arguments and the descriptions of the propositions. "I doubt that very many people spend much time reading it except by their bedside as they fall asleep." Since banning paid signature gatherers had been ruled out by the courts, Hull recommended that the state consider raising the number of signatures required to qualify an initiative. Hull's sentiments were echoed that same week at the other end of the country by Maine's governor, Angus King, an Independent who complained that deceptive questions misled the state's voters. The solution, he suggested, lay in making it more difficult to qualify a proposition for the ballot, either by requiring more signatures, mandating that a specified number of signatures be collected from each county, or barring circulators from collecting signatures at polling places.[4]

In Oregon, initiative reform has been a major preoccupation of late. In the winter of 1996 the City Club of Portland issued an influential report on the initiative and referendum that recommended five constitutional amendments. Drawing upon the testimony of thirty-five witnesses, academics as well as public officials and activists, the committee proposed requiring a three-fifths supermajority for constitutional amendments, limiting the subject matter of initiated amendments to "the structure, organization, and powers of government," and creating a form of indirect initiative that would enable the legislature to offer the voters the choice of an alternative measure. These proposals were promptly endorsed by the newly formed if short-lived Oregon Initiative Committee. Composed of some of the state's most distinguished political leaders, Republicans as well as Democrats, the committee was designed to give the City Club's recommendations greater visibility and political clout. In the three legislative sessions held between 1995 and 1999, well over one hundred bills relating to initiative reform were introduced. The 2001 session witnessed more of the same.

Initiative reformers have sometimes been encouraged by public opinion surveys that reveal dissatisfaction with the operation of the initiative and support for an array of reforms. The City Club of Portland, for instance, relied on a poll of Oregonians conducted in February 1995 that found only 13 percent of respondents were "very satisfied" with the way the initiative process works. Over three-quarters agreed that "it's too easy for special interest groups to buy their way onto the ballot using paid signature gatherers," and endorsed a geographic distribution requirement for signatures as well as limits on paying people to gather signatures. Nearly seven in ten said they supported the idea of increasing the number of signatures required to qualify a constitutional amendment for the ballot, and six in ten said they would favor an increase even for statutory initiatives. Seven in ten worried that it had become so easy to amend the state constitution that "the basic rights of citizens" were at risk, and roughly the same percentage agreed that "there were so many complicated measures on the ballot last November that I don't trust the election results to reflect what the people would decide if they had time to really study each measure." Two out of three respondents rejected the view that the more measures the better, and six in ten rejected the idea that "the initiative process is fine just the way it is."[5]

A 1997 California survey showed parallel patterns of public discontent, or at least unease, with the initiative process. Six in ten voters believed that the issues on the ballot generally reflected the concerns of organized interest groups, whereas only a little more than two in ten believed propositions reflected the concerns of the average voter. Nearly seven in ten respondents felt that only some or a few initiatives were understandable to the average voter. Among the reforms that majorities claimed to support were: limiting spending on initiatives, requiring the Secretary of State to review and comment on whether a proposed initiative is clear and conforms to state law, and requiring a two-thirds popular vote to pass a proposition. These reforms were favored not just among the small minority of people who thought that statewide initiative elections were generally "a bad thing" for California but also among the very large majority who felt that the initiative was "a good thing."[6]

These polls, however, have proven to be poor predictors of voting behavior. Although 80 percent of survey respondents endorsed the idea of requiring that some minimum number of signatures be gathered in each of Oregon's five congressional districts, when the legislature referred this proposal to the electorate in 1996 voters rejected the plan. And the 78 percent of Oregonians who said they supported raising the number of signatures to place a constitutional amendment on the ballot quickly dissolved when the legislature placed a proposal to do just this on the 2000 primary ballot. In the end, only 42 percent of Oregonians voted in favor of raising the required percentage of signatures for initiative amendments from 8 to 12 percent, which was even less than the 44 percent that had approved the legislature's plan to require one-fifth of the signatures from each congressional district. Why the marked discrepancy between what people tell pollsters and what they do at the ballot box?

In part, the difference between survey response and actual vote can be understood as one instance of a larger pattern in initiative elections. Propositions generally begin with substantial support in the polls. Having given little thought to the question prior to the pollster posing it, many voters are inclined to acquiesce, deciding "it sounds good to me." Over the course of a campaign, however, as voters are exposed to arguments on the other side, much of the initial support typically erodes. The discrepancy between poll result and the vote may also be due to the fact that the survey questions did not specify precise numbers. Perhaps voters approved of the concept of raising the number of signatures but thought a 50 percent hike too extreme. Similarly, voters may have agreed in theory that gathering signatures in every congressional district was a good idea but felt the legislature went too far in requiring that one-fifth of the signatures be gathered in each of the five districts. Alternatively, voters may have just changed their minds. When questioned in February 1995, with the memory of the crowded 1994 ballot still fresh in their minds, voters may have been sympathetic to an increase in the requisite signatures, but perhaps by the time they came to vote in May 1996, more than a year later, the memory of initiative abuse had faded and, with it, voters' passion for reform.

Each of these explanations is plausible, but even considered collectively they do not resolve the puzzle of why initiative reform efforts have largely failed over the past decade despite substantial popular discontent with the operation of the initiative and referendum. The fundamental obstacle to meaningful initiative reform is that it runs into two of the most powerful strains in contemporary American political culture: libertarianism and populism. Suspicion of government and faith in the people converge in a reflexive distrust of politicians. Since it is legislators who are inevitably responsible for placing reform proposals on the ballot, opponents of initiative reform have little difficulty framing initiative reform as a struggle between the people and the politicians. And that is a fight that legislators will almost always lose.[7]

This is what happened in Nebraska in November 2000, when voters refused to approve legislative proposals to require two votes before a constitutional amendment becomes law and to bring forward by five months the deadline for submitting signatures. The rationale behind both changes was to promote greater public discussion of proposed initiatives. Legislative backers also emphasized the need to protect the constitution, which, they reminded voters, was a "sacred document." The arguments were compelling and the groups mobilized in support were imposing (e.g., the Nebraska State Education Association, Nebraska Council of School Administrators, Nebraska Association of County Officials, and the League of Nebraska Municipalities), but both measures were easily defeated. The opposition prevailed despite being outspent by a wide margin because it was able to define the election as a contest pitting the legislature against the people. As the opposition spokesman explained the result, "The voters are saying the Legislature doesn't have the right to interfere with the citizen petition process, and they're sending that message to the Legislature loud and clear."[8]

Although voters (as distinct from survey respondents) have generally shown little appetite for initiative reform, state legislatures continue, as they have always done, to amend the statutes regulating the initiative process. Most of the bills proposed never pass, of course, and most of those that do pass involve only minor changes. Yet even a partial list of statutory changes drawn from only the past four years (1997–2000) shows significant revisions in a number of states. In Montana, for instance, the legislature increased the power of the attorney general to prevent an initiative from circulating. Instead of a largely perfunctory review of the petition form, the attorney general is now empowered to determine whether a proposed initiative is legal and complies with the constitution, especially the single-subject rule. The Idaho legislature enacted a geographic distribution requirement and Utah made its more stringent. Circulation windows were made more restrictive in Idaho, Maine, and, most recently, South Dakota. Alaska, Montana, and Utah have each passed laws requiring financial disclosure reports for paid signature gatherers. In Utah the sponsor must detail the amount paid per signature, in Montana the sponsor is compelled to reveal the amount paid to each signature gatherer, and in Alaska the signature gatherer must indicate at the bottom of each petition page whether they are being paid and by whom. Alaska went still further by limiting the amount per signature a petition circulator can be paid. The Utah legislature also permitted itself to make technical corrections to initiatives submitted to the legislature.

Arguably the most important if unpredictable source of political change over the past decade has come not from the legislature or the people but from the courts. Among the most significant changes in the rules of engagement in initiative politics over the past two decades was eliminating the ban on paid signature gatherers that had existed in a number of states for decades. That change, as reported in chapter 3, came not from legislatures or from the people but from the judiciary. Eliminating the ban on paid signatures made life easier for initiative sponsors, but courts have also changed the rules in ways that have made the lives of initiative proponents more difficult. In September 2000, for instance, the Oregon Supreme Court, reversing its own 1993 decision, ruled that owners of private property, including owners of supermarkets and shopping malls, did not have to allow initiative petitioners to gather signatures on their property. The decision was described by Bill Sizemore, with typical hyperbole, as "a near-death blow to the initiative process." Voters, Sizemore added, "ought to enjoy voting on all the ballot measures this fall. This will be the last chance they get."[9] Although it is easy to dismiss such obvious exaggeration, it is nonetheless true that supermarkets and shopping malls have been favorite sites for many signature gatherers, and that the ruling—unless overturned by initiative petition, the legislature, or another court decision—may make signature gathering more difficult and expensive. Stricter interpretations of single-subject or single-amendment rules and more stringent scrutiny of ballot titles have also largely been court-driven changes in the process.[10]

A number of significant changes to the initiative process have also stemmed from administrative agencies. In 1998, for instance, the U.S. Postal Service issued new regulations that forbade signature gathering in front of any post office, a ruling that angry initiative activists challenged in court.[11] Oregon's decision in 1996 to count signature gatherers as employees rather than independent contractors, thereby increasing the costs of signature gathering, was made by the state Employment Department. More recently, in March 2000, the Oregon Elections Division directed county clerks not to count initiative signatures by "inactive voters," a category established by Congress in 1993. Initially used by the state for voters who moved and failed to reregister, the category was expanded by the state legislature in 1999 to include voters who had not voted for five years. The legislature's aim in pruning inactive voters from the rolls was to make it easier to reach the 50 percent turnout threshold that, ironically, had been imposed by a Sizemore-sponsored initiative in 1996. Since no law specified whether inactive voters could sign initiative petitions, that determination was left to the Elections Division and the courts. The ruling contributed to a substantial increase in the number of signatures ruled invalid, from an average of about 17 percent in 1998 to 25 percent in 2000. The result was a de facto hike in the signature requirement.[12]

Change, in short, is a constant if not always highly visible part of the initiative process. And that change will surely intensify as state officials and initiative activists grapple with the new possibilities and problems posed by technological advances, especially the Internet. The change hovering most immediately over election officials is the prospect of gathering and submitting signatures electronically. A number of states, including California, allow voters to download signature petitions that are posted on the web site of the initiative sponsor; though that may help get petitions in the hands of a few more people for a little less money, it is unlikely to disrupt the basic dynamics of signature gathering, particularly the increasingly heavy reliance on paid signature gatherers. But online signature gathering, whereby an individual could electronically sign and send a petition accessed on the Internet or sent to the person by e-mail, could radically transform the initiative process. Signature thresholds put in place to regulate access to the ballot could be rendered virtually meaningless by the new technology.

Initiative activists are understandably excited about the prospects of expanding public access to initiatives. Online petition gathering is widely seen as a way to invigorate grassroots, volunteer activism and diminish the advantages that economic wealth currently possesses in gaining ballot access. Some even foresee the slow demise of paid signature gathering. Instant verification and counting of signatures promises to eliminate the signature verification bureaucracy as well as the little understood methods of statistical sampling that are routinely employed in high-use initiative states to determine whether an initiative petition has the requisite signatures. In addition, proponents believe that online petition gathering can simplify the complex and often intimidating state regulations that govern signature gathering, from the size of the margins and font size to the weight and color of the paper. Because the Internet seems to promote a government that is more transparent and accessible to the average citizen, while also reducing the size of government and pruning the web of arcane administrative rules, both populists and libertarians hail the medium as a panacea for contemporary political ills.

Enthusiasm for the Internet is not entirely misplaced. The story of Helen Hill, with which I began this book, noted the ways in which Hill and her allies used the Internet to recruit like-minded individuals and to coordinate their efforts. Internet communication compensated, to some extent, for a lack of conventional interest group organizations or economic muscle. The web also offers citizens the opportunity for fuller and quicker access to campaign finance records. If campaign contributions are reported electronically, as they increasingly are, the government can relay this information to the public almost immediately. Even if few voters can be expected to take the time to look up such information, the press can access the information and disseminate it through traditional media outlets. Certainly for students of the initiative process the Internet is a precious gift that revolutionizes scholars' and activists' ability to track developments in all twenty-four initiative states.

That the Internet will, in some respects, improve American democracy generally and the initiative process specifically seems beyond question. But the Internet also poses serious dangers, particularly in regulating ballot access. Signature thresholds are, to be sure, a clumsy, imperfect instrument. Wealthy individuals and interests, as chapter 3 documented, can easily hurdle the barrier if they are so inclined. Yet for all their imperfections, signature thresholds do help to weed out frivolous proposals and protect the ballot from being inundated with half-baked ideas. If signing a petition was as effortless as responding to an online poll question, the effectiveness of existing signature thresholds would be seriously compromised.[13] To initiative enthusiasts, of course, that is exactly the point. Just imagine the possibilities: almost any citizen could place his or her idea before the people for a vote. The people would rule, citizens would once again believe that government was run for them rather than for a few big interests, and participation would soar. These activists look forward excitedly to a "new system where every citizen can propose and vote on every political decision," a system that will "raise humanity to a higher level and will change not only society but also the individual."[14]

It would be easy to pour cold water on these more extravagant fantasies of political transformation. The historically minded skeptic would point out that there is nothing novel about dreams of a withering away of the state or of dissolving power relations and giving all power to the people. Nor is there anything new in the hope that technology will help achieve these antipolitical ends. One could point to similar popular enthusiasms that have greeted past technological changes in communications, including newspapers, the telegraph, radio, and television.[15] One could dissect the flawed assumption that problems of voter competence or participation are rooted in a scarcity of information, and the corollary that if increased information were more readily available, people would become active citizens.[16] One could also, as many have done, point to the "digital divide" that continues to separate the affluent and well educated from those who are not so fortunate. Many of the predictions made about the Internet—that it will reduce the power of money, transform citizen participation and awareness, and invigorate the grass roots[17]—are almost certainly wrong, or at least hopelessly inflated.

But it would be a mistake to dismiss the millennial hype surrounding e-democracy as just another passing fad. For beneath the exaggerated flights of fancy and the technological utopianism lies a political philosophy that poses a fundamental challenge to the principles underlying the American system of representative democracy. It is a political philosophy shared and expounded by many, many initiative activists, one that says, in the words of Dennis Polhill, chairman of the Initiative & Referendum Institute, "America's political systems have served well, but are hopelessly archaic for dealing with the complex issues of the future." The future, in this view, belongs to the initiative and referendum, "the people's tool for change." It is a philosophy that celebrates, as does Grover Norquist, president of Americans for Tax Reform, that the "one big difference between initiatives and elected representatives is that initiatives do not change their minds once you vote them in." It is a philosophy, in the well-chosen words of David Broder, of "laws without government," of a system in which individual preferences are aggregated rather than negotiated, counted rather than compromised.[18]

The framers of the U.S. Constitution erected a political system built on radically different precepts. The people are the fount of all legitimate political authority, but they are not, as one prominent Oregon antitax activist has it, "the superior branch" of government.[19] Representative democracy was not a necessary evil but a positive good. The ideal was not just to mirror public preferences but to engage in reasoned debate about the public interest. The point of having selected individuals study, discuss, and debate public policy in a face-to-face forum was that they might reach a judgment that was different from the opinion or prejudice with which they began. Expert testimony might lead them to revise their beliefs, or the intense pleas of affected groups might unsettle their convictions. The rival interests of other constituencies would need to be heard and considered; compromises would need to be reached. Unlike Norquist, the founders thought that changing one's mind was a sign of political flexibility and maturity.

The framers also assumed that the political process generally works best when decisions are made slowly, deliberately, and with great care. In emergencies rapid action would be necessary, but in the normal course of events speed would only empower the passions of the moment and lead to ill-considered plans. Haste was the enemy of rational dialogue and effective public policy. Enduring policies were to be forged through the long, laborious process of building consensus. Legislative inaction, from this perspective, is not necessarily a sign of failure. Instead, the legislature's reluctance or inability to act may be a wise and necessary response to the clash of profoundly different interests and values. The American political system is built upon a premise articulated by Cicero over two thousand years ago: "It is better that a good measure should fail than that a bad one should be allowed to pass." It is a philosophy worlds apart from that expressed by initiative activist Tim Eyman, who defends the initiative process as "a laxative to a constipated political process."[20]

To Internet and initiative enthusiasts democracy is largely about counting votes. It's a very simple idea: whoever has the most votes wins, so long as the policy is not an unconstitutional infringement on the minority. No allowance is made for intensity of preference. Imagine three friends, two of whom wish to eat at McDonald's but don't feel strongly about where they eat, and one of whom wishes to go to Burger King because McDonald's makes him sick. Under the initiative process or most versions of electronic direct democracy, every preference is weighted equally. The majority rules, and so the three friends go to McDonald's, forcing the one friend either to go hungry or be physically ill. Under the legislative process of the framers, however, intensity of preference matters. The two friends may possibly try to coerce the third into eating at McDonald's, but more likely they will come up with a compromise. Not feeling strongly about the matter, the two friends may defer to the third and eat at Burger King. Or they may decide to eat at Burger King this time and McDonald's the next. Or they may look for a third option, perhaps Wendy's. Although Wendy's may be nobody's first choice, it has the advantage of not making the third friend ill, and the other two friends prefer it to Burger King. By accommodating intensity of preference rather than merely counting votes, democratic deliberation can produce policies that are acceptable to minorities as well as majorities. In contrast, issue voting in initiative elections or on the Internet promotes policies that pay scant attention to the consent of the minority, encouraging losers to take their grievances to the least democratically accountable branch of government: the courts.

Of course, legislatures do not always, or even mostly, operate in fact as they are supposed to in theory. Weighing intensity of preference may be the ideal, but the mobilization of resources often owes more to organization and money than it does to the intensity with which values and beliefs are held. The polarized partisanship among political elites often seems disconnected from the apolitical middle ground occupied by many American citizens. Amendments tacked onto legislation in the closing days of the legislative session receive nothing like the critical scrutiny envisioned by the framers of the Constitution. Disinterested policy expertise is often in short supply, particularly in states like Oregon in which professional staff are at a minimum and the legislature meets only once every two years. And term limits, of course, have only further undermined the expertise and experience of state legislators.

For all their failings, legislatures have the singular virtue of being capable of identifying, correcting, and learning from past errors. Citizens are accustomed to viewing legislatures as fallible, imperfect instruments, and so neither citizens nor legislatures see anything wrong or unusual in changing and improving current laws. There is nothing sacred about the status quo. Competitive elections between political parties are expected to result in changes in public policy. A government policy enacted by the legislature is treated as the law of the land, not as the godlike voice of the people.

The real problem with initiatives is not that they are more likely to produce poor public policy than are legislatures—though they may—but rather that mistakes made by initiatives are generally more difficult to correct. A successful initiative, unlike a legislative action, is widely assumed to be the authentic expression of the "voice of the people." Legislators or interest groups who dare to suggest amending or jettisoning a law enacted by initiative are vilified for violating the popular will, as if they were trying to alter one of the commandments brought down from the mountain by Moses rather than an imperfect government policy written by special interests. Even the modest attempt to have voters reconsider their decision brings howls of populist outrage.

Yet initiatives typically reveal more about the ideology and preoccupations of those who supply the initiatives than they do about the priorities and values of voters. Initiative sponsors, not voters, decide whether an issue will be a constitutional amendment or a statutory change. And it is the initiative sponsors who frame the issue and the choices in ways that significantly shape the answer. The importance of the ballot title in the voters' decision means that an election result is akin to a public opinion poll, in which the answer one gets largely depends on how the question is asked. If, as one initiative sponsor conceded, "it's all in the question you ask," then there is little reason to think that initiatives are more representative of the will of the people than is ordinary legislation.[21]

I introduced this book with the fond hope of persuading Americans to be at least as skeptical of the initiative process as they are of legislatures. But that turns out to be only half the task. The other, more difficult half is to teach citizens to appreciate the enduring value of representative institutions.[22] Enthusiasm for the transformative power of Internet democracy has made it more important than ever to communicate to the American public the contemporary relevance of the political principles that inform American representative democracy. But who will tell the people? With a few notable exceptions, those in the mass media generally focus on the failures and foibles of individual politicians and expend little effort in helping Americans understand the theory and practice of the legislative process. Legislators should know better, but they are more likely to run against the institution than they are to educate constituents about the value of representative legislatures or the need for partisan conflict, long debate, and messy political compromises. Even when politicians take seriously the task of civic education, public cynicism about politicians is such that the message is often heavily discounted if not ignored. Nor can we expect much better from those who have made the study of American politics their vocation, for political scientists have never been less well equipped to carry out civics lessons than they are at the turn of the twenty-first century. The abstract mathematical models that dominate American political science are impenetrable to most people, not to mention quite a few political scientists.

Populism and libertarianism are deeply rooted in American political culture.

They are not alien or un-American ideas. If they were, they would be easy to dispel. The pull of populist and libertarian beliefs means that politicians as a class will probably never be popular in the United States. Nor is that a bad thing. A degree of distrust of political leaders and government is healthy and helps account, in part, for the United States' extraordinary record of freedom and democracy spanning over two centuries. But these twin traditions have a dark side as well. Populism's glorification of "the people" as unified and monolithic makes little or no allowance for the conflict of values and interests that makes political bargaining and compromise necessary. Libertarianism's robust skepticism of coercive government power easily careens into a corrosive cynicism or even paranoid distrust of elected leaders and democratically accountable officials. By pitting the people against the politicians and promising a system of laws without government, the initiative process feeds and thrives on the most alarming aspects of both libertarianism and populism. Rebuilding public trust in American political leaders and institutions requires, among other things, exposing the antipolitical and antidemocratic assumptions and implications of these two strands of American political culture. Identifying the democratic delusions that shroud the initiative process in a sacrosanct veil is one small but necessary step in the larger project of restoring our collective faith in deliberative and representative democracy.

Appendix:
Initiative Use by Decade and State

	1900s	1910s	1920s	1930s	1940s	1950s	1960s	1970s	1980s	1990s	2000-1	Total
Alaska	—	—	—	—	—	—	2	7	8	13	2	32
Arizona	—	33	19	15	16	16	8	5	11	22	6	151
Arkansas	—	9	8	26	22	14	10	5	11	5	2	112
California	—	30	33	35	20	12	9	21	44	61	12	277
Colorado	-	37	18	19	9	8	9	19	15	37	6	177
Florida	—	—	—	—	—	—	—	2	4	9	1	16
Idaho	—	0	0	1	6	2	0	3	5	8	0	25
Illinois	—	—	—	—	—	—	—	0	1	0	0	1
Maine	—	1	2	3	2	0	0	4	12	11	3	38
Massachusetts	—	—	3	6	7	3	2	6	9	18	6	60
Michigan	—	3	3	16	5	4	1	11	8	6	2	59
Mississippi	—	—	—	—	—	—	—	—	—	2	0	2
Missouri	—	8	11	13	6	1	0	7	8	11	2	67
Montana	-	9	8	1	2	2	1	9	16	16	1	65
Nebraska	—	4	1	7	5	3	4	2	3	10	2	41
Nevada	—	1	1	3	1	6	2	1	8	13	2	38
North Dakota	—	7	25	45	21	17	14	11	11	19	0	170
Ohio	—	13	7	6	3	2	2	12	7	8	0	60
Oklahoma	1	17	8	16	9	6	10	5	4	8	0	84
Oregon	23	82	28	26	14	14	7	18	32	56	18	318
South Dakota	1	7	6	0	1	1	0	6	13	10	3	48
Utah	0	0	0	0	0	2	1	3	6	3	2	17
Washington	—	9	5	16	9	13	13	20	14	29	9	137
Wyoming	—	—	—	—	—	—	—	0	0	7	0	7
Total	25	270	186	254	158	126	95	177	250	382	79	2002

Notes

1. A Tale of Two Initiatives

1. Except where indicated, the narrative of Helen Hill's life and the life of Measure 58 is based on interviews conducted by the author, most importantly four interviews with Hill herself, on February 17, 1999, and July 8, 9, and 22, 2000. Others interviewed were Donna Harris of Creative Campaigns (July 12, 2000); Warren Deras, treasurer of the opposition measure group Concerned Adoption Professionals (July 14, 2000); Bill Pierce, former president of the National Council for Adoption (July 14, 2000); Nancy Simpson, manager of the adoption unit of Boys and Girls Aid Society (July 17, 2000); Shari Levine, executive director of Open Adoption and Family Services (July 18, 2000); Paula Lang, Program Manager of Pregnancy Support and Adoption Services division of Catholic Charities (July 19, 2000); Frank Hunsaker, the lawyer who carried the legal challenge to Measure 58 (July 20, 2000); Senator Frank Shields (July 24, 2000); and Kathy Ledesma, Program Manager for Adoption Services for the State Office for Services to Children and Families (July 24 and 26, 2000).

2. Spencer Heinz, "Ballot Measure Stirs Fears, Hopes as Adoptees Seek Birth Certificates," *Oregonian*, October 2, 1998, A18; Sam Howe Verhovek, "An Adoptee-Rights Hero Who Knows All the Arguments," *New York Times*, June 3, 2000, A7.

3. Kim Murphy, "Open-Adoption Initiative Is Facing Voters in Oregon," *Los Angeles Times*, November 3, 1998, A1.

4. The Bastard Nation mission statement is available on the group's website at *http://www.bastards.org/whoweare/mission1.htm*.

5. When asked again about the matter over a year later, Hill had revised her judgment, concluding that they would have won even had the opposition spent large sums of money.

6. Adam Pertman, "Oregon Voters Could Open Door to Adoptees' Past," *Boston Globe*, October 2, 1998, A1.

7. Verhovek, "An Adoptee-Rights Hero Who Knows All the Arguments."

8. Maya Blackmun, "Rights Clash in Adoption Disclosure Debate," *Oregonian*, March 22, 1998, B1.

9. *Jane Does v. State of Oregon,* 164 Ore. App. 543 (1999), quotations at 566, 558.

10. Except where indicated, this account of the genesis of Measure 8 is based on inter-views with the following individuals: Ruth Bendl (July 20, 2000); Bob Tiernan (July 25, 2000); Mari Anne Gest, a former lobbyist for Oregon Public Employees Union (OPEU) (July 19, 2000); Becky Miller (July 5, 2000); OPEU Research Director Paul McKenna (July 20, 2000); Bob Andrews, PERS legislative liaison from 1989 to 1995 (July 19, 2000); Gary Carlson, executive vice president of Associated Oregon Industries (July 25, 2000); and legis-lator Lee Beyer (August 1, 2000). Also utilized were the court transcripts in *Bendl v. Parks* (1998), A102499, Court of Appeals records office, Salem, Oregon.

11. Steve Duin, "Manipulating All Those Cynical Voters," *Oregonian,* November 14, 1993, D1; Gail Kinsey Hill, "Tiernan Remains Firm in Quest to Pare Public Employee Ben-efits," *Oregonian,* February 17, 1994, D1; idem, "Union Blues," *Oregonian,* September 28, 1994, B1.

12. Hill, "Tiernan Remains Firm in Quest to Pare Public Employee Benefits"; Steve Duin, "Place on Public Enemy List: No. 1," *Oregonian,* September 30, 1993, E7; Bill Sizemore, "Where Does Government Go After Measure 8?" *Oregonian,* December 15, 1994, D13.

13. Sizemore, "Where Does Government Go After Measure 8?"; Courtenay Thompson, "Schools Offer Raise of 6 Percent," *Oregonian,* November 8, 1994, B2; Gail Kinsey Hill, "Launching a Pre-emptive Strike," *Oregonian,* August 11, 1994, A1; idem, "1994 Voters Guide: Measure 8," *Oregonian,* September 21, 1994, B6.

14. Jeff Mapes, "Union Workers Are Mad About Bob," *Oregonian,* May 10, 1995, A12; Gail Kinsey Hill and James Meyer, "The Top of It: Measure 8," *Oregonian,* August 31, 1994, B4; Gail Kinsey Hill, "Supporters of Measure 8 Declare Victory," *Oregonian,* November 17, 1994, A25; Bill MacKenzie, "Measure 8 Supporters Cry Foul," *Oregonian,* December 18, 1994, B5. Tiernan and Sizemore responded to the unions' efforts to publicize contribu-tors' names by refusing to release these names and threatening felony intimidation charges against the public employee unions, as well as "a class action lawsuit on behalf of [their] contributors under the state's racketeering statutes." See Steve Suo, "Kitzhaber Will Try to Cool Measure 8 Tiff," *Oregonian,* December 14, 1994, C4; also see Editorial, "Wise Up, Measure 8 Backers," *Oregonian,* December 14, 1994, E10.

15. Hill, "Launching a Pre-emptive Strike"; idem, "Pension Measure Misses Target," *Oregonian,* December 11, 1994, A1.

16. Charles E. Beggs, "Measure 8 Backer Talks of Recall Drive," *Oregonian,* December 5, 1994, B5; Dennis McCarthy, "Lieutenant Says He's Been Paying the 6 Percent All Along," *Oregonian.* December 9, 1994, D2; Courtenay Thompson, "Public Employees Get Early Gift, Thanks to Measure 8," *Oregonian,* December 9, 1994, D2.

17. Gail Kinsey Hill, "Kitzhaber Won't Back Measure 8 Pay Boost," *Oregonian,* Novem-ber 29, 1994, A1; David R. Anderson, "Gresham Will Continue 6% Pension Payments," *Oregonian,* November 30, 1994, C2; Gail Kinsey Hill, "Putting Budgets to the Test," *Ore-gonian,* August 24, 1994, B2.

18. Charles E. Beggs, "Measure 8 Backer Talks of Recall Drive," *Oregonian,* December 5, 1994, B5; Hill, "Kitzhaber Won't Back Measure 8 Pay Boost"; Laura Trujillo, "County School Districts Sidestep Punch of Measure 8," *Oregonian,* November 21, 1994, B2; Gail Kinsey Hill, "Multnomah County OKs Pay Raises," *Oregonian,* December 2, 1994, B1.

19. Gail Kinsey Hill, "Unclear Answers Given on Sick Leave," *Oregonian,* August 4, 1994, B1; idem, "Ruling Says Elected Officials Also Covered by Measure 8," *Oregonian,* November 22, 1994, B1.

20. *Oregon State Police Officers' Association v. State of Oregon* 323 Ore. 356 (1996), quotations at 412, 375.

21. Jeff Mapes and Ashbel S. Green, "Court Sinks Public Pension Measure," *Oregonian,* June 22, 1996, A1; Associated Press, "Attorney General Won't Appeal Pension Measure," *Oregonian,* August 29, 1996, B5.

22. Janet Goetze, "Other Issues Make Tiernan Happy," *Oregonian,* November 7, 1996, D4.

2. The Initiative Revolution

1. Sarah M. Henry, "Progressivism and Democracy: Electoral Reform in the United States, 1888–1919 (Ph.D. diss., Columbia University, 1995), 55, 154; Richard G. Jones, "Organized Labor and the Initiative and Referendum Movement, 1885–1920" (master's thesis, University of Washington, 1963), esp. chap. 2; David D. Schmidt, *Citizen Lawmakers: The Ballot Initiative Revolution* (Philadelphia: Temple University Press, 1989), 7; Elliott Shore, *Talkin' Socialism: J. A. Wayland and the Role of the Press in American Radicalism, 1890–1912* (Lawrence: University Press of Kansas, 1988), 78.

2. Steven L. Piott, "The Origins of the Initiative and Referendum in South Dakota: The Political Context," *Great Plains Quarterly* 12 (Summer 1992), esp. 183–89; Jones, "Organized Labor and the Initiative and Referendum," 45–48; Schmidt, *Citizen Lawmakers,* 267–68.

3. J. W. Arrowsmith, "The Direct Legislation Movement in New Jersey," *Direct Legislation Record* 1 (May 1894), 2; Steven L. Piott, "The Origins of the Initiative and Referendum in America," *Hayes Historical Journal* 11 (Spring 1992), 8–11; Schmidt, *Citizen Lawmakers,* 6–7; Chester McArthur Destler, *American Radicalism, 1865–1901* (Chicago: Quadrangle Books, 1946), 24, 101–4; Robert E. Weir, *Beyond Labor's Veil: The Culture of the Knights of Labor* (University Park, Penn.: Pennsylvania State University Press, 1996), esp. xvi, 123, 214, 291; Norman Pollack, ed., *The Populist Mind* (Indianapolis: Bobbs-Merrill, 1967), 65; Howard H. Quint, *The Forging of American Socialism: Origins of the Modern Movement* (Columbia: University of South Carolina Press, 1953), 249; Shore, *Talkin' Socialism,* 76.

4. Piott, "The Initiative and Referendum in America," 7–8; James W. Sullivan, *Direct Legislation by the Citizenship through the Initiative and Referendum* (New York: Nationalist Publishing Company, 1893), i, 95, 105–6; Jones, "Organized Labor and the Initiative and Referendum," 54; see also Henry, "Progressivism and Democracy," 56–59.

5. Burton J. Hendrick, "The Initiative and Referendum and How Oregon Got Them," *McClure's Magazine* 37 (July 1911), 236–37, 239; Thomas C. McClintock, "Seth Lewelling, William S. U'Ren and the Birth of the Oregon Progressive Movement," *Oregon Historical Quarterly* 68 (September 1967), 201–7; Lute Pease, "The Initiative and Referendum—Oregon's Big Stick," *Pacific Monthly* 17 (May 1907), 565.

6. Pease, "Initiative and Referendum," 565–66; Paul Thomas Culbertson, "A History of the Initiative and Referendum in Oregon" (Ph.D. diss., University of Oregon, 1941), 54–55; McClintock, "Birth of the Oregon Progressive Movement," 207; Robert Douglas Johnston, "Middle-Class Political Ideology in a Corporate Society: The Persistence of Small-Propertied Radicalism in Portland, Oregon, 1883–1926" (Ph.D. diss., Rutgers University, 1993), 222–23.

7. Henry, "Progressivism and Democracy," esp. 57–58, 129, 159; Johnston, "Middle-Class Political Ideology," esp. 225; Sullivan, *Direct Legislation,* 106, 113.

8. Henry, "Progressivism and Democracy," 160–62; McClintock, "Birth of the Oregon Progressive Movement," 215–16; Tony Howard Evans, "Oregon Progressive Reform, 1902–1914" (Ph.D. diss., University of California, Berkeley, 1966), 62–63. Johnston, "Middle-Class Political Ideology," 225.

9. Henry, "Progressivism and Democracy," 146 n.56, 153–54 (emphasis added); Culbertson, "History of the Initiative and Referendum in Oregon," 57.

10. Henry, "Progressivism and Democracy," 63–64; Jones, "Organized Labor and the Initiative and Referendum," 58.

11. James D. Barnett, *The Operation of the Initiative, Referendum, and Recall in Oregon* (New York: Macmillan, 1915), 81, 78; Evans, "Oregon Progressive Reform," 212, 68, 155; Culbertson, "History of the Initiative and Referendum," 52; Pease, "The Initiative and Referendum," 568; Joseph N. Teal, "The Practical Workings of the Initiative and Referendum in Oregon," in *The Initiative, Referendum, and Recall,* ed. William Bennett Munro (New York: D. Appleton, 1920), 220–21, 231.

12. Henry, "Progressivism and Democracy," 239–40; Frederick C. Howe, "Oregon: The Most Complete Democracy in the World," *Hampton's Magazine* 26 (1911), 459–60; John J. Dinan, *Keeping the People's Liberties: Legislators, Citizens, and Judges as Guardians of Rights* (Lawrence: University Press of Kansas, 1998), 85; also see Piott, "Origins of Initiative and Referendum in South Dakota," 190.

13. Dinan, *Keeping the People's Liberties,* 84; Cronin, *Direct Democracy,* 38; Henry, "Progressivism and Democracy," 240; Evans, "Oregon Progressive Reform," 71.

14. Collecting accurate data on statewide initiative use is not easy, particularly in states with poor record keeping and/or in which initiatives were not clearly distinguished from referenda. For initiative use through 1976, the standard source is Virginia Graham, *A Compilation of Statewide Initiative Proposals Appearing on Ballots Through 1976* (Washington, D.C.: Library of Congress, 1978). Graham's Congressional Research Service (CRS) study was updated in a second CRS report by Lisa Oakley and Thomas Neale, *Citizen Initiative Proposals Appearing on State Ballots, 1976–1992* (Washington, D.C.: Library of Congress, 1995). Both compilations are valuable but neither are flawless, particularly as they relate to Arkansas and Colorado. For Colorado I have relied on data painstakingly compiled by Dan Smith of the University of Denver. For Arkansas since 1938 I used "Proposed Constitutional Amendments, Initiatives and Referenda, 1938–1998," compiled by the office of the secretary of state; it is available on the secretary of state's webpage. For pre-1938 Arkansas I have generally relied on Graham, though these numbers, due to poor record keeping by the state, almost certainly underreport initiative use in Arkansas during this period; see David Thomas, "The Initiative and Referendum in Arkansas Comes of Age," *American Political Science Review* 27 (1933), 66–75. I have also consulted the data ("Initiative Usage by State and Year, 1898–1998") compiled by the Initiative and Referendum Institute (*http://www.iandrinstitute.org*). Although the institute is an extraordinarily rich source of information on the initiative and referendum, its historical data contain many errors and need to be handled with extreme caution. Where available, I have also consulted historical data compiled by the chief election officer in the state, usually the secretary of state. For Oregon I relied on the *Oregon Blue Book, 1999–2000* (Oregon Secretary of State, 1999), and in the case of California I made use of Appendix A ("Direct Legislation Propositions,

1912–1998") in John M. Allswang, *The Initiative and Referendum in California, 1898–1998* (Palo Alto: Stanford University Press, 2000), 251–69. For elections since 1992 I have relied on secretary of states' webpages, the Initiative and Referendum Institute's webpage, and a compilation of 1990–96 initiatives provided to me by Professor Floyd Feeney of the University of California, Davis.

15. Philip L. DuBois and Floyd Feeney, *Lawmaking by Initiative: Issues, Options and Comparisons* (New York: Agathon Press, 1998), 82–83; David B. Magleby, "Direct Legislation in the American States," in *Referendums Around the World: The Growing Use of Direct Democracy,* ed. David Butler and Austin Ranney (Washington, D.C.: AEI Press, 1994), 224.

16. Magleby, "Direct Legislation in the States," 224, 228.

17. Patrick B. McGuigan, *The Politics of Direct Democracy in the 1980s: Case Studies in Popular Decision Making* (Washington, D.C.: Free Congress Research and Education Foundation, 1985), 114.

18. Michael C. Burton, "Bill Would Create Initiative and Referendum in Texas," February 28, 1997 (*www.lubbockonline.com/news/022897/bill.htm*); Bill McAuliffe, "House OKs Bill That Gives Voters Power to Pass Laws at the Polls," *Star Tribune* (Minneapolis), March 23, 1999, 3B. This argument is elaborated in Dustin Buehler, "The Drive for Direct Democracy: An Analysis of States Without the Initiative and Referendum" (senior thesis, Willamette University, 2000).

19. Dave McNeely, "'Impossible Dreams' Still on Senator's Agenda," *San Antonio Express-News,* January 26, 1999, 7B; Burton, "Bill Would Create Initiative and Referendum in Texas."

20. McNeely, "Impossible Dreams." The quotation is from Mike Ford, the chairman of Initiative for Texas, a group that has been pushing for a state constitutional amendment to establish the initiative and referendum in Texas.

21. Jack Wardlaw, "Voter Initiative Proposal Blasted: Business Groups Split with Foster," *Times-Picayune* (New Orleans), January 7, 1999, A3.

22. John Henrikson, "Voters Get a Grip on Government," *Statesman Journal* (Salem, Ore.), July 8, 1994, A2. City Club of Portland, "The Initiative and Referendum in Oregon" (Portland, Ore., February 16, 1996), 28. The report is available on the Web at *www.pdxcity club.org/report/init.*

3. The Business of Signatures

1. John Henrikson, "Voters Get a Grip on Government," *Statesman Journal* (Salem, Ore.), July 8, 1994, A2; Dan Bender, "Political Foes Ally for Citizens' Rights," *Statesman Journal* (Salem, Ore.), October 2, 1995, A2.

2. Philip L. DuBois and Floyd Feeney, *Lawmaking by Initiative: Issues, Options and Comparisons* (New York: Agathon Press, 1998), 102.

3. Although texts on the initiative and referendum routinely list North Dakota as the state with the most lenient signature requirement, the state's 2 percent requirement is roughly equivalent to a requirement that signatures be equal to 5 percent of the votes in the previous gubernatorial contest. For instance, South Dakota, which sets a 5 percent threshold for statutes and has a population of about 700,000, required 13,010 signatures in 2000, while

North Dakota, which counted 638,000 people in the 1990 census, required 12,776 signatures. By a very slight margin, then, North Dakota's requirement was actually more burdensome than South Dakota's.

4. Dubois and Feeney, *Lawmaking by Initiative*, 33–34; David Magleby, *Direct Legislation: Voting on Ballot Propositions in the United States* (Baltimore: Johns Hopkins University Press, 1984), 38–40.

5. In Oregon (as in Arkansas, Ohio, and Utah) there is no formal limit on the number of days petitioners can spend gathering signatures for an initiative, but as a practical matter the limit in Oregon is two years since an initiative campaign cannot begin to gather signatures until after the July deadline for the coming general election has passed. So, for instance, only signatures obtained after July 17, 1998, counted for initiatives being qualified for the 2000 ballot; signatures gathered prior to the July deadline counted toward the 1998 election.

6. Michael W. Bowers, *The Nevada State Constitution: A Reference Guide* (Westport, Conn.: Greenwood Press, 1993), 146.

7. This does not count Illinois, which, though it has marginally more people than Ohio, has had only one initiative in its history. Florida, which today is the second most populous initiative state, had no initiatives during the period Schmidt studied.

8. "Studies Show Initiatives Are Nonpartisan, Grassroots Politics," *Initiative News Report* 5 (November 30, 1984), 1–2, 5–9. Alaska accounted for close to half of the campaigns in small states that relied on paid signature gatherers for more than 10 percent of the signatures.

9. "Studies Show Initiatives Are Nonpartisan, Grassroots Politics," 2.

10. *Libertarian Party of Oregon v. Paulus*, Civ. No. 82-521FR, slip op. at 4 (Sept. 3, 1982). The case was brought by the Libertarian party, which wanted to use paid petitioners to collect the signatures required to qualify the party's candidates for the ballot. U.S. District Court Judge Helen Frye ruled that Oregon's ban on paid signature gatherers was an unconstitutional restriction on the Libertarian party's right of free speech. Although Frye's decision did not specifically address ballot measures, it was widely assumed that the ruling applied to initiative and referenda as well, and so the Oregon legislature responded the following year by dropping its long-standing ban on paid canvassers in initiative and referendum elections. In 1984, after a federal judge upheld Colorado's ban on paid petitioners in a case (*Grant v. Meyer*) dealing specifically with an initiative, Oregon's secretary of state, Norma Paulus, spearheaded an effort to reinstate the ban on paid signature gatherers for ballot measure campaigns only. In 1985 the bill passed by better than a two-to-one margin in the Oregon House but died in the Senate. The measure resurfaced in the next legislative session and again passed the House by a large margin and failed in the Senate.

11. *Meyer v. Grant* 486 U.S. 414 (1988). The ban was modified by a 1983 Colorado Supreme Court decision, which struck the word "inducement" from the statute that had banned "direct or indirect payment in consideration of or as an inducement to circulation of a petition" (*Urevich v. Woodward* 667 P.2d 760). That decision stemmed from a suit filed by the Association of Community Organizations for Reform Now (ACORN), which in 1982 had tried to qualify an initiative for the ballot and had requested that petition circulators collect financial donations at the same time they sought ballot signatures. The circulators were offered 30 to 40 percent of the contributions they collected. A Denver district judge said ACORN violated the ban on paid circulators, but the Supreme Court both reversed the decision—arguing that "ACORN's method falls outside the statute, because its solicitors are not paid in consideration of circulating the petition, but rather in consideration of the financial

contributions they solicit"—and struck the term "inducement" as overly broad (UPI wire report, July 18, 1983).

12. *Meyer* also nullified a short-lived ban on paid signature gatherers in Nebraska, which had been enacted earlier in the 1980s.

13. *LIMIT v. Maleng* 874 F. Supp. 1138 (1994).

14. *State v. Conifer Enterprises* 82 Wash. 2d 94 (1973); *State of Oregon v. Ronald K. Campbell* 265 Ore. 82 (1973). The first time a court struck down a state restriction on paid circulators came in 1976, when the California Supreme Court (*Hardie v. Eu* 18 Cal. 3d 371) invalidated a law (enacted as part of the Political Reform Act of 1974, which was passed by initiative) limiting expenditures on behalf of an initiative to no more than twenty-five cents a signature. In reaching its decision, the California court explicitly followed the U.S. Supreme Court's landmark ruling on campaign finance in *Buckley v. Valeo*, which was issued earlier that year. The *Buckley* case is discussed in greater depth later in this chapter.

15. James Barnett, *The Operation of the Initiative, Referendum, and Recall in Oregon* (New York: Macmillan, 1915), 59–60; *State v. Olcott* 125 P. 303 (1912), quotation at 306.

16. Barnett, *Operation of the Initiative,* 61–63.

17. Barnett, *Operation of the Initiative,* 62; Philip L. Dubois and Floyd F. Feeney, *Improving the California Initiative Process: Options for Change* (Berkeley: The California Policy Seminar, University of California, 1992), appendices B and C; V. O. Key Jr. and Winston W. Crouch, *The Initiative and Referendum in California* (Berkeley: University of California Press, 1939), 546–47, 562.

18. Proceedings of the Thirteenth Annual Convention of the California State Federation of Labor, October 7–12, 1912, 91; cited in Charlene Wear Simmons, "California's Statewide Initiative Process," California Research Bureau, 1997, 7.

19. Prior to 1966, California had an indirect initiative option that required only 5 percent of signatures. The option was little used and voters approved abolition of the indirect initiative at the same time they lowered the number of signatures for direct statutory initiatives, as recommended by a constitutional revision commission.

20. California Commission on Campaign Financing, *Democracy by Initiative: Shaping California's Fourth Branch of Government* (Los Angeles: Center for Responsive Government, 1992), 146; Simmons, "California's Statewide Initiative Process," 9; Peter Schrag, *Paradise Lost: California's Experience, America's Future* (New York: New Press, 1998), 210. The mountain lion sponsors experimented with using direct mail solicitations that included signature petitions and fund-raising appeals, but they found that combining signature collection with fund-raising was not an effective way either to gather signatures or to raise money. Eleven organizers were hired to coordinate the work of the army of volunteer signature gatherers, some of whom devoted the entire summer of 1989 to circulating petitions. See the account in William M. Lunch and Wesley Jamison, "The Lab Rat That Roared: The Mountain Lion Initiative in California and the Animal Rights Movement in the Nation" (presented at the annual meeting of the Western Political Science Association, San Francisco, March 1992), 9–11.

21. Communication with Penny Ysursa, Administrative Secretary, Election Division, Idaho secretary of state's office, October 18, 1999; Kevin Richert, "Signature-for-Hire Businesses Fueling Idaho Ballot Initiatives," *Idaho Falls Post Register,* December 7, 1995, A11; Marty Trillhaase, "Initiative Drives Get Costlier," *Idaho Statesman,* June 18, 1996, A1; idem, "Recognizing an Era Has Passed," *Idaho Falls Post Register,* February 11, 1997, A10.

22. Patti Epler, "Illegalities Won't Stop Initiative; Denturists' Measure Likely to Be Only One on Fall Ballot," *News Tribune* (Tacoma, Wa.), June 30, 1994, A1; Kathy George, "State's Citizens May Have Too Much Initiative," *Seattle Post-Intelligencer,* July 7, 1994, A1.

23. Joseph Turner, "Fall Ballot Likely to List 2 Initiatives," *News Tribune* (Tacoma, Wa.), June 26, 1995, B1; Kimberly Mills, "The Name Game: Initiative Process at Its Best with a Volunteer Effort," *Seattle Post-Intelligencer,* July 23, 1995, E1.

24. Joseph Turner, "Abortion Issue Likely on Ballot," *News Tribune* (Tacoma, Wa.), July 2, 1998, B1; Hunter T. George, "Initiative Campaigns Succeed Without Paid Signature Gatherers," *Columbian* (Vancouver, Wa.), July 2, 1998, B2; Susan Gilmore, "Abortion Initiative to Be on Ballot in November," *Seattle Times,* July 27, 1998, B1. Even as these volunteer efforts were succeeding quite comfortably, Rob Killian, a Tacoma physician who paid for every signature gathered for the medical marijuana measure, told reporters, "I don't know anyone who can get anything on the ballot anymore just with volunteer signature gatherers." Hal Spencer, "Marijuana, Wage Initiatives on Track," *Columbian* (Vancouver, Wa.), June 2, 1998, B5.

25. The most signatures in Washington history were gathered in a 1973 initiative campaign to roll back and cap legislative salaries. Riding a tidal wave of popular outrage against a legislative pay raise that had tripled legislators' salaries from $3,600 to $10,650 a year, a furniture salesman and political novice, Bruce Helm, spearheaded a volunteer effort that needed only two weeks to collect almost seven hundred thousand signatures.

26. Mills, "The Name Game."

27. Burt Hubbard, "Big Bucks Buy Spot on Ballot," *Denver Rocky Mountain News,* August 7, 1994, A4; Bill Orr, executive director of the American Constitutional Law Foundation, quoted in Elizabeth Garrett, "Money, Agenda Setting, and Direct Democracy," *Texas Law Review* 77 (June 1999), 1852 n. 31.

28. Daniel Smith, "Progressives Need to Show Initiative on Ballot Signatures," *Denver Post,* January 13, 2000, B7; Ann Schrader, "Abortion Limits Proposed; Coalition Submits Petitions for Pair of Ballot Initiatives," *Denver Post,* July 8, 1998, B1.

29. UPI wire report, July 23, 1982.

30. Because of the growth in the state's population, the number of signatures required increased somewhat between the 1980s and 1990s. In 1984, for instance, 46,737 signatures were required, while a decade later 49,279 signatures were needed. By 1998, however, the number of required signatures had reached 54,242, and heavy turnout in the 1998 election (the signature percentage in Colorado is determined as a percentage of the vote in the preceding secretary of state's race) meant that 62,595 signatures were required to qualify for the 2000 ballot.

31. Jim Schultz, *The Initiative Cookbook: Recipes and Stories from California's Ballot Wars* (San Francisco: Democracy Center, 1998), 33.

32. Washington secretary of state Ralph Munro, quoted in Scott Maier, "Big Bucks Back 2 State Initiatives; Paid Professionals Circulated Petitions," *Seattle Post-Intelligencer,* August 31, 1992, A1.

33. For instance, Phil Keisling, Oregon's secretary of state, complains: "The promise of the initiative is grassroots democracy. It's becoming greenbacks democracy"; quoted in Henrikson, "Voters Get a Grip on Government."

34. Key and Crouch, *Initiative and Referendum in California,* 444, 572, 487; also see David McCuan et al., "California's Political Warriors: Campaign Professionals and the Ini-

tiative Process," in *Citizens as Legislators: Direct Democracy in the United States*, ed. Shaun Bowler, Todd Donovan, and Caroline J. Tolbert (Columbus: Ohio State University Press, 1998), esp. 57–61.

35. Schultz, *Initiative Cookbook*, 33; California Commission, *Democracy by Initiative*, 152.

36. David Ammons, "Tabs & Taxes Initiative Headed for Ballot," Associated Press State & Local Wire, June 29, 1999; Robert Gavin, "Backers of $30 Tabs Raked in Piles of Cash; Half Came from Donors Giving Less than $100 Each," *Seattle Post-Intelligencer*, December 29, 1999, B1; Ann Donnelly, "Just Say No to Marijuana Legalization," *Columbian* (Vancouver, Wa.), July 12, 1998, B13; Deidre Silva, "Initiatives May Face More Rules," *Spokesman-Review* (Spokane, Wa.), February 1, 1999, A1.

37. Hal Spencer, "Records Show Labor as Main Force Behind Wage Initiative," *Columbian* (Vancouver, Wa.), July 14, 1998, B9; George, "Initiative Campaigns Succeed Without Paid Signature Gatherers."

38. Lynn Fritchman, spokesman for a group trying to qualify an Idaho measure that would have outlawed the use of bait and dogs in hunting bears, explained that they wanted to avoid paying for signatures because "we know the National Rifle Association is going to spend a whole bunch of money to defeat this, and we want to have some money left at the last month to combat that." See Marty Trillhaase, "Money Helps Gather Signatures," *Idaho Statesman*, November 12, 1995, B1. In the end, though, as the volunteer campaign faltered, Fritchman's group was forced to pay for signatures in order to qualify for the ballot. See Kevin Richert, "Bear Group Is Paying to Collect Signatures," *Idaho Falls Post Register*, April 30, 1996, A1; Bill Loftus, "Bear Advocate Says He Has Enough Signatures," *Lewiston Morning Tribune*, June 26, 1996, A1.

39. Kelly Kimball, head of one of the largest and most successful signature-gathering firms, Kimball Petition Management, estimates that paid signature gatherers have signature validity rates of between 60 and 70 percent, while well-trained volunteers typically have rates between 75 and 80 percent. Direct-mail petitions typically do best of all, usually ranging between 85 and 90 percent. See California Commission, *Democracy by Initiative*, 149; Lowenstein and Stern, "First Amendment." In Oregon in 1998 and 2000, the validity rate for signatures submitted to the secretary of state's office for verification was about ten percentage points higher for volunteer-only signature drives (87 percent) than for campaigns that relied on paid signature gatherers (76 percent). These validity rates are higher than Kimball's estimates because the campaign coordinators generally check the work of individual signature gatherers and attempt to weed out invalid signatures before forwarding the signatures to the state for verification. Both the Oregon secretary of state's data and Kimball's estimates, however, point to roughly the same gap in validity rates between volunteer and paid signature gatherers.

40. Schultz, *Initiative Cookbook*, 32; telephone interview with Mabon, January 12, 1999.

41. Sally Farhat, "Signatures Collected to Lower Tab Fees—Sponsors of I-695 to Turn in Petitions," *Seattle Times*, June 22, 1999, B1; Steve Lipsher, "Ballot Drive a Job for Pros," *Denver Post*, September 19, 1994, A1.

42. Lipsher, "Ballot Drive a Job for Pros."

43. One professional signature gatherer who had worked in at least six different states testified in court that "it's mostly the placement of the petition, and how much the petitioner pushes it [that determines what gets signed]. You're only going to get them to sign 3 out of 10 petitions so you figure your 3 most profitable petitions [are the ones you push]." Testimony of Michael Rhodes, in *Affinity Communication v. Virlina Crosley*, hearing at [Oregon] State

Employment Office, July 10, 1999, 98. Also see David Broder, "Taking the Initiative on Petitions: Signatures for a Price," *Washington Post National Weekly Edition*, April 20, 1998, 11; Schultz, *Initiative Cookbook*, 34; California Commission, *Democracy by Initiative*, 147.

44. Craig B. Holman and Robert Stern, "Judicial Review of Ballot Initiatives: The Changing Role of State and Federal Courts," *Loyola of Los Angeles Law Review* 31 (1998), 1243 n. 29; Charles M. Price, "Afloat on a Sea of Cash," *California Journal* 19 (November 1988), 484; California Commission, *Democracy by Initiative*, 132.

45. An example of the latter is Ohio Governor George Voinovich's failed attempt to qualify a campaign finance measure. With less than a month left and still far short of the required 104,000 signatures, the campaign turned in desperation to a professional signature-gathering firm, but even a campaign war chest totaling two hundred thousand dollars and a price of better than one dollar per signature was not enough to rescue the effort by the December 23 deadline. See Benjamin Marrison, "Campaign Reform Drive Faces Hurdle," Cleveland *Plain Dealer*, December 14, 1994, B5.

46. Daniel Hays Lowenstein and Robert M. Stern, "The First Amendment and Paid Initiative Petition Circulators: A Dissenting View and a Proposal," *Hastings Constitutional Law Quarterly* 17 (Fall 1989), 199.

47. California Commission, *Democracy by Initiative*, 154.

48. California Commission, *Democracy by Initiative*, 132, 147 n. 60. Lowenstein and Stern, "First Amendment," 203, 204 n. 128; Garrett, "Money, Agenda Setting, and Direct Democracy," 1849. That any or virtually any issue can make it to the ballot if the backers have the money is attested to by multiple sources. See Larry Berg and C. B. Holman, "The Initiative Process and Its Declining Agenda-Setting Value," *Law and Policy* 11 (October 1989), 458; Lowenstein and Stern, "First Amendment," 175, 199; David B. Magleby and Kelly D. Patterson, "Consultants and Direct Democracy," *P. S.:Political Science & Politics* 31 (June 1998), 161; California Commission, *Democracy by Initiative*, 35; Garrett, "Money, Agenda Setting, and Direct Democracy,"1852; City Club of Portland, "The Initiative and Referendum in Oregon" (Portland, Ore., February 16, 1996), 27; P. K. Jameson and Marsha Hosack, "Citizen Initiatives in Florida: An Analysis of Florida's Constitutional Initiative Process, Issues and Alternatives," *Florida State University Law Review* 23 (Fall 1995), 446 n. 269.

49. California Commission, *Democracy by Initiative*, 157–59, 455–57; Berg and Holman, "The Initiative Process and Its Declining Agenda-Setting Value," 455–57.

50. City Club of Portland Report, "The Initiative and Referendum in Oregon," 27; Michael Roman, "Ruling Not Expected to Boost Initiatives," *Rocky Mountain News* (Denver, Co.), January 13, 1999, A18; Betsy Z. Russell, "Grass-Roots Ballot Initiatives Withering," *Spokesman-Review* (Spokane, Wa.), July 8, 1998, A1.

51. "The Price of Petitioning," *Oregonian*, July 25, 1996, A15.

52. "Big Givers Dominate Initiatives," *State Government News* 35 (September 1992), 25; California Commission, *Democracy by Initiative*, 279–80, 274. The 1998 figures are calculated from the campaign finance data available online from the California secretary of state's office.

53. California Commission, *Democracy by Initiative*, 158, 265, 274.

54. Jameson and Hosack, "Citizen Initiatives in Florida," 447–48; Steve Woodward, "It's Not Always the Money That Matters," *Oregonian*, November 9, 1996, A1; Dubois and Feeney, *Lawmaking by Initiative*, 181–88; Garrett, "Money, Agenda Setting, and Direct Democracy," 1847.

55. On the increasing importance of parties and partisanship in initiative elections, see Daniel A. Smith and Caroline J. Tolbert, "The Initiative to Party: Partisanship and Ballot Initiatives in California," *Party Politics* 7 (December 2001), 781–99. Particularly valuable in understanding how voters makes decisions in initiative elections is Shaun Bowler and Todd Donovan, *Demanding Choices: Opinion, Voting and Direct Democracy* (Ann Arbor: University of Michigan Press, 1998).

56. *Buckley v. Valeo* 424 U.S. 1 (1976), quotations at 19–20, 25, 29.

57. *National Bank of Boston v. Bellotti* 435 U.S. 765 (1978), quotations at 765, 790; *Citizens Against Rent Control v. City of Berkeley* 454 U.S. 290 (1981), esp. 297–300.

58. *Meyer v. Grant* 486 U.S. 414, quotation at 414.

59. *Meyer v. Grant* 486 U.S. 414, quotations at 415, 425; also see Lowenstein and Stern, "First Amendment," esp. 200–205.

60. *Grant v. Meyer* 741 F.2d 1210 (1984), quotation at 1213; Caroline Tolbert, Daniel H. Lowenstein, and Todd Donovan, "Election Law and Rules for Using Initiatives," in *Citizens as Legislators*, 36; Lowenstein and Stern, "First Amendment," 215.

61. *Meyer v. Grant* 486 U.S. 414, quotations at 421–22.

62. Lowenstein and Stern, "First Amendment," 182, 197–99; Schmidt, *Citizen Lawmakers*, 199; *Grant v. Meyer* 741 F.2d 1210, quotation at 1214.

63. *Grant v. Meyer* 741 F.2d 1210, at 1212–13; Tolbert, Lowenstein, and Donovan, "Election Law," 35–36; Lowenstein and Stern, "First Amendment," 183.

64. *Victoria Buckley v. American Constitutional Law Foundation* 119 S. Ct. 636 (1999).

65. In truth, such badges, with or without names, are unlikely to be effective. As DuBois and Feeney point out, circulators might very well "seek and obtain signatures by using the disclosure as the basis for an appeal for voter support to help them achieve some worthy personal goal (e.g., pay the rent, go to college, travel abroad) wholly unrelated to the content of the petition." See DuBois and Feeney, *Lawmaking by Initiative*, 102; also see Lowenstein and Stern, "First Amendment," 220.

66. *Victoria Buckley v. American Constitutional Law Foundation* 119 S. Ct. 636, quotations at 647, 657, 659; also see *WIN v. Ripple* 213 F.3d 1132 (2000). It is perhaps not entirely a coincidence that the three dissenting justices in *Victoria Buckley* worked as judges or lawyers in initiative states. The only justice in the majority who hails from an initiative state is Anthony Kennedy.

67. *Victoria Buckley v. American Constitutional Law Foundation* 119 S. Ct. 636, quotations at 638. At the time of *Victoria Buckley,* some twenty states required that party or candidate petitioners be registered voters, including Arizona, California, Colorado, Connecticut, Idaho, Illinois, Kansas, Michigan, Missouri, Nebraska, New Jersey, New York, Ohio, Pennsylvania, Rhode Island, South Dakota, Virginia, West Virginia, Wisconsin, and Wyoming. Since *Victoria Buckley,* Arizona and Idaho have repealed the requirement, and federal district courts in Illinois have struck it down twice. Both district courts based their decision on *Victoria Buckley.* See *Ballot News,* August 3, 1999, and September 1, 2000.

68. *Victoria Buckley v. American Constitutional Law Foundation* 119 S. Ct. 636, quotations at 659, 661.

69. *Victoria Buckley v. American Constitutional Law Foundation* 119 S. Ct. 636, quotations at 643, 659; "Court Denies Appeal on Marijuana Petition," *Bangor Daily News,* July 29, 1998. In July 1999 federal district court judges in North Dakota and Mississippi upheld state residency requirements for circulators; see *Ballot News,* September 1, 1999, and August

3, 1999. Residency requirements were also upheld in Maine by the state supreme court in July 1998 and by a federal court the following year.

70. *Victoria Buckley v. American Constitutional Law Foundation* 119 S. Ct. 636, quotations at 642.

71. "Voters on Their Own in Initiative Process," *San Francisco Chronicle,* January 18, 1999, A22.

72. *LIMIT v. Maleng* 874 F. Supp. 1138 (1994); *Term Limits Leadership Council v. Clark* 984 F. Supp 470 (1997); *On Our Terms '97 PAC v. Secretary of State of the State of Maine,* U.S. District Court, Docket #98-104-BDMC (1999). Wyoming prohibited payment per signature in 1996, but the restriction has yet to be challenged in court, according to Peggy Nighswonger, elections director in the Wyoming secretary of state's office (e-mail communications, March 13 and 27, 2000).

73. *Initiative & Referendum Inst. v. Jaeger,* U.S. District Court, A1-98-70 (1999); Dale Wetzel, "Judge Throws Out Petition Restrictions Challenge," *Bismarck Tribune,* August 3, 1999, A3. In February 2001 the U.S. Court of Appeals for the Eighth Circuit affirmed the district court's judgment (*Initiative & Referendum Inst. v. Jaeger* 2001 U.S. App. LEXIS 2186). The effect of the law is hard to estimate, but North Dakota is one of the few states where volunteer campaigns remain the norm. Of the eight initiatives on the ballot in North Dakota between 1996 and 1998, five were qualified by volunteers exclusively (data provided by Cory Fong of the North Dakota secretary of state's office).

74. *Portland Press Herald,* December 12, 1999, B6; *LIMIT v. Maleng* 874 F. Supp. 1138, quotation at 1140–41; *Meyer v. Grant* 486 U.S. 414, quotation at 426.

75. "Process Belongs to States," *Bismarck Tribune,* August 12, 1999, A4; *Portland Press Herald,* December 12, 1999, B6.

76. Denver lawyer Neil O'Toole, quoted in Richard Carelli, "Court Considers How Much States Can Regulate Ballot Initiatives," AP wire report, October 14, 1998.

77. *Canvasser v. Employment Department,* CA A100171, Court of Appeals of Oregon (1999); Sizemore quoted in David Kravets, "Signature Gathering Facing Court Fight," *Statesman Journal* (Salem, Ore.), February 5, 1999, C3. In February 2000 the Oregon Supreme Court let stand the Court of Appeals' ruling. The original hearing before the administrative law judge opened a revealing window on the underworld of signature gathering. Rhonda Buffington had set up a political consulting business (Affinity Communication) and obtained a contract with a large California signature-gathering firm, Kimball Petition Management, to coordinate the campaigns for three measures that Kimball had contracted to get on the ballot. Buffington's duty was to recruit individuals to gather signatures. She hired an office staff of four persons, whom both sides in the case agreed were properly considered employees, and about four hundred people, most of whom she did not know and who by the time of the hearing had "scattered to the far ends of the country." Most of the people who were gathering signatures for Affinity were also gathering for other firms, and according to testimony, some of these circulators were carrying "as many as 22 petitions." See *Affinity Communication v. Virginia Crosley,* hearing at [Oregon] State Employment Office, July 10, 1999, 26.

78. *Initiative & Referendum Institute v. Secretary of State of Maine,* U.S. District Court, District of Maine, Civil No. 98-104-B-C, 25–27.

79. *Meyer v. Grant* 486 U.S. 414, quotation at 423.

80. At the same time, Idaho changed its signature requirement from 10 percent of the number of votes in the last gubernatorial election to 6 percent of the number of registered

voters in the last general election. The total number of signatures required under these two standards was roughly the same: in 1996 petitioners needed 41,335 signatures, while in 1998 they needed 42,026. The change was made to be consistent with the new geographic distribution requirement. It was also hoped that registered voters would be a more stable basis for calculating signatures than the gubernatorial vote (e-mail communication with Penny Ysursa, March 3, 2000).

81. Louis Brandeis, *Other People's Money* (1933), as quoted in *Buckley v. Valeo* 424 U.S. 1, at 67, and *Victoria Buckley v. American Constitutional Law Foundation* 119 S. Ct. 636, at 657.

82. Lowenstein and Stern, "First Amendment," 200 n. 116; DuBois and Feeney, *Lawmaking by Initiative*, 102–4.

83. Tolbert, Lowenstein, and Donovan, "Election Law," 37; Lowenstein and Stern, "First Amendment," 219–23; DuBois and Feeney, *Lawmaking by Initiative*, 104–6; Garrett, "Money, Agenda Setting, and Direct Democracy," 1873–76.

84. DuBois and Feeney, *Lawmaking by Initiative*, 105; also see Sue Thomas interview in Patrick B. McGuigan, *The Politics of Direct Democracy in the 1980s: Case Studies in Popular Decision Making* (Washington, D.C.: Free Congress Research and Education Foundation, 1985), 117.

85. Barnett, *Operation of the Initiative*, 75; also see Key and Crouch, *The Initiative and Referendum in California*, 562.

86. Daniel H. Lowenstein, "Election Law Miscellany: Enforcement, Access to Debates, Qualification of Initiatives," *Texas Law Review* 77 (1999), 2007; Philip L. DuBois and Floyd F. Feeney, *Improving the California Initiative Process: Options for Change* (Berkeley: The California Policy Seminar, University of California, 1992), 85–88. DuBois and Feeney, *Lawmaking by Initiative*, 106–9.

4. In the Name of the People

1. Patrick B. McGuigan, *The Politics of Direct Democracy in the 1980s: Case Studies in Popular Decision Making* (Washington, D.C.: Free Congress Research and Education Foundation, 1985), 119.

2. Tom W. Smith, "That Which We Call Welfare by Any Other Name Would Smell Sweeter: An Analysis of the Impact of Question Wording on Response Patterns," *Public Opinion Quarterly* 57 (Spring 1987), 75–83; William A. Lund, "What's in a Name? The Battle Over Ballot Titles in Oregon," *Willamette Law Review* 34 (Winter 1998), 143–67.

3. Lydia Chavez, *The Color Bind: California's Battle to End Affirmative Action* (Berkeley: University of California Press, 1998), 80, 145–46; for poll results, also see 19–20, 99, 104, 106.

4. Chavez, *Color Bind*, 247; Julie Mason, "Court Backs Proposition A Ballot Wording," *Houston Chronicle*, November 27, 1997, A1; Ron Nissimov, "Judge Rejects Last Fall's Vote," *Houston Chronicle*, June 27, 1998, A1; idem, "Judge Shies at Revising Ballot on Affirmative Action Herself," *Houston Chronicle*, August 14, 1998, A37; idem, "Affirmative Action Ruling Is Overturned," *Houston Chronicle*, December 22, 1999, A1.

5. *Oregonian*, September 23, 1996, A8. Measure 47 was greatly helped by the arrival of property tax bills in mailboxes only days before ballots and voter guides arrived in the mail.

6. Chavez, *Color Bind*, 118, 160.

7. Bill Sizemore, quoted in David Postman, "Legislators Try to Limit Initiatives That Try to Limit Them—14 Citizen Measures on Oregon Ballot Last Year," *Seattle Times,* July 19, 1999, A1.

8. Charles Bell and Charles Price, "Are Ballot Measures the Magic Ride to Success?," *California Journal* 19 (September 1988), 380–81; California Commission on Campaign Financing, *Democracy by Initiative: Shaping California's Fourth Branch of Government,* (Los Angeles: Center for Responsive Government, 1992), 62–63, 275–76.

9. John Balzar, "Victims, Officials Kick Off Initiative to Speed Up Trials," *Los Angeles Times,* May 26, 1989, Metro section, pt. 2, 3; Mark Simon, "Don't Look Now—Election 1990," *California Journal* 20 (November 1989), 443–46.

10. James A. Barnes, "Comeback Kid II," *National Journal,* September 10, 1994, 2074–78; Jim Schultz, *The Initiative Cookbook: Recipes and Stories from California's Ballot Wars* (San Francisco: Democracy Center, 1998), 88; Chavez, *Color Bind,* 37; Los Angeles Time Poll, Survey #348. Proposition 187 was originally the idea of Ron Prince, an Orange County accountant, who believed illegal aliens are "killing us in California" (Patrick McDonnell, "Prop. 187 Turns Up Heat in U.S. Immigration Debate," *Los Angeles Times,* August 10, 1994, A1). Prince claimed that his crusade against illegal immigrants was sparked by a searing personal experience in which he lost half a million dollars to a housing contractor who was not a legal resident (see Jonathan Freedman, "Save Our State? It's More Like Spite Our State," *Los Angeles Times,* July 19, 1994, B7; and Alex Pulaski, "Ballot Items on Illegals Fought," *Fresno Bee,* May 29, 1994, B1). When a journalist checked out the story, however, it turned out that the contractor in question was a legal Canadian immigrant (married to a legal Nicaraguan immigrant), an auto mechanic and friend of Prince's, and that the money Prince actually lost in their housing venture (to build an extension on the friend's house and then a house for Prince) was only a small fraction of what Prince had told reporters (Gebe Martinez and Doreen Carvajal, "Creators of Prop. 187 Largely Escape Spotlight," *Los Angeles Times,* September 4, 1994, A1). Prince would have been just another crank outside Vons vainly trying to secure signatures but for the intervention of two lobbyists, Harold Ezell and Alan Nelson, who had been high-ranking officials in the U.S. Immigration and Naturalization Service during the Reagan administration. Ezall and Nelson saw the initiative as a chance to force the U.S. Supreme Court to revisit its 1982 ruling in *Plyer v. Doe,* in which a bare majority had decided that children of illegal aliens were constitutionally entitled to a public school education (Steve Albert, "Can States Stop Aid to Immigrants?" *The Recorder,* June 2, 1994, 1). The two former Reagan officials redrafted the measure and introduced it to the conservative wing of the Republican party. A host of conservative Republican officeholders from southern California clambered on board, including assemblyman Richard L. Mountjoy, who gave the initiative more than twenty-five thousand dollars. The California Republican party also quickly endorsed the measure and contributed over eighty-five thousand dollars in nonmonetary contributions for mailers and postage (Kevin Johnson and H.G. Reza, "County Kicks in One-Fifth of Immigration Initiative Funds," *Los Angeles Times,* August 3, 1994, B4).

11. Chavez, *Color Bind,* esp. 2–3, 39, 56, 68–76; quotations at 56, 75.

12. Catherine Bridge, "How Labor Turned the Tide on 226," *The Recorder,* June 12, 1998, 1; Ilana DeBare, "How Measure Evolved and Attracted Its Many Backers," *San Francisco Chronicle,* April 6, 1998, A15; David S. Broder, *Democracy Derailed: Initiative Campaigns and the Power of Money* (New York: Harcourt, 2000), esp. 92–104, 128, 142, 154.

13. Vlae Kershner, "Budget Initiatives Follow Separate Paths," *San Francisco Chronicle,*

September 14, 1992, A4; Virginia Ellis, "Welfare Measure That Boosts Governor's Power Sparks Costly War," *Los Angeles Times,* October 25, 1992, A3; Daniel M. Weintraub, "Wilson Regrets Tactic of Fusing Prop. 165 Issues," *Los Angeles Times,* January 12, 1993, A3.

14. John Jacobs, "Wilson's '98 Goals No Lame-Duck Agenda," *Fresno Bee,* December 21, 1997, B11; Robert Gunnison, "Strike 2 on Wilson Juvenile Crime Bills," *San Francisco Chronicle,* April 16, 1997, A16; Ed Mendel, "Wilson Initiative Targets Bad Teachers, Big Classes," *San Diego Union-Tribune,* December 12, 1997, A1; Nanette Asimov, "Complex Prop. 8 Creates Divisions," *San Francisco Chronicle,* October 21, 1998, A1; Nick Budnick, "Wilson Gets Tough on Juveniles," *The Recorder,* December 11, 1997, 3; Dana Wilkie, "Wilson Stands Out at Conference," *San Diego Union-Tribune,* November 23, 1997, A2; Robert Salladay, "Wilson to Target Education in Final Year," *San Francisco Examiner,* December 24, 1997, A1; Matt Isaacs, "For Pete's Sake," *SF Weekly,* January 12, 2000.

15. John Balzar, "Van de Kamp Ponders Political 'Swamp,' " *Los Angeles Times,* October 17, 1989, A3; Schultz, *Initiative Cookbook,* 86.

16. Edward Epstein, "Feinstein Starts Initiative Drive For Education," *San Francisco Chronicle,* December 25, 1997, A1.

17. Dan Morain, "California Elections: Proposition 184; 'Three Strikes': A Steamroller Driven by One Man's Pain," *Los Angeles Times,* October 17, 1994, A3. Even though the initiative was identical to the Three Strikes law passed by the legislature in early 1994, the initiative's backers continued to push the initiative because they believed the legislature would be far more reluctant to amend a law passed by the people than one passed by the legislature. Another reason the qualification effort went forth, explained a consultant for the campaign, was that Huffington "wanted very much to use it as a campaign issue."

18. Doug Willis, "Davis, Top Fund-Raiser, Doesn't Want to Change the Rules," Associated Press State & Local Wire, March 3, 2000; Lynda Gledhill, "Unz Bows Out of U.S. Senate Race," *San Francisco Chronicle,* December 1, 1999, A3.

19. Charles Price, "The Virtual Primary," *California Journal* 26 (November 1995), 39. The blanket primary was subsequently declared unconstitutional by the U.S. Supreme Court in *California Democratic Party v. Jones* 530 U.S. 567 (2000). The court ruled that the blanket primary violated political parties' First Amendment right to freedom of association.

20. Brad Cain, "Ambitious Lawmaker Stirs Pot on Crime, Social Issues," Associated Press State & Local Wire, February 6, 1999.

21. City Club of Portland, "The Initiative and Referendum in Oregon" (Portland, Ore., February 16, 1996), 28. Also see Leslie Helm, "Factories With Fences: Oregon's Ambitious Prison Work Program Is Being Closely Scrutinized for Ways to Manage the Rising Cost of a Growing Prison Population," *Los Angeles Times,* January 5, 1997, D1; Michelle Roberts, "Fight Brews Over State's Inmate Work Program," *Oregonian,* December 22, 1998, D1.

22. Amalie Young, "House Republicans Tour State Prison Work Programs," Associated Press State & Local Wire, February 17, 1999; emphasis added.

23. Sue Thomas, "Lawmakers as Petitioners," *Initiative Quarterly* 3 (Spring 1984), 4.

24. Ibid.; Broder, *Democracy Derailed,* 206.

25. Daniel A. Smith, *Tax Crusaders and the Politics of Direct Democracy* (New York: Routledge, 1998), 142, 153. Romer's efforts were also absorbed in opposing a high-profile antigay initiative as well as a school voucher initiative.

26. Charles Bell and Charles Price, "Are Ballot Measures the Magic Ride to Success?" *California Journal* 19 (September 1988), 381.

27. A seventh initiative, Measure 7, was written by OTU but was handed off to a prop-

erty rights group, Oregonians in Action, in the closing stages of the qualification campaign so that Sizemore could focus on what he considered the organization's most important measures. On election night, as it became clear that OTU's six initiatives were going down to defeat, Sizemore scrambled to associate himself once again with Measure 7, declaring it "our most important measure" and "our most powerful and our favorite measure."

28. "Technicality Hurts Gun Check Petition," *Statesman Journal* (Salem, Ore.), May 13, 2000, A1.

29. Jeff Mapes, "Sizemore Points Canvassers at Five Initiatives for 2000," *Oregonian*, May 28, 1998, D5.

30. Sizemore testimony, Oregon Senate Committee on Rules and Elections, April 25, 1995; also see Sizemore's testimony on SJR3 before the Oregon Senate Committee on Rules and Elections, February 9, 1999.

31. Phil Keisling, quoted in David Postman, "Legislators Try to Limit Initiatives That Try to Limit Them," *Seattle Times*, July 19, 1999, A1. Becky Miller, Sizemore's administrative assistant, explained, "We generally only operate through constitutional amendments because that is the only way for the people to directly voice their opinions. Statutory initiatives are subject to legislative interference and interpretation" (phone interview conducted by Courtney Gregoire, January 31, 2000).

32. Becky Miller, quoted in Dave Hogan and Harry Esteve, "Unions Enjoy Election Victories," *Oregonian*, November 12, 2000, B4; Dave Hogan and Steve Suo, "Business Groups Help Drive Campaign Spending into Record Territory," *Oregonian*, October 23, 2000, A1.

33. James Meyer and Lisa Grace Lednicer, "Kitzhaber Announces Three Initiatives to Help Schools," *Oregonian*, September 10, 1999, A1; Steve Law, "School-Fund Measure Cancelled," *Statesman Journal* (Salem, Ore.), April 12, 2000, A1; Jeff Mapes, "Kitzhaber Gives up on School Buffer Fund Proposal," *Oregonian*, April 12, 2000, A1; Harry Esteve, "Kitzhaber, Sizemore Go Another Round," *Oregonian*, April 17, 2000, A1; Brad Cain, "Trounced by Kitzhaber in 1998, in Some Ways Sizemore Now in the Driver's Seat," Associated Press State & Local Wire, May 6, 2000.

34. Jeff Mapes, "Sizemore Warms to Run for Governor," *Oregonian*, October 7, 1997, A1; James Meyer, "Sizemore Idea Is Popular, But He Isn't," *Oregonian*, April 20, 1997, A15.

35. Michele Mclellan, "Sizemore's Campaign for Governor Increases Interest in His Background," *Oregonian*, April 26, 1998, G1.

36. Ibid.; Harry Esteve, "Personalities Overshadow Issues in Oregon Governor's Race," Eugene *Register-Guard*, October 19, 1998; Nena Baker, "Sizemore Takes Hits Trying for Home Run," *Oregonian*, October 18, 1998, A25; Nena Baker and Brent Walth, "Sizemore Leaves Trail of Debts," *Oregonian*, April 19, 1998, A1. See also the comments of Colorado's Douglas Bruce, as quoted in Dan Smith, *Tax Crusaders*, 166.

37. David Kravets, "Despite Defeat, Sizemore Still Fights Tax Battle," *Statesman Journal* (Salem, Ore.), April 14, 1999, A1; Harry Esteve, "Kitzhaber, Sizemore Go Another Round."

38. Peter Wong, "Shetterly, Sizemore Square Off," *Statesman Journal* (Salem, Ore.), April 15, 2000, C1; Bill Sizemore, "The People Have the Power," *Oregonian*, April 29, 2000, D8.

39. Nena Baker, "Sizemore Firm Tallies Measure Money," *Oregonian*, July 22, 1998, B1; also see Broder, *Democracy Derailed*, 206–7. Sizemore's I&R firm also retained another sixty thousand dollars for overhead from money it was paid to qualify two other initiatives: Measures 65 and 61.

40. Smith, *Tax Crusaders,* 142, 146.

41. Ibid., 147; Scott Mackey, National Council of State Legislatures, quoted in Katie Kerwin, "Colorado Has Toughest Spending Law," *Denver Rocky Mountain News,* August 6, 1997, A8.

42. Smith, *Tax Crusaders,* 155; Sue Lindsay, "Bruce Goes Directly to Jail," *Denver Rocky Mountain News,* August 4, 1995, A5.

43. David Postman, "Colorado's Lessons on I-695: Voting on All Tax Increases Isn't Disastrous But It's Complicated," *Seattle Times,* October 11, 1999, A1.

44. However, the legislative referral, which was clearly motivated by distrust of Bruce, also had the ironic and unintended consequence of placing obstacles in the way of those who wished to overturn Bruce's 1992 tax limitation measure. In 1996 a proposed repeal of Bruce's TABOR amendment was rejected by the state's title-setting board on the grounds that the repeal initiative violated the single-subject rule. The board was unmoved by the proponents' argument that since TABOR contained multiple subjects, any measure to repeal it in its entirety must also necessarily deal with multiple subjects. See Fred Brown, "Referendum A Protects Amendment 1," *Denver Post,* February 28, 1996, B7.

45. The absence of a challenge to version 166 was apparently not by design; rather, the individual who had been responsible for the previous ballot title challenges was reportedly sick at the time (e-mail communication with Dan Smith, May 24, 2000).

46. Jim Lynch, "The Sassy Mouth of the Masses," *Seattle Times,* August 15, 1999, A1; Marsha King, "State, Local Preferential-Treatment Programs Targeted," *Seattle Times,* August 4, 1997, A1; Florangela Davila, "Carlson Tapped to Lead Campaign for Initiative 200," *Seattle Times,* October 9, 1997, B1.

47. According to the Washington Research Council, the state's tax burden in 1996 was thirteenth in the nation; see Washington Research Council, *How Washington Compares, 1999 edition (http://www.researchcouncil.org/HWC/HWC99/Tables/Totaltaxes.htm).*

48. Joseph Turner, "2 Car-Tax Initiatives Sputtering," *News Tribune* (Tacoma, Wa.), May 23, 1998, B1.

49. Angela Galloway, "Salesman Eyman Has a Car-Tax Deal for You," *Seattle Post-Intelligencer,* October 4, 1999, A1; Craig Welch, "Driving Force Behind I-695 Thinks Fast But Talks Faster," *Spokesman-Review* (Spokane, Wa.), September 1, 1999, A1.

50. Angela Galloway, "Proud Sponsor of I-695 Plans Exit from Political Stage," *Seattle Post-Intelligencer,* November 4, 1999, A4.

51. King, "State, Local Preferential-Treatment Programs Targeted."

52. David Postman, "Eyman's Initiative Coffers Swell Up," *Seattle Times,* May 11, 2000, B1.

53. Turner, "2 Car-Tax Initiatives Sputtering."

54. I-722, like I-695, was struck down by a superior court judge on the grounds that it contained two different proposals and thus violated the state's single-subject rule.

55. Rebecca Cook, "Eyman Drops HOV Lanes From His Roads Initiative," Associated Press State & Local Wire, May 9, 2000. Eyman refiled the measure only two months before the signature deadline. A genuine grassroots campaign would have found such a delay fatal to its chances for qualification, but for Eyman, who now had the resources to employ Bockwinkel's firm, the delay raised the per-signature cost without jeopardizing the measure's place on the ballot.

56. Howard Buck, "Taking the Initiative: Tim Eyman Casts for Change," *Columbian*

(Vancouver, Wa.), January 3, 2000, A1; David Postman, "Transit Targeted by I-695 Author," *Seattle Times,* December 16, 1999, B1; King, "State, Local Preferential-Treatment Programs Targeted"; Welch, "Driving Force Behind I-695 Thinks Fast But Talks Faster"; Galloway, "Salesman Eyman Has a Car-Tax Deal for You"; Lynch, "The Sassy Mouth of the Masses."

57. Buck, "Taking the Initiative: Tim Eyman Casts for Change"; Tim Eyman, "Voters Can Solve Problems Politicians Can't or Won't," *Seattle Times,* January 7, 2000, B5; David Ammons, "Initiative King: Eyman's Going for Two More Hits in 2000," Associated Press State & Local Wire, December 17, 1999; David Ammons, "Eyman Relishes Role of Pitchman for Populist Revolt," Associated Press State & Local Wire, October 2, 1999.

58. Buck, "Taking the Initiative: Tim Eyman Casts for Change"; David Ammons, "Campaign 2000: Cantwell In; Who'll Take on Locke? Eyman?" Associated Press State & Local Wire, January 22, 2000; David Ammons, "It's True. Tim Eyman Might Need Initiatives Anonymous," Associated Press State & Local Wire, December 17, 1999; Knute Berger, "Dumb-ocracy," *Seattle Weekly,* April 13, 2000, 7. In March 2000, a superior court judge invalidated I-695, a ruling upheld later that year by the Washington Supreme Court. But the legislature and the governor, bowing to "the will of the people," quickly rushed through legislation that upheld the thirty-dollar fee for car tabs. See David Ammons, "Cheap Car Tabs? It's a Done Deal," Associated Press State & Local Wire, March 22, 2000.

59. Measures of media coverage were obtained from a search of all Washington newspaper sources in Academic Universe by using a keyword search for each major political figure in Washington politics. In the six months between November 1, 1999, and April 30, 2000, 204 stories were retrieved on Eyman, which was second only to Governor Gary Locke (1,207). Next were Attorney General Christine Gregoire (177), gubernatorial candidate John Carlson (87), co-Speaker of the House Clyde Ballard (86), House Appropriations co-chair Tom Huff (74), Senate Ways and Means co-chair Valoria Loveland (64), Senate Majority Leader Sid Snyder (49), and Secretary of State Ralph Munro (34).

60. Catherine Tarpley, "Bus-ted," *Seattle Weekly,* March 9, 2000, 16. "Kamikazes" was the nickname Eyman gave to the signature gatherers and other volunteers who worked to get I-695 on the ballot. Interestingly, prior to the Oklahoma City bombing in 1995, Douglas Bruce carried business cards in which he proudly identified himself as "Terrorist." After the bombing Bruce changed the cards to read "Patriot" (Smith, *Tax Crusaders,* 154).

61. "American Democracy: How Far Can You Trust the People," *The Economist,* August 15, 1998, 23.

62. "Summary Report of Campaign Contributions and Expenditures, General Election, November 3, 1998," published by Elections Division, 141 State Capitol, Salem, Oregon.

63. Phone interview with author, January 29, 1999.

64. Report 98-F, California General Election Campaign Receipts, Expenditures, Cash on Hand and Debts for State Candidates and Officeholders (July 1, 1998 through December 31, 1998); Report 98-E, California's Statewide Ballot Measures on the November 3, 1998, General Election Ballot: Campaign Receipts and Expenditures Through December 31, 1998; Report L-98-3, Lobbying Expenditures and the Top 100 Lobbying Firms: January '97 through December '98. The reports are available on the webpage of the California secretary of state.

65. In 2000, for instance, the promoters of an Arkansas initiative authorizing casino gambling and establishing a state lottery promised voters that the lottery would generate sufficient profits to cover the in-state college tuition costs of every high school graduate in the state. Voters, though, saw through the implausible claim and decisively defeated the measure.

66. Rob Carson, "Voters Again Say No to Slot Machines," *News Tribune* (Tacoma, Wa.), November 6, 1996, B3; Lisa Kremer, "Election 1996," *News Tribune* (Tacoma, Wa.), October 18, 1996, A1.

67. Phil Sutin, "Industry Spent $10 Million to Back 'Boats-in-Moats,' " *St. Louis Post-Dispatch,* December 4, 1998, C5; Rick Alm, "Casino Group's War Chest Sizable," *Kansas City Star,* October 29, 1998, B1; Jo Mannies, "Political Parties Try to Capitalize on New Power," *St. Louis Post-Dispatch,* October 30, 1998, A7; *Nixon v. Shrink,* January 24, 2000, No. 98–963.

68. The campaign expenditure numbers are based on data compiled by Dan Smith of the University of Denver.

69. Not counting Colorado, the five successful gambling initiatives in the 1990s have been in Missouri (1994, 1998), Arizona (1996), Michigan (1996), and California (1998). Initiatives to expand gambling have been defeated in North Dakota (three in 1990), Ohio (1990, 1996), Utah (1992), Florida (1994), Washington (1995, 1996), and Oklahoma (1998). This does not include three state lottery initiatives (Nebraska in 1990, Arkansas and Oklahoma in 1996) in the 1990s, each of which failed. Lottery proponents had much greater success in the 1980s, passing lottery initiatives in a number of states, including Arizona in 1980, California and Oregon in 1984, and Florida in 1986. In 2000 gambling initiatives failed in Arkansas and Maine and passed in South Dakota.

70. Yes on E Committee, Post-General CS, December 6, 1996; Michigan First! Committee, Post-General CS, December 5, 1996; Vote No on Proposal E Committee, December 5, 1996; Campaign Finance Reports Online, Bureau of Elections, Michigan Department of State; Amy Lane, "Casinos' Lucky Numbers: Prop E Backers Had Money to Back Up a Winning Hand," *Crain's Detroit Business,* November 25, 1996, 1; idem, "Campaign-Finance Reports Show Pro-Casino Push," *Crain's Detroit Business,* December 9, 1996, 1; "Michigan Briefs," *South Bend Tribune,* October 16, 1996, B2.

71. Philip L. DuBois and Floyd Feeney, *Lawmaking by Initiative: Issues, Options and Comparisons* (New York: Agathon Press, 1998), 143. By not identifying itself by name in the initiative, Scientific Games got around a California constitutional provision that prohibited naming any private firm in a constitutional amendment. That provision, ironically, was enacted through a legislative referendum in direct response to a 1964 initiative by Robert W. Wilson, which proposed a state lottery and specified that it would be run by Wilson's American Sweepstakes Corp., which would retain 13 percent of revenues. Unlike Scientific Games, Wilson did not try to disguise his greed, admitting, "Sure, we want to make a buck." The lottery initiative, he boasted, would make his company "bigger than Standard Oil." See Paul Lieberman, "Another Roll: Gambling Advocate Launches Ballot Drive for Casinos," *Los Angeles Times,* January 26, 1992, A3.

72. Author's interview with Gordon Miller, January 21, 1999; Summary Report of Campaign Contributions and Expenditures, 1994 General Election. The measure was subsequently struck down by the courts as an unconstitutional abridgment of free speech.

73. Barnes Ellis, "Aloha Manufacturer Gives Conservatives Big Boost," *Oregonian,* June 20, 1994, B1.

74. Steve Law, "Bendl/Parks Initiatives Get Low Marks from Law Deans," *Business Journal,* September 6, 1996, 4.

75. *Bendl v. Parks* A10224999, Court of Appeals Records Office, Salem, Oregon; Gail Kinsey Hill, "Millionaire Defamed Employee, Jury Finds," *Oregonian,* March 4, 1999, D1;

Ashbel S. Green, "Appeals Court Reinstates Jury Verdict; the Finding Restores a $135,000 Award for a Fired Political Activist," *Oregonian, January 6, 2000, B5.

76. Howard Fineman, "Why Billionaire George Soros Is Trying to End the Drug War as We Know It," *Newsweek,* February 3, 1997, 24; Campaign Finance Report 96-F, Financing California's Statewide Ballot Measures: 1996 Primary and General Elections (*http://www.ss.ca.gov/prd/bmc96/prop215.htm*); Broder, *Democracy Derailed,* 191–97.

77. Mark Fritz, "Split Grows Inside Pot's Grass Roots," *Los Angeles Times,* January 21, 1998, A1; David Schaefer, "Marijuana Initiatives Blooming," *Seattle Times,* August 20, 1998, B1; Initiative Committees, Contributions and Expenditures, *1998 Election Financing Fact Book,* Washington State Public Disclosure Commission, Olympia, Washington, p. 15 (*http://web.pdc.wa.gov*); Summary Report of Campaign Contributions and Expenditures, 1996 General Election.

78. Chris Moeser, "Props. 104, 105 Both Push People Power," *Arizona Republic,* October 20, 1998, A1; Hal Mattern, "Push Begins for Voter Protection Act," *Arizona Republic,* September 18, 1997, B1; Jeremy Voas, "Say It Ain't Joe," *Phoenix New Times,* June 12, 1997; Campaign finance information is taken from the Arizona secretary of state's webpage (*http://www.sosaz.com/cfs/CampaignFinanceSearch.htm*); also see Broder, *Democracy Derailed,* 195–96.

79. The campaign finance records for the political action committee, Protecting Colorado's Water and Economy, are available on the Colorado secretary of state's web page at *http://www.dos1.state.co.us/campaign.* On Anschutz, see Jerd Smith, "The Man With the Cash," *Denver Rocky Mountain News,* December 21, 1997, W5, and Andy Van de Voorde, "The Miracle Worker," *Denver Westword,* January 29, 1998.

80. Author's interviews with Gary Kutcher, June 5–6, 2000, and James Musumeci, February 16, 1999.

81. Susan Gordon, "2 Groups Seize the Initiative to Alter Schools," *News Tribune* (Tacoma, Wa.), May 30, 1995, B1; Dick Lilly, "2 Couples Put Money on School Initiatives," *Seattle Times,* August 30, 1995, B1; Peter Callaghan, "Lobbyist Couple Do Spady Work for Law Creating Charter Schools," *News Tribune* (Tacoma, Wa.), January 21, 1996, D1.

82. Rebekah Denn, "Allen Helps Bankroll Initiatives," *Seattle Post-Intelligencer,* May 25, 2000, A1; Linda Shaw, "Allen Pushes Charter Schools," *Seattle Times,* May 25, 2000, A1. In the end, the initiative narrowly lost, despite the three million dollars spent by Allen.

83. Author's interview with Aaron Durland's mother, February 16, 1999.

84. Brendan Riley, "Ballot Proposal Seeks Ban on Prostitution in Nevada,"Associated Press State & Local Wire, January 26, 2000; Martin Griffith, "Search Continues for Missing Anti-Brothel Crusader," Associated Press State & Local Wire, November 10, 1999.

85. Barbara Serrano, "Citizens Are Taking Initiative," *Seattle Times,* March 27, 1994, A1; "Initiatives to the People, 1914–1919," Initiative History and Statistics, Office of the Secretary of State, State of Washington (*http://www.secstate.wa.gov/inits/iphist.htm*) and "Proposed Initiatives to the People-2000," Initiative History and Statistics, Office of the Secretary of State, State of Washington (*http://www.secstate.wa.gov/inits/people2000.htm*); Charles M. Price, "In the Shadow of Jarvis and Gann: Citizen Initiators Tilt at the Electoral Windmill," *California Journal* 26 (April 1995), 41.

86. David Postman and Dionne Searcey, "Lawmakers Talk Tax Cuts," *Seattle Times,* January 11, 2000, B1; "Initiatives to the People, 1914–1919," Initiative History and Statistics, Office of the Secretary of State, State of Washington (*http://www.secstate.wa.gov/inits/iphist.htm*); Price, "In the Shadow of Jarvis and Gann," 41.

5. Majority Rules

1. *The Book of the States, 1998–99* (Lexington, Ky.: The Council of State Governments), 5–6 (table 1.2); also see Philip L. DuBois and Floyd Feeney, *Lawmaking by Initiative: Issues, Options and Comparisons* (New York: Agathon Press, 1998), 72. It must be acknowledged at the outset that state constitutions are favored with nothing like the public reverence that attaches to the U.S. Constitution. Indeed, if some surveys are to be believed, nearly half of the public is not even aware that its state has a constitution (G. Alan Tarr, *Understanding State Constitutions* [Princeton: Princeton University Press, 1998], 2). The U.S. Constitution has been amended 27 times in over two hundred years, whereas the average current state constitution has existed for one hundred years and has been amended about 120 times. Only nineteen states still have their original constitution, and a few states like Georgia and Louisiana have gone through ten or more constitutions (23–24; the average length of a state constitution is calculated from *The Book of the States, 1998–99*, 3 [table 1.1]). The frequent amending of state constitutions, moreover, is not due solely or even mostly to the initiative process. The longest and most amended constitution belongs to Alabama (220,000 words and over 600 amendments in a hundred years), a state that does not possess the initiative power. California has the second most amended state constitution (493 amendments between 1879 and 1997), but less than one-tenth of those amendments came from citizen initiatives. Every state constitution in the nation has been amended far more often by the legislature than by initiative. Even in Colorado, where over 40 percent of the constitutional amendments submitted to voters have come through the initiative process, the actual impact of initiatives on the constitution is diminished because the success rate of legislative amendments is so much higher than that of initiated amendments.

During the last two decades in Oregon, about 40 percent of constitutional amendments have been proposed by initiative, yet only a little over one-quarter of the amendments passed by voters came by way of the initiative process. The impact of the initiative on the Oregon state constitution is more impressive, however, if one focuses on the immediate past. Between 1994 and 1998, 57 percent of the 44 proposed amendments to Oregon's constitution were placed on the ballot by initiative. Despite the lower success rate of initiative amendments (36 percent as compared to about 63 percent of legislative amendments), 43 percent of the amendments in Oregon during these years came by initiative. Moreover, these numbers understate the impact of the initiative process on the constitution since many legislative amendments are efforts to fix deficiencies in initiative amendments. This was true with both legislative initiatives in 1997, one of which remedied a 1994 constitutional initiative that required prisoners to work and the other of which clarified a 1996 constitutional initiative that reduced property taxes. Seven of the nine legislative amendments on the ballot in 1999 were actually separate parts of a 1996 initiative (Measure 40) that had been struck down in court for containing multiple amendments. The legislative sponsor of these seven amendments, Kevin Mannix, was also the chief petitioner of Measure 40. In sum, though the role of the initiative in amending the constitution should not be exaggerated, it cannot be ignored either, particularly in states like Oregon and Colorado where initiated constitutional amendments have become commonplace.

2. J. Allen Smith, *The Spirit of American Government* (1907), quoted in John J. Dinan, *Keeping the People's Liberties: Legislators, Citizens, and Judges as Guardians of Rights* (Lawrence: University Press of Kansas, 1998), 65; Stephen Holmes, *Passions and Con-*

straint: On the Theory of Liberal Democracy (Chicago: University of Chicago Press, 1995), 162, 171.

3. Austin Ranney, *Channels of Power: The Impact of Television on American Politics* (New York: Basic Books, 1983), 74; Pauline Maier, *The Old Revolutionaries: Political Lives in the Age of Samuel Adams* (New York: Knopf, 1980), 176; James Sterling Young, *The Washington Community, 1800–1828* (New York: Columbia University Press, 1966), 54.

4. William C. Mitchell, "The Ambivalent Social Status of the American Politician," *Western Political Quarterly* 12 (September 1959), 683–98; Maurice Klain, " 'Politics'—Still a Dirty Word," *Antioch Review* 15 (Winter 1955–56), 457–66; Ranney, *Channels of Power,* 75; Seymour Martin Lipset and William Schneider, *The Confidence Gap: Business, Labor, and Government in the Public Mind,* rev. ed. (Baltimore: Johns Hopkins University Press, 1987), 74–79.

5. James A. Morone, *The Democratic Wish: Popular Participation and the Limits of American Government* (New York: Basic Books, 1990).

6. Subcommittee on Courts and Intellectual Property of the House Committee on the Judiciary, *Hearing on the H. R. 1170,* 104th Cong., 1st sess., April 5, 1995. The bill passed in the House but never made it out of committee in the Senate; it reemerged in 1997 as a part of H.R. 1252, the Judicial Reform Act, but again fell short.

7. DuBois and Feeney, *Lawmaking by Initiative,* 78–80. In California the legislature can make changes on its own only if the initiative explicitly allows for this. When an initiative does allow for legislative change, it virtually always requires a legislative supermajority and insists that the legislative amendment be "consistent with and further the purposes of the initiative" (79, 80 n. 12).

8. Julian N. Eule, "Checking California's Plebiscite," *Hastings Constitutional Law Quarterly* 17 (1989), 156–57; James D. Barnett, *The Operation of the Initiative, Referendum, and Recall in Oregon* (New York: Macmillan, 1915), 174–75; DuBois and Feeney, *Lawmaking by Initiative,* 45 n. 26. The quotation is from former California Supreme Court Justice Joseph Grodin, who failed to hold on to his seat in a retention election in the 1980s.

9. Eule, "Checking California's Plebiscite," 154; idem, "Judicial Review of Direct Democracy," *Yale Law Journal* 99 (May 1990), 1503–90. The Eule thesis is discussed critically in Robin Charlow, "Judicial Review, Equal Protection and the Problem with Plebiscites," *Cornell Law Review* 79 (March 1994), 527–630.

10. These same restrictions apply to constitutional amendments referred to the people by the state legislature. The initiative in Illinois, though, is limited to amendments pertaining to "structural and procedural subjects contained in Article IV." In the three decades since Illinois gained the initiative power, only one initiative has ever reached the ballot: a 1980 initiative that reduced the size of the legislature. The measure passed with 69 percent of the vote.

11. Three other states have requirements that theoretically could result in a supermajority requirement for statutes. Massachusetts, Washington, and Nebraska require that the majority be at least 30, 33.3, and 35 percent, respectively, of those who go to the polls (David Magleby, *Direct Legislation: Voting on Ballot Propositions in the United States* [Baltimore: Johns Hopkins University Press, 1984], 46). Voter drop-off would have to be in the neighborhood of 35 to 40 percent for these provisions to begin to have any effect, and then only in a very tight contest. Once upon a time such high drop-off rates were not unheard of. Massachusetts, for instance, experienced 50 and 41 percent drop-off on the two initiatives on the ballot in 1932, one regulating nomination procedures and the other legalizing the practice of chiropractics (neither initiative was affected by the 30 percent threshold because one was

defeated and the other won by a better than two-to-one margin). In the past two decades, however, drop-off on statutory initiatives in Massachusetts has never been higher than 15 percent and, as often as not, is under 10 percent. A more consequential threshold of 40 percent has been adopted by Mississippi, where the initiative can only be used for constitutional amendments. Under this 40 percent requirement voter drop-off would still have to be at least 20 percent before an initiative with a majority could fail.

12. Richard Carelli, "Challenge to Wyoming Voter Abstention Law Rejected," The Associated Press State & Local Wire, December 14, 1998. The case was *Brady v. Ohman* 105 F. 3d 726 (1998).

13. These drop-off rates were derived from data kindly provided by Dan Smith of the University of Denver. Also see Joseph Lubinski and Daniel A. Smith, "Direct Democracy During the Progressive Era: A Crack in the Populist Veneer?" typescript, pp. 10–11.

14. In 1996 Oregon voters narrowly defeated an initiative that would have forbidden the legislature, for a period of five years, from altering a statute that had been passed by the voters. Any alteration to the initiative during this five-year period would have to be referred to the voters. After five years the legislature could amend or repeal the statute on its own, but only with a three-fifths vote of both houses of the legislature.

15. *The Book of the States, 1998–99*, 5–6 (table 1.2); Dubois and Feeney, *Lawmaking by Initiative*, 34, 73.

16. One possible way out of the dilemma, suggested by the California Commission on Campaign Financing, is to permit a simple majority vote to delete language from the constitution and, when desired, to add it to the statute books instead. The supermajority requirement would be reserved for additions to the constitution. See California Commission on Campaign Financing, *Democracy by Initiative: Shaping California's Fourth Branch of Government* (Los Angeles: Center for Responsive Government, 1992), 192.

17. J.H.M., "Judicial Activism and Municipal Bonds: Killing Two-Thirds with One Stone?" *Virginia Law Review* 56 (March 1970), 296–306, 331–34; Donald P. Lacy and Philip P. Martin, "The Extraordinary Majority: The Supreme Court's Retreat from Voting Equity," *California Western Law Review* 10 (Spring 1974), 561–63.

18. "Passing Tax Increases the Hard Way," *State Legislatures* 22 (July-August 1996), 9; Steven Hayward, "The Tax Revolt Turns 20," *Policy Review* 90 (July-August 1998), 9–12. Having achieved tax supermajorities in a number of states, some antigovernment activists are now looking to a new frontier of spending supermajorities. Conservative law professors John O. McGinnis and Michael B. Rappaport have developed an argument favoring supermajorities for spending bills as a means of limiting government spending, particularly spending that benefits special interest groups ("Supermajority Rules as a Constitutional Solution," *William and Mary Law Review* 40 [February 1999], 365–470). Elizabeth Garrett counters that supermajorities for spending bills might actually lead to more logrolling and more catering to special interests because lawmakers would be forced to assemble larger (and hence more expensive) coalitions ("A Fiscal Constitution with Supermajority Voting Rules," *William and Mary Law Review* 40 [February 1999], 471–504).

19. Cf. the recommendation made by the California Commission on Campaign Financing in *Democracy by Initiative*, 25–26, 192–93. Measure 63 was subsequently struck down by the Oregon Court of Appeals, but not because of the supermajority provision. Rather, the court found the complex initiative contained multiple constitutional amendments that were not "closely related"; see *Swett v. Keisling* 171 Ore. App. 119 (2000).

20. The change in Nevada's system occurred in November 1962, when voters approved

a constitutional amendment, referred to them by the legislature, that eliminated the requirement that an initiative proposing a constitutional change first had to be presented to the legislature and the governor. In place of the indirect initiative the legislature devised the idea of successive majorities.

21. Dubois and Feeney, *Lawmaking by Initiative,* 72. In November 2000 Nebraska voters soundly rejected a legislative referral that would have required votes in two separate elections before a constitutional amendment could take effect. The proposal would have applied to legislative referrals as well as initiative petitions, although a legislative amendment could have been voted on twice in the same year (in the primary and general elections), whereas initiative amendments would have had to wait two years until the next general election for the second vote.

22. Jack McFarren, "How Question 6 Reversal Happened," *Reno Evening Gazette,* November 5, 1990, 3.

23. Peter Schrag, *Paradise Lost: California's Experience, America's Future* (New York: New Press, 1988), 173–77.

24. "Swackhamer Restates Question 9 Position," *Reno Evening Gazette,* September 4, 1980, 6; Terri Gunkel, "Question 9 Foes Hit the Streets," *Reno Evening Gazette,* October 29, 1982, C4; "Question 9 Protest Planned Thursday," *Reno Evening Gazette,* October 27, 1982, D4.

25. California, Alaska, North Dakota, and Oklahoma are the only states that currently permit initiatives to appear on primary ballots, but only in California are initiatives routinely voted on in primary elections. The states that allow initiatives in odd-numbered years are Washington, Maine, Ohio, and Mississippi.

26. Dubois and Feeney, *Lawmaking by Initiative,* 90–91; [Massachusetts] Legislative Research Council, "Report Relative to Revising Statewide Initiative and Referendum Provisions of the Massachusetts Constitution," February 4, 1975, 93–94.

27. Dubois and Feeney, *Lawmaking by Initiative,* 30; *Statewide Ballot Measures, 1919 Through 1998,* published by William Francis Galvin, Secretary of the Commonwealth, Elections Division, Boston, Massachusetts, December 1, 1998.

28. In Massachusetts, if the legislature fails to enact the statute that is proposed by initiative, the petitioners can get the initiative onto the ballot by gathering an additional quantity of signatures equal to half of 1 percent of the votes cast for governor at the preceding biennial state election.

29. The other states that use the indirect initiative are Alaska, Maine, Michigan, Mississippi, Nevada, Ohio, Utah, Washington, and Wyoming. In Utah and Washington the petitioners are given a choice between using the direct and indirect initiative.

30. Thomas E. Cronin, *Direct Democracy: The Politics of Initiative, Referendum, and Recall* (Cambridge, Mass.: Harvard University Press, 1989), 48; Thomas C. McClintock, "Seth Lewelling, William S. U'Ren and the Birth of the Oregon Progressive Movement," *Oregon Historical Quarterly* 68 (September 1967), 206–7; Magleby, *Direct Legislation,* 31.

31. Dubois and Feeney, *Lawmaking by Initiative,* 49–57.

32. This double majority scheme would run into constitutional problems in the United States since it violates the "one person, one vote" concept first articulated by the Supreme Court in the early 1960s. In 1969 the New Mexico Supreme Court used the "one person, one vote" idea to strike down the state's requirement that a constitutional change could not be made without a two-thirds vote in each county. The constitutional problem was not the

supermajority requirement; in fact, the court upheld the state's requirement that a proposed amendment must also be approved by three-fourths of the ballots cast. Rather, the trouble with the provision was that it gave equal weight to counties with unequal populations, thereby making the vote of a person in a sparsely populated county worth more than the vote of a person in a densely populated area (Lacy and Martin, "The Extraordinary Majority," 565). Using the "one person, one vote" standard, the only thing that prevents the Supreme Court from declaring the U.S. Senate unconstitutional is Article 1 of the Constitution. State legislatures, which lack this constitutional protection, are forbidden from representing geography rather than people.

33. Dubois and Feeney, *Lawmaking by Initiative,* 49–57. The double majority requirement, however, has not proved to be a major obstacle in the passage of constitutional amendments proposed by the Swiss legislature. Between 1874 and 1991 three-quarters of the 118 constitutional amendments proposed by the Swiss parliament were enacted into law, as well as 65 percent of its 26 counterproposals (49).

34. Dubois and Feeney, *Lawmaking by Initiative,* 52.

35. At the cantonal level, where statutory initiatives are permitted, laws reached through the initiative process are never given legal priority over statutes enacted through the legislative process. No cantonal assembly is prevented from amending initiative statutes (Dubois and Feeney, *Lawmaking by Initiative,* 80 n. 14).

36. Whether this is true in practice is a matter of vigorous debate among scholars. See, for example, Elisabeth Gerber, "Legislative Response to the Threat of Popular Initiatives," *American Journal of Political Science* 40 (February 1996), 99–128; and Edward Lascher, Michael Hagen, and Steven Rochlin, "Gun Behind the Door? Ballot Initiatives, State Policies and Public Opinion," *Journal of Politics* 58 (August 1996), 760–75.

37. *Senior Citizens League v. Department of Social Security* 228 P.2d 478 (1951); *Fritz v. Gorton* 517 P.2d 911 (1974); *Washington Federation of State Employees v. State of Washington* 901 P.2d 1028 (1995); *Amalgamated Transit Union Local 587 v. State of Washington* 11 P.3d 762 (2000); Angela Galloway, "Tax-Cut Initiative Voided by Judge," *Seattle Post-Intelligencer,* February 24, 2001, A1.

38. In two cases, however, the California Supreme Court refused to hear an appeal from appeals court rulings in which the "reasonably germane" test had been used to invalidate an initiative. The first of these was a 1988 case, *California Trial Lawyers Association v. Eu* (200 Cal. App. 3d 351), in which the appeals court struck from the ballot a no-fault automobile insurance initiative that totaled 120 pages and 67 sections. Nestled unobtrusively in this long and complex revision of the insurance laws was a section that regulated campaign contributions by insurance companies and consumer groups, and this the court reasonably found to be not germane to the purpose of the initiative. The insurance companies quickly rewrote the measure, taking out the offending clause, and still managed to qualify it for the 1988 ballot. The second case involved a postelection review of a 1990 ballot measure that regulated household toxics, health insurance for seniors, nursing homes, initiative advertising, and corporate investment in South Africa. These disparate provisions were bundled under the subject of the public's right to know, but the courts ruled that while the measure required disclosure to consumers, voters, and investors, this was not sufficient to make these provisions "reasonably germane" (*Chemical Specialties v. Deukmejian* 227 Cal. App. 3d 663). In December 1999, for the first time in its history, the California Supreme Court leaned on the precedents set by these two cases to use the single-subject rule to invalidate an ini-

tiative, one that had already qualified for the May 2000 ballot and been assigned a ballot number. The court ruled that the proposition contained at least two purposes that were not "reasonably germane": (1) reducing legislative pay and changing the process by which legislative salaries are set, and (2) giving the power to reapportion legislative seats to the state supreme court. Each of these and other provisions in the measure required voter approval to go into effect, but this commonality, the court ruled, was not enough to make the disparate provisions "reasonably germane" (*Senate of the State of Cal. v. Jones* 21 Cal. 4th 1142). The court did not explicitly repudiate the permissive standard it had applied in the 1970s and 1980s, but it is hard to see why legislative pensions and term limits are "reasonably germane" yet legislative pay and reapportionment are not. Without overruling the standard articulated in the single-subject decisions of the 1970s and 1980s, the California high court appears to have moved toward a decidedly more stringent understanding of the term "reasonably germane."

39. Dubois and Feeney, *Lawmaking by Initiative,* 131–32, 134; *Fair Political Practices Commission v. Superior Court* 25 Cal. 3d 33 (1979), quotation at 43; *Brosnahan v. Brown* 32 Cal. 3d 236 (1982); *Legislature v. Eu* 54 Cal. 3d 492 (1991).

40. *Raven v. Deukmejian* 52 Cal. 3d 336 (1990), quotation at 364; also see Marilyn E. Minger, "Putting the 'Single' Back in the Single-Subject Rule: A Proposal for Initiative Reform in California," *U.C. Davis Law Review* 24 (Summer 1991), 879–930; and Steven W. Ray, "The California Initiative Process: The Demise of the Single-Subject Rule," *Pacific Law Journal* 14 (July 1983), 1095–1111.

41. Daniel H. Lowenstein, "California Initiatives and the Single-Subject Rule," *UCLA Law Review* 30 (June 1983), 936–75.

42. *Fine v. Firestone* 448 So. 2d 984 (1984), quotation at 989; Joseph W. Little, "Does Direct Democracy Threaten Constitutional Governance in Florida?" *Stetson Law Review* 24 (Spring 1995), 398 n. 32.

43. As the California Supreme Court pointed out, "Given the widespread public debate of initiatives, the explanations in the ballot pamphlets and in the media, and the huge volume of legislative business—over 1,000 bills enacted each year—it is unreasonable to assume that initiative measures receive less scrutiny than proposed legislation" (*Fair Political Practices Commission v. Superior Court* 25 Cal. 3d 33, quotation at 42).

44. In splitting the measure into two separate initiatives, the Nevada court did not rely on a single-subject rule. Rather, the justices focused on the misleading nature of the initiative, specifically its failure to explain clearly the effect the initiative would have on judicial terms, and its failure to distinguish the judiciary from the legislature and the executive. "We have the real concern," the court wrote, "that a casual reader will not understand that the proposed limits apply to judges and not just to officers elected to the political branches of government. Some voters who want term limits for 'politicians' may actually prefer a career judiciary." An initiative's "failure to inform voters as to its nature and effect" was "sufficient ground" to strike down an initiative, but the court opted instead to remedy possible voter confusion by splitting the measure in two (*Nevada Judges Association v. Lau* 910 P.2d 898 [1996], quotations at 903).

45. *Armatta v. Kitzhaber* 327 Ore. 250 (1998), quotations at 255, 277, 283.

46. See, for example, the reactions quoted in David R. Anderson, "State Court Throws Out Crime Measure," *Oregonian,* June 26, 1998, A1.

47. The requirement that jurors be registered voters was smothered by the legislature, so

voters did not get the opportunity to vote on this particularly questionable part of Measure 40. Instead, the legislature agreed on an alternative measure that would prohibit citizens convicted of a misdemeanor "involving violence or dishonesty" within the last five years from serving as jurors. Both Measure 40 and the legislative referral, Measure 75, included a fifteen-year ban on convicted felons. The ban on felons already existed under state law, so this part of the measure, like a number of other parts of Measure 40, didn't change the law so much as constitutionalize it. Voters who were unaware that felons were already barred from jury duty might have had difficulty voting no, fearing that it meant they would be approving trial by felons. Including the felon provision thus served to forestall an informed discussion about the substantial practical difficulties of implementing a prohibition against jury duty by citizens convicted of "dishonest" misdemeanors.

48. The decision had an immediate impact on the secretary of state's preelection review of initiative petitions. Using the "separate-vote" test of the 1998 *Armatta* decision, the secretary of state's office rejected seven initiatives in under a year, which was roughly equal to the number of initiatives that had been turned down in the previous eight years combined (Steve Law, "State Keeps Initiatives Off Ballot," *Statesman Journal* [Salem, Ore.], October 25, 1999, A1). Lower courts have also begun to use the *Armatta* decision to weed out several ambitious initiatives. In November 2000 the Oregon Court of Appeals (*Swett v. Keisling* 171 Ore. App. 119) relied on *Armatta* to invalidate Measure 62, and a few months later a circuit judge did the same to invalidate Measure 7, an initiative that would require government to compensate landowners for any government regulation that lowers property values (Dave Hogan and Tomoko Hosaka, "Judge Tosses Measure 7," *Oregonian*, February 23, 2001, A1).

49. Dubois and Feeney, *Lawmaking by Initiative*, 136–37, emphasis added. Prior to *Fine v. Firestone*, in fact, the Florida Supreme Court had twice determined in 1976 and 1978 that the initiative single-subject rule should be interpreted in the same way as the single-subject rule for legislation.

6. The Initiative Goes to Court

1. Kenneth P. Miller, "The Role of Courts in the Initiative Process: A Search for Standards" (paper presented at the annual meeting of the American Political Science Association, Atlanta, Ga., September 1999), 12; idem, "Judging Ballot Initiatives: A Unique Role for Courts" (paper presented at the annual meeting of the Western Political Science Association, San Jose, Ca., March 2000), 9. Miller's findings are based on a study of every successful initiative in California, Colorado, Oregon, and Washington between 1960 and 1999.

2. More precisely, between 1995 and 1999 20 percent of the 149 ballot title cases filed were dismissed for one reason or another, 38 percent were certified as written, and 42 percent were rewritten by the court. The data presented in this section were provided by Jennifer Hannan, of the Appellate Court Records Section of the Oregon Judicial Department, and Keith Garza, staff attorney for the Oregon Supreme Court.

3. Author's interview with Keith Garza, August 3, 2000.

4. *Rooney v. Kulongoski* 322 Ore. 15 (1995).

5. Ibid., quotations at 58–60, 25. Those three are Justice Durham, who joined Unis' 1995 dissenting opinion; Justice Van Hoomissen (see his dissent in *Starrett v. Myers* 330 Ore. 147

[2000]), who in the 1995 *Rooney* decision had sided with the majority; and Justice Riggs (see his concurring opinion in *Nelson v. Myers* 330 Ore. 92 [2000]), who was elevated to the court in 1998.

6. In order to appeal in Oregon, the interested party must have offered testimony, either in writing or in person, at the hearing for the ballot title.

7. These numbers are based on cases retrieved from a search using Lexis-Nexis Academic Universe. I have excluded those cases in which the issue was purely procedural and did not involve the court making a judgment about the validity of the ballot title or whether the initiative violated a single-subject rule.

8. *In re An Initiated Constitutional Amendment Respecting Rights of the Public to Uninterrupted Services by Public Employees* 609 P.2d 631 (1980), at 632, quoting from *Bauch v. Anderson* 497 P.2d 698 (1972); *In re Proposed Initiative Concerning Drinking Age* 691 P.2d 1127 (1984), quotation at 1132; also see *Say v. Baker* 322 P.2d 317 (1958), which, the court in *Bauch* said, "epitomized" Colorado's case law on ballot titles.

9. *Aisenberg v. Campbell* 1 P.3d 720 (2000), quotations at 723. *Garcia v. Chavez* 4 P.3d 1094 (2000). Two justices claimed the initiative violated the single-subject rule because it contained "at least three distinct and unrelated purposes: (1) instruction of Colorado public school students in the English language, with an option for parents to waive their children out of the 'English immersion' program; (2) reallocation of school districts' constitutional authority to control the instruction of their students; and (3) elimination of bilingual education programs."

10. The statute, which has remained basically unchanged throughout the latter half of the twentieth century, says only that "the court shall remand [the case] with instructions, pointing out where the Title Board is in error." An early precedent for having the court direct the board to use specific language was established in *Cook v. Baker* 214 P.2d 787 (1950), where the court rejected the board's title as insufficiently brief. The court offered its own, more concise language, though it was clearly hesitant to do so. "We *suggest*," the justices politely began, "the following, which *we consider* adequate, and which *in our opinion* complies with the requirements of the law" (emphasis added). A dissenting judge severely chastised the majority, pointing out that "the suggestion of a proper ballot title by this court is beyond our function." The late-twentieth-century Colorado court, in contrast, has expressed no doubts about the propriety of telling the board how to write titles.

11. *In re An Initiated Constitutional Amendment etc.* 609 P.2d 631 (1980), quotation at 632; *In re Proposed Initiative on Parental Notification of Abortions for Minors* 794 P.2d 238 (1990), quotation at 242; *In re Title, Ballot Title, Submission Clause, & Summary by the Title Board* 877 P.2d 848 (1994), quotations at 850–51.

12. *Arizona Legislative Council v. Howe* 965 P.2d 770 (1998), quotations at 775. In Arizona the secretary of state is charged with writing the ballot title and a summary of the effect of a yes or no vote. The Legislative Council is charged with drafting a neutral analysis of the measure and its effects. The title, summary, and analysis are written only after the proponents of the measure have gathered and submitted the required signatures.

13. *Fairness & Accountability in Ins. Reform v. Greene* 886 P.2d 1338 (1994).

14. Jeffrey A. Singer, "Ruling Unfairly Singled out Prop. 107," *Arizona Republic*, October 4, 2000, B9; Robert Robb, "Court Is Improperly Refereeing Initiatives," *Arizona Republic*, August 13, 2000, B11; Paul Davenport, "Supreme Court Overturns Descriptions of Ballot Measures," Associated Press State & Local Wire, August 8, 2000; idem, "Court

Strikes Part of Description of Bilingual Education Measure," Associated Press State & Local Wire, August 18, 2000.

15. *Stavros v. Office of Legislative Research and General Counsel* 2000 UT 63 (2000). The LRGC's ballot title for Initiative A read: "Shall a law be enacted to: (1) declare English to be the official language of Utah; (2) make English the sole language of government and require all official state and local government documents and actions to be in English, with specified exceptions; (3) require the State Board of Education and the State Board of Regents to make rules for the public and higher education systems that assist non-English speaking persons to learn English and that encourage foreign language instruction; and (4) require an accounting of any state funds affected by implementation of this proposed law?" The court's rewrite read, "Shall a law be enacted to: (1) declare English Utah's official and sole language for state and local government documents and action; (2) exempt those documents and actions required by the United States and Utah constitutions; federal law and regulations; law enforcement, public safety, and health requirements; public and higher education; certain judicial proceedings; economic development and tourism; and libraries; (3) require public and higher education to enact rules to promote learning and using English and encourage learning foreign language; and (4) return to the General Fund monies appropriated or designated for services in another language, and require accounting?" For Initiative B, the LRGC wrote, "Shall a law be enacted to: (1) change provisions relating to the forfeiture of property involved in the commission of any of the crimes specified in the Initiative: (a) to give additional protection to persons whose property is sought to be forfeited, including persons accused of any of the specified crimes; (b) to impose additional limitations and requirements on the forfeiture of property; and (c) to change how the proceeds of forfeited property are distributed; and (2) narrow the class of racketeering defendants subject to an alternative fine and reduce the maximum allowable amount of that fine?" The high court overhauled the ballot title to read, "Shall Utah law be amended to: (1) forbid forfeiture (seizure and sale) of property involved in crime where an innocent owner neither knew of nor consented to the crime; (2) create uniform procedures to protect property owners where forfeiture is sought by the government; (3) require the government to prove property is subject to forfeiture, and to reimburse owners for damage to property in custody; (4) require distribution of forfeiture proceeds, after deductions for court costs and victim losses, to schools instead of counties or the state; (5) clarify valuation methods for forfeited property, and require tracking and reporting of all money from its sale?" In both cases virtually nothing of the LRGC's language was retained by the court.

16. Greg Burton, "Court Won't Interfere in Initiative B's Impact Statement," *Salt Lake Tribune,* September 2, 2000, D2; "Group Asks Supreme Court for Further Changes in Voter Guide," Associated Press State & Local Wire, August 30, 2000.

17. Shannon Johnston, "Judge's Action May Set Precedent for Ballot Titles," *Seattle Times,* February 15, 1994, B3.

18. Associated Press, "Ballot Title Changes for Partial-birth Ban," *Columbian* (Vancouver, Wa.), May 10, 1998, B2; David Ammons, "Wording of Ballots Affects the Outcome," *Columbian,* August 2, 1998, B2.

19. Fla. Stat. Ann. 101.161.

20. The only other states that allow initiatives for constitutional but not statutory changes are Mississippi and Illinois, neither of which use the initiative process to any significant extent.

21. *Advisory Opinion to the Attorney General—Limited Marine Net Fishing* 620 So. 2d 997 (1993), quotations at 1000.

22. *Advisory Opinion to the Attorney General Re: Voter Approval of New Taxes* 644 So. 2d 486 (1994), quotations at 492–94.

23. Ibid., quotations at 497–98.

24. William Yardley, "Connerly Plan Attacked in Court," *St. Petersburg Times*, March 7, 2000, A1.

25. Jim Saunders, "Court Snuffs Connerly's Anti-Affirmative Action Drive," *Florida Times-Union* (Jacksonville), July 14, 2000, B1; Janet Marshall, "Court Kills Affirmative Action Vote," *Ledger* (Lakeland, Fl.), July 14, 2000, B1. It is quite possible and more than a little ironic that the Florida Supreme Court, in keeping Connerly's anti–affirmative action initiatives off the ballot, may have cost Al Gore the presidential election.

26. *Adams v. Gunter* 238 So. 2d 824 (1970), quotation at 835.

27. In 1998 the court struck Amendment 4 from the ballot because of problems with signatures, and they did not need to reach the ballot title question. One initiative in 1996, a campaign finance measure, was not challenged in court.

28. David Y. Thomas, "The Initiative and Referendum in Arkansas Come of Age," *American Political Science Review* 27 (1933), 66–68; *Hodges v. Dawdy* 104 Ark 583 (1912), quotation at 598; *Brickhouse v. Hill* 167 Ark. 513 (1925).

29. *Westbrook v. Mcdonald* 184 Ark. 740 (1931), quotations at 759–60.

30. *Shepard v. Mcdonald* 189 Ark. 29 (1934), quotations at 31, 35.

31. *Kurrus v. Priest* 342 Ark. 434 (2000), quotations at 443, 440–41.

32. Miller, "The Role of Courts in the Initiative Process"; idem, "Judging Ballot Initiatives."

33. *Fouts v. Hood River* 81 P. 370 (1905), quotation at 374; *State ex Rel. v. Richardson* 85 P. 225 (1906), quotations at 229–30; also see *Baxter v. State* 88 P. 67 (1907) and *State v. Kline* 93 P. 237 (1907).

34. *Oregon v. Pacific States Tel. & Tel. Co.* 99 P. 427 (1909); *Kadderly v. Portland* 74 P. 710 (1903), quotation at 720.

35. James D. Barnett, *The Operation of the Initiative, Referendum, and Recall in Oregon* (New York: Macmillan, 1915), 173.

36. *Pierce v. Hill* 45 S. Ct. 571 (1925).

37. Miller's data indicate that there have been nearly as many voter-approved initiatives challenged in court in the 1990s as there were in the preceding three decades, though the percentage invalidated has not changed substantially. See Miller, "The Role of Courts in the Initiative Process" and "Judging Ballot Initiatives."

38. Howard Jarvis et al., "Rebuttal to Argument Against Proposition 62, in California Ballot Pamphlet, Proposed Statutes and Amendments to California Constitution with Arguments to Voters" (1986), quoted in Stacey Simon, "A Vote of No Confidence: Proposition 218, Local Government, and Quality of Life in California," *Ecology Law Quarterly* 25 (1998), 529 n. 57; *City of Westminster v. County of Orange* 204 Cal. App. 3d 623 (1988), quotation at 630; *Santa Clara County v. Guardino* 902 P.2d 225 (1995), quotation at 251; Jamie Beckett, "State Court Voids Santa Clara Sales Tax," *San Francisco Chronicle*, September 29, 1995, A1; "Appeals Court Upholds Dismissal of Taxpayers' Suit Against La Habra," *Metropolitan News-Enterprise*, August 31, 1999, 5; also see *City of Woodlake v. Logan* 230 Cal. App. 3d 1058 (1991).

39. *Bramberg v. Jones* 978 P.2d 1240 (1999).

40. Marsha Cohen, symposium on "The Criminalization of Medicinal Marijuana," *Hastings Women's Law Journal* 11 (Winter 2000), 103.

41. Michael Vitiello, "Proposition 215: De Facto Legalization of Pot and the Shortcomings of Direct Democracy," *University of Michigan Journal of Law Reform* 31 (Spring 1998), 730–31; Edward Epstein, "Lockyer Gives Quiet OK to S.F. Pot Clubs," *San Francisco Chronicle,* March 20, 1999, A15.

42. Vitiello, "Proposition 215," esp. 718–29 (Dennis Peron quoted at 725 n. 99). Peron's argument that his club was a "primary caregiver" was initially accepted by a superior court judge (*People v. Dennis Peron,* Docket No. 980105, Jan. 10, 1997, as quoted in Vitiello, "Proposition 215," 723 n. 92) but was later rejected by a California court of appeals (*Lungren v. Peron* 59 Cal. App. 4th 1383 [1997]), a decision that the California Supreme Court declined to review. Shortly after the *Peron* decision, the federal government filed lawsuits against six cannabis buyers' clubs, and a federal district court judge (*U.S. v. Cannabis Cultivators Club* 5 F. Supp. 2d 1086 [1998]) granted an injunction against the operation of the clubs on the grounds that they likely violated the federal Controlled Substances Act. The United States Court of Appeals for the Ninth Circuit (*U.S. v. Cannabis Buyers' Cooperative* 190 F.3d 1109 [1999]) remanded the case, strongly implying that the district court needed to modify its injunction to allow for a medical necessity defense. The U.S. Supreme Court then stepped in and issued an emergency order halting the distribution of marijuana by cannabis clubs (*United States v. Oakland Cannabis Buyers' Cooperative* 121 S. Ct. 21 [2000]), and in May 2001 it rejected the court of appeals' argument that there was a medical necessity exception to the Controlled Substances Act's prohibition against the manufacture and distribution of Schedule I drugs (121 S. Ct. 1711). In a separate case relating to Proposition 215 (*Conant v. McCaffrey* 2000 U.S. Dist. LEXIS 13024), a federal district court judge ruled on First Amendment grounds that the federal government could not revoke a doctor's license for recommending marijuana even if the recommended option was illegal.

43. For a similar discussion, see Miller, "Judging Ballot Initiatives," 19–20.

44. Ibid., 19.

45. *Legislature v. Eu* 816 P.2d 1309 (1991), quotations at 1341–42. Mosk was on far stronger ground in arguing that Proposition 140 violated the single-subject rule. In addition to the term limits and pension provisions, the measure also slashed the legislature's budget by 40 percent. Even under California's lenient interpretation of the single-subject rule, it is difficult to see how legislative pensions and budget are related to term limits.

46. *Bates v. Jones* 958 F. Supp. 1446 (1997), quotations at 1467, 1471.

47. *Jones v. Bates* 127 F.3d 839 (1997), quotations at 848, 844, 856, 863.

48. There are, in fact, good reasons to think voters did know what they were voting on, as the dissenting judge pointed out. Although the California initiative (unlike the Oregon term limits initiative approved at the same time) did not explicitly use the words "during a lifetime," the same is true for the Twenty-second Amendment to the U.S. Constitution, which states only that "no person shall be elected to the office of the President more than twice." Moreover, the official "Argument Against Proposition 140" in the ballot pamphlet insistently hammered home the point that legislators would be "banned for life." Proponents and opponents explicitly contrasted Proposition 140 with a less sweeping term limits measure on the same ballot that would have allowed legislators to return to office after one term out of office. An expensive advertising campaign, as Justice Sneed pointed out, made sure the issue was "widely discussed and publicized" (*Jones v. Bates* 127 F.3d 839 [1997], quotation at 866).

49. *Bates v. Jones* 131 F.3d 843 (1997), quotation at 847.

50. Reynolds Holding and Robert B. Gunnison, "Term Limits Upheld," *San Francisco Chronicle,* December 20, 1997, A1; Ed Mendel, "California Law on Term Limits Gains Final OK," *San Diego Union-Tribune,* March 24, 1988, A1.

7. The Myth of a Golden Age

1. Tony H. Evans, "Oregon Progressive Reform, 1902–1914" (Ph.D. diss., University of California, Berkeley, 1966), 88–95.

2. Ibid., 95–101.

3. Ibid., 78–81; James D. Barnett, *The Operation of the Initiative, Referendum, and Recall in Oregon* (New York: Macmillan, 1915), 167.

4. Evans, "Oregon Progressive Reform," 134–35.

5. Allen H. Eaton, *The Oregon System: The Story of Direct Legislation in Oregon* (Chicago: A. C. McClurg, 1912), 27–28; Evans, "Oregon Progressive Reform," 132.

6. Evans, "Oregon Progressive Reform," 148–49; John J. Dinan, *Keeping the People's Liberties: Legislators, Citizens, and Judges as Guardians of Rights* (Lawrence: University Press of Kansas, 1998), 110–11.

7. Frederick V. Holman, "The Unfavorable Results of Direct Legislation in Oregon," in *The Initiative, Referendum and Recall,* ed. William B. Munro (New York: D. Appleton, 1920), 286–87.

8. Evans, "Oregon Progressive Reform," 136–37, 155.

9. Ibid., 221, 280, 283–84.

10. Barnett, *The Operation of the Initiative,* 80.

11. Ibid., 57; George Haynes, "A Year of the People's Rule in Oregon" (1910), in *The Initiative, Referendum, and Recall,* 275.

12. Evans, "Oregon Progressive Reform," 214–16.

13. Ibid., 269, 294; Lincoln Steffens, "U'Ren the Law-Giver," *American Magazine* 65 (1908), 527–40.

14. Since the 1908 initiative proposed a modified single tax, U'Ren refused to support it, explaining that he "never stood for and would not consent to stand for a half way measure" (Robert C. Woodward, "W. S. U'Ren and the Single Tax in Oregon," *Oregon Historical Quarterly* 61 [March 1960], 50). U'Ren was the leading spokesman for the 1912, 1914, and 1916 single tax initiatives.

15. Barnett, *The Operation of the Initiative,* 14, 42; Evans, "Oregon Progressive Reform," 219.

16. Barnett, *The Operation of the Initiative,* 66–68, 75. The Corrupt Practices Act placed strict limits on the amount of money a candidate could spend in a run for office. An attempt, in the 1913 legislative session, to place similarly strict limitations on expenditures in initiative campaigns was defeated (90). Modeled on the British example, the Corrupt Practices Act also forbid candidates from electioneering on election day (Evans, "Oregon Progressive Reform," 175).

17. Barnett, *The Operation of the Initiative,* 13–15.

18. Eugene *Register,* December 21, 1913, and *Oregonian,* December 18, 1913, quoted in Barnett, *The Operation of the Initiative,* 61; also see *Oregonian,* March 27, 1908, quoted in Barnett, *The Operation of the Initiative,* 62.

19. Barnett, *The Operation of the Initiative*, 90; Woodward, "U'Ren and the Single Tax," 59.

20. California Commission on Campaign Financing, *Democracy by Initiative: Shaping California's Fourth Branch of Government* (Los Angeles: Center for Responsive Government, 1992), 37 n. 17.

21. At the municipal level, however, the initiative played a more important role in bringing Progressive reform to California. Twenty cities, including Los Angeles (in 1903) and San Francisco (in 1898), had adopted the initiative and referendum before the statewide initiative was approved in 1911. See V. O. Key Jr. and Winston W. Crouch, *The Initiative and Referendum in California* (Berkeley: University of California Press, 1939), esp. 428–29; and John M. Allswang, *California Initiatives and Referendums, 1912–1990: A Survey and Guide to Research* (Los Angeles: Edmund G. "Pat" Brown Institute of Public Affairs, 1991), 7.

22. Spencer C. Olin Jr., *California's Prodigal Sons: Hiram Johnson and the Progressives, 1911–1917* (Berkeley: University of California Press, 1968), 13, 44.

23. After 1926 four states enacted the recall, only one of them (Montana in 1976) through the initiative. Two of the states (Alaska in 1959 and Georgia in 1978) owed the recall to a constitutional convention, and in one (Idaho in 1933) the deed was done through a legislative referral.

24. Olin, *California's Prodigal Sons*, 46–49.

25. Key and Crouch, *The Initiative and Referendum in California*, 464.

26. Thomas E. Cronin, "The Paradoxes and Policies of Citizen Initiatives," *Willamette Law Review* 34 (Summer-Fall 1998), 738; Dinan, *Keeping the People's Liberties*, 107; Lynn A. Baker, "Direct Democracy and Discrimination: A Public Choice Perspective," *Chi.-Kent Law Review* 67 (1991), 708. Cronin also mistakenly claims that "after several failed attempts, initiative petition in Colorado . . . granted the vote to women" (Thomas E. Cronin, *Direct Democracy: The Politics of Initiative, Referendum, and Recall* [Cambridge, Mass.: Harvard University Press, 1989], 97; also see 199). In fact, woman suffrage came to Colorado by the legislature referring a constitutional amendment to the voters.

27. On Arizona, see Ida H. Harper, ed., *History of Woman Suffrage*, 6 vols. (1922; rpt. Salem, N.H.: Ayer, 1985), volume 6:10–15.

28. While still a territory, the Wyoming legislature passed a bill allowing for woman suffrage, which, when signed into law by the governor in 1869, made Wyoming the first territory or state in the Union to have full woman suffrage. When applying for admission as a new state, Wyoming held a constitutional convention that drew up a new constitution containing woman suffrage. The constitution was submitted to the voters for approval in 1890, making Wyoming the first state to enact full woman suffrage. Wyoming voters never received an opportunity to vote on the suffrage amendment separately, either in 1869 or in 1890 (Carrie C. Catt and Nettie R. Shuler, *Woman Suffrage and Politics: The Inner Story of the Suffragette Movement* [New York: Charles Scribner's Sons, 1926]), 74–82; Susan B. Anthony and Ida H. Harper, *History of Woman Suffrage* [1902; rpt. Salem, N.H.: Ayer, 1985], 4:994–1011). Woman suffrage was defeated in every case in which a state constitutional convention gave voters the opportunity to vote separately on the suffrage amendment: Colorado in 1877, Washington in 1889 and 1898, South Dakota in 1898, New Hampshire in 1902, and Ohio in 1912.

29. Harper, ed., *History of Woman Suffrage*, 6:508–19; Catt and Shuler, *Woman Suffrage and Politics*, 196–210.

30. Catt and Shuler, *Woman Suffrage*, 175–77; Harper, ed., *History of Woman Suffrage*, 6:27–58.

31. Anthony and Harper, eds., *History of Woman Suffrage*, 4:970–74; Harper, ed., *History of Woman Suffrage*, 6:673–86.

32. Legislative referrals were rejected in North Dakota, New Jersey, Pennsylvania, Indiana, Illinois, Iowa, Nebraska, Rhode Island, Massachusetts, Wisconsin, West Virginia, Maine, Louisiana, and Texas. In Ohio and New Hampshire the woman suffrage amendment was referred to voters by a constitutional convention. In Missouri an initiative gave voters the opportunity to enact woman suffrage.

33. If the initiative did not directly secure woman suffrage, might it have had an indirect effect, a "gun behind the door" pressuring state legislatures to act? This argument, advanced by Lee Ann Banaszak (*Why Movements Succeed or Fail: Opportunity, Culture, and the Struggle for Woman Suffrage* [Princeton: Princeton University Press, 1996], esp. 184), has a superficial plausibility since initiative states were more likely to adopt woman suffrage than noninitiative states. Upon closer inspection, however, the argument breaks down. Six of the initiative states allowed women to vote only in primary elections (Arkansas) or in presidential elections (Missouri, Ohio, Nebraska, North Dakota, and Maine). Presidential suffrage in each case was achieved through the legislature taking action after the people of the state had rejected the legislature's referral of a constitutional amendment for full woman suffrage and/or had rejected suffrage initiatives. None of these legislative actions can be reasonably understood as a response to the threat of a popular initiative. Five initiative states that secured full woman suffrage prior to passage of the Nineteenth Amendment (Colorado, Idaho, Utah, Washington, and California) did so *before* they possessed the initiative power. Leaving aside Oregon and Arizona, where suffrage was directly enacted through the initiative process, there were only five initiative states (Montana, Nevada, Michigan, Oklahoma, and South Dakota) in which full woman suffrage was achieved subsequent to the state acquiring the initiative power and in which legislative action could possibly have been impacted by the threat of a woman suffrage initiative. But in all but one of these cases it is clear the initiative process played no role in the legislature's action. Nevada passed women suffrage in 1914, but since the state's first initiative did not appear until 1918, it is exceedingly unlikely that the threat of initiative loomed large in legislators' minds. The initiative was used frequently in South Dakota, but the legislature had referred six suffrage amendments to the voters, all of which had been defeated. The legislature, by any measure, was clearly out in front of the public. In any event, prior to 1972 South Dakota only allowed statutory initiatives and thus could not have achieved full suffrage by initiative amendment. Montana, too, forbid constitutional changes from being made by initiative (that changed with the new state constitution, adopted in 1972). In Michigan voters had rejected suffrage referrals in 1912 and again in 1913, and it was only after the legislature took things into its own hands by enacting presidential suffrage in 1917 that the voters finally relented to a legislative referral. That leaves only one state, Oklahoma, in which the threat of a popular initiative could possibly have influenced legislative behavior. The woman suffrage movement in Oklahoma did in fact use the newly created initiative process to place a suffrage initiative on the ballot in 1910, but the initiative was decisively rejected by the people. In 1915 there was a brief effort to start another initiative petition, but the effort never got off the ground (Harper, ed., *History of Woman Suffrage*, 6:527). In 1918, when the state legislature finally referred a woman suffrage amendment to the voters (it passed unanimously in the senate and was approved by over 85 percent of the house), there were apparently no plans for or prospect of another initiative petition. In sum, although support for woman suffrage and the initiative were clearly linked to similar geographic or cultural factors, there is no

evidence that the initiative functioned as a gun behind the door that helped to bring about woman suffrage.

Epilogue

1. California Commission on Campaign Financing, *Democracy by Initiative: Shaping California's Fourth Branch of Government* (Los Angeles: Center for Responsive Government, 1992); Citizen's Commission on Ballot Initiatives, *Report and Recommendations of the Statewide Initiative Process* (Sacramento, January 1994); California Constitution Revision Commission, *Final Report and Recommendations to the Governor and the Legislature* (Sacramento, August 1996). The latter report included a strongly worded dissenting view signed by eight of the twenty commission members. Each of the eight were appointed by either the Republican governor or the Republican assembly speaker. All five of the Democratic appointees supported the final report. Another review, conducted by Philip DuBois and Floyd Feeney for the California Policy Seminar, was published as Dubois and Feeney, *Improving the California Initiative Process: Options for Change* (Berkeley: California Policy Seminar, University of California,1992).

2. "Hertzberg Creates Speaker's Commission on Initiative Process," Press release, October 26, 2000 (*http://www.cainitiative.org*).

3. Steven K. Paulson, "Education Group Formed to Reform Initiative Process," Associated Press State & Local Wire, October 23, 2000; "Lawmakers Target Initiatives," *Denver Rocky Mountain News,* October 24, 2000, A7.

4. Paul Davenport, "Governor Expresses Unease about Initiatives," Associated Press State & Local Wire, August 16, 2000; Mike McCloy, "Hull Urges Establishing Limits on Initiatives Requested by Voters," *Arizona Republic,* August 17, 2000, B7; "Taking the Initiative," *Bangor Daily News,* August 19, 2000.

5. City Club of Portland, "The Initiative and Referendum in Oregon" (Portland, Ore., February 16, 1996), Appendix C, 61–68.

6. Michael G. Hagen and Edward L. Lascher Jr., "Public Opinion about Ballot Initiatives," Graduate Program in Public Policy and Administration, California State University, Sacramento, Working Paper 98–02. Also see Philip L. DuBois and Floyd Feeney, *Lawmaking by Initiative: Issues, Options and Comparisons* (New York: Agathon Press, 1998), 4.

7. The one clear exception during the past decade has been Wyoming, where in 1998 voters approved a legislative referendum that made the state's geographic distribution requirement far more restrictive.

8. Robin Tysver, "Group: Make Amendment Process Harder," *Omaha World-Herald,* November 2, 2000, 18; Jake Bleed, "Nebraskans Reject Two Sections of Petition Amendment," *Omaha World-Herald,* November 8, 2000, 23.

9. Peter Wong, "Court Reins in Petition Drives," *Statesman Journal* (Salem, Ore.), September 15, 2000, A1; David Sarasohn, "Initiative Industry Loses Branch Offices," *Oregonian,* September 17, 2000, G4. The case (*Stranahan v. Fred Meyer* 331 Ore. 38), involved a 1989 arrest of a signature gatherer, Lois Stranahan, outside a Portland Fred Meyer store. Stranahan sued Fred Meyer and won $2 million from a jury in 1995, though the trial judge later reduced the award to $375,000. The award was then upheld in 1998 by the court of appeals. The Oregon Supreme Court's *Stranahan* decision not only reversed the award but also overturned a 1993 state supreme court ruling (*Lloyd Corporation v. Whiffen* 315 Ore.

500) that because they are the equivalent of public squares, shopping malls must be open to signature gatherers. The court reasoned in the 1993 case that the right to initiate laws and constitutional amendments "implicitly included the right to solicit signatures for initiative petitions in the common areas of large shopping centers." But seven years later the court decided it had been in error, and that there was "*nothing* to support the conclusion set out in [the case] that persons soliciting signatures for initiative petitions may do so on certain private property over the owner's objection." The 1993 decision, the court now proclaimed, was in "error, and it is disavowed" (*Stranahan,* 45, 65; emphasis added).

10. The notable exception is Colorado, where the court's increased reliance on the single-subject rule was a direct response to a 1994 constitutional amendment requiring that "any measure proposed by initiative or referendum be confined to a single subject." The legislature passed the amendment and referred it to the voters, who overwhelmingly approved it.

11. The court challenge was filed in June 2000, with the Initiative and Referendum Institute as the lead plaintiff. The case (*Initiative & Referendum Institute v. United States Postal Service*) was still pending before the U.S. District Court for the District of Columbia as of this writing.

12. Also contributing to the increase in the number of signatures thrown out (and hence required) was a new statistical sampling method adopted by the state in 1999, a change initiated by the state supreme court and subsequently shaped by the legislature and the secretary of state. Back in the 1960s, when initiative petitions were relatively uncommon, Oregon checked every signature on initiative petitions, as still occurs in better than two-thirds of initiative states. However, in 1973 the legislature permitted the state to use a sampling method except when the count was close, and in 1986 the legislature mandated statistical sampling for every initiative petition. The legislature required that no petition be invalidated unless two separate sampling processes showed that it lacked the required number of signatures, but otherwise left the secretary of state free to devise the sampling method and the size of the sample. (The second sample had to be larger than the first, but beyond that the statute remained silent.) The secretary of state implemented the new legislation by adopting an administrative rule requiring that on the second sample there must be an 80 percent probability that an initiative petition lacks the required number of valid signatures before it can be rejected. That rule was challenged in 1998 when the secretary of state placed a property crimes initiative on the ballot even though the state's sampling method showed it to be 173 signatures short. The supreme court agreed with the appellants that allowing initiatives onto the ballot even though there was better than a 50 percent chance that the measure had not in fact qualified violated the statutory directive to verify that a petition contain the required number of valid signatures before placing it on the ballot (*Hymes v. Keisling* 327 Ore. 556 [1998]). The legislature promptly changed the law so that rather than assume a duplication rate of 2 percent on the second sample, as had been done previously, the secretary of state must now count the actual number of duplicates in order to devise an estimated signature duplication rate for each petition. In making this change, the legislature's aim (Kevin Mannix, author of the invalidated Measure 61, was also the chief sponsor of the legislation) was to make the process fairer so that it did not punish petitioners who had already combed through their petitions and discarded duplicates. But the new sampling method adopted by the secretary of state also had the effect of increasing the number of signatures being thrown out. In the case of one Sizemore initiative, the secretary of state threw out as duplicates nearly 5 percent of the 108,632 signatures submitted, which is more than double

the 2 percent duplicate penalty under the old system. See Steve Law, "Initiative Rule Faces Challenge," *Statesman Journal* (Salem, Ore.), February 5, 2000, A1.

13. Mike Gravel, a former U.S. senator from Alaska, who heads the group Philadelphia II, advocates allowing popular initiatives to qualify not only by citizen petition but also by public opinion poll. The aim of the group is to "enable ordinary citizens to make laws and legislate policy in every government jurisdiction of the United States." See Brian Weberg, "Instant Democracy for Everyone," *State Legislatures* 26 (July–August 2000), 22.

14. Aki Orr's "Direct Democracy Manifesto," as quoted in Weberg, "Instant Democracy," 22.

15. For a good discussion on this theme, see Richard Davis, *The Web of Politics: The Internet's Impact on the American Political System* (New York: Oxford University Press, 1999), 27–37. Davis' book is an invaluable antidote to Internet millennialism.

16. The flawed assumption underlies much of the analysis in Jan A. Schevitz's paper, "The Fourth Branch of Government: An Analysis of the Initiative and Referendum Process and How the Internet Might Improve It," May 2000, esp. 21–22; available under "In-Depth Studies" on the web page of the Initiative and Referendum Institute (*http://www.iandrinstitute.org*).

17. For a sample of such predictions, see Dick Morris, *Vote.Com* (Los Angeles, Ca.: Renaissance Books, 1999).

18. These two quotations can be found on the Initiative and Referendum Institute web page under "Famous Quotes" (*http://www.iandrinstitute.org*). "Laws Without Government" is the title of the last chapter in Broder's *Democracy Derailed: Initiative Campaigns and the Power of Money* (New York: Harcourt, 2000). When confronted with the shortcomings of the initiative process, many defenders seek to disarm criticism by falling back on the argument that it provides another check to the American system of checks and balances. Although this may work as an argument in favor of the popular referendum by which voters can nullify laws passed by the legislature, it is not clear how a mechanism that allows individuals to bypass entirely the legislative and executive branches of government, as the direct initiative does, can be understood as providing an additional check on the system.

19. Don McIntyre, quoted in Ashbel Green, "Lawmakers Weigh Changing Measures," *Oregonian,* February 22, 1997, B1.

20. Robert Henry, "Deliberations About Democracy: Revolutions, Republicanism, and Reform," *Willamette Law Review* 34 (Summer–Fall 1998), 534; Knute Berger, "Dumbocracy," *Seattle Weekly,* April 13, 2000, 7.

21. This revealing remark was made by Dave Hunnicutt, director of legal affairs for Oregonians in Action (OIA), the group that spearheaded the campaign for Measure 7, the so-called takings initiative on the Oregon ballot in 2000. Approved by 53 percent of the voters, Measure 7 required that government compensate property owners for regulations that lower the value of the property. Confronted with postelection polling and focus groups claiming that for the great majority of Oregonians this was an issue about which they cared little and understood less, a skeptical Hunnicutt indicated that he would "like to see the polling data and the report from the focus group. Anybody who does this for a living can tell you that a poll is only as good as the questions you ask. . . . Given the questions I can probably predict the poll answers. . . . I'd be more than happy to poll this and come back this time next year and come back with poll results that will be entirely different." Hunnicutt's admission that answers can be readily changed by manipulating the question inadvertently undercut OIA's claim that Measure 7 clearly reflects the will of the people. Instead, Measure 7 is

revealed to be a proposal that matters a great deal to a small band of activists and hardly at all to the vast majority of people, and one which benefited enormously from having a ballot title that resonated with core American cultural values without mentioning the impact implementation would have on land-use planning, zoning laws, or environmental regulations. Hunnicutt's comments, which were in response to polling and focus group evidence presented by Patricia McCaig of Cli Strategies, were made at a forum on Measure 7 held at Willamette University on April 18, 2001.

22. Similar pleas are voiced by Alan Rosenthal in *The Decline of Representative Democracy: Process, Participation, and Power in State Legislatures* (Washington, D.C.: Congressional Quarterly Press, 1998), and by John R. Hibbing and Elizabeth Theiss-Morse in *Congress as Public Enemy: Public Attitudes Toward American Political Institutions* (Cambridge: Cambridge University Press, 1995).

Index